T I M E   M A T T E R S

TIME

Andrew Abbott

MATTERS

ON THEORY AND METHOD

The University of Chicago Press

Chicago & London

ANDREW ABBOTT is the Gustavus F. and Ann M. Swift
Distinguished Service Professor and chair of the Department
of Sociology at the University of Chicago. He is author of
*The System of Professions: An Essay on the Division of Expert
Labor* (1988), *Department and Discipline: Chicago Sociology at
One Hundred* (1999), and *Chaos of Disciplines* (2001), also
published by the University of Chicago Press.

The University of Chicago Press, Chicago 60637
The University of Chicago Press, Ltd., London
© 2001 by The University of Chicago
All rights reserved. Published 2001
Printed in the United States of America

10 09 08 07 06 05 04 03 02 01   1 2 3 4 5

ISBN: 0-226-00102-4 (cloth)
ISBN: 0-226-00103-2 (paper)

Library of Congress Cataloging-in-Publication Data

Abbott, Andrew.
    Time matters : on theory and method / Andrew Abbott.
        p.   cm.
    Includes bibliographical references and index.
    ISBN 0-226-00102-4 (hardcover : alk. paper)—ISBN
0-226-00103-2
    (pbk. : alk. paper)
    1. Sociology—Methodology. 2. Sociology—Philosophy.
3. Time—Sociological aspects. I. Title.

HM511 .A33   2001
301'.01—dc21
                                                    00-012680

To Clio

CONTENTS

ACKNOWLEDGMENTS

Because the prologue tells a personal story, there is need for only the briefest acknowledgments.

My thanks go to the dozens of people from whom I have learned and with whom I have argued about these matters over the years. In one sense the thirty or so people mentioned in passing in chapter one symbolize this much larger group. Writing that chapter has made me more than ever aware what a corporate endeavor it is to write a book.

I must thank also family and friends, particularly my wife Sue, who has lived through (survived?) and supported the writing of all this, and Woody, who has become more and more emphatically his interesting self throughout the time since the first paper in this group was published.

In revising these papers for publication, I have merely corrected a few grammatical infelicities. I have changed the appearance of the papers somewhat by moving to a common style for the scholarly machinery. To make them easier to read, I have put all that scholarly machinery into footnotes. This has occasionally resulted in minor changes in text. But I have not updated bibliographies and references, other than to replace conference presentations with published versions where I have known it possible. Partly, this choice came from a sense that it's not fair—particularly in the more polemical papers—to take advantage of later material. But it also reflects my sense that once begun, such an updating of references could only end up in my rewriting everything. The revision for publication and the writing of the conclusion were done during a short stay at Nuffield College in Trinity term 2000. Nuffield's Warden and Fellows have offered me much academic hospitality over the years and I thank them for it.

I have dedicated the book in classical fashion to Clio, the muse of history. Sometimes she had only to appear or glance at me to seize my whole being. Yet her secret remains hidden within her.

May 2000
Nuffield College

An Autobiographical Introduction

To publish such a book as this is to confess that one cannot give it a proper introduction. If the thematic structure exists for an introduction, one could and should write a full-scale monograph. But that is becoming an endless struggle, and hence I make in this collection an attempt at a progress report. In such a case, autobiography is the easiest way to set the stage, making thematics emerge from history. The epilogue tries to pull the major themes from the ensemble.

Ironically, the question of how thematics relates to history is in fact the central topic of this book, all of whose chapters concern in one way or another the relation between social scientific and historical thinking. At the same time, it is clear that chance has shaped the book as well. So I cannot say, in the last analysis, whether the grand theme or the petty historical chances have made the result. When my parents lived in tiny Medfield, about fifteen miles from Boston, they once invited a city friend named Fred Hickok to dinner, giving him elaborate directions. He went the wrong way at the first turning, but then followed the rest of the directions correctly and arrived on time at our house by a completely different route from the one my parents had intended. Perhaps like Fred Hickok I too could have ended up where I am today by a completely different pathway. Maybe there is a cunning of reason. Then again, maybe there isn't. Maybe the little contingencies matter.

My story starts with a course I taught in 1981 on historical sociology. But like a Victorian novelist, I will first introduce my protagonist. And before that I must make an equally Victorian prefatory comment about the style of this introduction.

That style is a detailed one, where small events swirl around in several subplots that eventually weave into a complete story. I hope by relating the details to let the reader see how coherence (well, relative coherence) emerges from seeming chaos. After all, one doesn't live intellectually in an abstract world disconnected from the daily round of teaching and grading and getting roasted by referees. I include therefore the small events—the rages and disappointments, the half-finished drafts, the phone calls from friends that sent me in new directions. I include as well the false starts and the ideas that failed. And I have not organized the whole into a grand narrative, but have left the subplots as they were, since I have usually pursued at least three or four lines of research at once and the mutual commentary of these lines of work turns out to be one of the driving forces of my story as a whole. I have started my story well before the first paper of this collection, because that relatively clear statement arose out of the conversation between earlier methodological and theoretical papers. Finally, I have not included here any of my purely methodological papers, although in this prologue I have discussed their writing, since it played a crucial role in producing the line of philosophical argument that dominates the book.

All this means that this autobiographical introduction is the longest chapter of the book, filled with anecdotes of professional life, descriptions of intellectual ditherings, and, of course, summaries of the actual papers here included. I can only plead in extenuation that perhaps such a detailed examination of the life course of a set of ideas can give younger scholars a sense of how an intellectual program actually unfolds in the life of an academic. The endpoint is not what one imagined at the outset. Nor are the routes rationally chosen.

So much for preamble. Here's the story. The reader may judge whether it is driven by the little accidents, the grand theme, or something in between.

I begin with the protagonist. Like many would-be intellectuals of the Sputnik era, I wanted to be a scientist through high school and to that end buried myself in calculus, modern algebra, and the like. On the side I read Camus and Dostoyevsky like other would-be intellectuals. But a splendid English teacher (a poet and translator named Dudley Fitts) pushed me towards the humanities, and I majored in History and Literature in college, all the while spending most of my course time dabbling in the various social and behavioral sciences. The long and short of it is that I had intellectual attention deficit disorder and finished college with no clearer idea of what I wanted to study than I had when I began. I knew I wanted to study. I just didn't know what I wanted to study or how I wanted to study it. It is now fairly easy to see that what I really wanted to do was to figure out who I was and why, my preconceived notions about those matters having been overthrown by the upsets of the 1960s. But what I thought at the time was simply that this whatever-it-was called sociology would let me study things I cared about in whatever way I pleased. So I became a sociologist. Perhaps it helped that my college didn't have a sociology department at the time. What I didn't know couldn't displease me.

At Chicago my original dissertation plan was to analyze the mental hospital that I had worked in and studied for my first five graduate years, treating that hospital as a community or small town, rather than in the traditional fashion as a (failed) formal organization. My advisor Morris Janowitz greeted this idea with his famously contemptuous mumble. In a rage I proposed a thesis based on one sentence of that original proposal, a sentence stating that psychiatrists had become absentee landlords of the mental hospitals. This became of necessity a historical thesis, which was easy enough because I had already done extensive primary historical work as an undergraduate.

All of which brought me to a first-floor classroom in Scott Hall at Rutgers in the fall semester of 1981, with the buses roaring outside the sunny window—my first graduate class. Present were about six students and my daunting colleague Michael Moffatt, an anthropologist who had asked permission to sit in. (I think he was looking for comic relief, being then in the middle of the fieldwork that led to his book on American college life, *Coming of Age in New Jersey*.) I had decided to thematize historical sociology into a number of basic topics and to do one per week. There were weeks on Interpretation, Sequence, Historical Sociology, Objectivity, Narrative, and so on. Of course I only got through two or three of these topics.

I had still not finished my own thesis at this point. Like everything I have done, it had multiplied like a virus and had now become four almost separate theses. The first of these undertook a comprehensive prosopography of American psychiatry in the period 1880–1930 (I had created biographies for one thousand workers in nervous and mental disease), coupled with some simple mathematical modeling of career patterns and their implications for professional demography. A second section examined the growth of communities of outpatient psychiatrists and neurologists in four cities, looking at diaries, notebooks, organizational minutes, and so on. A third examined in excruciating detail the changes in psychiatric conceptions of certain diseases as viewed in successive editions of textbooks, and a fourth examined changes in the social functions of psychiatry by looking in detail at caseloads and trying to infer the relation of patient complaints to changes in modern life.

Although I could see that there was some essential difficulty that kept these sections separate, I did not at the time know that that difficulty lay in the different temporalities of the historical processes involved. I thus had little idea how to put this particular Humpty Dumpty together again; I would eventually figure that out in 1992, much too late to publish the thesis as a book. (That later realization would, indeed, itself lead to the demise of yet another book project.) As far as my thesis was concerned, I should have followed the advice of the medical historian Charles Rosenberg, who at about this time read the manuscript and advised me to publish it as four separate books and retire.

But to return to nervous me, teaching my course with my undone thesis and my brand spandy-new *(sic)* themes. I decided at some point in that course that I wasn't good enough to work on all my themes at once. I would choose one and focus on it. That one, chosen a little arbitrarily I think, was sequence and order. Historians cared about sequence and order. Sociologists didn't. Why?

So I set out to write a comprehensive analysis of the problem of sequence in social science, looking on the one side from history towards sociology, and on the other from sociology towards history. I was not as systematic about this as I should have been or as I tell graduate students to be. (I didn't look up "sequence" in the *Social Science Citation Index* until quite late in the process, for example.) Rather, I wandered off into a number of interesting literatures, most of them encountered through the usual contingencies of everyday academic life. I talked to this one and that one about my interest in sequence and got some fascinating responses.

From the historians, I sought reflections on narrative. In fact, historians didn't give a damn about narrative and sequence at the time. Social science history and Marxist history were all the rage, both of them mistrustful of narrative and events. But substantive interests had led me to the Davis Center at Princeton, then focusing on the history of professions. There I met Wilfred Prest, an Australian historian of the legal profession and fellow at the center, who told me to read *History and Theory*—"lot of good stuff there." He was right. These were the cusp years between the analytic philosophy of history and the new culturalism, and so I found pages of thoughtful work as yet unburdened with polemical freight. I read every issue of the journal from 1976 to 1980, more or less cover to cover.

Another chance contact, a purely social phone call to graduate school friend Patricia Cox, a specialist in early Christian literature, led me to deconstructionism. (I suppose you need deconstructionism if you study patristics; the number of texts is fixed, but the need for dissertation topics goes on forever.) The book Pat recommended was out of the library, and the person who had it out (a kindly librarian violated confidentiality rules to tell me this privately) was my English Department colleague Pat Tobin, a literary theorist who was also director of the College Honors Program (this *will* be relevant, I promise.) With her gusty enthusiasm, Pat Tobin swept me up into the high structuralist view of order and sequence, the view of Propp, the early Todorov, Barthes, and friends.

On the sociological side, I looked first at the theoretical traditions, which were quiet enough on the phenomenon of sequence. There were a few ideal sequence conceptions—explicit in Weber and Stinchcombe, implicit in other writings—and these were easy enough to catalogue. I then considered methodologies, working through the various methods standard in sociology and asking myself what sense they made of sequential phenomena. Luckily, my ancient mathematics education proved to be up to reverse-engineering these methods, and I found that in general sociological methods rested very uneasily with respect to sequence of events. I also explored some more esoteric areas—ARIMA methods (then unknown in sociology) and dynamic programming (which would later be my bread and butter, but under another guise). Again luckily, one of my random self-education efforts in my mental hospital days had led me to explore Markovian models (of patient populations), and so I was reasonably well informed about these more "historical" methods for studying the social world. They had sequence but not much: only one step at a time. In a similar framework, at least at first, were event history methods, which had just gone public in the justly celebrated Tuma, Hannan, and Groenveld *AJS* article of 1979. (In later years, these were recast as simple durational methods but at the time they were explicitly motivated as an examination of one cell of a Markovian transition matrix.)

I stuffed all of this material—from Danto to Propp to Box-Jenkins and Tuma—into my first piece on the subject of sequence, a compendium called "Sequences of Social Events," which I delivered at the Social Science History Association (SSHA) and eventually published in *Historical Methods* in 1983. *AJS* gave me an R&R on it, but historical demographer Dan Smith (editor of *Historical Methods*) had offered to publish it with only one revision; he wanted me to cut the opening, a textual analysis of a passage from a history of nursing that illustrated the importance of sequential assumptions. I have occasionally wondered whether the *AJS*, too, would have accepted it if I had sent it back without the textual introduction. It's like Cleopatra's nose; perhaps the "whole face of [my] world" would have been different.[1] Inter-

1. Pascal, *Lettres provinciales* no. 162. "The nose of Cleopatra; if it had been shorter all the face of the earth would have changed."

estingly, detailed textual analysis was later to become a main weapon in my
rhetorical arsenal. And the connection with *Historical Methods* and with the
SSHA (which I had discovered quite accidentally through psychiatric historian Nancy Tomes, a fellow of David Mechanic's mental health research op-
eration at Rutgers) became crucial to me. In the 1980s, the SSHA was my
only audience for work on sequence methods; adventurous historians like
Dan Smith, Eric Monkkonen, and Randy Roth were my main interlocutors.
For the more general project of trying to figure out a theory of history, my
main interlocutor was closer to home. The office next to mine at Rutgers,
where sociology and anthropology were a merged department, contained
the brilliant linguistic anthropologist Susan Gal, who was obsessed with
language change and was always ready to challenge and redirect my ideas.

To this point, it may seem that chance took the lead. Now the thematics
took over. I sent the "Sequences" piece around to all my friends to read.
(While they were doing so, Messrs. Janowitz and Shils finally allowed me to
declare victory with respect to my dissertation—a useful development now
that I had been teaching at Rutgers for over three years without a degree.) I
got two responses to the sequence paper. My qualitative friends, as yet un-
leavened by the historical and cultural yeasts of the mid-1980s, politely
told me it was interesting and why didn't I do something real—something
Marxist, for example? (Five years or so later they were telling me that I
ought to get interested in narrative.) My quantitative friends mostly told me
to shut up. If I didn't have anything better to suggest, I should stop yelling at
them.

In response, I began to look around for some better things for my quantitative friends to do. Again, an old acquaintance proved crucial. My high
school classmate Phipps Arabie had become a psychometrician at Illinois
and in a social phone conversation one day I muttered something about being interested in sequence. Phipps told me about the literature on seriation
in archaeology and also said that Joseph Kruskal at Bell Labs was working
on a very powerful new set of sequence techniques. I followed his advice to
the seriation material, which consisted of simple techniques for finding the
most characteristic order in sequences of nonrecurrent events. It was sum-
marized in a crazily interdisciplinary volume that brought archaeologists,
historians, and mathematicians together to seriate the works of Plato, analyze types of tumuli, and categorize artifacts, all this using methods that
seemed wonderful and strange indeed.

The seriation literature enabled me to start a bunch of empirical projects. At the recommendation of my graduate classmate Terry Halliday, I

had begun to think of myself as a sociologist of professions rather than a sociologist of knowledge. So I looked for an empirical application of these seriation methods to professions. I saw that the techniques could be used to address a famous problem in the history of professions, the question of whether professions always acquired their various institutions—licensing, examinations, schooling, associations, ethics codes, and so on—in the same order. Harold Wilensky's celebrated 1964 paper had so argued, but did not have a very convincing methodology. Here was the convincing method. So I sat around one vacation at my parents' house applying Alan Gelfand's simple seriation algorithm (from the archaeology/mathematics book) to the Wilensky-type data various research assistants had dug up for me.

Unfortunately, there was a problem. Wilensky's "events" included things that could occur only once (founding a national association) and things that occurred many times (founding a medical school). If we looked for the first occurrence of each, the one that occurred more often would come first on sheer probabilistic grounds even if the expected "shapes" of the likelihoods over time were the same. It was like taking a sample of one versus a sample of four hundred on the same distribution and asking which sample included the smallest element. (Much later, I was to see that this particular piece of mathematics had important implications for affirmative action.) Now on the one hand, all this was great fun and in my attention deficit disorder way I temporarily became a fan of the mathematics involved—the theory of extremals and order statistics. On the other hand, my recognition of the problems of order statistics put me in a bind. By now I had written two whole book chapters about the order of professionalization, based on Gelfand's seriation method and using order statistics. They were chapters two and three of what became *The System of Professions*, the theoretical monograph on professions that was my main substantive work at the time. Indeed, these two chapters had gone out to the friends who were reading the manuscript for me. But the problem of order statistics was fatal to these chapters.

At least I had learned by now that when you ran across a problem that destroyed a body of your work, you published an article about how important it was. So I wrote a paper entitled "Event Sequence and Event Duration" for a 1983 MIT conference (published in *Historical Methods* in 1984) that tried to analyze the issues involved in conceptualizing and measuring sequence data. In this paper I argued about the need for careful "colligation" (the narrative version of conceptualization) and measurement of sequence data. With respect to colligation, I focused on the problems of finding a single coherent narrative level for the story/sequence (thereby avoiding the Wilensky problem), as well as on development of a substantively sound version of the story supported by a careful analysis of the duration and dispersion of the events in that story.

The most important idea of this paper was its explicit distinction between "events," which I defined as abstractions (the equivalents of concepts in standard methods), and "occurrences," the actual happenings we use to indicate that an "event" has taken place (the equivalents of indicators in the standard methods). Hence "medical education" was an *event* (concept) of which "the founding of a medical school" was one possible *occurrence* (indicator). The analysis was exactly equivalent to the standard view of measurement in sociology, then being adumbrated as part of the spread of LISREL. (My new colleague Rob Parker was a great LISREL fan, so measurement was in the air at Rutgers. But the event/occurrence idea itself showed up in a conversation I had with Bruce Carruthers, one of the graduate students from my Historical Sociology course.)

The measurement part of the paper focused on the trade-off between applying order statistics, medians, and rates to the occurrence distribution of the various events one was trying to order. I analyzed this with a simulational analysis based on the various possible patterns for those occurrences. I would later develop this argument in an empirical piece on sequences of institutionalization in American medical communities, but at the time I think nobody could see what the fuss was about. The 1984 paper's philosophical argument has profound implications for areas like life course and stress research, but I certainly couldn't have persuaded life course and stress researchers at the time. Indeed, in 1999 I was to be attacked in print by my friend Larry Wu, the event-historian, for among other things ignoring these very kinds of concerns, which I had in fact explored at length a decade and a half before.

Reflecting about conceptualization and measurement of sequence data was subtle and interesting. But its inevitable consequence was the sad decision—taken in the shower one morning—to throw away two whole chapters of *The System of Professions*, nearly a year's work. I saved parts of the first, which ended up in the published book's first chapter. But the other chapter, with its flawed methods, was gone for good. Too bad—I rather liked its conclusion that there was a sequence to American professionalization, but not to British. I just don't know if it's true.

Interestingly, I couldn't bring myself to remove from the first pages of *The System of Professions* the paragraphs claiming that the book had a methodological subtext as important as its substantive surface. These had been much more appropriate when the second and third chapters had been about conceptualizing and measuring professionalization as a sequence. But in fact the book's main theoretical message was that thinking of professions as developing independently was foolish. Indeed that message came across more clearly after the professionalization chapters were cut. I rewrote the historiographical claims to emphasize the idea of "theorizing about interdependence and contingency," but when I reread them today I still see them as a relic of the earlier vision of the text, something that should have been removed, but wasn't.

Around this time I finally gathered the courage to call Joseph Kruskal, whom Phipps Arabie had mentioned in connection with new sequence methods. It felt like calling God; Kruskal had invented multidimensional scaling and who knows what else. But he was polite enough and sent me a preprint of the first chapter of his book with David Sankoff on optimal matching techniques. Here I reencountered dynamic programming and suddenly found myself a member of the then tiny interdisciplinary community of people (biologists, computer scientists, cryptographers, and various camp followers) interested in something called "sequence methods." I eventually got software for doing such "optimal matching" from David Bradley, who had written a set of programs for his biologist brother to use in studying variations in sparrow dialect (yes, this is for real) by comparing the sequence of cheeps, whits, and whoos in the birdcalls. We converted the software from CDC to VAX FORTRAN and by 1986 I had my first optimal matching paper in print, an analysis (with anthropologist John Forrest, whom I had met at a country dance camp) of sequence patterns in morris dances, the traditional English ceremonial dances. We published this paper—with little difficulty—in the adventurous *Journal of Interdisciplinary History*. Heaven only knows what the *AJS* would have thought. I didn't waste my time with them. A bizarre postscript to the story came when I sent a copy of the paper to Joe Kruskal; he turned out to have done morris dancing as a young man.

So in the mid-1980s, I was advancing (I wasn't sure towards what) on both the theoretical and the methodological fronts. Indeed, I was so excited about what I was doing that I assembled an undergraduate course called "The Idea of Order," in which I tied together Barthesian criticism, Collingwoodian historicism, optimal matching, and all sorts of other things. Deconstructionist Pat Tobin welcomed me into the college honors program, where I taught the course for three years. In its first avatar there turned up an intense young woman named Alexandra Hrycak, of whom more below.

By this time I had begun to recognize that my basic problem was the relation between history and sociology, but I was somewhat confused that nobody else seemed to think that this general relation was much of a problem. Theda Skocpol was energetically leading the historical sociologists at the time, and I have the impression she thought I was a curious—although perhaps useful—crank because of my preoccupation with issues that were as much philosophical as theoretical and methodological. Her own concerns were relentlessly substantive, and led her and her followers towards their excellent work on the welfare state and a gradual shift into political science. But they were in reality little concerned with the philosophical problem of history.

As for myself, I decided to try again to synthesize the basic disagreements I had with standard methods. This time I would focus on the underlying assumptions those methods made about the social world. So I read a bunch of standard articles in the best journals using an "interview protocol" that posed questions about what those articles assumed. I read twenty or thirty articles, compared the results, sifted for the best thematic organization, and then assembled a paper using one or two articles to illustrate each theme. I delivered this to the SSHA in 1985. It wasn't published until 1988, when, with my son looming in my wife's belly, I began to fear that all my half-written papers would never appear in print once Woody arrived to occupy our attention. So I hurriedly sent it off to a place likely to publish it, *Sociological Theory*. This is the first paper in this volume, "Transcending General Linear Reality."[2]

I organized "Transcending" along a broad front, a list of important assumptions much the same as the topics of my 1980 course. Narrative sequence was again just one of the basic philosophical problems at issue. By now, I had seen clearly that my growing methodological work of identifying "typical sequences" in bodies of sequence data could address only one of these problems. With respect to the others, I was myself making assumptions that I had elsewhere excoriated. For example, the methods I was developing quite obviously assumed that sequences were independent of each other, as they also assumed a positivist ability to uniquely identify sequence elements. In the same year that "Transcending" appeared, I published *The System of Professions* with its clarion recognition of contingency and interde-

2. Throughout this chapter, I shall refer to the various papers in this volume by short abbreviations after I have given the full title once. Although I believe these titles are unambiguous, let me list them, in order, here: "Transcending," "Seven Types," "Causal Devolution," "Conceptions," "Cases," "From Causes," "Temporality," "Turning Point," and "Things."

pendence. It was indeed awkward to be peddling methods making assumptions I was elsewhere attacking. (In 1996, this was pointed out in print by Mike Hanagan and Louise Tilly, who, kindly enough, saw this split as a [lamentable] historical change in me rather than an unresolved inconsistency in my work.)

"Transcending" also established a useful rhetorical genre for me. It was the first of many papers that followed the *analyse de texte* format I had learned when practicing the New Criticism under Dudley Fitts in high school. It combined detailed reading and critical analysis with a specific focus on dissecting the assumptions of a particular argument. This was a pattern I would follow in numerous later papers, including several that appear here.

I felt a little guilty publishing "Transcending" in *Sociological Theory*. This was preaching to the converted, as I well knew. But I had a sneaking sense—true enough as the sequel would show—that Max Planck was right when he said that "old theories are never disproved, their adherents die." Given my temper, it was better to preach to the converted than to rage at the incomprehensions of referees from hostile paradigms. Young people will try anything, but middle-aged dogs don't like new tricks.

"Transcending General Linear Reality"

"Transcending" proceeds by asking what are the assumptions about social reality that are implicit in standard sociological methodologies, what I called general linear reality (GLR). These are not the mathematical assumptions, but rather the ontological and metaphysical ones.[3] The paper discusses six such basic assumptions. First, GLR assumes that the social world is made up of fixed entities with changing attributes. Second, causality is believed to flow from large to small: from background variables to a particular dependent variable, or between variables of equal temporal size. GLR does not allow little things to cause big things (so much for Cleopatra's nose). Third, GLR assumes that a given attribute of an entity has one and only one (causal) meaning, at least in one study. (It was the variation in this meaning *across* studies that eventually became the central topic of "Seven Types of Ambiguity," the paper that follows "Transcending" in part one of this volume.) Fourth, GLR assumes that the order of events doesn't make a difference. This fourth assumption was to be the focus of my temporality work for the next ten years. The fifth assumption is GLR's belief in

3. Occasionally these assumptions are ontological or metaphysical assumptions entailed by the mathematical assumptions, as, for example, the assumption of casewise independence.

casewise independence, and more broadly its rejection of structural determination. This was of course the whole burden of *The System of Professions*,
as it was of the burgeoning network literature. The sixth assumption is of
independence of context, an assumption I was to specify in later papers as
proceeding from the odd idea that main effects exist. They are, of course,
mere analytical conveniences, not realities. My particular concern here—
and years of experience since have proved it a real one—was that even many
sociologists, to say nothing of their students and the public, lose sight of this
analytical character of main effects and come to think of things like "gender" and "bureaucracy" as having some kind of reality, merely because we
measure "their" effects.

I present in "Transcending" three alternative general ontologies for sociology: demographic, sequential, and network. These are mere sketches,
but they evoke three fundamentally different ways of thinking about the social world, ways that I think could get sociologists out of some of the traps
into which standard methods have seduced them. Rereading this paper today, I am struck by how often I have repeated these ideas, and how little effect they seem to have had. I could write the same paper with contemporary
examples today. People still think "new methods" are a substitute for reflecting about their assumptions re social reality.

In the years 1985 to 1987 I was unable to devote much time to issues of
temporality, method, and explanation because something else was occupying my attention. For a job talk in 1982 (I got the job but decided not to
leave Rutgers), I had had the offhand thought that maybe professions
worked as a vacancy chain system (about which more below). This offhand
thought became the nucleus of a "quick and dirty little book" (as I told myself) in 1983–84. This book rapidly metastasized into a huge and ambitious
volume (*The System of Professions*), much as my thesis had grown from one
sentence in my original proposal to a 250,000-word dissertation. Some sections of *The System of Professions* got written at breakneck speed, but others
took forever, and there were lots of them. The notes alone took five months,
and book production spoiled most of 1987.

Thus it was not until 1988 that I finally wrote up an optimal matching
application for a "real" sociological dataset. The dataset itself was an accident. Alexandra Hrycak had become my RA on a project to code the lives of
hundreds of German baroque musicians in order to look for vacancy chains
in the system. Vacancy chain systems are mobility systems of uniquely identified positions in which no one can move until a vacancy is created. As a
result vacancies—not people as in the standard mobility model—have

the initiative. Vacancy chains were then a fascination of mine; I had loved them ever since reading Harrison White's vastly clever *Chains of Opportunity* sometime in the mid-1970s. I had done an article with my colleague Randy Smith on vacancy chains among college football coaches (Randy is a sports junkie) and, as I mentioned, had based *The System of Professions* originally on a vacancy chain insight. I figured I would look for chains in German musicians. As a producer and consumer of classical music, I was fascinated by the old story of Kuhnau's death leading to Bach's hiring and the consequent hiring of somebody else to replace Bach, etc.

Alas, a grand total of four complete vacancy chains showed up in the German musicians data (detailed careers of six hundred people.) The thing was a bust. But I decided we could use optimal matching to look for career patterns. This became Alexandra's Henry Rutgers Honors Thesis, written under my direction (goading? screaming?) in an endless string of all-nighters and weekends in spring of 1988. I wrote a publication draft of a joint paper and sent it off to the *AJS*. The saga of this paper—from its initial flat rejection by the *AJS* to its eventual publication there—is best left undiscussed. It proved again how right Planck was. And Jim Coleman was right as well when he said to me four or five years later: "Nobody's gonna pay any attention to what you're saying as long as you write about dead German musicians." It wasn't a "real" dataset after all, in most sociologists' eyes.

As the late 1980s wore on, I focused again on temporality, on assumption number four of "Transcending."[4] The three papers of part two all came out of this more focused analysis of methods and presuppositions about temporality in the four years from 1988 to 1992. Throughout this period I entertained the idea of writing a book about temporality. It was confused in various ways with other potential books. One of these was a book about the broad-front differences of methodologies and even of disciplines. As early as 1985 I had been playing with ideas about systematizing the differences between the various disciplines and their approaches to social life, in papers for a new center at Rutgers founded by the wonderfully intellectual (and supportive) literary critic George Levine. I had written empirical papers of this type about the stress literature (in 1987, published in *Sociological Forum* in 1990) and the disciplinary relation of history and sociology (in 1990, published in *Social Science History* in 1992). I had done and redone a theoretical analysis of disciplines in a paper whose first draft dated from 1985. So my notion of the temporality book as of 1990 was that it would be, like the re-

---

4. My return to the broad-front approach later would produce the two other papers of the first section of this book. I shall discuss them below, in their chronological place.

jected chapters of *The System of Professions*, organized as a zoom in from an introduction organized around broad-front issues of disciplinary difference to a main body specifically focused on temporality. Obviously "Transcending" would be in this book in revised form, along with the disciplines material, and so on. Various other pieces of this torso were finished, in particular a background sketch on sequence literatures across the social sciences, half a chapter on causality, and an *analyse de texte* looking at three articles, all on the same subject (work commitment) one by an economist, one by two sociologists, and one by a historian.

This temporality book came to nothing because in 1992 I wrote an ASA paper (never delivered because I became too sick to go—was this psychosomatic?) in which I began to recognize that I had been fundamentally wrong about certain aspects of temporality and, more important, that one couldn't write a truly theoretical book about temporality without writing about social structure at the same time. The intellectual reason for this I will give below, but for the moment let me outline the subsequent history of the material blown up by this particular piece of homemade fireworks. Because temporality was now inseparable from structure, the zoom design of my temporality book became a mistake, and all my work dealing with the broad-front conceptual analysis of methods and disciplines was adrift. I realized eventually that the disciplines line of work could be put together under the concept of fractal distinctions, which I had developed partly in the disciplines work and partly in a broader theoretical paper (unpublished, but written in 1987) on fractal social structures. Through many rearrangements and theoretical retrenchments as well as the writing of two new conceptual papers and one new empirical analysis, all this gradually became the book *Chaos of Disciplines*, finally cleaned up in 1997–99 and published in 2001.

The temporality material for the destroyed time book was also adrift. Some of the pieces I reused. I plundered the "sequences in other disciplines" material for an *Annual Review* article in 1995 and the causality material eventually resurfaced in the late 1990s, as I note below. The other material disappeared into the graveyard of my files. Thus the 1992 ASA paper was indeed a watershed in my work on temporality. The three papers of part two capture my work just before that watershed.

The first of these came when I was asked to write a paper for a conference organized by Howie Becker and Charles Ragin on the topic "what is a case?" This was an insomniac special, written in the very early mornings before our new baby shattered the local silence. I decided to do an *analyse de texte*, in this case a more or less linguistic analysis of three articles in what was at the moment the latest *AJS*. The paper wrote itself. I called it "What

Do Cases Do?" partly because that was what it was about, but partly because I had come to like question titles, particularly admiring Joan Robinson's *What Are the Questions?*

"What Do Cases Do?"

"Cases" begins by analyzing three articles with a simple procedure. I read the theoretical sections of the articles, underline the narrative and action verbs, and then show what are the subjects of those verbs. A striking result is that in the two standard-methodology articles variables rather than actors do the acting, except when unexpected things happen, in which case authors fall back on telling stories about actors. Even in those cases, however, parametric properties of the actors are actually all that change; the actors themselves are conceived essentially as rational automata. By contrast, in an article giving an institutional analysis of gender inequality in hierarchical pay systems, there are many narratives involving real individuals and actors, all with complex personal structures.

The paper goes on to analyze the single-case narrative as a methodological strategy, elaborating the account set forth in "Transcending." Drawing on the sources for my 1983 sequence article, I give accounts of narrative explanation within the frameworks of structuralism and the analytic philosophy of history. Through this analysis I begin to clarify what exactly is involved in the concept of "variables," a topic that reaches back to Blumer's celebrated paper on that subject. My paper then tries to bridge the gap between independent and interdependent narratives by developing a trichotomy of (a) stage theories (independent narratives that I would later call natural histories, following the old Chicago school terminology), (b) career theories (semi-independent narratives), and (c) interactional systems (in which interdependence is so great that one cannot think about single narratives at all, the kind of system I had analyzed in *The System of Professions*). I later extended this analysis by providing a second dimension for interdependence, that of space, in my ASA Sorokin lecture, written about this time but not published until 1997. (It is now the concluding chapter of *Department and Discipline*.) In "Cases" I also hint at a general language for transformations among social structures at different levels. This was part of a research program in occupational coalescence that grew out of *The System of Professions*, a program of which I shall say more below.

"Conceptions of Time and Events"

The second of the part two papers, "Conceptions of Time and Events," was written for the SSHA in 1989 and published in *Historical Methods* the next year. The paper aims to establish some points that had emerged as crucial for me in my polemic with standard methods. By now this was a more focused debate, for event history methods had become standard graduate school fare and were commonly believed to "answer" the question of temporality. My first point is simply that one should differentiate clearly between thinking about the world in sequences (patterns) and in variables (causes). I use the concept of careers to illustrate the difference. On the one hand is my conception of whole careers as single units to be analyzed at once. On the other is the by-then standard Markovian conception of careers (implicit in event history methods) as the accidental results of a stochastic process run through a certain number of time intervals. What is at issue is the nature of the regularities to be found. The cases should be seen as fish in a lake (i.e., as moving dots in an n-dimensional state space). If they swim in certain regular patterns, linear models (and their temporally stochastic derivatives) can capture those patterns. But if they are constrained by weeds always to swim around certain parts of the lake in certain ways, then only sequence methods can discover the patterns. If the exact shape of past history has binding effects on the future, too, there will be "long" patterns in the sequences, visible only to whole-sequence-based methods.

"Conceptions" goes on to two other important demonstrations. The first of these is a demonstration that most things that could happen don't. This point was crucial to my polemic against "general linear reality." The general linear model for data is a single statement that applies everywhere in the data space. This means you write a statement that governs many things that don't occur, which could be very wasteful scientifically. Perhaps one can more quickly simplify a data space by simply categorizing it. Seen in its broadest terms, this argument is a brief for description against "causal analysis," a topic I would more fully explore in "The Causal Devolution," the third paper of part one. But at this time I saw it mainly as a brief for sequence analysis. If most of the possible data sequences that can occur are not observed (if most possible tracks through the data space are not followed), then sequence analysis might well be a faster way to simplify the space than would be writing a linear model for data in that space.

It was too complicated to quickly demonstrate that "most things that could happen don't" with over-time data, so the paper does it with cross-sectional data on the fifty states, taken from the *Statistical Abstract*. It was great fun, particularly since my prediction turned out to be true at a level that surprised even me. The paper uses the same data to illustrate my second important point: that the concept of outlierness is a fractal. Removing one set of outliers just makes new things outliers. This is less an important polemical point than a simple *jeu d'esprit*. I was angry about the idiotic pictures of "uncorrelated" data displayed prominently in statistics and sociology textbooks. They usually showed highly nonrandom data, spread quite uniformly about the space in a way that random data never is. So I demonstrate in the paper that uncorrelated data can be filled with regularities and, furthermore, that the problem of having outliers is actually a fractal quality of any real dataset.

Both these arguments were and are profound challenges to standard methods. In particular, this paper provides a deep challenge to event history methods with their philosophical pretense that repeated measures on single individuals count as independent observations. Not only is this statistically worrisome (as I have noted in a number of papers, the issue being the use of maximum likelihood estimation in the presence of the extremely high correlations among variables induced by repeated measures). It is also just philosophical idiocy. If Illinois doesn't pass a certain kind of law in forty years and then passes it in year forty-one, no cancellation in the world should persuade us that we have forty-one independent observations.

"Conceptions" goes on to discuss the issue of "time horizon," the different sizes of time period over which a given variable is thought to have an effect. The paper sees clearly that GLR makes radical assumptions about the temporal "size" of variables. But it does not really state how these could be avoided. An absolutely Markovian view of the social world (everything happens instantaneously and there are no "big" events) presents real problems (there obviously are big events). But it is not clear how to avoid the Markovian view without buying into the equally problematic assumptions of GLR (that events can be influenced only by equal-sized or bigger ones). The paper is thus a good one, in that it sees two sides to profound issues, but a bad one, in that it comes to no conclusion.

The third of these papers, "From Causes to Events," tried to put my whole temporality program in context. The published paper (1992 in *Sociological Methods and Research*) was assembled out of two 1991 papers—one for the ASA and one for Harrison White's first "Shaker Inn Conference," held a few miles from my parents' house in New Hampshire. This conference was memorable mainly because Washington called Bruce Bueno de Mesquita away from the conference table to "run his models" and "tell us what's going to happen in Russia," where Gorbachev had just been imprisoned in his dacha. It was also memorable for the incredulous stares on the faces of Bueno de Mesquita and other rational choice scholars when Eric Leifer said in the course of his characteristically offhand talk that "skill means arranging your life so you never have to make a rational choice." The "causes" paper also marked a personal watershed of a sort, for in it I self-consciously gave up my earlier pretense that I had a unique view of these issues, in particular forcing myself to give Peter Abell his due as a coworker in the vineyard.

"From Causes to Events"

"Causes" once again sets forth the distinction between a narrative and an analytic conception of social reality. By this time, the word "narrative" had come to mean (in the disciplines at large) different things than it had when I first worked in this area, however. Transformations in history had brought narrative back to the center of historiographical thinking, sometimes as bogeyman (as in "grand narratives"), sometimes as hero (as in "narratives of the people without voice"). To qualitatively inclined readers the term "narrative" had irrevocably subjective connotations. Many who encountered my paper were therefore bewildered and put off by the phrase "narrative positivism" in its subtitle. For the narrative conception of social reality that it sets forth is still "positivistic" in that it does not necessarily assume the multivocality of social life nor does it believe that formalized comparison and even hypothesis testing about narratives are impossible.

The paper evokes quickly a history of causalism that I was to set forth much more fully in "Causal Devolution" several years later. It also calls on the analysis of methodological assumptions in "Transcending," summarizes concerns about the nature of events that dated from my earliest (1983 and 1984) sequence papers, and evokes the theoretical analysis that concluded "Cases." The main novelty of the paper is its forthright review of empirical methodologies for generalizing about narratives, covering many areas I had dealt with in very early papers, but organizing them under the contrast between modeling approaches and descriptive approaches. Under the latter I distinguished between Peter Abell and David Heise's somewhat more formal techniques and my own rough-and-ready use of optimal matching. As it has happened, and somewhat as I expected, the elegance and complexity of Abell's and Heise's methods has hurt their adoption. Optimal matching is simpleminded in many ways, but it has proved portable in ways that homology analysis and event structure analysis have not.[5]

After this review of the papers of part two, it is useful to step back and see

5. For a current review of sequence analysis in social science generally, the reader should see Abbott 1995b. On optimal matching in particular, see Abbott and Tsay 2000.

what else I was doing in that period. As usual, my other activities played a big role in determining what happened next in this particular line of work, that is, in my response to the crisis of my 1992 ASA paper.

In the period of the part two papers, I was also moving ahead on the purely methodological front. I wrote several applications of optimal matching and sequencing methods to basic sociological datasets, mostly with friends and students. Stan DeViney and I analyzed sequences of the development of welfare states, showing that there weren't any correlates of the sequence patterns. John Forrest and I analyzed versions of the Native American "Star Husband Tale," replicating in an afternoon a categorization that had taken Stith Thompson several years. We also did some reliability work on the effects of coding variation on optimal matching applications. On my own I dug out an old dataset on medical institutions in American cities that I had created in my first seriation days and reanalyzed it using multidimensional scaling to do the seriation (as I should have done in the rejected chapters of *System of Professions*). This paper answered at last the old question of whether professionals' first move was towards control of work or development of professional knowledge. The answer was control of work. The earlier (simple seriation) version of this analysis had been part of my 1984 event sequence paper, from which I had cut it at publication time because I found the empirical analysis unpersuasive. But I retained from the earlier paper the explicit attention to the problem of measurement theory in sequence analysis, which remains the most important aspect of this empirical application.

At the same time, I was moving into new methodological waters. I had long been interested in figuring out what we might call, following the earlier metaphor, the problem of constrained fish—the question of whether there might be parts of narrative sequences (careers, life courses, etc.) that everyone had to traverse the same way. Rob Sampson had come to Chicago at the same time as I and was interested in criminal careers. A subsequence driving people into criminality (a turning point, as it were) was something that interested him. But no one had an algorithm for multiple subsequence alignment, an algorithm to find turning points in sequences. In desperation one day, I called up Stephen Altschul, whose name seemed to appear on 90 percent of the interesting articles I had run into on sequence alignment. He asked me if I took *Science* magazine. I told him yes, and he replied, a little stiffly, that he and others had just published such an algorithm there. (I should have been reading the thing, not just scanning it!) This proved to be a Gibbs sampling algorithm, which I immediately managed to replicate on my PC, in one of the most lucky programming outings I've ever had. Some old acquaintances turned up in the literature on Gibbs sampling (a way of using Markov chains to sample data spaces too big or too complex to explore otherwise); Alan Gelfand—whom I had encountered long before in the seriation literature—proved to be one of the apostles of the new technique. Gibbs sampling also provided a powerful metaphor for thinking about how social processes work, although I haven't written anything from that metaphor yet. With Emily Barman I did write a Gibbs-based article (designed for one journal, but eventually appearing in another in 1997) on orders of subsections in *AJS* articles. Sadly, the study of criminal careers with Sampson bogged down in technical difficulties.

So the years of part two and afterwards were years in which I did a fair amount of methodological development. I was overwhelmingly aware, by the time I finished the three papers of part two and did the methodological work just mentioned, that my own new methods had their profound assumptions about independence of cases. But what caused the crisis for me was rather my recognition that I was implicitly presuming a kind of reality to narrative regularities that was philosophically quite worrisome. The past, quite simply, doesn't exist. It's gone. The world really is Markovian at some level; there is only the immediate past and its passage into the present. How then can one have narratives that are wholes—enduring things with influence over the future? Do we really want to think that if you've gone 80 percent of the way down some path, you have to go the rest? Or to think that that's a useful model for thinking about social reality in general? Yet that view was implicit, at least in some ways, in my argument that narrative regularity was the right way to think about social processes. Indeed, it was at the heart of "Conceptions."

How can events in the past influence the present? Obviously "through memory" was one answer. My friends in the discipline of history—in particular Bill Sewell, with whom I was coteaching during what was for both of us our first quarter at Chicago in the fall of 1991—could accept this easily enough. History was for them a cultural affair; the symbolic endurance of the past was enough to guarantee its influence in the present. But I wanted more than that. I wanted structural influence for the past. I wanted not to have to invoke culture at this point, only later. But the structural past is well and truly gone. It can have its influence—this was one of those cases where you form the sentence then you try to figure out what the words in it actually mean—only if it somehow encodes itself into the present on a continuing basis.

It was in my abortive 1992 ASA paper that I first began to sketch out a concept of this encoding. I still haven't figured it out completely, but I have figured out that it provides the key to a number of long-standing puzzles. It provides the grounding for the long-term influence of narrative on the future, for the effect of the deep past. It also provides the reconciliation for the four separate parts of my Ph.D. thesis, for it allows historical processes of varying sizes to have influence on one single present.

But the immediate implication of this idea, as I noted above, was that any book about temporality had to be a book about social structure at the same time. Indeed, I am in the middle of writing such a book at this moment, in the same way I was in the middle of writing *Chaos of Disciplines* in 1990, when all the ideas were wandering around in my head but I had no idea which of them would go in that particular book.

The turn to structure of course didn't mean that I stopped thinking about temporality. I had to reflect what exactly we mean by the passage of time. I was by this time (1992–93) involved again in archival historical work, for Marta Tienda had asked me to do a history of the *AJS*. My theoretical concerns naturally shifted somewhat with my empirical preoccupations. I became less bothered by the technicalities of optimal matching and its assumptions, realizing that like other methods it would be used if it gave interesting results and ignored otherwise, whatever its assumptions. But I became more concerned with the issue of the shape and nature of social things. Just exactly what was I writing the history of when I wrote a history of the *AJS*? In the middle of the *AJS* effort, I was asked to write about the Chicago school, and began to wonder what kind of a beast that was as well. Oddly enough, these historical studies fit in directly with work I had planned when I came to Chicago in 1991 but had gradually left behind. I had planned to take the German musicians data, combine it with my (newly coded) thesis data on American psychiatrists, and do a study on the bases of occupational coalescence. The central questions were to be when and how occupations actually became social things. I wrote a few draft papers on this subject, but in the rush of other obligations, the empirical side of the project gradually got shelved. (I would later steal various parts of the theoretical drafts for other papers.) In any case, the historical question of the continuity of social things had a prehistory for me, now underscored by the endless (and endlessly pleasurable) archival work on the *AJS*. The archival and historical side of this work would ultimately take form in the book *Department and Discipline*, which I tried to frame—perhaps unsuccessfully—around the issue of the nature of historical entities. The theoretical material, along with the empirical studies of occupational coalescence, remains largely unfinished.

But my concern here is with the reflections on temporality that arose out of the intellectual crisis induced by my 1992 ASA paper and the fact that I experienced that crisis in the context of a turn towards archival rather than formal methodological work. By 1994, having spent a year or so fiddling the wreckage of the abortive time book into the first version (later completely revised) of what would be *Chaos of Disciplines*, I began to turn to temporality proper. As usual there was a handy occasion.

"Temporality and Process" was written in first draft in the summer of 1994 for the annual conference of the Norwegian Sociology Association. By this time I had become familiar with my pattern of grandiose beginnings followed by desultory wanderings and panicked cleanups. The various grand designs for books on time that I had done in the early 1990s had produced, among other things, the notion that I ought to read the philosophy of time. I had a large bibliography, but the good sense not to begin to read it all. Only one book. For reasons I don't remember, I read Whitehead's *Process and Reality* cover to cover, perhaps ten pages at a time, in 1993. What led to this, I don't know. I was a complete insomniac at the time, under the burden of simultaneously editing *Work and Occupations*, being Master of the College's Social Science Division and Deputy Dean of the Social Sciences Division, teaching three courses a year, doing my research, and helping raise a five-year-old. Most mornings I arose at 5:30 and either did administrative work or read my ten pages of Whitehead. I did not have the sanitized and reorganized new edition of *Process and Reality*, so the text was overwhelmingly confusing.

For the paper itself, I followed my old *analyse de texte* format, picking three writers to "read" in depth: Bergson, Mead, and Whitehead. For Bergson and Mead I simply worked through the relatively short texts involved (*Time and Free Will* and *The Philosophy of the Present*, respectively). I had already read the monumental Whitehead. Actually, only the Bergson and Mead sections of the paper were written by the time I got to the conference at spray-girt Tjøme. But the experience of the conference led to a serious rewriting of the paper, producing the version here. Midway through the conference we were taken on a day-long bus tour of the local sights—the field where they found the Oseberg Viking ship, Edvard Munch's house at Åsgårdstrand, and the town of Tønsberg, where everything from the widows' and orphans' home to the hospital and almshouse seemed to be named for a man called Svend Foyn. What had Svend Foyn done, we asked? He invented the grenade harpoon, they said. So that's where all the widows and orphans came from, we thought! So I recast the paper by using the underlying texts to analyze the particular event of inventing the grenade harpoon.

"Temporality and Process in Social Life"

The resulting paper, written in fall 1994, was published later (much later, as is usually the case with collections) in the conference volume *Social Time and Social Change*, edited by Fredrik Engelstad and Ragnvald Kalleberg. This paper is perhaps less summarizable than any other I have written. It starts with a brief statement of the invention of the grenade harpoon, the tool that finally enabled the hunting of the great whales. (The specific gravity of the great whales at death means they sink. When a harpooned blue whale weighing two hundred tons sinks in three thousand feet of water at the end of two thousand feet of line, one does not want to be in a small whaleboat with the line cleated home. The grenade harpoon enabled whalers to shoot from the mother ship, which had enough buoyancy to keep even the largest whale from sinking. Foyn's harpoon gun was such a device.)

I reflect in the first section of the paper on the Eleatic paradoxes of time, and in particular on the conception of historical "epochs," periods within which a certain set of social laws holds true. Epochs seem like a useful way to divide labor between history and sociology; sociology applies within an epoch, history explains why there are epochs. But if epochs in fact exist, how could any force traverse them that would change their fundamental laws?

Reading Bergson leads me to focus on the nature of experienced duration as indexical, multiple, and inclusive. It is centered on a perceiver, and thus is indexical. It is of many different, overlapping sizes, and hence is multiple. It is ranked by size, but always concentric, and thus is inclusive. But Bergson has no account of others' time, only of ego's. And thus he has no account of social time. He also has no account of how determination fits into the freedom that seems inherent in personal time.

After considering and rejecting a number of contemporary versions of temporality (including Ricoeur's), I turn next to Mead. Mead accepts Bergson's reading of time as multiple, inclusive, and indexical. But he insists on the nearly infinite plasticity of the past, seeing its irrevocability as a quality assigned to it by us after the fact. At the same time, he has no account of how the potential muddle of pasts generated by many observers is worked into a socially more or less stable perception. In the last chapter of *Philosophy of the Present*, however, Mead begins to develop a concept of the "distance" between individuals and to argue that it is this distance—which makes messages from similar (in Newtonian terms) presents reach us at different moments—that gives us the basis for developing a social sense of time. This difference of presents enables us to escape the inherent granularity of actual temporal experience.

From Whitehead I take mainly his conception of ontology. For Whitehead, the world is a world of events. These events can be defined into the stable lineages that we call (social) things. The crucial effect of this move is to destroy the micro/macro problem as a difficulty in social theory. For now both individuals and social structures of all kinds are produced instantaneously out of relationships defined on the endless flow of events. Moreover, the problem of historical epochs has been resolved. Since change is the norm, it is easily explained. One has rather to explain stability. In the remainder of the paper I sketch out the implications of this Whiteheadian ontology, which is indeed one foundation of the much larger theoretical book I am writing. Here I begin to put some skin on the bones of the concept of encoding (from my 1992 ASA paper), although on rereading I can see that this paper may remain too faithful to the Whiteheadian language for the casual reader.

My new view of temporality meant I could start to play with new ideas about structure. This meant returning to the problems about entities and structures raised by assumptions one, five, and six of "Transcending." (These are the assumptions about the existence of entities and about their independence of each other and of context.) These issues of entities and structures are the focus of the two final papers of part three.

Unlike most of my papers, "On the Concept of Turning Point" has no involved history. I was asked by Fredrik Engelstad (of the Norway conference) to respond to a paper of John Goldthorpe's in a volume of *Comparative Social Research* that Fredrik was editing. Although John was soon to become an acquaintance (I spent the spring of 1997 at Oxford's Nuffield College where he is an Official Fellow), I knew him less for his methodological writings than for his celebrated work on stratification. I thought John had in this case set up some straw men. But one of them was me, and so I have left in the version published here the short beginning of my paper, which responds to the issues John's paper raised. But my paper basically used Goldthorpe's critique as an excuse to launch its own argument. I had long been bothered by the philosophical status of the concept of turning point. It seemed to be one of those terms that meant whatever the writer wanted it to mean, particularly in the life course literature. I thought a good going-over would help us make it a more useful term. But I ended up writing only the first part of the paper on the title topic, turning in the second to a theory of structure that proceeded out of the concept of turning point and that could justify both my "narratives are real" stance *and* a structural reality, but without involving the intricacies of my concept of encoding.

"On the Concept of Turning Point"

After the introduction about John Goldthorpe and his concerns, "Turning Point" bases itself on mathematical concepts of turning points for both continuous and discrete processes. One of the essential insights here is that the concept of turning point is a "narrative concept." It cannot be conceived without reference to two points in time. (One can't know at the time that a turning point has occurred; if we could do that, we would all be beating the stock market all the time.) The paper then goes on to develop a concept of "trajectories," those parts of a process that *aren't* "turning points." It notes that these are the portions of the social process that are most susceptible to analysis by standard methodologies, but points out that the turning points may in fact be more crucial. Much of social reality, I argue, can be imagined as a structure in which actors proceed through trajectories to their ends, then face the striking and to some extent randomizing moments of turning points. Here was a different division of labor with standard methods; standard methods could analyze the easy part (the trajectories), sequence methods the consequential part (the turning points).

The second part of the paper raises the issue of whether choice models—another Goldthorpian theme—really are a sensible way to think about the unfolding of the social process. It then goes on to further adumbrate the view of social structure emerging in "Temporality." Again actors and structures are defined as networks of events. An important subtheme here is the multiplicity of events; when I act, men act, professors act, people over fifty (sigh) act, etc. As in "Temporality," I try to undercut the language of "large" and "small" in social structure by insisting that these sizes have more to do with temporal endurance (the social structures we call large are the ones with long endurance) than sheer populousness (we do not necessarily think social structures "large" if they merely involve many people).

The third paper of part three, "Things of Boundaries," arose from the intersection of two 1995 obligations. On the one hand Dick Scott of Stanford invited me to speak at the Asilomar conference, an annual academic party he used to give for Stanford graduate students interested in organizations. On the other hand I had promised to write something about boundaries for an issue of *Social Research,* one of these things where they round up the usual suspects and hope at least one or two of them have something new to say. I was unenthused, because I knew that boundaries had become very trendy; academic life generally was flooded with "boundary transgressions" unleashed by the confused reasoning humanists call theory. But then my morning shower once again produced a great idea. Everybody was talking about boundaries as the key to everything. Why not pull the judo move of throwing them with their own weight? I would jettison the idea of things altogether and assume that boundaries came first, then we made things out of them. So this paper began with the old heuristic trick of forming a phrase by means of a purely syntactic discourse rule—in this case the phrase "things of boundaries"—and then figuring out what that phrase could possibly mean semantically. It was the same strategy I had used for the concept of encoding.

Fortunately, I saw that I had all sorts of intellectual junk lying around that would do something with the phrase "things of boundaries." First, I had the shreds of another attention deficit disorder foray, this one into topology in the mid 1970s. I remember being very interested in something called the "theory of sheaves" at the time. I even wrote a (fortunately lost) paper pretending to apply this theory to something, for a far-off student conference of the Chicago sociology department. In any case, if I was going to imagine things without boundaries I would be heading back into algebraic topology, which I had tried to teach myself from some impenetrable monograph of the American Mathematical Society in mid-1970s. There were a few useful memories left.

Second, and much more important, I had go. Here was a game that basically consisted of trying to make things out of boundaries. Just as my knowledge of the theoretical underpinnings of classical music had always been my secret way of theorizing about multilevel social processes (a fact I more or less confessed in the footnotes of my 1983 sequence paper), go would be my secret way of thinking about things of boundaries. I had taken up go in the early 1990s, for the worst of all possible reasons. I had known about it because I had read Japanese literature for many years, and go figures prominently both in classic works like the *Tale of Genji* and modern ones like *The Master of Go*. But sometime in the early 1990s I decided that somebody like me simply had to be a player of some unusual game. Just as I had taken up classical guitar because it suited the image I wanted to project as a teenager, here I was at forty-five taking up a board game because it was profound and unusual and therefore fit a persona I was still trying to manufacture. I had played chess briefly as a kid, but I was too stupid and couldn't figure it out at all. But go was great, simple yet profound. I learned it by playing against my computer, which did not, like my childhood friend and occasional chess rival George Bourgeois, keep reminding me how stupid I was.

So this paper was very much the typical paper that one writes at this time of life. Relatively open obligations come together with longstanding pieces of knowledge gathered for some other reason or for no reason at all. As usual, I turned to the professions for the empirical example to work out the details, in this case the profession of social work. As with *System of Professions*, I originally planned a hyperdetailed version of this argument at the empirical level, but the data never quite worked out. I did do a more empirical version as the *Social Service Review* lecture in 1995, but even that lacked the empirical detail I wanted. A fun side of "Things" was the chance it gave me to cite an old grad school dormitory friend, the evolutionary biologist Mike Wade, whose group selection models fit nicely into the arguments of the paper.

"Things of Boundaries"

"Things" motivates its problems by noting the strong assumptions about the existence of solidary professions that I had made in *System of Professions*. The paper also invokes the processual ontology of "Temporality," with its insistence on viewing the world of entities as in perpetual flux. The paper then gives a number of examples of "things of boundaries"; for example, I define a profession as a set of turf battles that are yoked into a single defensible position in the system of professions. The argument then turns to the curious logical problem of defining boundaries without having things for them to bound, a difficulty that requires redefinitions of basic words. In particular, I replace the concept of boundary with the concept of "site of difference."

The paper then gives an extended example, the formation of the profession of social work. I show that social work emerged at least in part through the yoking together of several different kinds of differences into a definable social organization. The last part of the paper considers various possible definitions of this "yoking together," one of the central processes in my account of entity emergence. It also considers at length the "thinglike" quality of entities as this is conceived within the framework of processual thinking. Here I stole the theoretical guts of a much earlier (1990) ASA paper on the subject of occupational coalescence. I consider the various ways of conceiving of occupations in terms of the presence or absence of three basic attributes: a particular group of people, a type of work, a form of organization. The paper closes with a short comment relating my views of social entities to those of other standard accounts of social organization.

My 1992 crisis over the relation of temporality and social structure meant that broad-front issues returned to my intellectual foreground. I had to address the other aspects of the "Transcending" agenda. As I have said earlier, I took up the problems of entities and structures (assumptions 1, 2, and 5 of "Transcending") in the papers of part three. Another direction of that agenda was the third "Transcending" assumption, about univocality of meaning. The broader issue here, of course, was of the inevitable ambiguity of things—in short, the question of culture. I had been maintaining a kind of false boundary towards this question for some time at this point. Not that I wasn't writing about culture. *The System of Professions* was quite self-consciously about cultural systems, and the material that would become *Chaos of Disciplines* was mostly cultural as well. But I had been refusing to connect culture into the temporality question at the theoretical level for fear of falling into what seemed to me the facile answer that the "memory" of social systems is predominantly cultural. Yet the rapidity and success with which others—most notably my friend Bill Sewell—took this position and developed it left me feeling I needed to move forward on the cultural front. Indeed Paul Ricoeur's *Time and Narrative* had also made me very nervous, for it drew on literatures—the analytic philosophy of history and literary structuralism—of which I had thought myself pretty much the only current consumer in social theory. It was lucky, I thought, that Ricoeur did not see the purely structural problem of temporality.

I first began to theorize directly about ambiguity in a 1993 paper for a session Susan Watkins had organized at SSHA on new directions for computing in social science history. At some point later I discovered that NORC maintained a complete list of all the studies that had ever used the GSS, together with a list of all the variables they had used. Somehow a crazy idea lurched up from my memories of Rob Parker as prophet of LISREL and measurement models. He had said how important it was to choose the proper multiple indicators for a concept and drew lots of pictures with bunches of indicators pointing up at single concepts. But obviously, different people used one given indicator to indicate many different concepts. What if I turned the whole measurement diagram on its head and asked what were the many conceptual meanings that were attached to a particular variable? All of a sudden I saw one could reverse-engineer the whole quantitative system, discovering how quantitative science worked with ambiguity of meaning by looking at the uses of variables across studies. It was an afternoon's programming to write a program to read the NORC file (it was then in pure text) and retrieve the information. There were some size problems in the dataset, but I was off and running.

"Seven Types of Ambiguity"

So was born "Seven Types of Ambiguity," the second paper of part one. The first part of this paper was my latest statement of the exact relation between narrative and analytic approaches to social reality, complete with a list of seven places where ambiguity and multiplicity of meaning blurred the translation from the one to the other. (The title was stolen from a book of literary criticism that I had enjoyed back in my college years as a major in history and literature.) There is no need to list those seven types of ambiguity here, but they are, in practice, all problems familiar to careful practitioners of the standard empirical methodologies. Some are related to time, others to indication. Some arise at a particular level of explanation, some between levels.

The second section of the paper considers all the articles published to that point (1997) using the religious intensity variable of the General Social Survey. I begin with a cluster analysis of the most common variables used in these studies, showing them to fall into a very clear set of clusters. I then turn the categorization around and categorize articles in terms of the variables they used, separating the articles into four waves in time. These are presented as cluster analyses and show a number of remarkable things. They illustrate in large all the forms of ambiguity earlier discussed. More important, they show how once we look at literatures as wholes, a single variable acts as a node in a complex network of possible relationships among variables—sometimes dependent, sometimes independent, sometimes intervening. They also show that scientific literatures may begin with small clear tests of important variables, but then move towards a "centrist" model that includes dozens or hundreds of variables. Because of this inevitable drift towards the garbage can use of variables, each literature probably distinguishes itself from the others only in terms of which node it happens to treat as dependent. At the same time, a surprising finding is that real "literatures" don't seem to exist in the data. Given lists of variables are used for wholly different purposes by different investigators.

"Ambiguity" was another sermon to the converted. Positivism hardly flourishes in *Theory and Society*. To make trouble, I therefore steered the paper somewhat against the grain by arguing that one could use the kind of analysis I had done to retrieve from positivistic work information about the real ambiguities of social life. In this sense, a certain form of meta-analysis (like the statistical kind invented by my colleague Larry Hedges, but differing in intent) would provide access to a whole new range of "positivist" information about the ambiguities of meaning in our social structure. Needless to say, there has not been a large response to this proposal.

Also part of my return to broad-front analysis was "The Causal Devolution," which took up issues of causality that had also been raised in "Transcending." First a word about the title. For me "devolution" was just a fun word because of the assonance with "revolution," which is standard in pretentious titles of this type. I had a vague notion that the idea of causalism had devolved on sociology, in the true sense of "devolve," but I was also aware that nobody would know exactly what the word meant, any more than I could remember it without looking it up. I only knew it myself because I had read once about Louis XIV's "Wars of Devolution." Don't ask me what devolved or to whom—as I recall, the Sun King himself used the word in order to be ambiguous. In any case, I liked the word and everybody likes a mystery.

Adrian Raftery asked me to speak in a lecture series he organized to honor Herbert Costner on his retirement, and this paper was the result. Parts of the paper had earlier lives. There had been a section on causality in the abortive time volume of 1990, which I had later expanded for an SSHA paper in 1995. This was the Durkheim discussion. To this I added a detailed history of causalism in sociology, much expanded because of my increased archival knowledge (from the AJS project) and taking off from the polemical history of sociology I had written for my Sorokin lecture in 1992 (which eventually became the last chapter of *Department and Discipline*). So this is another paper with multiple roots in many places of earlier work.

I wrote this piece while at Nuffield College in the spring of 1997. Faced with those three long months alone in a wonderfully supportive intellectual environment, I had the choice of cleaning up a lot of half-done projects or starting something new. Characteristically, I chose to start *Time and Social Structure*, the systematic book implicit in my 1992 ASA paper. Cleaning things up would in any case be impossible, as I couldn't take all the necessary files with me. Only when I came back did I force myself to a schedule that led me to finish *Department and Discipline* and *Chaos of Disciplines* in the following two years.

My obligation to Adrian came in the middle of these three months. Being forced to put down the purely theoretical book for the analysis of causality made me realize that a pure theory book was a mistake. A synthesis would have to work all the way from pure theory into methods, and a reinterpretation (possibly a rejection) of our concept of causality would be a necessary part of that transition. So I began to see (and still do see) this piece as a study for an important chapter in the still far-from-completed *Time and Social Structure.*

"The Causal Devolution"

"Devolution" begins with an extended analysis of the concepts of causality employed in Durkheim's *Suicide.* It is thus, like several other papers here, rooted in an *analyse de texte.* I show Durkheim's arguments to have drawn on typically nineteenth-century positions, but to have revised them in specific ways. My basic argument is that the causal claims of Durkheim's book, quite by historical accident, turned out to be organized exactly along the form taken by the analysis of variance, put forward by Fisher and colleagues shortly after Durkheim's death. This enabled Durkheim's book to become the emblematic text of sociological causalism in the 1960s. Oddly enough, Durkheim himself thought of his arguments as highly *historical,* because in his head he was arguing against immanent evolutionists like Spencer. Causalism proves to be an indexical belief.

The paper continues with a history of the vicissitudes of the concept of causality in sociology. As only a few remember, the initial quantitative revolution in sociology was explicitly anticausalist. Causalism came back in with path analysis in the 1960s. I discuss this history in some detail. The paper then gives a quick review of the contemporary philosophy of causality, revisiting the literature on the philosophy of history, but placing it in a broader context of causal philosophies from Humeanism to logical positivism and ordinary language philosophy. The paper closes with a sermon about sociological methodologies. This starts by pointing out why the causal methods have never sat well with theorists; they ignore social action. I then make a strong plea for description and even simulation as legitimate genres of social investigation.

"Devolution" is the most recent paper in this collection. Yet I find that there are points even in it with which I am beginning to disagree. In particular, as part of developing the ideas for yet another chapter of *Time and Social Structure* I have evolved a new way of thinking about types of explanation in social science. I have felt for some time that we must broaden our conception of explanation, and hope that phrasing my challenge to hegemonic methodologies as a change in how we think about explanation will make it more comprehensible to those who have rejected it.

For the moment, however, the essays collected in the present volume contain the heart of my analysis of time and social structure. That analysis is heavily slanted towards the time side, but touches as well on issues of explanation, culture, and social structure itself. I have tried in this introduction to tell the genesis of these ideas carefully, less so that the essays can be understood in their personal context than so that people setting out on careers might realize exactly how fortuitous one's research life can be. It is true that I set out on this journey wanting to have a grand design and aiming to build up to a comprehensive account of social life. But had I sat down to write that in 1980, I would never have accomplished anything. Rather I pushed a bit on one side, then on another, climbed a hill this way, slabbed the ridge over that way, and so on.

I have also emphasized the part played in this story by a lot of characters who appear, have some effect, then disappear. Sometimes they reappear later. If I were writing a well-organized Victorian narrative, this wouldn't happen. The truly important people would be made important throughout. Prolepsis would carefully introduce crucial minor characters so that they created a proper frisson on their real appearance, and so on.

Of course, this isn't how life happens. I am not sorry, then, to have burdened the reader with the odd reference to Fred Hickok or Phipps Arabie or Pat Cox or Joe Kruskal or whomever. Particular actions of theirs happen to have been quite consequential for me, even as other actions of theirs were quite consequential for legions of people I haven't met. I have tried to tell the story so that the reader sees its openness towards chance, its embeddedness in a vast flow of contingent social experience. There is no Barthesian well-written story, although, as Ricoeur saw so well, well-written stories are our standard way of reflecting about how the world works.

In fact the story I tell here very much follows the theories I write. The research enterprise as I have experienced it is quite Whiteheadian. Given pieces of work are redefined by later work. Old drafts are taken up into new things and transformed. Most of my pieces take their places in several lineages of analysis, serving one function in one part of my work, another in another. The general result is a network of thinking directed overall at a single overarching problem but by no means organized in a straight-ahead fashion. I must therefore plead guilty to the charge, made by my friend John Padgett in a wry aside some years ago, that I have published all of my intermediate results. Indeed, because of this networked character, my work sometimes appears to me, its author, as having a quality of pastiche that I hope is not there for the reader. (Vis-à-vis John's statement, however, I am not sure I believe there is any result that is not an intermediate result.)

If I can invoke yet another metaphor, I have as a scholar been a Gibbs sampler. Gibbs sampling is a way of using conditional probability information to yield marginal information. You set up the conditionals as a Markov chain, iterate the chain and voilà, by the fundamental theory of Markov chains, you end up with marginals. I have been just like this. I don't know exactly where the "final end" of my project is, the way John perhaps thinks I ought to. In the meantime, I try to improve one lineage at a time. I conduct that improvement by looking at how that particular lineage is progressing, given all the ideas I get from everything else I'm working on. I then use that (conditional) information to pick a route for the development of that particular lineage. Then I write it up. Then I go on to some other lineage of my work and do the same thing there, only now taking my just-written advance on the present lineage as part of my conditional information about the next one. It's rather like a Gibbs sampler, only I live it. It turns out, of course, that Gibbs samplers can be made into very effective optimization machines. They lack the clear analytic logic of Newtonian optimization. But they work better in complicated and ill-behaved spaces.

I have an idea that processes like these work throughout the social system. At the same time, I am worried about imagining this as a process of optimization. For the rereading of these pieces, both the ones included here and, more important, the ones from the early 1980s that I have omitted, leaves me with a lingering fondness for the earlier versions. It is as if the theme of history and sociology, or of narrative and analysis if you will, is not a final end to be somehow reached, but an opera score to be performed and reperformed. I have produced the opera many times—in one disciplinary costume or in another, with arguments ranging from old veterans to reigning divas to rank novices, in famous journals and in intellectual summer stock. And if the performances have become with time more complex and profound, if my deeper understanding of the opera's structure enables my recent performances to comprehend more and more of what the opera can potentially say, there still remain to my first performances a bravura and an energy that I cannot now summon.

I suspect it is this way with all the great issues of social science, perhaps of knowledge itself. We are not discoverers, but performers. We have our time, perhaps, in the public eye. But other performers and other performances will come. For us it is enough to have mounted the work as often as we could and to have recognized that in fact there is no original score, only the endless succession of productions.

PART ONE

Methods and Assumptions

Transcending General Linear Reality

A growing chasm divides sociological theory and sociological research. While the general linear model and other new techniques have reshaped empirical work, renewed acquaintance with the classics has transformed theory. These contradictory transformations have bred acrimony. Some have sought to reduce social statistics to the status of a substantive theory, while others accuse theorists of proliferating vague alternatives. The debate has been taken up by interactionists, macro theorists, and many others over the years. But the split did not assume its current proportions until the challenging and once-laborious mathematics of linear and characteristic equations became computerized. Quantitative work has since come to dominate central disciplinary journals, while theoretical and qualitative work has increasingly founded its own journals and/or chosen book form.[1]

In this paper I identify one intellectual source for disagreement between theorists and empiricists. I shall argue that there is implicit in standard methods a "general linear reality" (GLR), a set of deep assumptions about how and why social events occur, and that these assumptions prevent the

This paper was originally presented at the Social Science History Association in Chicago on 23 November 1985, and was originally published in *Sociological Theory* 6 (1988): 169–86; reprinted with permission of the American Sociological Association. I thank Ron Angel, Joel Devine, Larry Griffin, Bill Gronfein, Erik Monkkonen, Doug Nelson, and Rob Parker for comments on the original paper.

1. See Collins 1984 on statistics as a substantive theory and Blalock 1984a:138 ff. for a critique of theorists. For the interactionist critique, see Blumer 1931, 1940, 1956. For a macrotheoretical perspective, see Coser 1975. Wilner (1985) discusses quantitative dominance. That commodification is central to methodological preeminence is easily demonstrated. Blalock's text (1960) is the classic sociological source on regression and other methods currently commodified in SPSS and similar packages. A contrasting source on uncommodified methods applying mathematical techniques to sociology is Coleman 1964. In the 1966–70 period, Blalock had 162 citations to Coleman's 117 in *Social Science Citation Index*. The figures for later years are: 1971, 54 to 39; 1975, 117 to 24; 1980, 121 to 24; 1984, 104 to 15. That Coleman's excellent book has never been reprinted testifies to the same fact.

One caution should be raised concerning terminology throughout the paper. The labels "theorist" and "empiricist" (or "methodologist") are arbitrary polar terms designed to refer quickly to ideal-typical positions. They do not, obviously, embody a formal sociology of sociology.

analysis of many problems interesting to theorists and empiricists alike. In addition to delineating these assumptions, I shall consider alternative methods relaxing them. The paper closes with a brief discussion of three alternative sets of methodological presuppositions about social reality. Through this analysis, I aim not to renew pointless controversies, for I believe the general linear model (GLM) is a formidable and effective method. But I argue that the model has come to influence our actual construing of social reality, blinding us to important phenomena that can be rediscovered only by diversifying our formal techniques.[2]

I General Linear Reality

The phrase "general linear reality" denotes a way of thinking about how society works. This mentality arises through treating linear models as representations of the actual social world. This representational usage can be opposed to the more cautious use of linear models in which the analyst believes that some substantive causal process logically entails patterns of relations between variables, patterns which can then be tested by that model to discover whether the actual state of affairs is consistent with the substantive mechanism proposed. These two uses will be called the representational and entailment uses, respectively. The discussion of section II will outline precisely what theoretical assumptions are implicit in representational usage. To begin the analysis, however, we must first sketch the mathematics of the model.

The general linear model makes some particular variable dependent on a set of antecedent variables up to an error term:

$$y = Xb + u \tag{1}$$

Lowercase letters here represent vectors and uppercase ones matrices. The row dimension of y, u, and X is the number of cases observed (m), while the

2. Much of theorists' disaffection with methods reflects not opposition to quantification, but the common belief that standard linear models are the only possible formalization for theories. Although there are other approaches, few have wide application (see Freese 1980 and Freese and Sell 1980 for reviews of formal sociological theorizing). Most classic work on theory and theory construction (e.g., Hage 1972; Abell 1971; even Stinchcombe 1968) has employed the GLR view of social reality. I should note that I assume throughout that theory exists to provide comprehensible and logically rigorous accounts of facts. Definitions of comprehensibility, logicality, and facticity are of course debatable. Some theorists believe that empiricists' "facts" are uninteresting or artifactual while some empiricists believe that theorists' theories are incomprehensible and esthetic. But despite their disagreements about content, the two sides agree that theory aims to explain why facts are what they are. I shall also assume that the basic criterion of rigor is logical formalism. Although there are many types of logic, I wish to exclude esthetics as the basic criterion of theory and the correlated notion that much theory is in principle unformalizable.

column dimension of $\mathbf{X}$ and row dimension of $\mathbf{b}$ is the number (n) of antecedent variables. We can disregard the constant term without loss.

In formal terms, the model is a linear transformation from R^n into R^1. The transformation itself makes no assumptions about causality or direction; any column of $\mathbf{X}$ can be interchanged with $\mathbf{y}$ if the appropriate substitution in $\mathbf{b}$ is made. Using the transformation to represent social causality, however, assumes that $\mathbf{y}$ occurs "after" everything in $\mathbf{X}$. In cross-sectional application, use of the model postulates a "causal time" that takes the place of actual time.[3]

That the range of the linear transformation has but one dimension is a constraint imposed by problems of estimation. One can easily conceive a general-form GLM:

$$\mathbf{X}_t = \mathbf{X}_{t-1}\mathbf{B} + \mathbf{U} \tag{2}$$

Here the index embeds the variables in actual time. Each succeeding value of *each* variable reflects a unique mix of all the antecedents. $\mathbf{B}$ becomes a square matrix of dimension n, and the full transformation is thus from R^n into R^n. This more general GLM underlies most panel studies, although the relevant coefficients can be estimated only by deleting on theoretical grounds some fraction of the dependence this model postulates. Loosely, this second model envisions the situation as a school of fish (the cases) swimming in some regular pattern (the transformation) through a multidimensional lake (the variable or attribute space).

To use such a model to actually represent social reality one must map the processes of social life onto the algebra of linear transformations. This connection makes assumptions about social life: *not* the statistical assumptions required to estimate the equations, but philosophical assumptions about how the social world works.[4] Such representational use assumes that the social world consists of fixed entities (the units of analysis) that have attributes (the variables). These attributes interact, in causal or actual time, to create outcomes, themselves measurable as attributes of the fixed entities. The variable attributes have only one causal meaning (one pattern of effects) in a given study, although of course different studies make similar attributes mean different things. An attribute's causal meaning cannot depend on the entity's location in the attribute space (its context), since the linear transformation is the same throughout that space. For similar reasons, the past path of an entity through the attribute space (its history) can have no influence on its future path, nor can the causal importance of an at-

---

3. For an elegant analysis of time in such models, see Robinson 1980.
4. For a polemical analysis of the statistical assumptions, see Leamer 1983.

tribute change from one entity to the next. All must obey the same transformation.

There are, of course, ways of relaxing some of these assumptions within
standard methods, all of them at substantial cost in interpretability. But it is
striking how absolutely these assumptions contradict those of the major theoretical traditions of sociology. Symbolic interactionism rejects the assumption of fixed entities and makes the meaning of a given occurrence depend on
its location—within an interaction, within an actor's biography, within a sequence of events. Both the Marxian and Weberian traditions deny explicitly
that a given property of a social actor has one and only one set of causal implications. Marx's dialectical causality makes events produce an opposite as
well as a direct outcome, while Weber and the various hermeneutic schools
treat attributes as infinitely nuanced and ambiguous. Marx, Weber, and work
deriving from them in historical sociology all approach social causality in
terms of stories, rather than in terms of variable attributes. To be sure, Marx
and Weber discuss variable attributes in some of their purely conceptual
writing, but their most currently influential works are complex stories in
which attributes interact in unique ways—the *Protestant Ethic*, the *General
Economic History*, the *Eighteenth Brumaire*, and even much of *Capital*.

The contrast between these assumptions and those of GLR suggests
that theorists may reject empirical sociology because of the philosophical
approach implicit in representational use of the GLM. In the rest of this paper, I shall consider the assumptions of that use, drawing examples from
work by some of the best exponents of the GLM. For each assumption, I
will discuss its nature, the attempts made to relax it within standard methods, and the types of alternative methods extant or possible. My focus
throughout on the problems with GLR and the potentialities of its alternatives does *not* imply any derogation of its very great successes, and in particular any derogation of the studies I use as examples. But by exploring the
theoretical limits of the GLM, I hope to suggest new lines of development
in empirical sociology.

II The Fundamental Assumptions
A. *Fixed Entities with Attributes*

A central assumption of the GLM is that the world consists of entities
with attributes. Entities are fixed; attributes can change. In practice, standard empirical work overwhelmingly concerns biological individuals,
governmental units, and other entities considered to be "stable" by common cultural definitions. The GLM is less often applied to social groups

like occupations, professions, and social movements whose members and social boundaries are continually changing.

The entities/attributes model for reality can best be understood by contrasting it with its most common alternative, the central-subject/event model. A historical narrative is organized around a central subject. This central subject may be a sequence of events (the coming of the Second World War), a transformation of an entity or set of entities into a new one (the making of the English working class), or indeed a simple entity (Britain between the wars). The central subject includes or endures a number of events, which may be large or small, directly relevant or tangential, specific or vague. Delineating a central subject and the relevant events—the task of colligation—is the fundamental problematic of classical historiography.[5]

Precisely the same phenomena are organized by the entities/attributes and central-subject/event approaches, but in different ways. Consider the problem of the spread of the multidivisional form (MDF) among American firms as analyzed by Fligstein.[6] There is a set of entities—the firms—which at any given moment have fairly clear boundaries. Firms can be thought of as having properties—size, rate of asset increase, domination by certain kinds of individuals, business strategies. We can imagine generalizing across the "cases" in terms of these "variables" and asking about the relation of the variables to the use of MDF. Yet we could also think about the history of a given "area" of firms, say the utilities area. We will see some entities in that area disappear through merger, others appear through internal differentiation and separation. Firm sizes will fluctuate through this appearance and disappearance as well as through variation in continuous entities. Some dominant individuals will control certain firms continuously, while other leaders will move from one firm to another through the mergers and divisions. Strategies will come and go, shaped by interfirm contagion and by period events like the depression. The histories of individual firms will be seen to follow unique paths shaped by the contingencies of their environments. In such a view, what GLR saw as variables describing entities become events occurring to central subjects.

This example shows a profound difficulty with the fixed entities approach; it ignores entity change through birth, death, amalgamation, and division. One way the MDF can arrive is through merger; yet merger removes entities from the sample and replaces them with new ones. It is not merely a strategy, but an event changing the sample frame. The social sci-

5. On central subjects, see Hull 1975. On colligation, see McCullagh 1978.
6. Fligstein 1985.

ence of demography does indeed deal with appearance and disappearance of entities, and demographic models are now being applied to organizations in the work of the Stanford school of organizational ecologists.[7] Yet the event history models so applied are essentially simple GLMs treating rates of change (usually of organizational death) as dependent variables and using a log-linear group of independent variables to predict them. Entities are grouped in synthetic cohorts and existence becomes yet another variable attribute to be predicted. Moreover, while such demographic methods address the appearance/disappearance problem, they do not address the merger/division problem in any formal way.

Classical demography also provides preliminary models for the other major problem with treating entities as fixed, the fact that names often stay the same while the things they denote become different. This problem is most evident in the situation of exchange between aggregate entities.

Consider the attempt of Simpson and others to estimate the ability of occupations to recruit and retain cohorts of workers.[8] The entities analyzed are occupations, characterized by the attributes of (1) strength, skill, and educational requirements, (2) product markets, industrial dispersion, and sex-specific growth, (3) earnings and earning growth potential, and (4) unionization or licensure. The dependent variable is an occupation's relative retention of a twenty-year age cohort, measured by the ratio of the odds of a cohort member's being in that occupation in the base year to those odds twenty years later, suitably standardized for death, relative occupational growth, and so on. Four twenty-year time-frames are analyzed, starting in 1920, 1930, 1940, and 1950.

There are two central problems with this daring design. First, the occupations themselves do not denote a constant body of work or activities. Simpson et al. have addressed this by excluding groups for which census classifications are not commensurate throughout the period. But this rules out, for example, the occupations reshaped by technology—a substantial fraction of the occupational structure, and a fraction that may in fact be determining what happens to the rest. Yet even those remaining in the sample changed drastically. Accounting, for example, began this period as a solo profession doing public auditing and ended it as a bureaucratized one doing nearly as much work in taxes and corporate planning as in auditing. The name stayed the same; the thing it denoted did not.

7. On MDF as strategy, see Fligstein 1985:383. For a review of organizational ecology, see Carroll 1984.

8. Simpson et al. 1982.

Second, the original cohort members present in an occupation after twenty years are not necessarily the same individuals who were in it at the outset. Evans and Laumann have shown that even the professions have extraordinarily high turnover and that they continue to recruit until well into middle age.[9] Thus, the individuals aggregated under the labels are not necessarily the same individuals at one time as at another. Retention is confused with migration. Moreover, the cohort barriers are so wide that as each cohort ages twenty years, some individuals go from the start of their careers to their career midpoints, while others go from midpoint to near retirement. The cohorts—themselves presumed entities like the occupations—are thus no more coherent entities than are the occupations themselves.

One might handle such problems by disaggregation. But this is the counsel of despair. Both occupation and cohort do have some sort of reality, some sort of causal power. To disaggregate and model the occupations as properties of individuals would forfeit any sense of occupations' reality as structures. The classic answer to such multilevel problems is ecological regression.[10] But to assign coherent group-level terms to individuals—as is standard ecological practice—is completely impossible. The individuals don't stay in the same aggregates over time, and the aggregates themselves change—both by migration of their members and by change in emergent properties like type of work. These transformations make ecological parameters meaningless.

Some writers have noted the possibility of combining demographic and attribute methods to deal with such problems. In such methods, underlying demographic dynamics provide members—with their own attributes—to an emergent level of aggregates, which in turn have *their* own attributes. Event history methods to some extent so mix demographic and attribute models. On the theoretical side, a number of writers have argued that iterative processes of interaction between micro-level units in fact provide the structure that is macrostructure. Thus, there are a variety of preliminary attempts to address these issues, but clearly much work—both theoretical work on the formal structure of central-subject/event approaches and mathematical work on how to realize them—is required to develop this area further.[11]

9. Evans and Laumann 1983.

10. For a review, see Blalock 1984b.

11. For an emergents/aggregates model, see Coleman 1964:162 ff. On event history methods, see Tuma and Hannan 1984. Theoretical writers on the micro/macro problem include Cicourel (1981), Giddens (1984), and Collins (1987).

B. *Monotonic Causal Flow*

Between the various attributes of entities that it analyzes, GLR assumes that causality flows either from big to small (from the contextual to the specific) or between attributes of equivalent "size." Cause can never flow from small to large, from the arbitrary to the general, from the minor event to the major development. This assumption has several constituent parts.

The assumption of monotonic causal flow begins with the assumption of "constant relevance." A given cause is equally relevant at all times because the linear transformation, in most models, doesn't change over time periods (because the reestimation required is impractical). Of course, the **B** matrix of the general-form GLM *can* change, but GLR practitioners seldom take the position, common in historical writing, that "at time t, x was important, while later, the conjuncture of things made y more important." That kind of thinking—in which **B** is mostly zeroes and the nonzero elements differ from iteration to iteration—is not common. The first constituent of the monotonic causal flow assumption is thus the assumption, not necessary but nearly universal, of constant relevance.

Within this presumed constant relevancy structure, the GLM assumes necessarily that if a cause changes, so does its effect. But this means that if a causal variable fluctuates over a period of two weeks, a GLM cannot allow it to determine something that fluctuates over a period of two years. It can study the "contextual" effect of the latter on the former, using cross-sectional data to discover how different levels of "context" affected the behavior of the more rapidly fluctuating variable. But once context is removed, the use of linear models implies the assumption that causes and effects have meaningful fluctuation *over the same period.* This assumption has in turn become a GLR assumption, a theoretical belief in what I shall call the unity of time-horizon. ("Time-horizon" denotes the minimum length of time in which a *meaningful* change in a variable can be observed.) GLR allows contextual effects of various levels down to a uniform "basic" level for causal effects, but refuses any reversal of this hierarchy—any causing of the large by the small, the enduring by the fleeting.

The uniform time-horizons assumption can most easily be seen in time series analyses, where a simple GLM is estimated on a single entity using successive years as different cases. Consider the problem of distinguishing the effects of government revenue and expenditure policies on the distribution of income in society. According to Devine, neoconservatives see the state as reacting to the rising expectations of a pluralist populace, while

Marxists see the state balancing between rewarding the dominant classes and purchasing the complaisance of the dominated ones.[12] Liberals by contrast view the state as technocratically motivated and lacking any intent to redistribute income. Measuring income distribution with the capital/labor income ratio, Devine predicts it with several prior attributes of the society: (1) the prior income ratio, (2) "controls" for inflation, unemployment, unionization, real GNP growth, and minimum wage, and (3) federal fiscal flows—revenue and expenditures for military personnel, for veterans benefits, for "technoscale" (military research and procapital infrastructure) and for "human scale" (transfer payments, education, and other collective goods). The federal fiscal flows are taken to measure intent, operationalizing the three theoretical frameworks of neoconservatism, Marxism, and liberalism. Devine's temporal structure for estimation is quite complex: inflation, real GNP growth, and unemployment are measured contemporaneously with the dependent variable: prior income ratio is measured the year before: unionization, revenue, and expenditures for military personnel, veterans, and "technoscale" are measured two years before. "Human scale" is split; the transfer payments are measured contemporaneously, while the collective goods are lagged two years. Devine specifies this complex lag structure after finding that simpler versions (e.g., lagging all fiscal variables for one year) produced less stable estimates. He justifies this choice with the argument that the longer lag "allows for adequate diffusion of state spending and extractive capacity," except in the case of transfer payments, where the effect is immediate.[13]

The problem with the whole approach is that the values of these measures at any given time are not freely variable. Annual inflation and GNP growth are linked in "recessions" that take several years to grow and die. Because laws link "human scale" payments to entitled populations, those payments fluctuate with demographic changes in age and other entitlement variables, which in turn reflect events ranging in size from the two-decade baby boom to much shorter fluctuations in unemployment. Military spending reflects wars and other foreign policy ventures again of widely varying durations. Thus, the observed values of the various "independent" variables at any given time (subject of course to the lag structure) are linked in arbitrary ways to their values at other times, the linkage being provided by the structure of what a historian would call "events." Because of this linkage, one cannot regard the independent variables as measures of the state's vari-

12. Devine 1983.
13. Devine 1983:614.

ous intents, nor the dependent variable as a measure of the realization of those intents. The independent variables don't really stand for the state's free expression of its intents, but rather for what it can intend *given* the various events it finds itself within. One could imagine measuring these events with moving averages, but the "width" of the moving averages would have to change with the temporal duration of the events involved. Thus the linkages of various yearly levels of variables into larger "events" undermines studies assuming uniform time-horizons, as do nearly all empirical uses of the GLM. Events of equivalent causal importance just don't always take the same amount of time to happen.

In fact, the problem is not limited to time series studies. Consider the cross-sectional problem of understanding the relation between wife's outside employment and marital instability. Booth and others have studied this process in 2,034 married couples aged under fifty-five years, measuring the following attributes of the marriages:

(1) "controls"—husband education, wife education, years married, number of children under eighteen.

(2) roughly five "steps" to marital problems—(a) hours wife worked, (b) other income and wife income, (c) marital division of labor and spousal interaction, (d) marital disagreement and marital problems, and (e) marital happiness and marital instability.

Hours wife worked was (apparently) measured over a three-year period, the income variables over a one-year period, and the remaining "process" variables by scales at the time of study. The various "steps" in the process of marital instability are set up in a classic path diagram (following the order just given), and are supported by causal narratives such as:

> marital interaction may be decreased by wife's employment. Household tasks that used to be handled by the wife while the husband was at work may cut into time previously allotted to joint activities.[14]

The model assumes that these various attributes of marriages fluctuate over equivalent time periods, or that the attributes earlier in the list fluctuate more slowly than those later. Yet in fact there is no conceptual reason to think that employment rates fluctuate more slowly than do, for example, marital problems or marital happiness. One can easily imagine a long period of gradually increasing marital instability in which episodes of wife employment punctuate attempts to reinstate a traditional division of labor. It *is* conceptually reasonable to expect wife employment to fluctuate at the same

14. Booth et al. 1984:569.

rate as wife income, but many of the other time-horizon assumptions in this "process" are erroneous. These problems compound the sequence problems to be discussed below. When attributes of entities fluctuate over different periods, it becomes impossible to specify the causal or temporal order that they actually follow. Moreover, the act of aggregation in GLR study further assumes that these attributes have similar time-horizons in all cases— for example, that one marriage's instability fluctuates at the same rate as another's.[15]

As a levels assumption, the time-horizon assumption bears directly on the micro/macro issue. GLR requires all causes to lie either on one temporal level, or on levels that decrease in the same direction as causality flows. Recent theoretical writing on the micro/macro problem objects strenuously to such a view. Collins has taken a basically aggregative approach to the problem, but Giddens and others have emphasized the role of micro-iterations in creating macro entities. It is clear that such relations can be formalized only within different methodological approaches, as in the work of Heise or in the work inspired by the dissipative structure theory of Prigogine.[16]

Not only do these causal flow assumptions disable GLR-type analysis of micro generation of macrostructure, they also prevent GLR from recognizing small events that assume decisive importance because of given structural conditions. Pascal tells us that if Cleopatra's nose had been a little shorter, the whole face of the earth would have changed. GLR cannot envision such occurrences. A few models for addressing them are being developed, such as threshold models. Attempts to treat sudden events within a continuous-variable, GLR-type framework have had mixed success.[17]

C. *Univocal Meaning*

To its restrictions on the relations between variable attributes GLR adds restrictions on the individual attributes. For many theorists, the most

15. One consequence of the monotonic causal flow assumptions is that every GLM study is implicitly a panel design. By modeling certain variables as causally subordinate to others, cross-sectional GLMs assume that the subordinates have had time to equilibrate to changes in their causes. On the implicit stochastic-process character of cross-sectional models, see Tuma and Hannan 1984:89 ff.

16. General writings on the micro/macro problem can be found in Alexander et al. 1987. See Collins 1981 for an aggregative approach and Giddens 1984 for an iterations-based one. See Heise 1979 for Heise's methods, and Schieve and Allen 1982 for work related to dissipative structures.

17. On threshold (tipping) models, see Granovetter 1978. Such models are more widespread in economics, see the celebrated Schelling 1978. For a model placing sudden events in a GLR framework, see Schieve and Allen 1982, chap. 8.

problematic assumption of GLR-based empiricism is its insistence that a given attribute have one and only one effect on another attribute within a given study. Theorists commonly treat terms like anxiety or wealth as having multiple meanings within the same explanation. The recent renewal of hermeneutic approaches in social theory gives this reservoir of meaning infinite depth. In strict contrast, GLR restricts our attention to one causal meaning of a given variable on another.

This contrast is well illustrated by Kohn and Schooler's work on the reciprocal effects of job conditions and personality.[18] The authors wish to show how flexibility and independence on the job determine and are determined by personality flexibility and strength, both at a given time, and (by assumption) over the individual's career. Kohn and Schooler's personality constructs are ideational flexibility (operationalized with an earlier-developed scale), self-directedness, and distress. The two latter constructs are developed by factor analysis out of separate indicators as follows:

> self-directedness is reflected in not having authoritarian conservative beliefs, in having personally responsible standards of morality, in being trustful of others, in not being self-deprecatory, in not being conformist in one's ideas, and in not being fatalistic. . . . Distress is reflected in anxiety, self-deprecation, lack of confidence, nonconformity, and distrust.[19]

The two factors have a mild negative correlation. Kohn and Schooler go on to apply full-information maximum-likelihood methods to estimate reciprocal causal lines between the two, estimating the path from distress to self-directedness at $-.08$, and its reverse at $-.25$. They conclude that "[i]f one of the three dimensions of personality is pivotal, it is self-directedness"[20]

Contrast with this Freud's analysis of the relation between anxiety (distress) and ego independence (self-directedness). Freud argued that anxiety symptoms signified danger to the ego. In response to some danger, the ego invoked repression to block dangerous instinctual impulses. (In the Kohn and Schooler case, such an impulse might be rage against a constricting workplace.) For Freud, repression had two exactly contradictory effects; (1) it exercised and supported ego control by diverting the threatening feelings into symptom formation but (2) it forfeited ego control by placing the repressed material solely under the logic of the id. Since that logic decreed

18. Kohn and Schooler 1982.
19. Kohn and Schooler 1982:1276.
20. Kohn and Schooler 1982:1280.

that subsequent impulses, responding to different situations, would nonetheless follow similar lines of development, new and different dangers (e.g.,
in the workplace) would nonetheless lead to similar symptomatic results,
with a consequent *loss* of feeling of ego control.[21] The Freudian theory suggests simultaneous and contradictory causal relations from anxiety to self-
dependence. No theorist would want to forgo the dual pathways, because
the two contradictory effects will probably generate two different causal
sequences. Nonetheless, summation is the standard methodological solution, a solution particularly problematic in the case of contradictory effects,
where sums are likely to be small and statistically insignificant.

Michael Burawoy's trenchant Marxian analysis of the Kohn and Schooler
situation illustrates a different pair of simultaneous, contradictory causal
paths within it.

> Thus, the internal labor market bases itself in a complex of rules, on
> the one hand, while expanding the *number* of choices on the other.
> Nor should these choices be belittled by saying that one boring,
> meaningless job is much the same as any other. The choice gains its
> significance from the material power it gives to workers in their at-
> tempts to protect themselves from managerial domination. Workers
> have a very definite interest in the preservation and expansion of the
> internal labor market, as the most casual observation of the shop
> floor would demonstrate. Moreover, it is precisely that interest that
> draws workers into the bidding system and generates consent to its
> rules and the conditions they represent, namely, a labor process that
> is being emptied of skill.[22]

Here, the psychological attributes flexibility and self-determination simultaneously increase both worker control and management dominance. These
two different effects can only partially be separated by saying that the former is short run and the latter long run, for in fact they are nearly simultaneous.

As these examples show, perhaps no other assumption of the GLR seems
as inimical to classical theory as that of univocal meaning. Recognition of
multiple meanings is central for sociological methodology because complexity of meaning is central for the qualitative theories currently dominant.
The most common empirical solution of the multivocality problem is to
disaggregate by finding intervening indicators that differentiate the causal
paths. But not only is this procedure not always possible, it also moves the

21. See Freud 1936:11–28, 1963b. On contradictory instincts, see Freud 1963a:97 ff.
22. Burawoy 1979:107–8.

causal focus from antecedent to intervening variables, a shift theorists may reject.

There are several formal ways to address the problem. One might assume that each variable produces an ensemble of effects on another and that some other process chooses which of these will obtain in the particular case. (In the Freudian example, such a model governs the choice of particular symptom formation.) If the determining process is endogenous, then the multiple meaning problem becomes the interaction problem; some combinations lead to one type of outcome, others to another (see sections II.E and II.F below). If the determining process is exogenous, one can perhaps model it directly.

A second general approach insists on allowing more than one effect at once. There is some work relevant to this problem within the network framework. Several writers have combined structural models based on different rating methods into complex models for relations between various units of analysis. This is, implicitly, a disaggregation strategy. Another disaggregation approach is to separate the two effects temporally. Thus, Cantor and Land have recently conceptualized the effects of unemployment on crime as a negative effect through opportunity (more people are home to protect their goods) and a positive one through motivation (people without work must turn to crime). They separate the effects by arguing that institutional support systems buffer the latter effect, which is thus estimated at a one-year time lag. Finally, certain forms of nonmetric analysis may support the direct inclusion of multiple effects; these may be the only approaches that do not require disaggregation. A few authors, notably Hayward Alker, have followed the lead of Schank and Abelson's artificial intelligence approach to modeling processes of understanding, aiming directly at replicating complex understandings.[23]

In defense of current methods, we should recognize that the multiple meaning problem is in part a problem of presentation and emphasis. Even the most complex of multiple causal relations (e.g., "determination in the last instance" in the writings of Poulantzas and Althusser) must in fact be disassembled into constituent relations to be logically interpreted.[24] The

23. For a disaggregation analysis, see Boorman and White 1976. The temporal separation example is Cantor and Land 1985. On nonmetric analysis, see Katzner 1983. For Alker's work, see Alker 1982, 1984; Alker, Bennett, and Mefford 1980; and Mefford 1982. On scripts, see Schank and Abelson 1977.

24. On determination in the last instance, see Poulantzas 1978 and Althusser and Balibar 1970.

theorists' style with such concepts is to retain their unity and treat them as causally ambiguous or complex. The methodologists' style is to disaggregate and treat the variables indicating the various causal paths as the independent variables of interest. Yet while methodologists need not recognize the "essentially subjectivist" position that human affairs are in principle nonformalizable, it is clear that serious work must be done on the problem of univocality.

D. *The Absence of Sequence Effects*

The preceding GLR assumptions, which concern causality as mediated through variable attributes of entities, are complemented by a set of assumptions about independence between entities, attributes, and time periods. These latter are not quite as inherent to the GLM itself as are the entity assumptions, but insuperable difficulties of estimation and modeling have made them, de facto, constitutive assumptions of the GLR way of thought. The first of these independence assumptions concerns sequence.

A fundamental assumption of GLR is that the order of things does not influence the way they turn out. According to the general-form GLM, the state of entity x_i at time $t + 1$ (that is, the pattern of its attributes at $t + 1$) is determined by applying the transformation matrix **B** to its state at time t; how it got to that present is not relevant to its current future. Such an assumption challenges fundamental theoretical intuitions about human events. The whole idea of narrative history is that the order of things matters, an idea that undergirds the interactionist and ethnomethodological paradigms as well.[25]

The sequence assumptions of GLR are in fact quite complex, depending on whether we are concerned with the "causal" sequence of the variables within a cross-sectional application of the simple GLM or the temporal sequence of states of entities in the general one. To see the assumptions about cross-sectional causal sequences, consider the problem of relating the racial mix of an industrial sector to its productivity, investigated by Galle, Wiswell, and Burr.[26] Each sector can be described by the following properties: (1) capital expenditures per worker, (2) mean educational level of workers, (3) mean age of workers, (4) percentage of blacks among workers, and (5) productivity. These properties are observed in the early 1960s and in 1972; annualized rates of change are then created for all but age. The cross-sectional models treat the productivity rate as depending on all the others within time

25. Gallie 1968; Sacks, Schegloff, and Jefferson 1974; Sudnow 1971.
26. Galle, Wiswell, and Burr 1985.

period and the over-time models use the change rates to predict both change in productivity and productivity in 1972.

The authors believe their cross-sectional GLM allows them to make conclusions about the productivity of black workers; they assume that black workers as individuals have or lack productivity and that their being recruited to an industrial sector then affects the productivity of that sector. But it may well be that in some cases more or less productive *sectors* needed labor when labor market conditions favored hiring black workers, whether the latter have an inherent productivity or not. In some sectors, that is, the causal arrow is undoubtedly reversed. But the GLM must assume that the sequence of variables is the same in every sector (case). Here, that means assuming that the dependent variable is dependent in every case. In more complex path models, it means assuming that the paths of causality are the same in every case. Although carefully noted by Blau and Duncan many years ago, this radical simplification has been ignored since.[27] Worse yet, familiarity with the GLM has led many of us to believe that reality actually works this way, that causality must always be in one direction across all cases.

The temporal situation is quite similar. Consider the problem of understanding the relation between personal unemployment and criminal behavior, examined by Thornberry and Christenson.[28] The entities are individuals and their attributes are two variables integrated over one-year periods— their percentage of time unemployed and their number of arrests. Data cover the years from age twenty-one to age twenty-four, and include some exogenous variables not of interest here. The authors take a general-form GLM approach, deleting a few coefficients to achieve identification. Each path is "justified" by a little causal story. For example:

(1) Unemployment reduces commitment and involvement with conventional activities and hence leads to criminal activity. "A person may be simply too busy doing conventional things to find time to engage in deviant behavior."[29]

(2) Crime creates further barriers to conventional means to success, among which is employment. "Employers, for example, ought to be less willing to provide jobs to current and former offenders."[30]

These causal paths aggregate a set of stories. Thus, individual A com-

27. Blau and Duncan 1967:167. Duncan was always very clear about his assumptions.
28. Thornberry and Christenson 1984.
29. Hirschi 1969, quoted in Thornberry and Christenson 1984:400.
30. Thornberry and Christenson 1984:401.

mits a first crime and goes on to a serious criminal career, never looking back, never bothering to seek legitimate work. Individual B spirals in an ever deepening circle of greater unemployment and more crime each year. C goes wrong at the start (perhaps because of a random crime or perhaps because unemployment drove him to crime), but is then frightened by the criminal justice system and never errs again. Each of these stories comprises several one-step theoretical elements of the kind just given, linked into a sequential story. But aggregating these sequences throws away the narrative patterns that link the elements into individuals' stories. Suppose everyone who has *two* consecutive years of many crimes becomes a permanent criminal. A general-form GLM with a one-year transformation period cannot see that, because the past at time $t + 1$ is not relevant to the future at $t + 1$ except through its influence on the present of time t.

A central assumption of GLR, then, is that the order of things does not make a difference. In the first place this means assuming that the "more causally powerful" attributes are the same in every case. In the second, it means assuming that the particular observed sequence of attributes over time does not influence their ultimate result. Unlike most GLR assumptions, this sequence assumption has seen some serious study.[31]

A number of methods permit specific forms of sequential dependence. ARIMA models allow a variable to depend on its own past as well as on past random disturbances, although usually restricting attention to one entity and one variable.[32] (Reverting to my earlier metaphor, this is like following one fish's complete path through the lake.) Markov models for sequential data divide the attribute space into a limited number of states (parts of the lake) and specify the likelihood of moves from each state to any other. If the number of states is small, the future can be made to depend on the *sequence* of n past states, although the number of transitions to be estimated for such models rises with the nth power of the original number of states. Although such nth-order Markov processes operationalize theoretically important concepts of time, they are in fact rare. In particular, the recent florescence of event history models—which are usually discrete-state, discrete-time Markov models—has not to my knowledge involved use of information on the exact sequence of past states to predict current and future developments.[33]

31. Abbott 1983; Abell 1987.

32. Box and Jenkins 1976.

33. On higher-order Markov processes, see Bishop, Feinberg, and Holland 1975. For an example, see Brent and Sykes 1979. A review of the event history literature is Tuma and Hannan 1984. I have not mentioned another general sequence method, dynamic programming.

Theorists and empirical workers alike have called for methods that can classify or cluster sequential data, such as the histories of individuals, occupations, and revolutions. For sequences of unique events in continuous or discrete time, various forms of uni- and multidimensional scaling have long been used. Abbott has applied them to the sequence of events in the histories of professions. Sequences of repeating events may be analyzed by optimal matching methods, which Abbott and Forrest have recently applied to sequential cultural rituals, arguing for their general applicability to social data. Although both scaling and matching methods work with intercase distances and hence force small samples, they provide a serious start on the problem of identifying common sequences.[34]

E. *Casewise Independence and Related Assumptions*

Other independence assumptions of the GLR concern cases and variables. Although commonly seen as statistical assumptions, these are also conceptual presuppositions. The first is that there is not "excessive" dependence between elements in a given row of the data matrix **X**. By increasing parameter variance, collinearity makes the GLM unable to distinguish the effects of variables closely related to each other. The GLR proscription of collinearity directly violates the view, common among theorists, that social determinants lie in closely related bundles; Weber's causal concept of "elective affinity" and his related notion of ideal types are the most obvious examples. Another celebrated bundling controversy pits elitists against pluralists over the degree to which different bases of status tend to parallel one another.[35]

In formal terms, the collinearity problem concerns the "level" of variation. Highly correlated independent variables can be treated as aspects of a single variable through factor analysis and other forms of scale construc-

---

Most solvable dynamic programming problems are handled by making Markovian assumptions for the back solutions. See Puterman 1978. I should also note that there are multivariate ARIMA models (e.g., Tiao and Box 1981), although considerable interpretation is involved in their use.

34. A theorist calling for classification is Stinchcombe (1978). Applications of scaling to temporality are found in Hodson, Kendall, and Tăutu 1971. My professions paper was Abbott 1985. A revised version is Abbott 1991b. [But note the discussion of this work in the prologue.] My original optimal matching paper was Abbott and Forrest 1986. In addition to my sequence work (Abbott 1983, 1984; Abbott and Forrest 1986), there is an alternative, more formal analysis of sequences in Abell's recent work (Abell 1984, 1987; Proctor and Abell 1985), which employs homomorphisms to measure sequence resemblance. Demographers are generally handling sequencing by enumeration, rather than by the direct approaches adopted by Abell and myself (see, e.g., Hogan 1978; Alexander and Reilly 1981; Marini 1984). An interesting sequential formalism of interaction is Heise 1979.

35. On elective affinity, see Howe 1978. For ideal types, see Weber 1949:89–104.

tion. But the GLM falters if variables like income have causal functions simultaneously as members of "emergent attributes" like general status and as independent variables. Hence GLR as a view of reality tends to limit not only entities (see section II.A), but also variables to one level, unlike many theoretical conceptions.

Correlated error terms are a second statistical problem with conceptual implications. Correlated errors usually arise through temporally or spatially structured data. They can be remedied, up to a point, by the use of special estimators. Behind the issue of error correlation, however, is a conceptual problem with a long history—Galton's problem of distinguishing effects of diffusion *between* units from effects of similar mechanisms *within* units. In fact, the standard remedies for serial correlation require theoretically postulating its exact structure; there are no purely statistical grounds (beyond the esthetic criterion of parsimony) for distinguishing between different temporal autocorrelation models. As for space, only now are substantial models for spatial autocorrelation combined with local causation being developed. Spatial autocorrelation makes it even more evident that the correlated error problem is ultimately conceptual, not statistical.[36]

Perhaps the most important independence assumption of GLR, however, involves the casewise independence of the dependent variable, assumed in the assertion that the independent variables determine the dependent variable up to an error term. A wide variety of sociological theories treat dependent variables as structurally constrained. In such theories independent variables are sufficient to explain the dependent up to an error term only *given* the necessary conditions specified by the constraints.

Versions of the constrained-dependent-variable problem are common. Thus, Peterson and Hagan study the effect of race, education, marital status, class, age, and a host of other factors on criminal sentencing, using simple GLM specifications for two dependent variables.[37] The first is the probability of sentencing (a probit model), the second the length of sentence. The units of analysis are drug offenders sentenced between 1963 and

36. Models combining spatial autocorrelation with local causation are Loftin and Ward 1981, 1983, and Hubert, Golledge, and Costanzo 1981. The standard source on spatial autocorrelation is Cliff and Ord 1981. Methods that originated in the study of atomic, unrelated individuals run an obvious risk of ignoring contagion, particularly spatial contagion. When sociologists move from the realm of largely disconnected individuals to networks of actors (e.g., from estimating the effect of education on social status to analyzing the reasons for the survival of newspapers [Carroll and Delacroix 1982]), the newly central contagion effects disappear because the models hide them. Yet contagion effects are among the central determinants of behavior, as network studies (e.g., Coleman, Katz, and Menzel 1966) tell us.

37. Peterson and Hagan 1984.

1976 in a particular Federal District. The constraint lies in the availability of prison cells. The independent variables freely determine sentence and length *once* availability is taken into account, availability being itself a function of past sentencing procedures, among other things. Availability may operate only as a general limit with a similar effect on all cases. But more often sentence severity will vary in different cases and at different times because of varying likelihoods that certain sentences can actually be served.

Some of the many possible constraints on dependent variables have received serious study. Most such study has separated the problem of specifying constraint from that of analyzing causal mechanisms once the constraint is given. For example, the structural and exchange mobility literature specifying the constraints on occupational achievement is generally separate from the status attainment literature describing achievement itself. The two topics are separate sections in the major syntheses of Blau and Duncan and of Featherman and Hauser. Simply distinguishing the constraints of structural mobility from the free motion of exchange mobility has proved perplexing, and Sobel, Hout, and Duncan have recently proposed adding the third concept of "unreciprocated mobility." Some have followed the reverse path of specifying constrained *attributes* influencing mobility. A more detailed approach to constraint has been taken in Harrison White's vacancy models and related Markovian mobility models.[38]

A considerable methodological literature treats social structure as itself causal, reasoning that social causes must move along lines connecting individuals. The network literature takes this approach, as do a variety of formal mathematical models. Methodologies addressing this problem include block-modeling, multidimensional scaling, and other formal network models.[39]

F. *Independence of Context*

A final independence presupposition of GLR is that the causal meaning of a given attribute cannot, in general, depend on its context in either space or time. Its effect does not change as other variables change around it, nor is its causal effect redefined by its own past. Mathematically, this assumes that the

---

38. For summaries of the various achievement literatures, see Boudon 1973 and Sobel 1983. Blau and Duncan 1967 and Featherman and Hauser 1978 are standard sources. See also Sobel, Hout, and Duncan 1985. The reversing proposal comes from Yamaguchi 1983. On vacancy methods and related models see H. C. White 1970, Stewman 1976, and Tuma and Hannan 1984.

39. Some formal models include H. C. White 1981 for markets, Padgett 1985 for justice systems, and Marsden 1983 for power in general. Methodological references are White, Boorman, and Breiger 1976 and Boorman and White 1976 for blockmodeling, Laumann and Pappi 1976 for multidimensional scaling, and Burt 1982 for a variety of related methods.

GLM ≈ dynamic programming calculus

matrix **B** of coefficients in the general-form GLM does not depend either on X_t or on X_{t-1}, X_{t-2}, etc. In actual GLM practice, this dependence is often allowed. The contemporaneous dependence is expressed by interaction terms; the past dependence by lag terms and change scores. But these techniques have their drawbacks, as we shall see. The GLM can consider only a narrow range of such effects, and GLR as a way of thinking about the world does not really incorporate them at all.

As an example, consider Bradshaw's analysis of dependent development in Africa.[40] A series of GLMs are here used to investigate a recursive "story" of dependent development that unfolds as follows:

> Multinational firms ally with indigenous elites to promote economic growth (E) and the development of a modern sector (M). This alliance can be seen in the impact of foreign investment (I), trade dependence (D), primary product specialization (P), and commodity concentration (C) on state expansion (X). The combination of growth and development leads to economic inequality (Q), which in turn leads to social turmoil (T).

Eight linear models are run—three with T as dependent, two each with E and M as dependent, and one with X as dependent. E and M prove highly stable over the two time periods analyzed (1960 and 1977), while T is quite volatile. X has some (small) effect on E, M, and T in 1977, although this is probably due to its dependence on E (and perhaps M) in 1960. It is clear that some of these variables receive their meaning from their context. Thus, as Bradshaw notes, if the state is expanding (X) *and* has the (foreign) resources (I) to transform the economy in a way rewarding to itself and the investors who support it, then E, M, and T will increase more than they would if either condition—state development or external investment—were absent. With either condition absent, the situation will not differ from that with both absent. One might alternatively theorize, however, that strong state development (X) and external investment (I) would lead to strong police and military forces (unmeasured), which could prevent turmoil (T) by threat alone—a suppressor effect contrasting to the conduciveness effect previously hypothesized. Such interactions are normally handled with multiplier terms in GLMs, a practice that renders the lower-order coefficients in the equation completely arbitrary, and that requires exceedingly delicate handling.[41]

40. Bradshaw 1985.
41. On the expanding state, see Bradshaw 1985:202. On interaction, see Allison 1977 and Southwood 1978.

Although the GLM itself can handle a few interactive effects or temporal dependencies when used with suitable care, GLR as a way of thinking has a harder time with them. In his detailed analysis of substantive models for interaction, Southwood shows the extraordinary complexity of even two-variable interactions when they are envisioned with proper care. With nine variables involved, and even a few particular interactive specifications considered, the models implied here surpass visualization. They mean that the sixty points describing the thirty cases at the two points in time make a particular shape in the nine-space of variables, with some specific deviation from regularity in that shape for each specific interaction. However straightforward the inclusion of multiplier terms in equations may be, the conceptual leap of imagining them is prodigious indeed.

Yet complex interactions permeate, indeed they define any real historical process. For a historian would define the place of, say, primary product specialization in any one of these countries in terms of the conjuncture of other variables at the time. Thus, in describing the impact of these variables on agricultural policy—a relative of Bradshaw's modern sector size—Bates says the following:

> Palm oil in Southern Nigeria in the 1960s was produced in a nation where marketing boards had been set up by the government in association with merchant interests. Government revenues derived from export agriculture, and popular demands for government services were strong; local processors consumed a growing share of the industry's output; farmers had few alternative cash crops, and production was in the hands of small scale, village-level farmers. The industry was subject to a high level of taxation. Only when farmers began to abandon the production of palm oil for other crops, and when the government found different sources of revenue, did the government relent and offer higher prices for the crop.
>
> The production of wheat in Kenya offers a striking contrast. Historically, the marketing board for wheat had been set up by the producers themselves, and prosperous indigenous farmers had played a major role in the nationalist movement which seized power in the post-independence period. The government derived a relatively small portion of its revenues from agriculture; farmers had attractive alternatives to the production of wheat; consumers had a strong preference for wheat products and alternative sources of supply lay in far distant markets. Wheat production was dominated by a relatively small number of very large farmers; and elite-level figures had direct financial interests in wheat farming. The result was a set of

policies providing favorable prices for wheat products and extensive subsidies for farm inputs.[42]

The attributes of Kenya and Nigeria come together in this discussion into two different conjunctures that produce strikingly different agricultural policies. It is the conjuncture that produces the results, not the superposition of interaction effects on fundamental "main" effects of the independent attributes. There really is no general causal story that Bradshaw can capture in a set of path models and that can in turn be modified by particular interactions. There are only the thirty particular stories. Even though the passage above does not give a particularly detailed or subtle historical account, it describes a situation that cannot be envisioned in GLR terms. The meanings of each attribute of each country are determined by the ensemble of other attributes at the time. To return to the analysis of section II.A above, social life happens in events—which can be seen as ensembles of particular values of attributes—rather than in a free play of attributes on each other.[43]

III Transcending General Linear Reality

The general linear model is a powerful tool for empirical research. And effective users recognize that there is, in fact, no warrant for treating it as a model for social causality. Rather, the GLM tests substantive models of social reality on the assumption that those models entail linear regularities in observed data. The substantive models involved need not take the point of view I have called general linear reality.

But in practice the GLM has generated a theoretical "back formation." Many sociologists treat the world as if social causality actually obeyed the rules of linear transformations. They do this by assuming, in the theories that open their empirical articles, that the social world consists of fixed entities with variable attributes; that these attributes have only one causal meaning at a time; that this causal meaning does not depend on other attributes, on the past sequence of attributes, or on the context of other entities. So distinguished a writer as Blalock has written "These regression equations are the 'laws' of a science." To say this is to reify an entailed mathematics into a representation of reality.[44]

Throughout this paper I have discussed some alternative methods that

42. Bates 1981:128.
43. The fictitious character of main effects was well understood during the creation of modern inferential statistics, but has been quite forgotten. For a sobering discussion, see Traxler 1976 concerning Neyman's objections to the idea of main effects.
44. Blalock 1960:275.

deal with some of the problems designated as interesting by theorists but excluded by GLR. I would like here to briefly present the theoretical positions that underlie these alternative methods. Each of course makes assumptions about the fully complex reality of the theorists, but each ignores different things than does GLR. All follow the same general strategy of relaxing one or more of the stringent philosophical assumptions here analyzed.

A. *The Demographic Model of Reality*

The demographic model principally relaxes the first, fundamental assumption of GLR, that of fixed entities with variable attributes. It allows entities to appear, disappear, move, merge, and divide. Demographic methods easily handle problems involving the appearance and disappearance of entities, and, as I noted above, these methods can in principle be combined with attribute-based methods to handle some of the central difficulties of entities/variables methods. Demographic methods are weaker with merger and division, however; even marriage is classically treated not as an amalgamation of two individuals, but as a state change in the life of one of them. Indeed, rather than presenting GLR-based methods with improved means for modeling the flow of entities, demography seems to be moving towards use of GLR models for state changes under conditions when entities can be assumed fixed.[45]

In fact, to develop a general demographic reality that has strength comparable to that of GLR requires extensive theoretical and methodological work. Methods that would sustain inquiry in this broad demographic sense require the serious conceptualization and measurement of complex entity processes, of what I earlier called "central subjects." We need rigorous concepts for how to delimit and measure social *actors*—how to separate social names and the things behind them; how to limit central subjects to a single level of interaction; how to specify that level of interaction. We need to decide how to define *events*—not simple ones like organizational death, but complex ones like organizational transformation, in which members of entities change even while the variable properties of the entity itself change. For once we relax the fixed entities assumption, admitting first simple events like appearance and disappearance then complex ones like merger or transformation, we advance directly towards redefining the social world in terms of central subjects to which events happen. This move towards a story-based model of the social world will ultimately force us to a sequential view of reality.

45. Examples for the new moves of demography are Rosenfeld 1983 and Morgan and Rindfuss 1985.

B. *The Sequential Model of Reality*

A sequence-based, central-subject/event approach reverses nearly all the GLR assumptions. It assumes, first of all, that the social world consists of fluctuating entities, accepting the demographic model just outlined. It deliberately makes order and sequence effects central. Moreover, it emphasizes the transformation of attributes into events. Thus, it interprets "30% of the cohort recruited by a certain occupation is retained after 20 years" not by comparing it to retention rates in other occupations, but by comparing it to previous and later rates in the same one; meaning is determined by story, not by scales that abstract across cases. The sequential model also avoids the assumptions about monotonic causal level. Extremely minor events (e.g., an assassination) can have large consequences because of their location in a story.[46]

The central conceptual task of the sequence approach, cognate with the conceptualization/measurement task of standard methods, is the colligation of events; how to separate hypothetical "events" (like hypothetical "concepts" in standard methods) from the occurrences used to indicate them; how to choose observed occurrences so as to best indicate the course of events. A large literature in the philosophy of history deals with the problem of colligation—the problem of defining commonly acceptable units and of grouping numbers of occurrences under a single general action. But there is little in social science beyond Abbott's brief study of the practical problems of measurement with social sequence data.[47]

The sequence model of reality does make the same kinds of assumptions about casewise independence as does GLR. My own analyses of professionalization sequences, for example, are flawed by the assumption that each profession develops independently of the others, a proposition I vigorously denied in other contexts. Perhaps the lone form of sequential analysis addressing the casewise dependence issue squarely remains White's vacancy chain model.[48]

46. In practical terms, methods studying sequential realities arise out of a common empirical situation particularly difficult for the GLM: the situation in which we are interested in how a process unfolds over time and in which there are relatively few (from 20 to 200) cases, with a large and heterogeneous collection of data available on them. Such situations include the comparative histories of organizations, of professions, of revolutions, of international policies, and dozens of other areas.

47. On colligation, see McCullagh 1978 and Olafson 1979, chap. 3. My own paper on it is Abbott 1984.

48. My professionalization analyses were in Abbott 1985, although, as I have noted, they proved wrongheaded in a number of ways. (In fact, they were never published, except, in part,

C. *The Network Model of Reality*

A third basic alternative to GLR emphasizes the relaxation not of the entities and sequence assumptions, but rather of the independence assumptions.
The network and structure literatures reject these assumptions, focusing
directly on the lines along which causes must flow rather than on the particular states and relations of the various causes. Although network models
make the same kinds of entity assumptions as GLR and lack in most cases
the historical structuring of the sequence approach, they embrace synchronic contingencies that GLR, as well as the demographic and sequential
approaches, must ignore. Since the network literature is large and well-
developed, my aim here is merely to identify it as embodying an alternative
conception of social causality. The interested reader can refer to numerous
reviews of it elsewhere.[49]

IV Conclusion

This paper has argued that sociological theory and methods are divided by
the unnecessarily narrow approach to causality implicit in the dominant
methods in the discipline. Although analysts studying social structure
through network data and workers studying entity processes through demographic methods have quietly developed alternatives, all too often general linear models have led to general linear reality, to a limited way of
imagining the social process. My aim in making this argument, as I said
at the outset, is not controversial. But since the paper has elicited strong
and even hostile response, I shall address in closing some particular objections.

The chief objections of theorist colleagues have been (1) these problems
are well-known and (2) even empirical work of the kind I here recommend
is not really possible within "human sciences." Although I have by no means
read the entire theoretical literature, the rejections of empiricism I have
seen do not in fact lay out the arguments I have made here, but take objection 2 as their principal ground. The "human sciences" position is indeed a
deeper objection, one that would require many pages to consider. My working answer is that (1) certain eminent and undeniably interpretive practitioners of the human sciences are ardent formalizers (e.g., Barthes) and (2)
in fact interpretation and formalization interpenetrate in all parts of this and

---

in Abbott 1991b.) I argued against independence in Abbott 1988a. The central work on vacancy chains is H. C. White 1970.

49. Reviews of the network literature include Marsden and Lin 1982; Knoke and Kuklinski 1982; and Burt 1982.

other disciplines. After all, most of the formal work I have cited on social sequences has been largely inspired by history and literary criticism.[50]

Quantitative colleagues have also objected (1) that the philosophical assumptions analyzed here are well-known, but in addition (2) that my alternatives are limited in applicability, and (3) that I should not present alternatives until they are better developed. I think all three of these judgments are mistaken. First, I have not seen these kinds of discussions in standard methodological sources. Lieberson's brilliant book (1985) deals with some of these issues, but never really leaves the philosophical framework of entities and variables. As for sequences, my own review of prior sociological work found virtually nothing and Abell, four years later, found little since. Careful practitioners of the GLM undoubtedly recognize the problems I have written about; Lieberson is an example. But to say that any of these problems is in the active consciousness of working sociologists belies the plain evidence of our major journals.[51]

As for the limited applicability of my alternatives, that is only apparent. The wide applicability of the GLM is itself an appearance, a consequence of the paradigm through which quantitative sociology apprehends reality. Alternatives seem applicable only to special cases, as Kuhn says, because our current methods prevent our seeing the myriads of situations to which they do apply. It is not that "there are certain special kinds of data to which sequence methods are appropriate." On the contrary. One can argue on the theoretical foundation of symbolic interactionism that a sequence-based methodology is the only one proper for the vast majority of social explanation.

Finally, one cannot require that alternative methods should not be considered until fully developed. The GLM did not emerge fully developed in Blalock or Duncan, much less in Sewall Wright; it became a full paradigm through a long process of development, criticism, and growth. To ask that alternatives achieve that development instantaneously is to deny the possibility of alternatives.

I have of course merely sketched the barest outlines of those alternatives here. But I hope thereby to have begun a serious consideration of the relation between methods and theory that can replace the shrill denunciations we sometimes hear.

50. For the human sciences position, see Giddens 1979, chap. 7. Barthes the formalizer is found in Barthes 1974.

51. My first sequence review was Abbott 1983. Abell's was Abell 1987.

Seven Types of Ambiguity

Many have argued that we have entered a postpositivist age. Having swept our intellectual horizons clear of measurement, we can move forward to view social reality in its full complexity. Yet social measurement is far from dead, either intellectually or practically. Indeed, reflecting about measurement may help us further develop the arguments by which the positivist enterprise is usually criticized.

In this paper, I analyze "positivistically" a phenomenon normally assumed to forbid the possibility of positivism: the multiple and seemingly incommensurable meanings assigned to human events. I discover in current positivist research a source of untapped information about those multiple meanings. This discovery does not deny the normal critique of positivism, but rather suggests that the antipositivist concept of ambiguity can be used to fold the seeming flatness of positivism into a complex and subtle terrain.

For some readers, bothering with the research produced by sociological positivism and its cousins in political science and economics may seem a waste of time. For them, its philosophical presuppositions are ruined. Its correspondence theory of truth is broken. Its "causality" has proved mere reification. Yet there are two problems with accepting the philosophical critique of positivism. First, even though positivist social science has been shown to be "in principle impossible," the vast majority of social science effort (and funding) is in fact spent doing it. Such research is often highly consequential, whether it be the market studies that shape consumer demand or the census figures that determine political districts.

The second problem involves the motivations of those who deny the efficacy of positivism. Proclamations against positivism often mask an arbitrary unwillingness to think formally about the social world. One asserts

I would like to thank Mary Ellen Konieczna for her research assistance in this project and Tom Smith for his help with the GSS. An early version of some of the ideas discussed here was presented at the Social Science History Association meetings in Baltimore on 3 November 1994. The paper was originally published in *Theory and Society* 26 (1997): 357–91; reprinted with permission of *Theory and Society*.

that the world is constructed of ambiguous networks of meaning, argues for the complexity of interpretations and representations, and then simply assumes that formal discussion of the ensuing complexity is impossible. But this is obviously untrue. Many people have thought formally about ambiguity, representation, and interpretation. Nothing in those phenomena militates against thinking in a rigorous, even disciplined fashion, as we see in the work of Empson, Barthes, and many others.[1]

There are thus good reasons for investigating not only the problems that ambiguity makes for positivism, but also the ways in which positivism can help us know ambiguity.

It is useful, before setting out on that analysis, to give some simple definitions so that reader and author may as far as possible understand the same things by the same words. By positivism, I mean the notion that social reality is measurable in some acceptable way. Thus, I set aside from positivism proper the more general concepts of quantitative analysis, causalist thinking, and so on. In my language, positivism means measurement.

By measurement, I mean the creating of a formal relation between differences in some aspect of reality and either an ordered set of numbers or a set of categories. The former is numerical measure, the latter categorical measure. In what follows I focus chiefly on numerical measure.[2]

Finally, by formalization, I mean representation of a complex thing by a simpler one whose properties are better known. Measurement is thus a subheading under formalization. It is not, however, necessarily entailed by formalization. The economists' indifference curves formalize the notion of trade-offs without measuring anything, just as do sociological theories of revolution or literary theorists' tropologies, although all three invoke typologies that ultimately presuppose categorical measure. As these examples show, abstraction and modeling are common means of formalization.

In this paper, I intend, then, to think about ambiguity formally. This means adopting the standard positivist conceptions of variables and indicators and turning them upside down in order to discover how the ambiguity of social life plays itself out within the framework provided by positivist research. I begin with a short discussion of the concept of measurement in positivism. I then set forth "seven types of ambiguity" in this model, following the lead of Empson. These types serve to guide my reading of the di-

1. Barthes 1974; Empson 1957. My title is chosen in homage to Empson, whose book I very much enjoyed when I read it in the 1960s.

2. It should be noted that categorical measure is by some writers not considered measurement at all. See Duncan 1984.

verse meanings assigned by positivists to one particular indicator—strength of religious attachment as measured in the General Social Survey (GSS). Analysis of the literature involving this indicator suggests a network theory of meaning within positivism and further shows how positivist sociology provides evidence about the multiply meaningful character of social life. In attempting to rid itself of ambiguity, positivism drives that ambiguity into the interstices between studies. By reading a large body of studies conjointly and carefully, I recover it, showing that positivist work can be read in as rich a fashion as can interpretivist work.

I Seven Types of Ambiguity

In the standard positivist model of measurement, visible indicators measure invisible concepts. The concepts are things like bureaucratization, education, and occupational prestige. These are nonmeasurable in the sense that there is no generally accepted correspondence between differing degrees of them and the real numbers. We "measure" them with operational things like percentage of actions governed by rules (to indicate bureaucracy), years in school (to indicate education), and judges' rankings (to indicate occupational prestige). Often, there are two or more of these indicators for any given concept. Some concepts are their own indicators: in most applications, income is such a concept. However, with such concepts, we are often less clear about the "conceptual" nature of the matter at hand, and often take the "measurable concept" as in fact indicating a nonmeasurable concept—class or "total income"—that stands behind it. Figure 2.1 shows this general model of social measurement.

Given this approach, there are two levels at which analysis proceeds. At the higher, conceptual level, a relation between the concepts is defined, usually called a "causal relationship." This relation is a syntactic one, in the sense that the various concepts operate on one another in some ordered fashion (shown here by the arrow in the figure). This syntax is familiar from the path diagrams common in sociological positivism. By contrast, the relation between concepts and indicators is semantic. The indicators point to the unknowable concepts; they represent them in practical, knowable, and operational form. (In the figure, syntactic relations are horizontal and semantic ones vertical.)

At the lower, indicator level, there is again a syntactic relationship, between the various indicators. But this relation is purely numerical. It is embodied in a collection of correlation coefficients and possesses in itself no order properties, no direction. (Since showing these relations between in

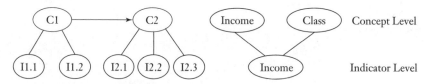

FIGURE 2.1 The standard model

dicators would require bidirectional arrows between every pair, I omit the "indicator syntax" from the figures altogether.) As many writers have pointed out, there is nothing in the syntactic relations of the indicators that provides any new information about the syntax among the concepts. All the information in positivism about "causal direction" is in fact provided at the conceptual level, by the investigator.[3]

Above the conceptual level stands another level, that of narrative. No serious positivist believes that bureaucratization and education and occupational prestige exist as real things that cause other real things to change. When they say education in part causes occupational prestige, positivists mean by this statement to provide a shorthand description of dozens of particular narratives whereby people with much education transform that education into membership in occupations of high social standing.

At this third level, actors of varying types undertake actions and enter interactions, which in turn have consequences, which in turn often involve other kinds of actors and so on. Thus, the "causal relation" of education and occupational prestige refers to or indicates a collection of particular narratives. The relation between levels is thus, again, a semantic one, but much more complex than the simple pointing that obtains between the lower two levels. The entire model at the level of concepts represents the entire chain of the story—indeed a collection of such chains—at the narrative level, as I have shown in figure 2.2.[4]

I am here chiefly concerned with the semantic relation between the two lower levels of indicators and concepts. This is normally what a positivist means by the relation of measurement. In fact, in some recent positivist work (e.g., in work using LISREL) it is customary to speak of a "measure-

3. The best known expositor of this argument is David Freedman (see, e.g., 1987). The Freedman critique is actually stronger than the critique mentioned here, for he has pointed out that the indicator-based estimates of the effect parameters (the causes at the conceptual level) are in fact conditional on the pattern of causes expected and thus cannot even disconfirm it.

4. I have written about this semantic relationship extensively elsewhere, e.g., in Abbott 1992c (chapter 4 of the present volume).

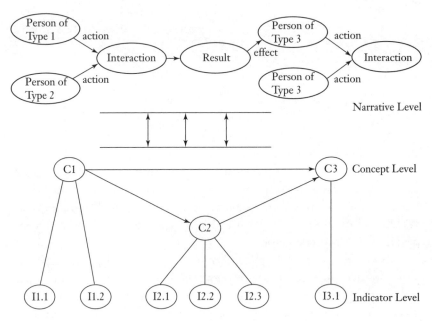

FIGURE 2.2 The augmented standard model

ment model." For it is often the case that there are several indicators of a
given concept (see figures 2.1 and 2.2). Religion, for example, can be indicated by church attendance, by daily prayer, by personal statements of belief,
or by more distant ("proxy") variables like ethnicity or region of origin. It is
common in positivist work to use such "multiple indicators" by reducing
them to a single indicator with scale construction procedures like summation and factor analysis.

But consider the reverse situation, the possibility that a given indicator
is attached to more than one concept. In such a case, one measurable thing
"means" several conceptual things at once. Years in school, for example,
"means" education, in the sense that we presume (somewhat against our
own experience as teachers) that time spent in school results in more or less
monotonic increase in education. But years in school also "means" exposure
to popular culture or experience with bureaucracy. Years in school even
"means" reduced time available for criminal activity, because those in
school are literally off the street. In fact, in many individual cases years in
school is probably a more accurate indicator of time available for criminality than it is of degree of education. This simple type of multiple meaning is
Empson's first type of ambiguity, a situation where one fact means several

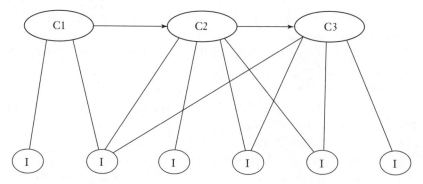

FIGURE 2.3 Ambiguous measure

things at once without those things resolving into any one meaning. I shall call this "semantic ambiguity," since it involves ambiguities in vertical links. Note that both multiple indicators and semantic ambiguity involve departures from a one-to-one correspondence between the two levels, the one through many indicators for one concept, the other through many concepts for one indicator (see figure 2.3). It is the widespread prevalence of *both* types that produces what I earlier called the network of meaning, where each concept is tied to many indicators and each indicator to many concepts.

In other cases, ambiguity arises because we regard social groups as inclusive. Thus, divorce rates can be taken to indicate something about the family (lessened commitment to marriage over the twentieth century, for example) or they can be taken to indicate something about the community (perhaps erosion of community stability over the same time period). In this case, the ambiguity about the meaning of the indicator arises in part through the inclusion of families within communities. This ambiguous location of a given indicator—as a property of different (although possibly concentric) social groups—can be seen as a second form of ambiguity, which I shall call "ambiguity of locus."

But the example of years in school is still more problematic. In part the multiple meaning arises here because of differing contexts of investigation. In the context of thinking about occupational achievement, schooling is important because it measures acquisition of a resource that narrative knowledge of social life tells us is centrally important in that achievement. In the context of investigating criminality, by contrast, years in school is important because school keeps young people off the street during the prime ages for criminal activity. But this second fact implies that even in the context of thinking about occupational achievement, the anticriminality effects of schooling are important, since criminal records affect not only employment chances but also opportunities for further schooling. In standard language these are indirect and reciprocal effects, respectively. There is thus here a semantic ambiguity, to be sure, but it is combined with ambiguous syntactic connections at the conceptual level. Analysts assign directional syntax to the concepts indicated by particular variables, assignments which of course vary from investigator to investigator. These changing causal contexts create an implicit ambiguity on the level of indicators. An indicator that is independent for one analyst is dependent for another. I shall call this "syntactic ambiguity."

Yet another source of ambiguity lies in time. The vast majority of positivistic social data is cross-sectional. Yet we often do not know whether an attitude item measures a recent attitude or a long-term idée fixe. Demographic characteristics like age and number of children may lack such ambiguity. But region, for example, has much temporal ambiguity unless we know duration of residence; the attitudes constituting southern-ness are not to be acquired in a moment, and thus southern residence will indicate "southern" attitudes only after a substantial period of residence. I shall call this "durational ambiguity," since it arises in the unknown temporal extent of the indicators observed.

A different kind of temporal ambiguity has to do with the third, narrative level of social analysis. There may be two or more different stories that give rise to a single variable syntax on the conceptual level. High levels of education can result in less criminal activity because education teaches people that crime is wasteful or wrong (and so they don't do it) or because it gives them an alternative means of income (and so they don't need to do it). This "narrative ambiguity" is well rehearsed in positivist work. But there is also a very direct narrative constitution of survey responses; every interview comes at a particular moment in a life narrative, a moment that shapes responses decisively. To be asked if one is happy during a stable period of one's life suggests a concern with week-to-week feelings. To be asked the same question in the midst of a major life change enters a far larger temporal province. Narrative ambiguity thus goes beyond the usual "multiple mechanisms" problem to involve survey responses themselves.

Other types of ambiguity arise again out of problems of semantics. That a given indicator may indicate two things within a study I have called semantic ambiguity. A more general problem is that a given variable may be linked with one set of variables in one study but quite a different set in others. This is not syntactic ambiguity—ambiguous location in a particular causal model—but rather the ambiguity involved, for example, in regarding abortion attitudes as part of "attitudes about women" in one study and part of "attitudes towards political liberalism" in another. In technical terms, this "contextual ambiguity" arises, like syntactic ambiguity, out of the manifold indeterminacy of the variable correlation matrix. Many possible lumpings are equally compatible with one such matrix, depending on our theories, our criteria, and our algorithms for constructing structures of salience.

But there is yet another variety of ambiguity hidden here. Indicators may not only mean different things in one study, or in different studies, they may also mean different things to different people in the world being investigated. Consider the variable of church attendance. People attend church for many different reasons: to express their religious beliefs, to get to know certain kinds of people, to provide an environment of certain values for their children. Yet the church attendance variable of the GSS tells us nothing about those reasons; at best, we can make inferences about them from other variables. This ambiguity seems like a generalization of syntactic ambiguity (as contextual is of semantic). But its heart lies in the interactional character of social life. To give another example, a graduate advisor may have a consistent pattern of actions with students. But what is warm mentoring for one student is claustrophobic control for another. The ambiguity arises in the openness of an action or attitude to redefinition in interaction. In the immediate case (of religious intensity), answers to a survey question are produced with an audience in mind. But the investigator doesn't know which audience that is. When one is asked whether one is a "strongly committed" Jew, for example, the answer might depend on who is asking the question or on a personally arbitrary scale or on a reference group or on an imagined "national scale." This general indeterminacy of meaning is my last type—"interactional ambiguity."

There are thus seven good reasons to expect ambiguity in the attachment of indicator measures to concepts. The usual image of a survey item is that it represents a "real" state of a "real" person. The seven types of ambiguity are seven ways in which this standard image is often mistaken.

Semantic ambiguity—one indicator signifies more than one concept

Ambiguity of locus—more than one description of the units involved in a measured indicator is possible

Syntactic ambiguity—a given indicator signifies concepts with different "causal status": dependent, independent, reciprocal, intervening

Durational ambiguity—the duration over which a given indicator
has characterized a unit of analysis is unknown but consequential

Narrative ambiguity—(a) two or more narratives imply the same
variable syntax at the conceptual level; (b) unknown biographi-
cal contexts shape the meaning of survey questions for respondents

Contextual ambiguity—an indicator is lumped as part of different
groups of indicators (contexts of meaning) in different studies

Interactive ambiguity—the meaning of an indicator is ambiguously
defined by the interactional context of its production, both in
the life world and in the survey setting proper.

Positivism is more or less aware of these ambiguities. Generally it addresses them by seeking nonambiguous indicators. There are various strategies for this—new surveys, dummy variables, switching regressions, for
example—all of which attempt to split the various ambiguous links apart by
attaching concepts to unique indicators in some fashion. As I shall show below, this procedure in reality merely exchanges one type of ambiguity for
another. I therefore wish to take a different approach, one that assumes ambiguity is a constitutive part of social life. I start with an indicator, rather
than a concept. And I attempt to discover all the many meanings attached to
it in positivist work. My seven types of ambiguity will help in that discovery.
But I shall also build a formal foundation for analysis.

As an important by-product, this analysis of ambiguity over time suggests important facts about scientific literatures. Indeed, we might begin by
conceptualizing literatures as attempts to find pathways through the network of ambiguities in positive inquiry about social life. The analysis that
follows shows some of the realities of those pathways.

II An Indicator and Its Associated Concepts

The General Social Survey not only provides a rich source of sociological
data, but also maintains records on all studies—published and unpublished—
that use GSS data. It is possible with this information not only to find all
these works, but also to retrieve automatically the list of GSS variables they
used. I have thus selected all the articles ever published using the RELITEN
variable (religious intensity): "Would you say you were a very strong, somewhat strong, not very strong [catholic, protestant, jew, other]?"

One hundred fifty-five substantive pieces have been written using the
RELITEN variable of the GSS. These include dissertations and conference

papers as well as journal articles, the latter making up about two-thirds of the total. I have undertaken two kinds of analysis with this data. First, I have undertaken cluster and scaling analyses that attempt to uncover groupings in these articles based on which GSS variables they used in common. I analyze four time periods (pre-1980, 1980–84, 1985–89, and post-1989) to see if these groups have changed over time. Second, I have read in detail thirty-three published articles from this group. These provide illustrations that flesh out the analysis whose skeleton emerges from the formal work.[5]

The 155 substantive analyses use a total of 774 different variables out of the 2,432 available in the various versions of the survey. Thus, while RE-LITEN is not one of the central variables of the survey (like sex and education, which appear in almost all scholarly work using the GSS), articles in which it figures nonetheless involve nearly one-third of the survey variables. Nearly half of the 774 variables used, however, appear in only one analysis. Three-quarters appear in five or less. Of those remaining, however, many are very widely used. Seeking to analyze about 100 variables, I found that the 97 most common variables had appeared in 17 or more of the studies. Indeed, these 97 variables account for 60 percent of all individual uses of variables in the studies here analyzed. (The median number of variables used per study is 25, the minimum 4, and the maximum 242.)[6]

These variables fall into fairly recognizable groups. I have verified those clumps by subjecting the data to cluster analysis, using a metric of "closeness between variables" as input to standard clustering algorithms.[7] I re-

5. I have used machine-readable ASCII copies of the index to the GSS bibliography, kindly provided by Tom W. Smith, Director of the GSS. For a general discussion of the GSS, see Davis and Smith 1994 (and later versions). There are 2,982 scholarly pieces in the bibliography, of which 181 use the RELITEN variable. I omit 26 items that are sociology or statistics texts or simply general reviews of trends in American society. In the 155 remaining, there are about 100 articles and chapters. (The rest are dissertations, theses, books, and conference papers.) For the detailed readings to be used here, I have thus read about one-third of this literature. Note that my approach presupposes that people answered the surveyors "fairly and honestly." That much of my analysis is "positivist." However, a positivist would regard the ambiguities in their responses as "errors," on the basis of which to construct probabilistic arguments and inferences. But I wish to treat them as links that help bind this one variable into a larger and complex network of meaning. Finally, all programming (and programming errors) and analysis are my responsibility.

6. I chose to analyze 100 variables because 100 is a practical number for investigation. The exact number is arbitrary, but one can't analyze too few variables without possibly losing the connections between this literature and diverse others, and one can't analyze too many variables without coming rapidly to analyze the whole dataset. One hundred seemed a practical medium.

7. Hierarchical cluster analysis is a means of placing objects into hierarchically organized groupings—represented by a tree or dendrogram—using as input the triangular matrix of

garded two variables as close to one another if they typically appeared in the same articles. In formal terms, the distance between two variables was Jaccard's coefficient; the number of articles in which both variables appeared divided by the number of articles in which one, the other, or both occurred. This omits from both numerator and denominator the studies in which both *don't* occur (including them would lead to the simple matching coefficient). However, since relatively few studies use more than 40 GSS variables, that any given two variables are both absent from a particular study is quite expected and gives us little additional information.

When clustered on this distance metric, the 97 common variables present a familiar picture. The list is given in table 2.1. The table also gives header labels for each group that will be used in tables below. It should be noted that these clusterings are not substantive, but largely arbitrary. (My intent here is more to introduce the cast of characters than to make a substantive point.) The given clusters are tight because a variety of structural factors favor the joint appearance of the variables listed within them. Some clusters contain subsidiary portions of single questions. Others betoken linked modules of questions that are rotated in and out of the GSS together. It is in some ways surprising that the clusters are not tighter.[8]

---

distances between each pair of cases. There are many algorithms for accomplishing this grouping, which often produce surprisingly different answers. I have done all clustering in this article using two such algorithms—single and average linkage—and have listed clusters that are strongly consistent across the algorithms. The two algorithms have quite different properties and emphasize different kinds of similarities in the data. Where they give similar answers, the clusterings can be taken as reasonably strong. "Cluster diameter" refers to the closeness of objects within a cluster relative to objects outside. Small cluster diameters indicate strong clusters. All of the cluster analyses given here have been interpreted with the aid of multidimensional scaling. The scalings are omitted from the paper to save space, but inform the discussion at some points.

8. In the 1980s, the GSS rotated many variables on and off the questionnaire on a two-year-on/one-year-off basis. After 1987, it included nearly all variables annually but not on all versions ("ballots," in GSS terminology) in a given year. Most of the present variables missed relatively few GSS years altogether. The median number of years off the instrument is two (of 21 administrations). All variables appear on at least two of the three ballots during the recent, varying-ballot period and a third appear on all three. However, within tight attitude clusters the design effect is usually clear, particularly for those variables that are subparts of a given question (like the tolerance variables).

It should be noted in this regard that there is no "real" level for a variable. That is, there is no firm conceptual reason why abortion attitudes should have nine "parts" in the GSS and anomie seven (of which only three appear here), etc. Yet these sizes influence the clustering. Note that this ambiguity is one in the life world, not merely in the survey world. For some people, attitudes on different parts of the abortion question may be as conceptually separate as attitudes on abortion are from confidence in public institutions for others. This ambiguity of attitude structure is a substantive reality of the life world and is hence part of the data for investigation, not a methodological problem to be solved.

TABLE 2.1

1. Demographic variables—age, education, race, sex, income, region of residence, marital status, size of community, and prestige of occupation. The GSS class and occupation variables do not cluster with this group, in part because they are not as commonly used.

2. Four subclusters related to "life satisfaction"
   * Three anomie variables (AN).
   * Satisfaction with family, city, friends, and hobbies, and health and extent of social relations with friends, etc. (SAT).
   * Marital and general happiness (HAP).
   * Confidence in science, the federal government, judges, legislators, and the army, with which also cluster belief in the fairness and trustworthiness of others (CON).

3. Eight subclusters of "attitudes"
   i. Nine variables measuring "civil liberties"—three settings (as speaker, library author, and college teacher) for three kinds of people (atheists, homosexuals, communists). For example, "should a communist be allowed to teach in a college or university?" (CIVLIB).
   ii. Three variables measuring racial attitudes, asking approval of busing, intermarriage, and a black as president (RAC).
   iii. Four variables capturing attitudes on crime and law—belief in capital punishment, criminalization of marijuana use, restriction of guns, and leniency of courts (CRI).
   iv. Four variables on sexual behavior—involving homsexuality, divorce laws, pre- and extramarital sex (SEX).
   v. Seven variables on various possible justifications for abortion: any cause, not wanting more children, rape, singleness, potential birth defect, mother's health, poverty (AB).
   vi. Four variables on general women's issues: approval of married women's work, of a female presidential candidate, of women in politics more generally, of women's remaining in the home (FE).
   vii. Seven variables describing attitudes on public spending: on arms, race issues, cities, environment, health, education, welfare (NAT).
   viii. Two variables on death—right to die and suicide (DEATH).

4. A small independent cluster—joined most closely with demographic variables—of two indicators of general political values—PARTYID and POLVIEWS (POL).

In this analysis, the religion variables do not lie in any close association with one another. (It is a striking fact that they are almost never summed up to make a scale.) When they are clustered by themselves, one clear clump comprises three rarely used variables with a common GSS rotation pattern: praying, reading the Bible, and feeling near God. The other religion variables tend to fall in a concentric hierarchy; the less commonly used ones are typically add-ons used when the others are already present. In ascending order, these variables, with their numbers of uses, are: religion at age 16 (20), confidence in clergy (24), membership in a church (25), belief in an afterlife (43), denomination (62), religion—Protestant, Catholic, Jew, other (120), and church attendance (122). Strength of religious attachment, of course, is definitionally present in all 155 studies.[9]

III The Changing Universe of Religious Intensity

Having discovered the basic relevant types of variables, I now cluster the data "in the other direction." That is, having ascertained the preliminary geography of the variables within which RELITEN takes its place, I ask about the terrain of *articles*. I thus ask not whether two variables tend to appear in the same articles but whether two articles tend to use the same list of variables. The measure is again Jaccard's coefficient: for any pair of *articles*, the number of variables common to both divided by the total number of variables that appear in one, the other, or both. Note that if there are coherent, tight groups of articles, we can think of these as examples of literatures, groups of articles talking to one another. I therefore use only the 97 predominant variables, which should be central constituents of such literatures. And I divide the articles into four time periods, hoping to discover potential changes in the shape of these literatures. There are 22 articles in the pre-1980 period, 51 in the period 1980–84, 48 in the period 1985–89, and 34 in the period after 1989.[10]

9. There are no design effects on the religion questions other than the first three. The rest appear in all GSS versions and all but one or two years. This preliminary survey of the variables that provide contexts for the RELITEN variable shows important absences. Social scientists apparently don't view religious intensity as part of the same context as the environment, or consumption and leisure behavior, or ethnicity, or present and former criminal behavior, or labor union activity—a long and important list. Rather, it is obvious that the main loci for positivist understandings of religion are on the one hand personal life satisfaction and on the other a variety of stands on public issues: on sex and gender in particular, but also on race, crime, civil liberties, and public spending. There are, to be sure, occasional studies using the other, absent variables: hours spent watching TV (eight such studies) and labor union membership (ten), for example. But the dominance of the topics of personal satisfaction and public attitude positions indicates that whatever the ambiguous meanings assigned to religious intensity, they generally do not reach into the other universes listed above.

10. I chose four time periods in order to see trends (if there were any) more clearly. The boundaries are arbitrary and attempt to balance between equality of temporal duration and of numbers of cases. Note that these time periods are wide enough so that the GSS rotation strategy has relatively little effect. None of these variables is completely absent from any period, indeed from more than half the years in any of these periods. What this means (by the intention of the GSS designers) is that most combinations of three "rotated areas" of variables are possible under these rotation constraints. (And given the two-on/one-off cycle, all combinations of two rotated areas are possible.) Design effects from common questions and common ballot po-

A. *Articles Pre-1980*

I begin with the 22 pieces using the RELITEN variable before 1980. Under Jaccard measure, these cases fall into two general clusters (with subclusters within them) whether clustered by single or average linkage. Cluster diameters are relatively large, however. Table 2.2 gives the subgroupings within the two general clusters and the variables characterizing those subgroups. Since the table (like those that follow) is extremely dense, we should pause to review its structure carefully. In this and subsequent tables, all variables listed appear in *all* studies in the subcluster, *unless* preceded by a digit, which indicates the number of studies in which they *do* appear. If there are no common variables in the category, it is blank. The numbers in parentheses *after* a variable header refer to numbers of variables. Thus, AN(7) means 7 anomie variables were used by all studies in a cluster; 2-Age means two studies in the cluster use the age variable. Where large subgroups of a cluster used several "other variables" in common, these are listed by subgroup (see the "other variables" column in table 2.3). Unless religion is specifically mentioned as a subject (in the last column of the table), the article indicated does *not* concern religion except tangentially; "abortion" as a topic means an article on attitudes towards abortion, in which religion may figure as one of many independent variables. (If religion *is* a central topic it is listed as such in the subject column, abbreviated as "R.") The number of variables given is the *total* number of variables used, and thus can exceed the 97 in terms of which the studies are clustered and scaled. Abbreviations are either obvious from context, listed in table 2.1, or, in the case of the religious variables, clear from the text discussion above.

A striking fact leaps out from the last column of the table. Knowing how the variables cluster does not, in general, tell us much about the subject of the study involved. The only subject-unified cluster in these groups is cluster 1, two very small-scale studies on religious practice and commitment. Cluster 6 has a general pattern of comparing groups, but the groups are not of consistent type; the cluster is bound together by the use of large numbers of variables in broadcast fashion.

---

sition are still present, but, as I noted above, they are in part tapping a constitutive ambiguity I wish to study. The basic question about design effects is whether they are providing a substantial fraction of the actual clustering of groups within periods. Given the vast numbers of possible articles that *are* possible given the existing design constraints, I think that they are not. The clustering is substantive. The reported clusters are evident in both clustering methods discussed in note 7. Cases that are clearly not in any particular cluster—cases that attach to the dendrogram very high up because they are generally far from nearly all others—are treated as outliers and not analyzed.

Table 2.2 Clusters of RELITEN Studies, 1973–1979

Cluster Number	Cluster Members	Total Variables	Religion Variables	Control Variables	Other Variables	Subjects
1	A, J	7–14	Att, Rel, Den	Sex	AN (1)	1. Religiosity 2. Belief in Afterlife
2	K, S, T, U	15–20	Att, Rel, Den	Age, Sex, Edu, Rac, Inc		1. R and Job Satisfaction 2. R and Status 3. Attitudes to Israel 4. Attitudes to Euthanasia
3	C, F	~25	Att, Rel	Cla, Inc, Occ, Rac, Sex, Works	FE (1)	1. Embourgeoisement 2. Attitudes to Sex Roles
4	B, L, V	20–50	Att	Age, Edu, Rac	AN (9), SAT (1), HAP (1)	1. Confidence in Congress 2. Minority Aging 3. Religious Participation
5	H, I	~50	Rel	Age	SAT (4), HAP (1), CIVLIB (12)	1. Racial Prejudice 2. Church Trends
6	O, Q, R	90–130	Att, Rel, Mem	ALL	Various from AN, SAT, HAP, CON, CIVLIB RAC, SEX, AB, FE	1. Unchurched vs. Churched 2. Religious vs. Nonreligious in New England 3. Types of Rural Groups
7	E, G, M	40–60		Age, Sex	AB (6), CON (1)	1. Childlessness 2. Attitudes to Abortion 3. Political Behavior
8	D, N, P					

This disconnection between the patterns of variable usage and matters of conceptual interest provides my first clear evidence of contextual ambiguity. In some of these studies, RELITEN enters with the control variables; it is a simple demographic characteristic interfering with other causal mechanisms of interest. In others, by contrast, age, sex, education, and other demographic variables stand alone, and RELITEN is a variable of independent interest. More broadly, religion is conceived in this set of studies as linked to a wide variety of areas. It is relevant to job satisfaction, to childlessness, to racial prejudice, to embourgeoisement.

Not only is RELITEN lumped in with a wide variety of variables for a wide variety of purposes, but it and other variables are clearly doing multiple duty as indicators. They mean one thing in one study, another elsewhere. In one study, attitudes on sexual practices indicate attitudes towards women; in another they indicate sexual attitudes alone, while other questions measure attitudes towards women directly. In some studies, RELITEN indicates "all" of religion. In many others, it is assisted by church attendance, whose use usually signals a desire to separate attitude (RELITEN) and action (attendance) in religious life. Thus we have considerable semantic ambiguity as well.

There is also evidence of syntactic ambiguity. The cluster unified by abortion variables (7) includes one article in which abortion attitudes are the dependent variable, one article in which they independently determine childlessness, and one article in which they are simply "related to" political behavior.

The studies divide into clusters in part by the extent and importance of the religion variables. Studies in clusters 1–3 are those in which religion variables make up a large portion of the common variables. (These articles are not necessarily about religion, however; articles on religious subjects appear throughout the clusters.) In clusters 2 and 3, a core of religion variables is augmented by small and uniform collections of control variables. Clusters 4, 5, and 7 are less unified by consistent religion and control variables than by consistent sets of other variables: satisfaction and anomie variables in cluster 4, satisfaction and civil liberties variables in cluster 5, and abortion variables in cluster 7.

These clusters show the beginnings of what might be thought of as "literatures." That is, we see articles using consistent sets of variables. But the conceptual structure of this space—given loosely by the subjects of the articles—reflects this variable structure only at the most general level. The gross division of the space into two "literatures"—one in which religion is a major conceptual attraction and one in which it is not—is possibly repeated at both conceptual and indicator levels. But within that, there is little or no correspondence between literatures as defined by topics and literatures as defined by variables. I should note also the emergence of two particular genres of article: the "religion proper" study (cluster 1) and the "throw it all in the hopper" intergroup comparison (cluster 6).

The three ambiguities evidenced in this first period—contextual, semantic, and syntactic—contribute to our difficulty in finding consistent literatures in the data. It is useful, indeed, to reflect about what a literature really is. One could define a literature as a body of work about a particular subject, or about particular variables, or about particular variables as used in a particular way (as dependent, for example). Or one could define a literature more as a conversation between scholars and indicate it by patterns of central substantive citations. In this latter context, social science becomes a very complex conversation, for given interlocutors don't exist. Studies can be responded to as easily by studies taking their ideas in completely new directions as by studies elaborating or detailing the same arguments. It may well be that what we usually call literatures are created largely retrospectively by review articles. Scientific conversation is simply a vast network or web, from which the reviewer selects a strand or strands to mold into one of a number of rhetorics: "all the work leading up to x problem," "all the descendants of the original studies of x," and so on.

B. *Articles 1980–84*

These were banner years for GSS studies involving religion. There are ten viable clusters here (see table 2.3).

The small-scale study of religion proper has disappeared in this period. Cluster 6 comes as close as any, and it has a high cluster diameter because it lacks internal consistency on variables of interest. The general survey or intergroup comparison, however, reappears (as cluster 10). Compared with the general studies of the earlier period, it has a feminist and civil liberties accent. (The earlier general studies were simple group comparisons.) Also continuing in this period, although less distinct, is the abortion cluster (cluster 8). We now see a "broker" study (C), which makes abortion part of a broader question of "sexual morality" and uses so broad an array of variables that it could be in either of clusters 8 and 10. Also intermediate between the abortion cluster (8) and the more general attitude cluster (10) lies a fairly consistent cluster (9) in which satisfaction and anomie variables play an important role. There is, however, another satisfaction-based cluster (7), in which satisfaction is related to a different set of things, often to attitudes about death. (See also cluster 4). Clusters 2 through 4 are unified by consistent sets of religion and control variables, and seem to lack internal consistency either in terms of subject or in terms of other variables used. Two peripheral clusters—1 and 5—are, by contrast, unified in both ways: the former concerning confidence in various social institutions (particularly the military) and the latter concerning political tolerance. Note that these are new clusters, not reproducing prior ones.

The political tolerance studies provide us with an instance of interactional ambiguity. One might ask, tolerance of whom? The variables tell us. The GSS asks questions about whether one would allow certain kinds of people to speak in one's community, to teach in a local college, or to have their books in the local library. This question is asked about communists, socialists, atheists, and homosexuals (of whom the left is more tolerant) and about militarists and racists (of whom the right is more tolerant). When a respondent answers these tolerance questions, he or she answers them all as a group after hearing the prefatory phrase "There are always some people whose ideas are considered bad or dangerous by other people, for instance. . . ."

But in fact, these variables are used by investigators in wildly different proportion. In the 155 articles here studied, variables involving the typically left-tolerated groups were used 251 times, while those involving the right-tolerated groups were used 75 times. This means that none of the right-tolerated group variables plays a foundational role, and, indeed, none appears on my list of the 97 central variables in this literature.[11] Thus, the respondent answers these questions in a context emphasizing both left and right. But when the variables are used, that interactional context has disappeared and investigators are free to interpret tolerance of people whom the left is more likely to tolerate as tolerance in general. The studies then end up being quoted in general public discourse as showing that the right is intolerant.

Even more striking than their interactional ambiguity is the syntactic ambiguity of these studies. It is clear from the topics in these and earlier studies that religion in general and RELITEN in particular are typically treated as independent variables. But there are a number of studies in this period in which religious trends and behavior are dependent rather than independent. They are quite pervasive, appearing in clusters 1, 2, 3, 4, 6, 7, and 10.

11. The corresponding figures for the entire GSS bibliography are 1,908 and 687. These figures explain the strong association between liberalism and tolerance commonly found in these and other GSS studies.

Table 2.3 Clusters of RELITEN Studies, 1980–1984

Cluster Number	Cluster Members	Total Variables	Religion Variables	Control Variables	Other Variables	Subjects
1	V, i, p	15–25		2-Age, 2-Rac	Con (9)	1. Military Manpower 2. Military Manpower 3. R among College Students
2	P, Y, m, u, v	20–30	Att, 4-Rel 4-Den	Age, Sex, Rac, 4-Inc, 4-Mar, Community Size	U, V: MEM (3) P, Y: ERA Attitudes	1, 2. ERA Support 3, 4. Church Attendance 5. Ideal Family Size
3	B, l, y	15–25	Att, Rel Den	Age, Sex, Rac, Mar, Region, NChildren		1. Religiosity 2. Ethnicity 3. Sex and Ethnic Prejudice
4	A, a, b, c, k, q	15–30	5-Rel	Age, Sex, 4-Edu	a, b, k: DEATH (2)	1, 2, 3. Attitudes to Euthanisia (3) 4. Women's Roles 5. Blacks in the Military 6. R Among Elderly Women
5	I, R, Z	20–40	Att, Rel	Edu	CIVLIB (6)	1, 2, 3. Political Tolerance
6	F, W, t	8–15	Att	Rac	F, W: AN (3)	1. Political Attitudes and Anomie 2, 3. Religiosity
7	N, T, d, f, s, w, x	20–40	4- Att, 4-Rel	Age, Rac, 6-Edu, 5-Sex	s, w, x: AN (3) T, d, w: DEATH (1)	1, 2. Life Satisfaction 3. Religious Imagination

8	C, D, H, e, j	15–70	3-Att, Rel	4-Rac, 3-Sex	N, T, f, w, x: SAT (2) N, d, f, x: Organization Memberships	4. Death Ideologies 5. Confidence in Government 6. Euthanasia 7. Race Differences
					AB (6)	1. R and Sexual Morality 2. R and Life Satisfaction 3, 4, 5. Abortion
9	G, J, K, U	55–85	3-Att, 3-Rel (3)	3-Age, 3-Mar, 3-Occ, 3-Community Size	POL (1), SAT (1) J, K: AN (3), SAT (3) G, J, K: CRI (3) J, K, U: POL (2) G, K, U: NAT (1)	1. Unreligious People 2. Achievement 3. Childless families 4. Support for the Political Right
10	E, Q, X, g, h, r	50–90	5-Att, 5-Rel, 4-Den	5-Region, 4-Age, 4-Inc	AB (3), FE (4) CIVLIB (3), CRI (1) E, Q, X: CIVLIB (6) E, X, h, r: RAC (4)	1. R in Society 2. Attitudes to Abortion 3. R Commitment 4. Pro-family Ideology 5. Southern Attitudes 6. Opinion Trends
11	L, M, O, S, n, o					

To ascertain the nature and consequences of this syntactic ambiguity, it is useful to consider the evidence of the studies read in detail. Of the 33 articles read in detail, 19 employ RELITEN as independent, some using it simply as a generic demographic control, others (typically those on political attitudes) treating it as substantively central. Another five studies are "characterizations of types of people" (activists, southerners, bureaucrats, the elderly), and take no view of causality. In them, religious intensity is simply an enduring characteristic of people like any other. Another three use RELITEN as an independent variable, but in the prediction of other religious behaviors and values: mystical experience (of which it explains surprisingly little) and church attendance (of which it is overwhelmingly the best predictor, accounting for about a quarter of the variance). Another two studies consider RELITEN as an intervening, not fully independent variable. One of them, an analysis of mystical experiences by Greeley, raises the issue of casual direction explicitly, asking whether mystical experience might not lead to stronger religious commitment, rather than the other way around. Finally, three studies treat RELITEN as a variable truly dependent on outside social forces. Stump makes it depend on regional migration, asking whether migrants retain the religious values of their old communities or take on those of their new ones. Rabinowitz and coauthors ask whether size of community influences levels of religious commitment. Iannaccone asks whether religious commitment is not an outcome of specific policies by churches.[12]

These final three studies throw the 19 studies that employed RELITEN as an independent variable into ambiguous relief. If RELITEN is a result of denominational policy or region of residence or size of community, then results treating RELITEN as a stable personal characteristic become suddenly unclear. Not only is there the syntactic question of the causal status of religious commitment, behind this lie both narrative and durational ambiguities. As the Greeley article suggests, there are many narratives (e.g., that of Saint Paul) in which enduring religious commitment results from particular moments and crises. And, since this is true, the duration of a current religious commitment is quite unknown.

My aim here is not to suggest that there is some right answer to be found by applying some appropriate technique, but rather to show that a careful reading of the positivist literature in fact finds the ambiguous complexity that we expect in social life. That the positivists themselves disown this am-

12. See Greeley 1987; Iannaccone 1994; Rabinowitz, Kim, and Lazerwitz 1992; and Stump 1984.

biguity as arising in insufficient knowledge and error should not blind us to the fact that the multivalent complexity of social life *does* find quite adequate representation in positivistic research. One must simply apply systematic techniques to find it.

RELITEN stands at a crossroads of meaning. While for most people and purposes it measures an enduring personal characteristic, part of a general matrix of opinions and values, for some it represents a recent event dependent on specific conditions. On the one side of RELITEN fan out lines of "causality" to attitudes on everything from crime to women's issues and life satisfaction, on the other flow into it personal experiences, environmental forces, region, and other determinants. One's particular denominational location influences the balance of these forces, and yet is itself subject to various forces and events. Again we discover this complexity not by disregarding positivistic research on religious commitment, but rather by reading it carefully.

In this group of studies, we have found major interactional and syntactic ambiguities, augmented by both durational and narrative ones. These make clear the means by which the network of meanings in the life world becomes encoded into the network of meanings in positivist analysis. All these ambiguities arise from twists of meaning and interpretation that yoke studies unexpectedly, or set them in unusual contrast, or spread them across a continuum. In this context, "literatures" begin to seem impossible, at least as mechanical phenomena generated by common variables. Literatures must arise in the specific intents of scholarly responses to earlier work. Yet the existence of a stream of work on a focused topic does not guarantee that the next response will not place old variables and findings in utterly new contexts.

C. *Articles 1985–89*

In the late 1980s, the various areas of work involving RELITEN came into clearer focus (see table 2.4). As in the preceding period, there is a coherent group of studies focusing exclusively on tolerance (cluster 1). There are also two clusters concerned almost exclusively with abortion (2 and 9). These two differ only in that the common variables (religion, race, education, and AB[4]) make up a much larger portion of the total number of variables in the first cluster. The second not only has a more diverse set of common variables (AB[7], FE[2], DEATH[1], SEX[1]), but also lacks the pattern of common controls. Thus, while there is a clear focus on abortion, there is no consistent agreement on how to study it.

TABLE 2.4 Clusters of RELITEN Studies, 1985–1989

Cluster Number	Cluster Members	Total Variables	Religion Variables	Control Variables	Other Variables	Subjects
1	K, l, h	15–30		Age	RAC (1), SEX (1) K, L: CIVLIB (3)	1, 2, 3: Social Tolerance
2	C, D, V, X, f, j, s, u	10–35	6-Rel	7-Edu, 6-Rac	AB (4)	1, 2, 3, 4, 5, 6: Abortion 8. Religious Participation
3	P, Y, Z, a, g, l	40–90	Att, Rel Den	Edu, Reg, Inc, 5-Community Size, 4-Age, 4-Sex	AB (1), Premar, Extra mar, Party, Polviews P, Y, Z, a: CRI (2) P, Y, l: AB (3), CIVLIB (3) Z, a, g, l: FE (4), RAC (4)	1. Abortion 2. Social Attitudes 3, 4. Southern Attitudes 4. Mormon Attitudes 6. Contemporary Religion
4	T, c, n	60–125	Att, Rel	Inc	SEX (3), HAP (1), NAT (1), POL (2), CRI (1)	1. Attitudes of Age Groups 2. Classes 3. Religions
5	M, N, k, o, p, q, r	15–40	Rel, 6-Att, Pray	Mar, Rac, 6-Age, 6-Sex, 6-Inc, 5-Edu	M, k, o, q: SAT (3) o, p, q, r: POL (2)	1, 2. R and Life Satisfaction 3. Attitudes to ERA

#		Range				
6	F, U, W	15–90	Att, Pray, Near God			4, 5. Attitudes to Suicide 6. Profile Ideology 7. R and Worldview
7	E, I, O, Q, R, e, t	15–20	Att, 5-Den 5-Rel	Age, Edu, 6-Sex, 4-Reg, 4-Inc		1, 2. Alcohol Usage 3. Race/Gender Consciousness 4. Contact with the Dead 5. R and immigration 6. Attitude change 7. Prayer in Schools
8	H, S, d, i	15–20	Rel	Edu, 3-Inc, 3-Community Size, 3-Age	POL (1) H, d: NAT (2)	1. Respect for Life 2. Marital Homogamy 3. Attitudes of Catholics 4. Irish Immigrants
9	A, b, v	30–120	Att, Rel		AB (7), FE (2), DEATH (1), SEX (1)	1, 2. Abortion 3. Value Retention
10	B, G, J, m					

Between the abortion clusters and the tolerance cluster lie clusters 3 and 4, both consisting of relatively broad surveys that are mostly of the "group differences" or "distinctive group" type seen in cluster 6 of table 2.1. The two differ in that cluster 4 is unified by a consistent but broad pattern of other variables, while cluster 3 is unified by a much more extensive pattern of common religion and control variables, with several different sets of other variables knitting various subclusters together.

Among the other clusters, the situation is less clear. In part, this reflects the fact that the overall clustering (evidenced in the two- and three-cluster solutions) is strongly shaped by the number of variables, in this as in other analyses. Jaccard measure is strongly influenced by size differences, and it is actually surprising that the clusterings are not more dominated by size (that is, that the numbers of variables in studies within clusters varies as widely as it does).

One force we might expect to overwhelm size is the force of coherent literatures. In a strong literature—what I am calling a conversation with specific intent—a core of variables would be augmented by other variables. One would begin with simple and striking results, then build a literature by further specifying these initial results. In such a "directional" literature, the choice of core variables would be much less random than that of periphery variables. Indeed, one might expect that scientific literatures would grow from a simple core of variables towards more and more complex sets of variables as investigators seek to make their results more precise and to reduce ambiguity. There is, however, little evidence of this directional process in my data here. Studies of particular topics show no tendency to a general increase in the number of variables they use as we move across time periods. There is no indication of "starting simple."

Moreover, even if this process of growth did occur, literatures would rapidly "grow into" one another as they reached out from their bases. As time passed, different literatures would gradually use more and more of the same variables; but what was control in one study would be center of attention in another. Indeed, it could be that clusters 4–6 in table 2.2 are clusters in which RELITEN was invoked merely as yet another external control; that is, that these clusters are *late* developments of *earlier* literatures focused on *other substantive variables*. The attempt within a given literature to reduce local syntactic ambiguity with respect to one special set of variables proceeds by gradually introducing new variables and therefore *inevitably involves an increase in contextual ambiguity*. One simply exchanges one form of ambiguity for another.

All this means that the number of variables a study uses—its size—*is* in fact of substantive interest; it is not an artifactual matter. (Indeed, that is one reason why I have used Jaccard measure.) For this reason, it is worth mentioning that the studies in clusters 5–8 in the third period are the "small scale" studies of that period. Cluster 7, for example, is a tight group sharing one or two religion variables and three (and often four or five) controls. These variables have, as the table shows, been put to a wide variety of substantive purposes, depending on the other variables (typically only five to eight of them) that have been introduced. Cluster 8 has fewer common controls and fewer common religion variables and leans towards political variables. Cluster 5 is much like 7, but has different common controls and again a mix of other variables (satisfaction and politics) helping glue it together. Cluster 6, sharing only three religion variables, including two unusual ones on private religious activity, recalls cluster 1 in the first period: its studies make religion absolutely central.

Study J in this period raises the important issue of ambiguity of locus. In this study, Cornfield attempts to predict strike and quit rates for 116 industries. All predictive variables are measured as characteristics of the industry, not of the individual, since industry is the unit of analysis. These determinants include truly individual-level variables like age of labor force and truly group-level variables like workforce homogeneity. In such a context, RELITEN becomes a group characteristic, a property of an emergent body.[13]

Of the 33 articles read in detail, 17 treat religious commitment as a purely individual phenomenon. It is measured individually and conceived purely as a property of the individual. Another nine treat religious commitment as the property of an individual, but not of a radical, contingent, monadic individual. Rather they envision a "typical individual"; a bureaucrat, a southerner, a widow, a black, etc. Here, the quality is more abstract. Religious commitment is not a local or contingent thing, but a part of a larger picture, a type around which individuals cluster. Two studies envision religious commitment as characterizing local networks (friendship groups and marriages). These recognize religious commitment as not freely variable within individuals, but as somewhat coerced by larger units. Finally a handful of studies—three to five, depending on how one draws the line—actually assume that religious commitment characterizes groups as much as it does individuals. For Iannaccone religious commitment is one thing a church can demand of its adherents; thus churches "have" strong commitment. For Miller and Sears,

13. Cornfield 1985.

religious commitment appertains to an individual's environment, rather than to that individual himself (the individual is taken to be a simple product of his environment). Such studies undercut the quiet methodological individualism of the mainstream. GSS data are gathered, of course, by individual units. But they are used to characterize groups as well as individuals. Their conceptual locus is ambiguous.[14]

Third-period studies thus confront us for the first time with clear ambiguities of locus. But they also provide examples of what appear to be more clearly defined literatures than we have seen before: concerning abortion and concerning tolerance. But while we can begin to theorize a life cycle for literatures beginning with radically simple results and moving towards more complexified, nuanced ones, our findings seem to show that this move merely exchanges local syntactic ambiguity for larger contextual ambiguity. There is a ceaseless dialogue between the radical and the comprehensive.

D. *Articles Post-1989*

The last period sees an expansion in the complexity and extent of the religion variables (see table 2.5), perhaps at last a sign of the maturing of a literature based on religious commitment. Once again, we see the obvious cluster of large-scale surveys and group difference studies (cluster 6). These lack any single common variables, but show much local similarity among large and diverse subclusters. The result is a clear and isolated unit. Among the low-numbered clusters, number of variables matters less than other things. The difference between clusters 2 and 3 on the one hand and 1, 4, and 5 on the other is that the latter group all include the attendance and religion variables, and in most cases have other common religious variables in various combinations. Clusters 2 and 3 mostly have attendance and Bible reading as their religion variables and have a somewhat less consistent set of control variables than do clusters 4 and 5. They also have substantive foci: on abortion (cluster 2) and attitudes relative to sexuality (cluster 3), although these are not perfectly consistent.[15] Cluster 5, by contrast, is a consistent "religion and X" cluster, showing the emergence of a standard set of variables—both religious and control—with which to attack the question of religion's impact on behavior. Cluster 4 is apparently the older, more familiar mixed genre of studies, with some slant towards politics.

14. Iannaccone 1994; Miller and Sears 1986.
15. These articles are presumably taking Bible reading as a proxy variable for fundamentalism with its conservative sexual attitudes. The Bible itself, as Boswell has decisively shown in the case of homosexuality, is a good deal more liberal on sexuality than those who haven't read it tend to think. See Boswell 1981.

Included in this last period is an interesting study illustrating the problems of narrative ambiguity. For Iannaccone, distinctive churches are strong because being distinctive forces their members to choose clearly between being in and being out. This reduces the probability of free riding and hence leaves the group with more benefits to reward adherents. The narrative here starts with a preexisting social group, the church, which wishes to increase its power and membership base. Religious commitment by particular individuals then flows out of the story that ensues. But there are other, quite different, stories for religious commitment. For Greeley, as I noted above, religious commitment can come out of a narrative that is highly individualistic and begins, possibly, with mystical experience. For Cornfield, religious commitment is a background characteristic of an industry that shapes strike behavior. For Bienenstock and colleagues, religious commitment arises through network homogeneity, just as for many others religious commitment, per contra, shapes likelihood to *join* networks.[16]

Combining Iannaccone's study with those on networks offers a hint of how to order this narrative labyrinth. For if distinctive churches become more so in order to produce strong adherents, then to the extent strong potential adherents exist ex ante and networks bring them together, church and members will both spiral towards an extreme position. Commitment of individual and of organization are produced by the same process. Of course, such an argument predicts that all social groups will so spiral, when in fact it is clear that this happens to only a small proportion of social groups. Clearly some horizon must be passed before the process begins. In formal terms, distinctiveness is an attractor, but only out to a certain "distance" in the space of possible adherents.

This last period thus closes my survey with an example of narrative ambiguity, which appears in an interesting tension with ambiguity of locus. There are multiple and interlocking stories, which occur at different levels.

E. *Summary*

Across the four periods, then, there seem to be some common patterns. First, we do see the gradual emergence of more complex studies of religious intensity itself. In the earliest period there is only a small cluster of studies purely on religious topics. The studies are small-scale and limited in their use of variables. By the last period, there are not only a small cluster of studies of this type, but in addition two larger clusters of studies with a broader

16. Greeley 1987; Cornfield 1985; Iannaccone 1994; Bienenstock, Bonacich, and Oliver 1990.

TABLE 2.5 Clusters of RELITEN Studies, 1990ff

Cluster Number	Cluster Members	Total Variables	Religion Variables	Control Variables	Other Variables	Subjects
1	N, O	15	Att, Rel, Pray, Clergy			1. R in America 2. Religious Life
2	I, T, f	15–35	Att I, f: Bible, Pray I, T: Den	Age, Inc I, f: Edu, Rac, Reg, Community Size	AB (6) I, F: FE (2), SEX (1)	1, 2, 3. Abortion
3	s, Z, a, g, h	25–40	4-Att, 4-Rel 3-Bible 3-Pray	Edu, Sex, 4-Age, 4-Reg, 4-Employ	FE (3)	1, 2, 3. Feminist Attitudes 4. Support for Military 5. Community Size and R
4	H, M, W, e	20–35	Att, Rel	Age, Degree, Mar, Rac, Sex, 3-Employ	H, W, e: POL (1)	1. Social Classes 2. Marital Satisfaction 3. Activists

5	A, E, F, G, L, R, U, b	15–20	Att, Rel, 7-Member, 6-Den, 5-Afterlife	Age, Edu, Inc, Rac, Sex, 7-Mar, 6-Reg	1, 2. Religious Change and Alcohol 3. R and Sex Attitudes 4. R, Class, and Alcohol Use 5. R and Health 6. Religious Commitment 7. Mystical Experience 8. R and Political Participation
6	B, C, J, Q, V, Y, c, d	31–240	6-Att	6-Edu	7-have FE (2) 6-have AB (1) 6-have NAT (4) 6-have SEX (2) 5-have CR (2) 5-have CIVLIB (3) 5-have RAC (2)	1. Conservatism 2. Attitude Polarization 3. R and Attitudes 4, 5. Attitude Trends 6. Attitudes of Bureaucrats 7. Attitudes of Italians 8. Theory of R
7	D, K, P, X				

range of variables in religion, one of those clusters having a solid and consistent list of controls as well.

Second, beyond this slowly growing core, religious intensity plays a variety of roles in a variety of contexts. A literature in which RELITEN relates to attitudes on abortion establishes itself early and remains throughout. But that literature eventually seems to divide over types of controls. Nor does it ever clearly hook up with a broader literature on the relation of religious commitment and attitudes towards women, although the two circle around one another on occasion. A small body of work on political tolerance appears and disappears, but is difficult to interpret because of the interactive ambiguity of the concept of tolerance.

While there are some hints of the development of literatures, however, consistent literatures often seem absent from this body of research. A consistent group of variables does not necessarily predict a consistent topic. Given lists of variables are being used for widely different purposes. We do not find the expected pattern of a small core of variables being built upon, except in the gradual development of the religion clusters. Rather, this is a story of complexity and duplication, of steps being retraced and detours being taken. Investigators build on the work of earlier investigators not by adding a few variables, but by introducing whole new clusters of variables. Each article, in some ways, stands in a whole new place. This cumulative process clearly leads many articles that began as responses to earlier traditions closer and closer to the general "throw-it-all-in" strategy characteristic of the "group differences" genre.[17]

IV Conclusion

In this paper, I have tried to show what becomes of the complexity of social life in positivist analysis. By looking at a body of work comprehensively and "from the ground (of an indicator) up," I have shown where ambiguity goes. It disappears into the cracks between studies. These cracks open because one indicator means slightly or completely different things to different

17. It goes without saying that this empirical analysis is colored completely by selection. That is, I have chosen a particular variable and seen the world from that variable's point of view. In network terms, this is equivalent to an ego-centered approach. While I myself lean towards structural network approaches, I think an ego-centered approach works here. After all, scientific literatures in part establish themselves not on structural bases but as conversations around a single issue. Nonetheless, selection may explain why only the religion literature appears to have any trajectory in this data. There is a sense in which ambiguity is what happens when we trace the weak ties out of a local "clique-like" literature into the larger arena of social investigation.

investigators, or because one investigator approaches a phenomenon as independent when another makes it dependent. They open because one investigator sees a variable in one context of other variables while another sees it in quite another, or because one investigator thinks an indicator characterizes a group when another thinks it characterizes individuals. They open because investigators decontextualize indicators in different ways, because they make different assumptions about the duration and narrative emplotment of indicators.

What enables positivism to move ahead and produce studies is a careful disattention to these cracks and fissures. It is the nature of a literature to try to flush certain ambiguities out of these cracks and to develop a set of conventional stands relative to those that remain. This is a matter of making basic assumptions, bringing in new variables to resolve ambiguities, and so on. But these conventions work only because other literatures are unknown. If one enters this world of investigation via the unity of indicator variables, the conventions disappear. Literatures interpermeate; they pervade one another's turfs of inquiry comprehensively. There are clearly "areas of variables" where two or three or more different social scientific communities are using the same indicators to do very, very different things.

As a result, any positivist will readily recognize my seven types of ambiguity and will note how literatures in positivism "routinely take account of these problems" in various ways. Ambiguity is, in this view, a problem to be resolved. But when it is resolved, what actually happens is the relegation of that particular ambiguity to the unknown world between the literatures. Oddly then, the project of rationalized positivism has the consequence of parsing out most of the ambiguity in social life and putting it in one very particular place. There it can easily be found by the kind of procedure used here.

That locating and identifying of particular conceptual ambiguities is the utility of this form of analysis. Although the investigation here may seem like a simple exercise in the sociology of sociology, in fact it offers a very quick route into the central conceptual problems of a literature. The great failure of the interpretivist attack on positivism has been its missing of this opportunity. The positivists have mapped out many of the crucial ambiguities and multiple meanings of social life, mapped them as difficulties and invisibilities. If we are careful, we can use their work to make these invisibilities visible.

At the same time, this analysis shows that the web of ambiguity constrains the life cycles of social scientific literatures. All "development" in scientific literatures consists in replacing one form of ambiguity with another. What we now require is a formal theory of whether this process simply replaces old ideas with new ones no more securely founded, or whether the ceaseless alteration of ambiguities in fact progresses in some sense. That is a larger topic than I can enter here.[18]

18. I have considered this problem at length in Abbott 2001.

The Causal Devolution

When we are all dead and forgotten, some scholar will sit in a quiet office at the end of a weary afternoon and gaze in perplexity at his notes on the sociological journals of the 1960s, 1970s, and 1980s. He wonders just what it was that sociologists believed. He writes:

> The people who called themselves sociologists believed that society looked the way it did because social forces and properties did things to other social forces and properties. Sometimes the forces and properties were individual characteristics like race and gender, sometimes they were truly social properties like population density or social disorganization. Sociologists called these forces and properties "variables." Hypothesizing which of these variables affected which others was called "causal analysis." The relation between variables (what these sociologists called the "model") was taken as forcible, determining. In this view, narratives of human actions might provide "mechanisms" that justified proposing a model, but what made social science *science* was the discovering of these "causal relationships."

Can this really have been what sociologists thought? He wonders. . . .

Luckily, of course, this future moment has not arrived. We ourselves understand all the hidden things we mean by the idea of causality, the things that aren't in fact apparent in our articles. We know quite well, for example, that the causal view just described is not the view of the classical social theorists. We know that this version of causalism is rather the vernacular social theory implicit in the methods courses that we all take within a year of ar-

This paper was drafted while I was at Nuffield College in the University of Oxford, as Norman Chester Fellow, in the spring of 1997. John Goldthorpe, Robert Sampson, and two anonymous referees for *Sociological Methods and Research* provided helpful comments. I would also like to thank audiences at the Institutt for Sosiologi at the University of Oslo and the Departments of Statistics and Sociology at the University of Washington for stimulating comments. The paper was written for the latter university's series of Lectures on Causality in the Social Sciences, in honor of Herbert Costner, and delivered in that series on 24 April 1997. It was originally published in *Sociological Methods and Research* 27 (1998): 148–81; reprinted with permission of Sage Publications, Inc.

riving at graduate school, a set of things we come to take for granted when
we apply standard empirical methods.

Initially, of course, we all remember the caveats. Regression relationships, as our instructors told us and as we tell our students, are the mere entails of real social action. Action is reality. But familiarity and practice send
the caveats packing. Economics articles, it is true, invoke formal action theories before settling into the comfortable technology of linear modeling.
But in the other empirical social sciences, an article's "theory" comprises
only a few narratives of "possible mechanisms." Either way, action and contingency disappear into the magician's hat of variable-based causality, where
they hide during the analysis, only to be reproduced with a flourish in the
article's closing paragraphs.

As a result, our empirical work would not be read by someone like my
future historian as grounded in the immediate social reality of action, the
way it seems grounded to us. To him, we live within a view of social reality
that we ourselves don't really believe. Our theoretical hearts are one place,
our empirical heads another.

To consider this disjunction, I begin by examining a classical discussion
of causality in sociology, that of Emile Durkheim's *Suicide*. I then review the
history of causality in sociological methodology and focus on the practical
aims behind the movement to causal analysis in the 1950s and 1960s. Con-
textualizing those aims leads me to the philosophical literatures on causality
and explanation. Breaking the usually assumed link between causality and
explanation, I then return to sociology and recommendations for the future
of methodology.

I should say a word about tone. Some readers of this paper have felt it to
be overargued. There are many neighborhoods in the city of sociology, they
say, enough room for causality and anticausality; there is no need to crush
causal argument. Others—causalists—have a simpler reaction; we knew all
this already.

In the years I have engaged in methodological debates, I have grown
used to both arguments: one thinks you have said too much, another that
you have said nothing at all. To the "many mansions" argument, I respond
that philosophically careless research practice is common in most of sociology's neighborhoods, from historical sociology to medical sociology to
stratification research. I have nothing but admiration for the creative audac-
ity that many years ago brought causalism into sociology in the first place.
But that an unthinking causalism today pervades our journals and limits our
research is an empirical fact. Of course there is room for many kinds of good
work. But there should be no room for thoughtless work.

To the argument that we know all this already, there is no response. Home truths are always old truths. That's no reason to avoid saying them, particularly if research practice ignores them. In any case, I did not intend this piece to be anticausal but to be reflective, to stand back from something that has become our common sense and ask why it has become so.

I Causality in the Classics: Durkheim

I begin with Durkheim. Not that his direct influence on images of causality was great. Untranslated until 1951, *Le suicide* assumed paradigmatic status only as the causal revolution gained momentum in the following decade. But by now three generations of sociologists have taken *Suicide* as a sacred text, and the book's great clarity makes both its virtues and its vices singularly accessible. It raises, at one point or another, nearly every important problem in the theory of causality.

In *Suicide* Durkheim insists from the start that causality embodies a kind of "forcing"—a determination—that is like the causality of classical mechanics. Thus, in the preface:

> When each people is seen to have its own suicide-rate . . . ; when it appears that . . . marriage, divorce, the family, religious society, the army, etc., affect it in accordance with definite laws . . . these states and institutions will no longer be regarded as simply characterless, ineffective ideological instruments. Rather they will be felt to be real, living, active forces, which, because of the way they determine the individual, prove their independence of him.[1]

Causality here means "living, active forces." It means determination. It means necessary and sufficient reason. Although Durkheim will later rely on more indirect types of causation, the ideal of social causality that he expresses at the outset is almost mechanical.

This mechanical image pervades Durkheim's writing on causality. His argument against cause by imitation rests essentially on a rejection of "action at a distance," the bugbear of classical physics. In the theory of imitation, he says:

> A cough, a dance-motion, a homicidal impulse may be transferred from one person to another even though there is only chance and temporary contact between them. *They need have no intellectual or moral community between them nor exchange services, nor even speak the same language, nor are they more related after the transfer than before.*[2]

1. Durkheim 1951:38–39. Except where noted, all translations used here are from the Simpson-Spaulding translation.
2. Durkheim 1951:123; emphasis added.

Imitation is thus rejected as a causal mechanism because it rests on a cognitive connection that is incapable of transmitting real influence between individuals, that is, because it constitutes action at a (social) distance. For Durkheim, it is the *sharing* of something—in particular of norms—that enables the passage of true causal force from one actor to another. Norms are an aether necessary to explain how social causality moves across seeming voids.

But Durkheim's approach at other times reflects less nineteenth-century physics than nineteenth-century medicine. Doctors then separated the causes of diseases into three layers: predisposing causes, precipitating (or "exciting") causes, and anatomical causes. Predisposing causes made people differentially likely to acquire certain diseases; certain climates were thought to affect lung diseases, for example, and excessive work was thought conducive to insanity. By contrast, precipitating causes "tripped the switch" in some of these predisposed people, thereby starting a disease. Alcoholism might trigger epilepsy or "disappointed affection" might trigger mania. Anatomical causes then produced the final common pathways in disease; they were the physical lesions that created the symptoms.[3]

Much of Durkheim's analysis of the social origins of suicide fits the predisposing cause model, and indeed Durkheim used that very word to specify his model:

> Chaque société est prédisposée à fournir un contingent determiné des morts volontaires. Cette prédisposition peut donc être le sujet d'une étude spéciale et qui ressortit à la sociologie.[4]

Here we seem to follow the doctors' model precisely; social forces make certain things more likely, while individual, contingent processes take care of the actual outcomes. But Durkheim has something more in mind, as we see in his discussion of heredity, the predisposing cause par excellence of late nineteenth-century medicine.

> When suicide is said to be hereditary is it meant merely that the children of suicides by inheriting their parents' disposition are inclined in like circumstances to behave like them? In this sense the proposition is incontestable but without bearing, for then it is not suicide that is hereditary; what is transmitted is simply a certain general

3. This discussion of causality relies somewhat on Abbott 1982, chap. 8.
4. "Each society is predisposed to produce a determined quota of voluntary deaths. This predisposition can thus be the subject of a special study, one under the jurisdiction of sociology" (Durkheim 1897:15, my translation).

temperament which, in a given case, may predispose persons to the act but without forcing them, and is therefore not a sufficient explanation of their determination.[5]

Durkheim emphatically rejects heredity as a cause of suicide, and precisely for its merely predispositional effects. The social causes that Durkheim will later introduce will be seen not as predisposing but rather as precipitating causes, by which Durkheim clearly means forces of determination, forces of joint sufficiency and necessity.

At times, Durkheim even seems to argue that social causes are *alternatives* to individual ones. Hence:

> No description, however good, of particular cases will ever tell us which ones have sociological character. If one wants to know the several tributaries of suicide as a collective phenomenon one must regard it in its collective form, that is, through statistical data, from the start.[6]

But in the last analysis, his approach does make the social causes a general framework within which individual forces exercise specific effects. Thus he says that:

> [records of presumptive motives of suicides] apparently show us the immediate antecedents of different suicides; and is it not good methodology for understanding the phenomenon we are studying to seek first its *nearest causes*, and then retrace our steps further in the series of phenomena if it appears needful?[7]

The immediate motives—which Durkheim is at pains to dismiss as what we would call intervening variables—thus simply ring changes on tendencies already established by larger forces.

Durkheim seems then to take a hybrid approach, a model of causality associated less with the physical or medical sciences than with the social sciences themselves. This is the model we social scientists are raised on, in which social forces directly determine underlying parameters, and individual cases then vary around them in response to local causality. We might call this the ANOVA model of causality, after the principal method embodying it. It is easy to point to passages in which Durkheim takes this ANOVA approach. Thus:

5. Durkheim 1951:93.   7. Durkheim 1951:148; emphasis added.
6. Durkheim 1951:148.

Certainly many of the individual conditions [i.e., causes] are not general enough to affect the relation between the total number of voluntary deaths and the population. They may perhaps make this or that separate individual kill himself, but not give society as a whole a greater or lesser tendency to suicide.[8]

Durkheim explicitly separates the two "levels" of causality.

[W]e do not accordingly intend to make as nearly complete an inventory as possible of all the conditions affecting the origin of individual suicides, but merely to examine those on which the definite fact that we have called the social suicide rate depends. The two questions are obviously quite distinct, whatever relation may nevertheless exist between them. . . . The [sociologist] studies the causes capable of affecting not separate individuals but the group.[9]

The fundamental difference between this position and the predisposing/precipitating model is that Durkheim, like other social scientists, wants to think of the social causes as determining, necessitous forces, not just as general probabilistic drifts. The general/particular causal distinction is made, but the location of force is changed. Where the nineteenth-century doctors often found the higher-level (predisposing) causes unchangeable and hence of merely academic interest, Durkheim's interest lies in precisely those higher-level (in his case, social) causes. For him, it is the immediate causes that are uninteresting.

It helps that data on these immediate causes—the so-called "motives" or "immediate stimuli" for suicide—are notoriously poor. Nonetheless, Durkheim rejects them. First, he presents statistics showing that overall suicide rates have risen sharply while these motives have not changed much at all. Then he presents statistics showing motives to be roughly the same for farmers and liberal professionals, when "actually the forces impelling the farm laborer and the cultivated man of the city to suicide are widely different."[10] He puts the matter bluntly:

The reasons ascribed for suicide, therefore, or those to which the suicide himself ascribes his act, are usually only apparent causes. . . . They may be said to indicate the individual's weak points, where the outside current bearing the impulse to self-destruction most easily finds introduction. But they are no part of this current itself and consequently cannot help us to understand it.[11]

---

8. Durkheim 1951:51.   10. Durkheim 1951:151.
9. Durkheim 1951:51.   11. Durkheim 1951:148.

Here Durkheim explicitly turns the predisposing/precipitating model on its head. Individual factors are now the predisposing ones; social-level factors are the exciting, effective, forceful causes.

The overall design of the great monograph that embodies this conceptualization of causality is familiar. After rejections of nonsocial arguments, Durkheim briefly considers what we would now call a descriptive or typological analysis—classifying suicides into categories and then analyzing them category by category. But here he finds too many diversities, too much missing data, too many errors on recording motivation. Better to reject this material altogether and pursue a purely social, causal analysis of suicide. In a central passage, he professes his faith:

Only in so far as the effective causes differ can there be different types of suicide. For each to have its own nature, it must also have special conditions of existence. The same antecedent or group of antecedents cannot sometimes produce one result and sometimes another, for, if so, the difference of the second from the first would itself be without cause, which would contradict the principle of causality. Every proved specific difference between causes therefore implies a similar difference between effects. Consequently, we shall be able to determine the social types of suicide by classifying them not directly by their preliminary described characteristics, but by the causes which produce them.[12]

This "classification by causes" governs the body of book 2, which closes with a final summary of the ANOVA view of causality:

Such are the general characteristics of suicide, that is, those which result directly from social causes. Individualized in particular cases, they are complicated by various nuances depending on the personal temperament of the victim and the special circumstances in which he finds himself. But beneath the variety of combinations thus produced, these fundamental forms are always discoverable.[13]

One can easily see why this book became the paradigmatic text of modern causal analysis, despite Durkheim's primitive statistical techniques. It is self-consciously scientific. It invokes the concept of causality. It combines

12. Durkheim 1951:146–7. Some points of this credo are obeyed through the book; types of suicides are separated by causes, for example. But the strict one-to-one causal relation assumed in the second sentence is later jettisoned, even though Durkheim is clearly honest in his professions here. And the explicit rejection of equifinality ("Every proved specific difference . . . ") is contradicted throughout by Durkheim's thoroughgoing functionalism.

13. Durkheim 1951:294.

the classical physicists' mechanism with the doctors' differentiation of local and global cause. It makes causality both universal and unique. And it lays out a model of causality that prefigures, almost word for word, the analysis of variance as set forth more than three decades later by Ronald Fisher and his statistical colleagues.

But we must hesitate before accepting this facile judgment, for it reads the present into the past. If we ask what *Durkheim* thought he was doing with all this talk of causality—talk that for us seems the very blazon of contemporary quantitative sociology—the answer is that Durkheim saw himself in a battle with immanent evolutionists like Spencer and Comte, scholars who saw in the course of events the mere working out of even grander and more universal forces than Durkheim's social powers. The *Rules of the Sociological Method* makes it very clear that Durkheim took up the cudgel of causality in the name of contingency and variation, in the name of the particular against the universal.[14] Odd as it may seem today, he thought he was urging the importance of real history, of actual events. Thus, what seems to us now like the ur-text of the sociological causalism of the last forty years was in fact seen by its author as a manifesto in favor of studying contingent social action as over against chronicling a unified, transhistorical development.

II Causality and Empiricism in Sociology

As I noted before, Durkheim's present symbolic importance belies what was in fact a negligible historical effect on social science's images of causality. The synthesis of causal analysis with quantitative methods so evident in *Suicide* in fact became widespread only in the 1950s, around the time *Suicide* was translated into English and republished by the Free Press. It was only then that the accidental affinity between Durkheim's theories and Fisher's mathematics made *Suicide* into the bible of causal analysis, repeatedly cited by Lazarsfeld, Stinchcombe, and other makers of modern sociological methodology. The new synthesis of causalism and quantitative analysis in fact arrived by a quite different route.[15]

Quantitative analysis was old in sociology, indeed in the social sciences more broadly, by the 1950s. But early quantitative analysis was neither causal nor inferential in the modern senses of those terms. The revolution of Fisherian statistics swept through the field of statistics itself only in the late 1920s. At that time, quantitative analysis in sociology took various

14. Durkheim [1895] 1964.
15. Lazarsfeld and Rosenberg 1955; Stinchcombe 1968.

forms—social trends under Ogburn, ecological analysis under the Chicago school, social distance scales under Bogardus—but none of these invoked the new Fisherian orthodoxy, although they did employ the correlational methods of the preceding generation of statisticians.

The new sociological statistics of the 1930s had three broad origins: biometrics, psychometrics, and econometrics. The biometric avenue is both the simplest and the most important. It was the biometricians who created modern inferential statistics between 1890 and 1930. Galton, Pearson, Fisher, Wright, and their colleagues invented correlation coefficients, regression methods, and path analysis. They also devised sampling theory and hypothesis testing, with its presumption of probabilistic reference models.[16]

In the early days, the biometric revolution was somewhat anticausal. The elder Pearson, for example, reduced causality to invariant succession in his celebrated *Grammar of Science*.[17] To be sure, within the experimental designs characteristic of early biological research the distinction between causality and association tended to blur. By isolating treatments from the influences of extraneous (we would say spurious) factors, experiments permitted a direct causal inference between treatment change and observed results. But much early statistical work—from that on intelligence to that on inheritance—was in fact conducted in nonexperimental situations and without any real theories of mechanism. It therefore tended to deemphasize causality and causal explanation. In particular, the main goal of the agricultural work was operational—how best to improve crop yield. Knowledge of mechanism was tangential to such work, which was effectively evaluation research without any theoretical pretensions.

The study of intelligence led to another set of statistical developments, this time within psychology. There, Thorndike, Spearman, and Thurstone developed scale and factor analysis. The psychometricians were even less causally oriented than the biometricians. The psychometricians' factor analysis reduced complex data to simple forms in order to reconcile quantitative data with intuitive categories. It ignored causality altogether. But this was hardly surprising. The major theoretical problem to which factor-analytic studies were addressed was the debate over the faculties of the mind—the

16. An early source on this subject is Bernert 1983. A more recent and important reference—particularly on sociological positivism—is Jennifer Platt's (1996) book on methods in American sociology. Bulmer 1984 is important for the earlier period. Stigler's (1986) history of statistics unfortunately cuts off in 1900, although it closes with a chapter on the elder Pearson and Yule.

17. Pearson [1892] 1937:102–14.

longstanding concern about whether there were separate "organs" of memory, desire, intellection, and so on. This was not a causal but rather a descriptive problem.

Econometrics provided a third entrance for statistics into social science. The earliest econometricians were fairly explicit associationalists. G. Udny Yule discussed "causation of pauperism" in the following operational terms in his *Introduction to the Theory of Statistics:*

> When we say, in fact, that any one variable is a factor of pauperism, we mean that *changes* in that variable are accompanied by *changes* in the percentage of the population in receipt of relief, either in the same or the reverse direction.[18]

Yule's text contained no index reference for causality or causation. It was only with the problem of reciprocal influence of time series that causal issues became central in econometrics. Writers like Slutsky, Frisch, and Tinbergen all spoke of their work as involving causes, but in all three cases causation essentially reduced to uniform association, as it did in the influential program document of Haavelmo on probability in econometrics. Issues of causation proper (issues going beyond association) arose in econometrics as questions of reversibility and direction, although lagged paths—characteristic from Tinbergen onwards—took care of many such problems. Some economists urged the separation of a theoretical level from a statistical one (as Keynes did in criticizing Tinbergen), arguing that causal ideas could come only from theory. Others believed causality could be analyzed only at the data level; the problem of specifying direction was in fact Wold's reason (from the late 1940s onward) for preferring the recursively structured path analytic paradigm. In the main, however, defining cause simply as uniform association was standard throughout the econometric literature, particularly in its simultaneous equations branch. Econometricians tended to use the language of cause more often than did the other new statisticians, but by it they meant only relationship or association.[19]

18. Yule 1912:192.
19. Haavelmo 1944. On Keynes and Tinbergen, see Morgan 1990:121 ff. On Wold's preference, see Morgan 1990:255. It was Trond Petersen who pointed out to me the importance of Herman Wold in this story. Wold was a central source for Blalock and spoke explicitly in causal terms. In this section on econometrics, I have relied to some extent on Morgan's book (1990), although not reading the sources quite as she does. It is tempting to speculate about the influence of quantum mechanics on econometrics' wholesale acceptance of the concept of probable causality. Tinbergen, after all, took a Ph.D. in physics and economics in 1929, when quantum mechanics was very much in the air. The idea of probable causality undergirding statistical associationism received its most important support from quantum mechanics, for in quantum

Thus the three main strands by which the new statistics emerged and entered the social sciences were somewhat mixed in their attitudes to cause. To the extent that the biometricians and econometricians talked about causality, it was identified with invariant relationships or associations. For their part, the psychometricians didn't care much about causality at all. This muted role for causality had also been characteristic throughout the quantitative sociology of the 1920s and 1930s. William Fielding Ogburn said that his Ph.D. thesis was "not a study to determine causes, but it is hoped that it may be used as a basis for a study of causes."[20]

In sociology, it was by contrast the old-style *qualitative* theorists who wanted to talk of causality. Thus, Robert MacIver's *Social Causation* (1942) attacked mathematicization precisely for losing sight of causality in a haze of associations. Much of MacIver's anger was directed against what he called the "mathematical limbo" of the more extreme versions of logical positivism, for example Morris Cohen's claim that "mathematical and logical relations form the intelligible substance of things." The extreme positivists in sociology—George Lundberg being the most vociferous—had argued that the concept of causality was anthropomorphic and "theological"; only association could be observed, never force or compulsion. Indeed the program of the early socio-logical-positivists included not only this extreme anti-causalism but an equally extreme operationalism that they had taken from the physicist Percy Bridgman.[21]

The concept of causality with which MacIver attacked these positivists was in fact closer to our concept of explanation than of causality. Causal assessment, he said, means seeking answers to the question "why does something or some regularity happen." Like Aristotle, he gave a number of different kinds of why questions, suggesting a number of generic types of causes. It is plain that the word causality meant for him something fundamentally different than it did for Cohen, Lundberg, and their like. Nor was MacIver the only such voice in sociology. In his principal methodological work, Znaniecki saw determined, "causal" processes as one of three basic types of social processes (the others being "ontogenetic" and "phylogenetic" processes) and made the Whewellian argument that causes could be discovered by analytic induction. Thus the Second World War found qual-

mechanics the reason for probable causes was not mere complexity, but in-principle failure of direct determination, as Reichenbach noted (1951:157–65).

20. Quoted in Bernert 1983:237.

21. MacIver 1942. The Cohen quotes are from MacIver 1942:49 and 53. The discussion on operationalism is at MacIver 1942:157.

itative, nonstatistical sociologists talking about causality and action, while quantitative, statistical sociologists focused mainly on association and were skeptical of causation. Yet after the war, the language of causality quietly drifted back into quantitative sociology. Causality reappeared as part of Lazarsfeld's gentling of the harshly scientistic paradigm associated with the social physics of Lundberg, Stuart Dodd, George Zipf, and others. The Lazarsfeld and Rosenberg reader of 1955 on *The Language of Social Research* established the modern concept of methodology (not least by consciously choosing that word) and made the investigation of causes central to that methodological process, citing MacIver alongside Lundberg, Dodd, and Durkheim, and indeed using MacIver's term "causal assessment."[22]

But the old skepticism remained. In the book's main section on multivariate analysis, the analyst is said to be pursuing "explanation," not causal assessment. Explanation here meant discovering general regularities, whereas causal assessment meant "applying available knowledge to the understanding of a specific case, be it a person or a collective." Lazarsfeld and Rosenberg gave examples of such causal assessment in a section on "empirical analysis of action," focusing on a favorite example, the process of purchasing a good. "Any bit of action," they tell us, "is determined on the one hand by the total make-up of the person at the moment, and on the other hand, by the total situation in which he finds himself."[23] In this formulation—which could easily have come from Herbert Blumer's symbolic interactionism—Lazarsfeld and Rosenberg view causality as a way of understanding and explaining particular action in particular settings.

The Lazarsfeld-Rosenberg skepticism about causality was echoed in Samuel Stouffer's contemporary review of quantitative methods. With surprising prescience, Stouffer noted the potential of game theory, decision theory, and stochastic processes for the future of sociology. He also covered recent developments in sampling, item scaling, experimental design, and official statistics. Multiple regression, in its infancy as a sociological method, rated a brief mention before much longer sections on factor analysis and significance statistics. But causality simply wasn't there. Even in Zetterberg's sketch of the scientific paradigm of sociology, causality played a very quiet second fiddle to explanation. Zetterberg's emphasis on axiomatic theory and deductive theory testing clearly derived from the logical account of science found in Cohen and Nagel and Hempel. Like Stouffer, he was deeply concerned with what we might call the semantics of research: the

---

22. Znaniecki 1934; Lazarsfeld and Rosenberg 1955. The choice of the word methodology is discussed at Lazarsfeld and Rosenberg 1955:4.

23. Lazarsfeld and Rosenberg 1955:387 (the first quote) and 393 (the second).

separation of theoretical and operational variables, the validity of definitions, and the reliability of measures. Causality—a matter of syntax—was
mentioned only briefly, in the discussion of longitudinal designs, and in fact
derided as a term "on the common sense level."[24]

But there were distinct changes in the second and third editions of
Zetterberg's scientific manifesto. By 1965, he was remarking that:

> [i]f the 1950's were particularly hospitable to taxonomies and de-
> scriptive studies, the 1960's seems [sic] more hospitable to theories
> and verificational studies.[25]

He introduced an extensive section on "propositions in sociology," in which
cause figures centrally:

> When we know or assume the direction in which the variates influ-
> ence each other, we can designate one as a *determinant* (cause or in-
> dependent variable) and the other as a *result* (effect or dependent
> variable).[26]

This statement seemed to follow the econometricians' acceptance of causality as simply invariant relation interpreted by a theoretical judgment about
direction. But Zetterberg included a lengthy analysis of "varieties of linkage
between determinants and results," discussing reversible and irreversible
relations, deterministic and stochastic relations, sequential and coextensive
ones, sufficient and contingent ones, and necessary or substitutable ones.

Sociology seemed to have passed a watershed. By the 1972 edition of the
Lazarsfeld and Rosenberg reader, the whole picture had changed. The lead-
off article of the book's section on multivariate analysis was a Hirschi and
Selvin chapter on "principles of causal analysis." The whole section on "empirical analysis of action" had disappeared (along with any coverage of qualitative research). Denzin's contemporaneous reader, *Sociological Methods*,
although reprinting Ralph Turner's elaboration of Znaniecki's analytical
induction, reprinted another chapter from Hirschi and Selvin, an attack on
"false criteria of delinquency." This chapter treated the associationalist conception as the only tenable possibility for a concept of causation, but assigned to association a quality of forcing or determination.[27]

24. Stouffer 1957; Zetterberg 1954; Cohen and Nagel 1934; Hempel 1942. The Zetterberg quote is 1954:60.
25. Zetterberg 1965:29.
26. Zetterberg 1965:64 (emphasis in original).
27. Lazarsfeld and Rosenberg 1972; Denzin 1970; Turner 1953; Hirschi and Selvin 1967.
Hirschi and Selvin's book was as much textbook on methods as a substantive critique of the
delinquency literature. In it, the new causalism is quite full-fledged.

The watershed, of course, was the implementation of path analysis. Path analysis had a long but subterranean history. Invented by Sewall Wright in the 1910s (the first full published exposition was in 1921), it was applied by Wright to problems in population genetics and econometrics. Although Wright used it widely and was followed by a few others in population genetics, path analysis remained generally unknown until the 1950s. The great statistician John Tukey wondered in 1954 "why I had not known about it before," and even as late as 1972 Goldberger argued that "statisticians have generally ignored Wright's work."[28]

Although Wright had worked in economics and had provided path analyses for his father's influential 1927 book on tariffs, economists too more or less ignored his work. Indeed his Chicago friend and economist colleague Henry Schultz knew of the methods but did not use them. As a result, economists routinely reinvented methods Wright had already developed (e.g., Tinbergen's "arrow scheme" of 1936). It was Herman Wold who around 1950 began explicitly to reintroduce path analysis to economics. Herbert Simon (another member of the Cowles Commission circle at Chicago in the early 1950s) also argued for path analysis, in two papers of 1953 and 1954, arguing that previously unreflective causality concepts in economics (e.g., in Haavelmo's celebrated 1944 paper) should be placed on a firm philosophical foundation. It is noteworthy that causality in this work was still defined in a very limited fashion. Wold defined it in rigidly operational terms, completely separating it from ideas of determination and forcing in his concept of a "generalized stimulus-response definition of causation." Simon in his 1953 paper likewise defined causal ordering in pure set-theoretic terms as the partial ordering of minimal subsets of variables.[29]

Path analysis entered sociology through Duncan and Blalock. In 1964 came Blalock's *Causal Inferences in Non-experimental Research*, which looked back to Wold and Simon. Reversing the positions of the 1940s and 1950s, Blalock treated causality as intrinsically linked with quantitative analysis, and with the analysis of general, not particular, phenomena. The opening pages of his book tell us just how dominant the causal model had become and how it had been redefined, losing the connotations of action that had been associated with it in Durkheim, MacIver, and even the early Lazars-

28. Wright 1921; Tukey 1954:35; Goldberger 1972:988.
29. On Schultz, see Morgan 1990:178, Goldberger 1972. On reinvention, see Morgan 1990:118. Simon's key papers were Simon 1953 and 1954. His argument about Haavelmo was at 1953:66 n. 6. Wold's definition of causality is in Wold 1964, the quote being from p. 274. Simon's definition of causality is in Simon 1953.

feld. There is no mention whatever of action, actors, or intentions. Causation is literally called a "forcing," and is something more than mere constant
conjunction or sequence. Like Durkheim, Blalock regards "causal laws" as
deterministic in the terms of classical physics, but clouded by error, by
which he means unspecified causes, individual variability, and so on. By the
word "theory," he means representations of reality in linear transformations. It is clear, in fact, that the philosophical prologue derives logically
from the statistical argument that follows it.[30]

Duncan's use of path analysis did not invoke an explicit concept of cause
as determination. He argued for "causal diagrams" that must be "isomorphic with the algebraic and statistical properties of the postulated system of
variables," suggesting that the algebraic properties came first. Indeed, he
quoted from Wright passages that prestated the celebrated critique David
Freedman would later give of misused path analysis:

> The method of path coefficients is not intended to accomplish the
> impossible task of deducing causal relations from the values of the
> correlation coefficients. . . . The method depends on the combina-
> tion of knowledge of the degrees of correlation among the variables
> in a system with such knowledge as may be possessed of the causal
> relations.[31]

The Blalock book (1964) and Duncan article (1966) proved to be citation
classics in the early 1970s, Blalock receiving a total of 115 citations and
Duncan's article 76 in the quinquennium 1971–75. Between them, they
launched a fleet of path diagrams.

Whatever Duncan's technical impact, his cautious use of causality was
eclipsed in the literature by the more determinative concept of Blalock. The
new emphasis on the concept of causality hinged on a redefinition; the term
"causality" could become important again in part because it had a new
meaning. Causality was now seen as a property of mathematical and statistical propositions rather than a property of reality, a fact clear in Blalock's
phrasing of discussions of causality specifically in terms of equations and
conditional probability, a phrasing that came directly from Simon and that
indeed echoed the long-standing associationalist definition of causality in
econometrics.[32]

30. Blalock 1964. The "forcing" quote is on p. 8, and the determinism discussion on p. 17.
31. Duncan 1966 is the key path analysis paper. The quote in text is from p. 3 and the block
quote from p. 15, quoting Wright 1934:193 and Wright 1960:444. Freedman's critique is laid
out in Freedman 1987.
32. Simon's discussions of causality can be found in Simon 1952, 1953, and 1954.

The shift also paralleled earlier trends in the philosophy of science. The logical positivists had sought to escape from the traditional epistemological problems of empiricism by redefining virtually all the central concepts of science, making them descriptions of scientific language rather than of empirical reality. Causality was one of several terms so treated. Thus, in Cohen and Nagel's immensely influential *Introduction to Logic and the Scientific Method* (1934), causality was defined as simply a kind of statement: a statement labeling an invariant relationship. Which specific aspect of this invariance was of interest would vary with the theoretical interests of the investigator, a point Blalock was to emphasize as well. A. J. Ayer took the same view in *Language, Truth, and Logic*, holding that "every general proposition of the form 'C causes E' is equivalent to a proposition of the form 'whenever C, then E.'"[33] The move towards the Durkheimian model of causality was thus not justified on the ontological grounds Durkheim himself had used, but rather on general philosophical grounds. The new model reinstated the idea of causality, but only (in theory) by making it a predicate of discourse, not of reality. At the same time, however, Blalock in practice quietly reinstated the Durkheimian concept of cause as forceful and determining, and his lead was followed by a generation of students unconcerned with the philosophical niceties that had restrained Duncan and many of the econometricians.

A summary makes this development more clear. For Durkheim himself, "causality" meant envisioning social reality as governed by real actions rather than by grand immanent forces. "Causes" were the local (although to our thinking still emergently social) forces determining these actions. For the early statisticians, "causality" had seemed of relatively little concern; they were interested in description or outcome analysis rather than in mechanisms. If anything, causality for them meant uniform association. For the logical positivists, causality in the lay sense was an anthropomorphic bugbear, to be purged from real science. They were militant supporters of associationalism and would accept the concept of "causality" only if it meant nothing more than association. For MacIver and other nonstatisticians, by contrast, causality seemed the essential heart of explanation in human affairs. Indeed, what they meant by causality was what the others meant by "explanation." Even for the early Lazarsfeld, "causality" meant something about understanding particular human actions. But the new causalism of Blalock and others accepted the causality concept of the logical positivists

33. Ayer 1946:55. For Blalock on aspects of invariance, see Blalock 1964:18.

(causality as a predicate of statements rather than reality and as a concept not referring to action) at the same time reinvesting it with both the quality of emergentism and the character of forcing or determination, both of which are present in Durkheim, although qualified by his sense of causality as tied up with action. As a result there emerged the full-blown ANOVA concept of causality. Ironically, philosophers are today reading the causal modeling literature for insight into "the nature and structure of probabilistic causation."[34]

I need not tell the reader that this view of cause is hegemonic in American sociology, although not, interestingly enough, in psychology or market research. We have ended up believing that social reality is determined in the main by certain general forces, and that these generalities are then specified by combinations of forces, and further limited by various aspects of "individuality," which in this sense is best understood as idiosyncratic higher-order interaction. Although we are, as I noted at the outset, very careful to tell ourselves and our students that this is really only the mathematical framework, in practice a surprising number of sociologists believe, for all intents and purposes, that this is the way the social world itself operates.

My discussion so far offers no account for why the Blalock-Duncan generation took up causal analysis in the form they did with the vigor they did. There seem to have been a number of reasons for this adoption.

One of these was a real belief in "science" as a stance for sociology. Thus, although Duncan regarded himself as a student of Blumer as much as of Ogburn, it was Blumer's insistence on rigor and science that appealed most strongly to him.[35] Blalock's similar faith in science speaks in page after page of his writing. To be sure, scientism was in the air. Logical positivism was

---

34. Irzik and Meyer 1987. I have not here discussed the large literature on probabilistic causality. Classical citations are Suppes 1970 and Salmon 1971. Nor am I considering the debates in statistics about causality that are associated with the names of Granger, Rubin, and Holland. (For a trenchant analysis of some of these issues, see Sobel 1996.) These arguments are well canvassed in the statistical literature and are somewhat removed from my concern with causality in the life-world and the proper relation of causal reasoning and explanation. As David Freedman says in a characteristically pungent phrase (in his denunciation of the TETRAD program for automatically generating path diagrams from data; 1997:76), "causation has to do with empirical reality not with mathematical proofs based on axioms." It is tempting to wonder whether the theory of probabilistic causality was an independent arrival or a rationalization of what had by the 1970s long since been common practice in both natural and social sciences.

35. See Duncan's many statements during the departmental debates of 1951–52, discussed in Abbott and Gaziano 1995.

triumphant in philosophy, and science had, in many people's eyes, won the Second World War. In social science, too, scientific stances seemed particularly strong. Polls were becoming universal. Market research was booming, both in the strongly quantitative Lazarsfeldian variant and in the softer, psychologistic style of Lloyd Warner and Burleigh Gardner. And scientism as an ideology went beyond a simple methodological stance. It was a general commitment, as evidenced by the arrival of double-blind reviewing in sociology journals in the mid-1950s.[36]

With respect to the new methodologies, this belief in science was very much a young man's game. In 1955, Duncan was 34, Blalock and Coleman 29, Goodman 27. Lazarsfeld was the grand old man at 54, dedicating the 1955 reader to "Charles Glock and his 'young turks' at the Bureau of Applied Social Research." Of course, sociology as a whole was young at the time because of its rapid expansion after the war. But there was a very generational flavor to the causal revolution. Duncan's famous public attack on Lloyd Warner's "unscientific" categories, written when he was 29 and coauthored with his graduate student colleague Harold Pfautz, was as much a young person's attack on the establishment as it was a blow in a quantitative/qualitative fight. Blalock first published his text *Social Statistics* at 34. Coleman's capaciously quixotic book on mathematical sociology came at 38.[37]

The youthfulness of the new causalism suggests another reason for its adoption, one for which I have a strong hunch, but scant evidence. Nicholas Mullins saw the new causalists as Cromwellian puritans.[38] But I think, by contrast, that the leaders of the new causalism were a little like Hilary climbing Everest. They did it "because it was there." The methods had been worked out by others. They could be quickly borrowed and applied. Trying them out would be easy. Who knew what might result? The young Turks did it, in short, for fun.

We get this "let's try it out" feeling again and again in Coleman's *Mathematical Sociology*, as we do even at times in *The American Occupational Structure*.[39] Duncan was explicit in the latter book about the extreme assumptions necessary for the analysis, but repeatedly urged the reader to bear with him while he tried something out to see what could be learned.

36. On the new forms of market research, see Karesh 1995. The rise of double blind reviewing is discussed at length in Abbott 1999a: chaps. 5 and 6.
37. Duncan's attack on Warner is in Pfautz and Duncan 1950. Coleman's book on mathematical sociology is Coleman 1964.
38. Mullins 1973.
39. Coleman 1964; Blau and Duncan 1967.

The memoirs one reads of Columbia in the early days of the Bureau of Applied Social Research all suggest a similar mood of experimentation—often contemptuous of outsiders, but lightheaded and giddy and energetic as only young people with a new truth can be.

To be sure, this try-it-out attitude was combined with the scientific puritanism Mullins so disliked. More consequentially, it was also combined with extraordinary exclusivity, for few senior sociologists could follow the mathematics necessary to undertake causal analysis on their own, and computerized commodity statistics were not yet available. As a result, the young causalists were rulers of a roost no one else could attack at an age when in more typical careers they would have been chafing for a decade or more under their elders' tutelage. It is little wonder that as the years passed they began to take their own creation with such remorseless seriousness.

This seriousness was passed on to their students, who had not had the experience of inventing causalism and therefore could not know at first hand its contingent, historical character. Rather they learned causalism in methods courses as the way science was done, and, within a few years, statistical packages would prevent their acquiring that tacit knowledge and sense of respect for the methods that comes with having worked them by hand. Duncan passed on to his students neither his desire for what he once called "a properly relativistic sociology" nor the comprehensive vision of social life that he had gotten from Blumer. He finished his career decrying nearly everything that people had done in following him. The causalists won all the battles, but lost the war.[40]

What was the war about? It was about providing a compelling and interesting account of social life. Causalism was a tactical avenue to that larger strategic aim. The great mistake of the causalists, in Duncan's eyes, was to have mistaken the tactical victories of "doing the science right" for the strategic victory of getting a better account of social life. To put it into the familiar terms of causalism itself, the mistake was to have taken the indica-

40. I have heard the "won the battles" phrase attributed to Duncan, but cannot verify its origin. For Duncan's attack on his followers, see *Notes on Social Measurement* (1984). The remarks on relativist sociology are in Duncan 1951. I do not have space in this article to deal with the lengthy defense of the causal interpretation of probabilities by Cartwright (1989: note that Cartwright was explicit that she had no defense for the causal interpretation of *data*; see, e.g., pp. 13, 35). Cartwright's detailed demonstration of the probability-cause connection seems to me to have difficulties because of its interpretation of disturbance terms, its bypassing of the issues of temporal orderability, and its forgetting that backwards reasoning from probabilities to causes is conditional on true knowledge of the causal situation. As many (starting with Whewell) have argued (and as Cartwright states in her second chapter), the theorizing act is always in the last instance autonomous.

tor for the concept. It is this losing sight of the main objective that I denote by my title—the "causal devolution."

But if the mistake was to have thought that a fairly narrow causality concept was the only way to undertake the explanation of social life, what are the alternatives? Here it is helpful to turn to the philosophical literature.

III Philosophy, Causality, and Explanation

The ANOVA view of causality common in social science in fact bears little relation to developments in the analysis of causality by philosophers. The classical analyses are those of Aristotle and Hume. With characteristic good sense, Aristotle noted that people meant a variety of things by "cause." Today, each of his four causes supports a major theoretical strand in social science. Material causes are studied by demographers, who believe that the explanations of social phenomena lie in the different qualities of the human materials going into them. Formal causes are studied by structuralists, who see in networks and patterns the determining shapes of human affairs. Final causes are studied by functionalists, with their interest in the purposes and ends of action. And efficient causes are the focus for choice modelers, who seek the final pathways by which action is determined. In most empirical social science, the first three (at least) are mixed together, although recently the last is entering the mix almost as often. Aristotle's notion of cause is thus a broad one, covering most of our activity as social scientists. Like MacIver's notion in the current century, his concept comes closer to our idea of "explanation" than to our idea of cause.

The Humean analysis is more specific. As is well-known, Hume directly attacked the notion of causality as a "forcing" of things to happen and as a necessary relationship in the real world. For him causality was a simple matter of invariable sequence or constant conjunction. Cause and effect had to be both adjacent and temporally successive, and, in addition, the relation between them had to be constant. But the necessity of it was purely in the mind of the beholder, for necessity could not be directly perceived. As the logical positivists were later to argue, causation denoted a kind of statement, rather than a kind of relationship between things. Even Kant could rescue causality from Hume's attack only by making it one of the categories of the pure reason, an a priori aspect of knowing. On this point, Durkheim—and with him most social, indeed most natural, scientists—completely ignored the Western philosophical tradition, for he took "forcing" and determination as central to his concept of cause.

Since Hume, the modern philosophy of causality has divided over a number of issues. Central among them are:

1. singular versus multiple causes
2. necessity versus sufficiency as the logical mode of causality
3. rational action versus mechanical determination as paradigms for causality
4. causality as simultaneous versus causality as sequential
5. determinate versus probabilistic causality.

I cannot review this literature—vast, controversial, and inconclusive—in so brief a space. But it is important to note that the social science notion of causality embodies one particular position within these inconclusive debates. It has generally made determination rather than action paradigmatic and has always presumed sequentiality: cause must precede effect. Problems 1, 2, and 5 have been resolved by a probabilistic version of the position of J. L. Mackie on plural causality. Mackie identified causality with what he called INUS conditions: "insufficient but nonredundant parts of an unnecessary but sufficient condition." The Mackie concept more or less justifies our common practice of apportioning causality in pieces: telling the public— or at least as they hear it—that criminality is 65 percent due to heredity or that intelligence is 35 percent due to nurture or whatever. The fact that the causes are insufficient in themselves covers us if they don't work separately. The fact that they are nonredundant parts of something covers our obvious assumption of plural causality. That they add up to something that is sufficient rather than necessary gets us out of directional difficulties.[41]

The philosophical literature, however, remains deeply divided on most issues of causality. Indeed, the greatest modern review of the practical problem of causality—Hart and Honoré's *Causation in the Law*—is deliberately, maddeningly catholic in its conceptions of cause.[42] But the book does make it clear that from a legal and practical point of view, the question of causality always arises as part of the question of explanation. And about explanation there is a separate and equally complex philosophical literature.

The modern philosophy of explanation rests on Carl Hempel's celebrated argument—set forth at the high-water mark of logical positivism in 1942—that explanation of particular events always takes the form of a syllogism whose major premise is a "covering law" and whose minor premise is

41. Mackie 1974 sets forth the idea of INUS conditions. For a review of causality ideas of this type in sociology, see Marini and Singer 1988.
42. Hart and Honoré 1985.

an assertion that a particular situation meets the hypothesis conditions of that law.[43] Thus, in Durkheim's case, sociology provided the theoretical major premise whereby certain social conditions entail certain necessary consequences: lack of social integration causes high suicide rates. The minor premise was the demonstration that a particular case fit the hypothesis of the major premise: Saxony lacked strict religion and hence lacked social integration. The syllogism then produced the inescapable conclusion that Saxony had a high suicide rate. Thus sociology "explained" that suicide rate.

Over the years, Hempel's argument has drawn considerable opposition. From the outset, Karl Popper argued that all social covering laws are trivial, the classic example being that "sane persons as a rule act more or less rationally."[44] For Popper, to invoke such a law was simply to restate the problem, not to explain anything. All the real explaining was done by side conditions that specified which covering laws hold, that is, which of a set of plural causes were doing the explaining and which were simply assumed in setting up the problem.

But the larger response to Hempel came from philosophers of history, who proposed a completely alternative view of explanation, based on narrative. There were three general versions. The first was the "understanding" model of Collingwood, Dray, and many others, which deals to some extent with Popper's issue of side conditions.[45] According to Collingwood, the historian aims to get inside a historical figure's own justification of action, to understand what was "reasonable" given that figure's tastes and conditions. The Collingwood position was thus a broad version of what would come to be known as rational choice theory; the historian figured out "what it made sense for the actor to do," given the actor's beliefs, knowledge, and psychology. This approach correlated with Collingwood's position that rational, intentional action was the paradigm of causality.

The understanding view was, however, seen by later philosophers of history as overly "idealist," given to dangerous subjectivism. A second view of narrative explanation, responding to this challenge, was the "followability" thesis of W. B. Gallie.[46] Like Collingwood's rational constructionism, this view attempted to describe how narrative history actually worked. On this argument narrative was itself explanatory by virtue of truth, consistent chronology, and a coherent central subject. Narrative was held to combine

43. Hempel 1942.
44. Popper 1962, 2:265. The argument is in Popper 1962, chap. 25.
45. Collingwood 1946; Dray 1957.
46. Gallie 1968.

things that are determined by general laws with things that are contingent, producing a plausible, because followable, story. This notion of "combination" was much looser than the formalities of the covering law model, but still left a place for general determinism that is missing in Collingwood.

A third position on historical explanation recognized a central problem in Gallie's followability view—the fact that knowing how the story turns out is central to a historian's "following the story." Louis Mink, for example, argued that history was one of three basic modes of thinking about the world: theoretical (the view of the natural sciences), categoreal (the view of philosophers), and configurational (the view of historians). What made configurational thinking unique was its insistence on putting particular pieces together into larger wholes. This was the process that Walsh and others had called colligation: the assertion that a group of conflicts should be collectively defined as a social movement, for example, or that a certain group of composers made up a school or a style. Conceived across time, colligation became the process of creating "configurations"—that is, histories or plots—of events.[47]

The literature on explanation in the philosophy of history can be seen in hindsight to have been part of the long tradition of two cultures positions reaching back to the *Methodenstreit* of the late nineteenth century. A fairly broad range of philosophers has argued that explanation in the human sciences is different from that in the natural sciences. The early statements of this position tended to be exclusionary (Windelband, Dilthey), but more recent ones have tried to suggest ways of merging interpretive and causal explanation.[48] This philosophical literature thus suggests that sociological views of explanation could benefit from frank discussion of whether and how it is possible to combine interpretive (intentional, teleological, etc.) explanation with causal (determinative, nomic, etc.) explanation. (By these multiple terms, I do not mean to imply that all these distinctions can be simply conflated, but to suggest that the issue of combining the two sides arises no matter how we happen to divide the two cultures.) The various concepts of explanation in the philosophy of history are examples of how we might proceed.

Most writers about interpretive explanation regard the issue of descrip-

47. Mink 1970, Walsh 1958. The term colligation is from Whewell 1968:129 ff. Whewell's analytic inductive account of the philosophy and history of science was replaced by the simple-minded induction of Mill, then by the work of Mach and Pearson (who nonetheless owed much to Whewell), and later by the more deductive accounts of the positivists.

48. See, e.g., von Wright 1971, chap. 4.

tions of events as both central and problematic in the activity of explanation. Before we can explain, we must describe. In particular, as Hart and Honoré argue, we generally seek to explain things when they deviate from some recognizedly normal state of affairs.[49] For them this "deviation from the normal" is as important a part of our idea of causality as is regular association. Such "deviation" is most obvious in our explanations of action, of course, but it appears as well in the simplest causal models in econometrics or the natural sciences; they all assume that the effects would not have arisen in any case, absent the cause. Thus not only does explanation presuppose description, it also presupposes description from a point of view.

As the analytic philosophy of history shows, it is important to realize that this point of view—and the description that results—is inevitably "narrative," in the sense of involving more than one point in time. For it is usually later events that define what were the salient causal aspects of a prior situation, that tell us what part of the description was important. To give a widely used example, we do not know until Oedipus's parentage is revealed that what matters about his marriage is not that it is with the most beautiful woman in Thebes but rather that it is with his mother.[50]

A final useful insight from the philosophy of explanation concerns our reasons for seeking explanation. Hart and Honoré's central aim in discussing "causality and the law" is to analyze the connection between our beliefs about causality and our attributions of responsibility. Now as it happens, despite the great dominance of scientific causalism in American sociological rhetoric, a central part of most published American sociology today is the attribution of responsibility. Certainly this is true in my own substantive field of studies of work and occupations, where attributions of responsibility for inequality are central to a majority of studies.[51] That being the case, sociology is deeply in need of careful reflection about the relation between causal analysis and attribution of responsibility. I am unaware of any such discussion. In this area we have much to learn.

IV Causal and Contingent Views of Social Reality

How can views of explanation that derive from interpretive philosophy and the philosophy of history provide viable alternatives to explanation of social

49. On description, see von Wright 1971:135. Hart and Honoré make their argument about deviation at Hart and Honoré 1985:29.
50. On the inevitability of narrativity, see Danto 1985:143. The Oedipus story is from Ruben 1990:105, quoting Mackie 1974.
51. See Abbott 1993.

life via our current concept of causality? To be sure, they stand much closer to traditional western social philosophy and to our modern social theorists than does the ANOVA view of causality that characterizes our quantitative work. They make action central. They mix determined and free acts. They embrace contingency. But to espouse them wholly would surrender the important knowledge we have gained about social determinants produced under the causality paradigm. We must recast our strategies of explanation, but without losing what we have gained. To do that, we must begin by asking what we want from explanation.

The main desiderata of explanation are consistency and interest. First, even though disciplines grow in fits and starts—pushing out here, surrendering there—our knowledge becomes great only when it has internal consistency. Our theories, our explanations, our methods, and our research programs should resonate with and support one another. In addition to this consistency, our knowledge of society should meet a second standard: it should produce—as Duncan and others wanted—a comprehensive, interesting, and compelling account of social life. That account should be interesting and compelling not only to us in our specialty, but also to the larger culture around us.

It is no secret that sociology at present meets neither the standard of consistency nor that of interest, although it has done so in the past and, with luck, will do so in the future. I have just discussed the profound inconsistency between our abstract theories and the concrete theories implicit in our methods. And surely none of us thinks that sociology has, at present, a publicly compelling account of social life.

I shall make one point about compelling public interest before closing the paper with my main topic of consistency. One central reason for sociology's disappearance from the public mind has been our contempt for description. The public wants description, but we have despised it. Focusing on causality alone, we refuse to publish articles of pure description, even if that description be quantitatively sophisticated and substantively important. Commercial firms pay millions for such work. Our society is in fact "described" in surpassing detail by proprietary market research. But we who like to imagine ourselves responsible for the public's knowledge of society despise description and indeed despise the methods that are generally used for quantitative description. Our social indicators are simply disaggregated variables, ready for input to causal analysis. The notions of complex combinatoric description, of typologies based on multiple variables: these fill the average sociologist with disgust.

Our disgust is disingenuous, for ease of computing has made of regression itself a descriptive method. When dozens of regressions can be run in an afternoon and when the average regression-based journal article reports perhaps five to ten percent of the runs actually done, we should stop kidding ourselves about science and hypothesis testing. And taken as a descriptive technique, regression is quite poor. Description aims to reduce a welter of data to something manageable. But regression reduces the dimensionality of the data space only by one. Worse still, that lost dimension usually retains most of its variation. So we haven't really even understood why that one thing happens. We *have*, to be sure, understood the effects of the independent variables on that one dependent dimension, and in an evaluation context—when we are trying to make decisions about whether to use fertilizer on the field or dopamine in the brain—regression is without question the method of choice.

But as a general method for understanding why society happens the way it does, much less as a strategy for simple description, causally interpreted regression is pretty much a waste of time. Scaling and clustering may throw away the vast majority of dimensionality, but by doing so they often produce compelling and powerful simplifications of complex data. When there are millions of dollars riding on results, the bettors go with descriptive methods, not regression. Market researchers use it to clean up details.

Of course, many of us feel the marketers are fools. Causal analysis is the only true science. Yet what produced biology's modern understanding of evolutionary trees? Accurate description and numerical taxonomy, known to us as cluster analysis. What has quintupled our ability to find drugs with specific powers? Sequence analysis, a descriptive technique. Most causal discoveries about protein mechanisms are premised on the descriptive geography of proteins produced by the sequence analytic community. Thus we should not assume that science must be about causality. Much of real science is description. Sociology will not be taken seriously again as a general science of social life until it gets serious about description.[52]

But my more important concerns are with consistency. I have argued that our methods imply theories of society that none of us actually believe. I have implied that we might escape the narrow concept of explanation implicit in our methodologies by employing alternative conceptions of explanation from the philosophy of history. I would like now to trace that path of escape.

52. For a similar position resting on a different argument, see Sobel 1996.

When I myself first turned towards "historical" explanation, I took it as a simple alternative. Instead of breaking social stories down into variables, I would leave them together, comparing and categorizing them as wholes. I would begin with stories as the historians did, but then I would generalize. Thus, I embarked on a ten-year quest for "characteristic plots," looking, for example, at sequences of local professionalization within medicine, at careers of individuals within an occupation, and at patterns in the evolution of the major welfare states.[53]

Needless to say, this endeavor attracted a lot of hostile press from people who called this work "mere description." I have already sketched the twofold response to that judgment: first there is nothing bad about description and second today's causal methods are effectively descriptions themselves. But my approach *was* wrong, for reasons both my critics and I failed to see. It wasn't "sociological." I knew full well that the foundational insight of sociology is that the social world is made up of situated actions, of social *relations*, not of independent stories. Social life is a process that continuously embodies itself in constraining structures. My methods assumed away those structures just as fast as did the causal methods I was attacking. I was *locating* social facts to be sure, but only within the individual stories of career or occupational cycle, only within time. I was not putting those careers and occupational cycles in motion in *relation* to one another. I was not locating them in social structure.

To be sure there are times when the broad assumption of casewise independence is reasonable and useful. So it was legitimate to compare the order of medical professionalization in Detroit with that in Boston and that in Altoona. But it had probably not been legitimate to treat the careers of German musicians as independent; they moved in a system where successes for some people meant failures for others. And it was no surprise that I found among the great welfare states not only no clear internal reasons for the sequencing patterns, but no obvious diffusion explanation for them either. For those states were bound up in the single cultural unit of Western Europe.

With any given social phenomenon, we can probably identify its independence of context in social space and social time. Phenomena that are completely free of context are the province of standard causal methods. Phenomena that are strongly conditioned by their temporal context but relatively free of environing social structure are the province of time series or

53. On local professionalization within medicine, see Abbott 1991b. On careers within an occupation, see Abbott and Hrycak 1990. On welfare states, see Abbott and DeViney 1992.

event history or sequence methods. Phenomena that are strongly conditioned by structural contexts but not by temporal ones are the province of network analysis and spatial autocorrelative methods.

But at the heart of sociology are those phenomena that are fully enmeshed both in social time and social space, what I have elsewhere called interactional fields.[54] It is because we study interactional fields that we are a discipline of social *relations*, concerned with the social *process*. The great empirical literatures of such analysis are the literature on small group interaction from Goffman onwards, the literature on urbanism and city patterns, and the literature on occupations and professions, as well as substantial portions of the literatures on crime and historical sociology.

What we should require of explanation is that it give us an account of how such interactional fields work. This account will not be purely causal. For nearly all of these literatures give a large place to free action, often to strategic choice in particular. Second, it will include temporal effects of many sizes, for in each of these areas a past of many depths shapes the present. Third, it will also include a complex understanding of social structure, for that too pervades interactional fields at many scales.

Middle range theories and empirical methodologies must, it seems to me, meet these three tests if they are to be consistent with our foundational vision of the social world. In terms of middle range theory, such work has in fact been done. Wallerstein's *The Modern World System* is essentially a theory of such an interactional field, with history and structure of varying sizes and powers. So also was my own book on professions.[55] Such books don't predict what will happen, indeed they suggest that interactional fields are probably too complex for us to predict. But they do show various internal patterns; they do sketch the "rules of the game;" they do portray the limits and possibilities of action in such systems.

We require quantitative methods that do the same thing. If I may use another forbidden word, we will have to employ simulation. Game theory won't get us very far, because it is ignorant, except in the most general terms, of a serious concern with structure and with complex temporal effects. But simulation may help us understand the limits and possibilities of certain kinds of interactional fields, and that would be profoundly sociological knowledge.

So, for example, in the world of professions, there are local contexts— local historically and local in terms of the competitors facing a profession—

54. Abbott 1997a.
55. Wallerstein 1976; Abbott 1988a.

in which it is very useful for a profession to be rigidly organized. There are other contexts in which it is not. When work is expanding rapidly, professions are better off being able to expand rapidly to meet it, for example. But the definition of which kind of moment it is for a particular profession resides in the evolution of the system. The phenomenon of locally expanding work is produced by the ensemble of strategic and nonstrategic actions by all the professions competing in a given area at a given time. Thus, there is no parameter we can put on the variable of rigidity of organization, for that parameter's power is situationally determined, emerging from the evolution of the system. It is not systematically time varying or space varying. There is no way to "window" it or see it as a property of anything other than the moment and the situation. Lazarsfeld was right that understanding "the actor in the situation" was the heart of analysis, but wrong to think that it was a simple matter of assembling enough general covering laws and applying them. Situations are all there is. A better strategy of explanation is understanding how an interdependent system evolves internally. Simulation may be the only way to do that.

More important, the "meaning of parameters" can itself change for strategic reasons, that is through deliberate action of actors in a system. Virtually all forms of current positivism assume that the meaning—causal or otherwise—of an event is fixed for the duration of analysis. But we all believe that one of the central, basic human actions is to redefine something, so that the very shape of the present, perhaps even the identities of the actors in the present, can be made new. Any serious methodology has to be able to encompass this kind of meaning change as well. Again, simulation seems the best alternative.

We seem then to be at a turning point. Our explanations are of little interest to the general public and are disconnected from our own general views of society. By broadening our concept of explanation we can address, once again, the foundational problems of our field.

I do not mean to denigrate the achievements of causalism. Causalism has been an immensely successful paradigm for sociological methodology, but the blunt fact is that it is now getting in the way of developments essential to the field. We have to refurbish and rethink our ideal of what it means to explain social life and we must reintegrate our theories and methods around that ideal.

PART TWO

Time and Method

What Do Cases Do?

This paper addresses three issues. It first asks what happens to the actions of "cases" in standard quantitative methods, showing that they lose their complexity and their narrative order. It then considers the kinds of studies that take those things seriously, particularly historical case studies, examining how case complexity and case action function in such studies. It closes with a consideration of how to generalize about complexity and narrative order across cases. As this summary makes clear, a central message of the paper is that we must disentangle the population-versus-case distinction from the analysis-versus-narrative one.

I am using "case" here in the sense of "instance." Instances can be of two kinds. First, a particular entity may be an instance (case) of a population. Here, we have "case" as single-element subset; the population is some set of social objects (persons, companies) and the cases are its members. But a particular entity may also be an instance (case) of a conceptual class. Here, we have "case" as exemplar; the conceptual class has some property (e.g., it is a structural type like bureaucracy) and the cases exemplify that property. Clearly these are different definitions with very different implications. As we shall see below, some sociologists assume that there are social objects that are not inherently "conceptual," while others do not.[1]

I would like to thank Charles Ragin, Howard Becker, David Weakliem, Claude Fischer, and Peter Abell for comments on the paper. In particular, Howie's comments reminded me of the great Chicago tradition I had overlooked in early drafts, an oversight all the more surprising given the influence of that tradition on my substantive work. This paper was originally presented on 2 March 1990 at a Northwestern University–sponsored conference organized by Ragin and Becker on the subject "What Is a Case?" It was originally published in *What Is a Case?*, ed. Charles Ragin and Howard Becker (Cambridge: Cambridge University Press, 1992), 53–82; reprinted with permission of The Cambridge University Press.

1. I am ignoring here the problem that the case relation is not a mapping, a problem rising with particular force under the conceptual definition of case. That is, "x is a case of y" can be simultaneous with "x is a case of z" and this may hold under a wide variety of relations between y and z. This is a most disturbing fact, but one whose implications would take me far away from my topic. Note, too, that even the subset definition of case is in fact subject to the same problems, for we do not have a well-defined, hierarchical set of categories for categorizing social entities. It is precisely in the reflection about what x is a case of that real theory arises.

By asking what cases do, I am assuming that the case is an agent. This idea is somewhat foreign to some sociological traditions. We don't generally think of the cases in the General Social Survey as agents with intentions and histories. But it is precisely my intent to begin with the question of what such cases "do" in the Weberian (etc.) sense of social action. What kinds of activities do they undertake? What do they try to accomplish? What kinds of agents are they?

I What Do Cases Do in Standard Positivist Articles?

A simple way to ascertain what cases do in standard empirical sociological studies is to open the latest *American Journal of Sociology* (November 1989 as of this writing) and analyze some articles in detail. (I will here consider the first three.) My procedure is simple. I find all the narrative sentences, the sentences whose predicates are activities or parts of the social process.[2] I then consider who are the subjects of these sentences, what kinds of activities are involved, and how the predicates are related to causality. I also consider when in the argument narrative sentences are likely to appear and how cases are (implicitly) construed by the authors.

The usual disclaimers apply. I am not attacking or debunking the particular authors involved. Their work's appearance in such a journal warrants its acceptance as disciplinarily proper and representative. And I am not trying to debunk the whole style of work involved. I merely wish to discover something about its "case" assumptions. I have used quotes extensively, since the exact locutions employed are of central importance. A thing may be said several ways; but it is precisely in the choice of one of those ways that assumptions about cases are most clear.[3]

In the first paper, Charles Halaby and David Weakliem are investigating the relation between worker control and attachment to the firm.[4] Their "cases" are workers. (Cases in this kind of literature are usually called "units of analysis," a term with considerably different connotations—of equivalence among individuals and of the preeminence of analytic categories—

2. See Danto 1985 for a technical definition of narrative sentences.
3. While these papers are technically a random sample—my procedure was exactly as described—some readers might feel that I "just happened to get some articles that looked like this." In fact, other papers would have produced pretty much the same set of observations, although perhaps in different ways. Indeed, I would imagine that the overall balance—two papers taking a strong "population/analytic" view and one taking a "narrative" one—probably overestimates the direct use of narrative in mainstream sociology.
4. Halaby and Weakliem 1989.

than those of "case.") Halaby and Weakliem investigate several hypotheses, and it is in these hypothesis discussions that we first find narrative sentences.

> The first hypothesis argues that worker control dignifies work. This may be evidenced empirically in the transformation that increasing control effects in the significance of work. In the absence of control, work is a mere instrumental activity, a means of subsistence: the worker works to produce wares. But with increasing control the work itself becomes a terminal value that is invested with significance in its own right as an expression of self. For reasons not always made clear . . . the value assigned to the work itself carries over into the employment relation, resulting in higher attachment.[5]

Note that "the worker works [only in order] to produce wares" is the only sentence in which cases act. Elsewhere, variables do the acting. In "the work itself becomes a terminal value . . . ," "the value carries over into the employment relation," and "the transformation that increasing control effects in the significance of work . . . ," variables are the subjects of the clauses. Presumably these are variable-based descriptions of psychic processes that take place "in the heads of the cases." Still, the variables, not the cases, do the acting here.

Halaby and Weakliem next propose the hypothesis that excessive supervision violates cultural norms:

> [Theorists] argue that supervisory practices that limit workers' independence and control of their work violate the "independence norm in American culture" and therefore result in dissatisfaction and turnover.[6]

Here, the variables are directly personified as agents. "[P]ractices . . . violate the . . . norm and result. . . ." We have moved away from the simple causal language ("becomes," "carries over," "effects") of hypothesis one to a more active vocabulary ("violates"). Again, this is presumably a psychic shorthand, yet there is no case agency even at the psychic level. The worker doesn't think about these things, the things themselves directly act in his or her psyche. The personality is merely the setting in which the causes act, not itself an agent acting (e.g., reflecting) on them.

The final major hypothesis is the authors' new theoretical contribution,

5. Halaby and Weakliem 1989:553–54.
6. Halaby and Weakliem 1989:554.

what they call a "match quality" hypothesis, emphasizing the fit between innate worker characteristics and job characteristics:

> Control of task-related job activities gives a worker the freedom to employ his skills and abilities more fully and thereby achieve more fully the maximum level of productivity commensurate with his productive resources. This means that the potential gains in productivity that might accompany a job change will tend to be low for autonomous workers. Such workers will therefore arrive at pessimistic estimates of the potential wage returns to job change and will exhibit higher levels of attachment to the current employers.[7]

Now this is different. In the preexisting theories, which are discussed first, we get extremely analytic statements couched in terms of variables. The "stories" (the psychic reflections of individual workers) that lie behind these variables' relations are left totally implicit. But here in the authors' own, new hypothesis, we start to see singular workers more clearly. They are reasoning and reflecting, and their reflections lead through a process that implies a particular relation between the variables studied (that is, a positive relation between worker control measures and job attachment measures). To justify that entailed relation between variables requires the creation of a plausible narrative about particular cases. Under such-and-such conditions, a worker of such-and-such a type will think so-and-so and hence act in such-and-such a way.

In the discussion, we find the same sort of division. On the one hand, we find some pseudonarrative statements that are actually simple descriptions of the correlations.

> [I]t is clear, then, that workers who experience a high degree of control over their work activities are significantly more optimistic about their chances of eliciting reward-equivalent offers from other employers, with their attachment to the current jobs suffering accordingly.[8]

Since the variables are responses to sentences of the "I think that . . ." type, they can readily be transformed into such pseudodescriptive statements. The worker need not be seen here as acting or thinking, but merely as the locale for the variables' doing their thing. There is no real action, for even though the workers "experience" a high degree of control, they merely "are" significantly more optimistic.

7. Halaby and Weakliem 1989:554.
8. Halaby and Weakliem 1989:576.

But we also have the following:

It should be noted that these results assume that worker control and match quality are causally prior to the intrinsic value of work. . . . Social theory largely ignores the possibility that workers may choose autonomous jobs and high-quality matches based on their prior orientation to work as an instrumental or terminal value. Indeed, it could be argued that regardless of a worker's prior orientation, it is only through the actual exercise of control and the full use of his productive capacities that the worker realizes self-actualization and the work has intrinsic value.[9]

This passage proposes an "alternative story," and here again, as we move away from the standard or the expected, we get actual worker activity, in this case choice of jobs.[10] The proposed narrative undermines the prior "causal story" of the variables (as opposed to the actual stories of the workers); the variables won't be entailed that way if this new narrative holds. And therefore a model with "other arrows" has to be tested. This second model is rejected because it gives some theoretically implausible results on one relation, which the original model does not.

It is important to note the role here of the alternative narrative. For any particular set of causal variable relations to hold, all agents (cases) must follow only one story. As Blau and Duncan admitted with commendable embarrassment, to estimate the regression coefficients that supposedly measure the effects of causes one has to assume that the causal model is exactly the same for every case, something that is obviously untrue.[11] Now two different narratives may entail the same set of variable relations. But if they do, analysts will seek other entailed variables to distinguish them. The ideal, that is, is a one-to-one relation between narratives and entailed variable models. But in that case "causality" effectively means narration; the notion that the two really differ (that variables are entailed by a narrative, rather than representing it) is a fiction. Even the move to variables as actors doesn't really get us away from narration, for every narrative with cases as actors entails a set of relations among variables (a narrative with variables as actors). Challenges to those relations arise when alternative case narratives entail al-

9. Halaby and Weakliem 1989:577.

10. Moreover, the action of the cases here is a peculiar one; they "vote with their feet." Note that this is one of the few actions always allowed to cases in quantitative approaches and that its results—selection bias—can vitiate such analysis altogether. An ironic evidence of disciplinary boundaries is the fact that the match quality hypothesis is the standard theory of worker separation in economics (see Mortensen 1988).

11. Blau and Duncan 1967:167.

ternative variable relations. The level of case narrative, paradoxically, is a necessary evil for these (as for other) authors, even though most activity in this study takes place at the level of variables, where things are considerably more tidy.[12]

The authors then find a major and unexpected direct negative effect of control on attachment and must decide what to do about it. Now my prediction, from the implicit theory I have been developing, is that their response would entail a move to direct narrative work. Here is the passage:

> [Decision-making and problem-solving skills accumulated by autonomous workers] . . . may give autonomous workers a competitive advantage over their less autonomous counterparts in the search for mobility gains. With match quality held fixed, autonomous workers would have more incentive to be oriented toward mobility, with their attachment suffering accordingly.[13]

Note that the description remains a narrative of variables. But we are starting to see the workers as individuals with actual incentives and hence potentiality for action. What follows completes the transition:

> [I]t would not be surprising if a receptiveness to change expressed itself as a heightened orientation to job mobility among autonomous workers. Such workers might realize that their productivity depends less on the identities of their employers and more on access to the means of production coupled with unfettered exercise of their skills. This would promote "attachment to skill" (e.g., profession, craft, etc.) insofar as such workers might not much care for whom they work as long as they have the opportunity to employ their productive resources.[14]

Here we start with variables as actors ("receptiveness . . . expressed itself as a heightened orientation") then move into a several-step, real narrative,

---

12. David Weakliem, who has commented on this paper with far better grace than I ever could have mustered in equivalent circumstances, makes this point in one of his comments:

> Even when we spoke of variables as actors we had the idea of an underlying narrative, and the statements about variables were just a shorthand for this. Where the underlying narrative was not familiar, we tried to spell it out, which explains why explicit narratives appeared only for new ideas or results.

Thus, narrative is indeed the level of "reality" (and hence a very necessary evil indeed), for which the rhetoric of variables is a shorthand. But note, as the singular noun implies, that the variables as actors permit only "an underlying narrative," not a variety of them.

13. Halaby and Weakliem 1989:582.

14. Halaby and Weakliem 1989:583.

with real actors, even though their acts are mere reflections about the real activity of changing jobs. Note that the reality of narrative is undermined by the subjunctive verbs; the authors are worried because such an alternative narrative has unmeasured steps. They are really happy only with very simple case action or direct "action" by variables.

In summary, most narrative sentences here have variables as subjects; it is when a variable "does something" narratively that the authors think themselves to be speaking most directly of causality. For anything unexpected, however, the level of real (case) narrativity rises, both in the number of steps in the narrative chain and in the replacement of variables as subjects by workers themselves. Finally, methodological restrictions allow only one narrative, which must cover the stories of all the cases, although the search for alternative variables betokens a covert assumption that causality is logically dependent on narration. We should recall that the realist metaphysics implicit in treating variables (universals) as agents was last taken seriously in the age of Aquinas. Of course, the official position of sociological positivism on variables is a nominalist one, but in this quite typical paper the "best" causal sentences are clearly realist ones in which variables act.

So cases do rather little here. What are their characteristics beside weak agency? They are made uniform by virtue of their following identical narratives. They are made enduring and fixed by the models, which treat them as such in all ways except those "varying" in the model. The rhetoric inevitably implicit in an individual study means that their only significant qualities are those defined by their relevance to the dependent variable of attachment. The cases are thus not complex entities whose character is simplified in this model, but characterless entities "complexified" by the variables that assign properties to them. To the extent that cases do emerge and act, they follow a very simple rational calculation scheme whose parameters are set by the actual realities of their situation. All the action lies in the parameters; the cases, even when they are reflecting workers, simply register the rational calculator's obvious decision among varying incentives.

We can test this analysis by applying it to the next paper, Eliza Pavalko's examination of interstate variation in the adoption of workmen's compensation.[15] Pavalko's piece has the additional merit of invoking another of the standard methods of positivism, event history methods. Perhaps this technique, whose name promises a focus on events and history, will deal more graciously with the activities of cases. Another interesting variation is that

15. Pavalko 1989.

the cases are states, rather than biological individuals; we must thus encounter the hydra of methodological individualism.

The author begins by discussing prior case studies, early analyses of policy adoption that generally followed the case method. She then gives us a justification for moving beyond these.

> Analyses of the actors and interests involved in the adoption of workmen's compensation have indicated some of the pressures for adoption. But this most visible level of politics cannot show underlying aspects of the political process that "shape the agenda of politics and the relative priority of issues and solutions" (Offe 1984, p. 159). To address this underlying level we need to shift our focus from individual actors to macroindicators that shaped politicians' perceptions of the need for workmen's compensation, the range of possible decisions and the consequences of their action or inaction.[16]

Immediately, then, we get a defense of the emergent, macro level against the methodological individualists, who attribute all activity to biological individuals, although in this case perhaps allowing for individual interest groups. Note that the shift is as much from the material to the cultural as from micro to macro; the macro (material) indicators are important for their cultural effects (i.e., on perception). That the move from micro to macro levels involves such information issues directly recalls the Halaby and Weakliem "cases," who, in their limited role as actors, made rationally reflective decisions *only within the bounds of their information.* Here, too, individuals are presumed to be straightforward rational calculators. And since all types of individuals exist in most states (legislators, businessmen, etc.), there should be no difference in policy adoption unless their knowledge varies across states. Since that knowledge is in turn largely shaped by the "real" environment, variables driving real differences in that real environment (i.e., variables at the state, emergent level) have causal priority in the system. The justification for treating the states as cases, that is, involves the simplifying assumption of a rational action paradigm for individual actors. (In fact, the author will ultimately move to such a model for states.)[17]

16. Pavalko 1989:593.

17. The micro/macro implications of the "case" concept are extensive, and I shall return to them later. But it is worth remark here that the approach taken by Pavalko means ignoring any micro processes within cases (here the states) if those cases are emergents. Turnover is a good example. A state could change all its legislators over the twenty-year period here studied and still, if the determining contextual variables didn't change, the predictions wouldn't change. One legislator is a characterless rational chooser like another. Of course, the proper procedure is to get extensive micro-level data on each state to complement the extensive macro

Pavalko's first hypothesis concerns business interests:

The employer's liability system was a problem for employers, particularly those in big business, because of high cost and unpredictability of long court battles.[18]

This variable gets no narrative justification at all. It is simply presented as an implied condition for action. Since actor a has interest x, actor a will do act y. Costly, unpredictable court battles will make big business want workmen's compensation, and hence workmen's compensation will appear. Of course there may be intervening steps, but the underlying notion is that even at the state level, it suffices to provide a one-step implicit justificatory narrative based on rational action assumptions. Virtually all the other variables get the same sort of treatment. A short, simple phrase establishing that a certain actor had certain interests or faced certain conditions is coupled with the assumption that actors will act on their interests, and together they produce a one-step narrative running from condition to action via interest. There are about a dozen variables so proposed.

Only one longer story is told. On my theory, that will prove to be, first, the author's and, second, the one that gets empirically supported. The predictions are correct. Eventually, we get a much more complicated narrative, too long to quote, which goes basically as follows. (I give it in exact order, which, as can be seen, is not proper chronological order.)[19]

1. workmen's compensation meant that guilt didn't need to be established.
2. which meant that changes in the labor process that increased both productivity and accidents could be rationalized as "inevitable outcomes of progress."
3. legislators were interested in increasing productivity because their jobs depended on it.
4. poor management of labor/management relations could result in low productivity.
   4a court disputes on accidents are an indicator of bad relations.
5. workmen's compensation, because of 1 and 2, could solve 4 and 4a.
6. hence workmen's compensation arrived.

---

data, but that necessity is a daunting one indeed. So one can easily understand why the concept of "case" assorts rather ill with micro/macro kinds of investigations.

18. Pavalko 1989:598.
19. Pavalko 1989:599.

After the empirical material, this story is again recounted, in proper narrative order this time. It is the chief subject of the paper's conclusions.[20]

Overall the narrative sentences in Pavalko's paper are quite similar to those in Halaby and Weakliem's. Most of them reduce activity to a one-step rational action model. Except for those in the last, complex story, none allows contingency over several steps or between variables or events. Even in the last story, everything dovetails to produce one result; there are no real accidents or contingencies. Nor do any of these narratives really involve actors with substantial complexity. The individual-level actors become rational action ciphers for their interests. The corporate-level actors—the states—are (like the "cases" of Halaby and Weakliem) characterless things. We don't have Iowa or Illinois or Idaho; we have states whose only properties are the values of "main effects" input to the method of partial likelihood. The cases' only significant qualities are those hypothesized to bear on workmen's compensation in this model. Furthermore, these qualities act in isolation from one another and without regard to narrative sequence. And finally, the level of narrativity again rises for the unexpected and the authorial.

There is one new aspect to the relation of case and narrative here, however. It has to do with how many cases there really are. In the body of the paper, we lose sight of the fact—clear in the opening discussion of a couple of cases (states)—that in fact we have simply 48 stories here. Estimating the parameters using standard partial likelihood methods pretends that what we really have is 369 cases. (Each state appears once for each year in which it lacks a compensation law as well as once for the year in which it acquires one.) All of these are seen as independent realizations of a stochastic process. Now to the historian there are only 48 stories at the group level, although obviously there are many more at the individual level. Those 48 stories are very complex ones; that is really the problem. But in the paper the 48 complex, chained narratives are made to seem like 369 independent, one-step ones and the "causal" steps in those 369 stories all become one-step rational action stories (as in Halaby and Weakliem). This occurs because the methods disregard the connections between the actually connected narrative steps that are documented in the historians' case studies. "Case," therefore, has a very different sense here than in a case study of workmen's compensation in, say, Massachusetts. To say that "Massachusetts is a case" raises one set of issues in both types of study. But Pavalko treats "Massachu-

20. Pavalko 1989:608–9.

setts in 1913" as a case independent of "Massachusetts in 1912." Not only spatial, but also temporal lines distinguish cases.[21]

Narratives in these standard positivist articles contrast very strongly with those in William Bridges and Robert Nelson's article on gender inequality in hierarchical pay systems, the third article in the November 1989 *American Journal of Sociology*.[22] Here the authors analyze a single "case" (the state of Washington civil service system). They apply quantitative methods to a universe of individual "cases" *within* that case, but only to establish that a baseline pay model doesn't work because of gender inequalities. The actual explanation of those inequalities occurs in narratives.

The narratives explaining gender inequalities are highly complex, featuring varying actors with varying interests, varying pasts, and varying motives. Not only do agents have the simple rational motivations of the other articles (as does the union, the American Federation of State, County, and Municipal Employees [AFSCME], for example). They also act on the basis of custom (the finance departments) and bias (numerous groups throughout the system). Bridges and Nelson view the whole system as too large to narrate or describe fully, but as having consistent results (gender inequality in pay) because of various systematically interlocked contingencies. For example, AFSCME lobbies in a particular way and opposes all splinter groups (and therefore specifically female splinter groups) because they contest its turf. But this in turn moves active "equity concerns" into the splinter groups, which feel they can't cooperate with agency heads, who tend, for historical reasons, to be male and hence problematic for the female splinter groups. This leaves AFSCME negotiating most of the other issues, including male pay grievances (because only the female ones are likely to be taken to the

21. One might adduce here the Heraclitean dictum about never stepping in the same river twice. But nonetheless, allowing temporal lines to distinguish cases seems a false procedure given our modern concepts of autoregression. Technically, the 369 "state-years" are regarded as independent not because the models are constructed that way, but because under certain conditions the equations for the temporal distribution reduce to that situation. One of the conditions is discussed by Allison (1982:82): the assumption that the vector of explanatory variables explains all variation in the hazard rate. Since this is unlikely, there will be serially correlated errors and problems of estimation. Pavalko has noted and discussed this problem (1989: 601 n. 5), although the caveats it raises disappear from her conclusion. The other condition is that of full rank for the matrix of explanatory variables, an assumption violated by any autoregression in the explanatory variables. Since the matrix includes repeated measures on substantive "cases" (i.e., states, here) this violation is virtually certain. (For example, whether or not the legislature is meeting follows a no-error autoregression scheme.) Econometricians have worried about this issue (see Kennedy 1985:38), but it does not feature prominently in sociological discussions of event history methods.

22. Bridges and Nelson 1989.

more vocal female splinter groups). Since AFSCME, again for various historical reasons, happens to negotiate pretty well and tends to succeed in getting raises when it is active, these raises therefore tend to be disproportionately for men.

In this article, then, we have narrativity and complexity. As before, but much less apologetically, they are introduced to account for results inexplicable in standard models, here the "administered efficiency" model for salary determination. Narrative allows interaction of attributes to take causal priority. It is not the variables of union success, union opposition to competitors, and percentage male in major power positions that determine, as main effects, the pay inequalities in a system. Rather it is the interaction of an AFSCME that is both successful and antisplinter and agency heads that tend to be male. Particular interactions, not independent variables, determine the course of social narratives.

What then do cases do in standard positivist analysis? For the most part, they do little. Narrative sentences usually have variables as subjects. For anything unexpected and for the authorial hypothesis, the level of narrativity rises in various ways. When cases do do something, it is generally conceived as a simple rational calculation. All particularity lies in the parameters of calculation. Since only the parameters change, there are no complex narratives; narratives are always one-step decisions. There are no real contingencies or forkings in the road. There are simply the high road of the variables and the rest—which is error.

Furthermore, cases themselves are largely undifferentiated and uniform, since in most models they all have to follow the same narrative, which is couched as a narrative of acting variables, not of acting individuals. Cases are characterless; they have no qualities other than those hypothesized to determine the dependent variable, and even those qualities act in isolation from one another. The case is constructed, built up parsimoniously out of main effects, rather than deconstructed by simplifying its complexity.

II The Single-Case Narrative

In a way, it is hardly surprising that cases can't do much and that they all act alike within this analytic world. In fact, we generally think that only individual case studies can really "be narrative" and that only population studies can really "be analytic." Let us consider, then, what cases do and how they are individualized in single-case studies where narrative *is* involved. Having done that, we will then be ready to see whether there are multicase approaches that can preserve some of the desirable properties that cases have in single-case studies.[23]

The first step of the single-case narrative is delimiting the case itself, what historiographers have called the "central subject problem"[24] There are many varieties of central subjects in historical case studies; for subjects need not be social actors or groups. They can be events (the First World War), social groups (the Oneida community), or even states of affairs (the structure of politics on the accession of George III). The crucial difficulty (a subject of much historiographical conflict) lies in drawing boundaries around the central subject given the continuous character of the social manifold. Note how this difficulty is avoided by the population/analytic approach, which tends to work with populations where cases are unambiguously distinct (biological individuals, states) and to feel uncomfortable with populations where they are not (classes, pressure groups).

Once the case is delimited, the unity of the "case" (as social actor, for example) is held to require that case attributes take their meaning from the "case-context." Thus, if 40 percent of psychiatrists are members of the APA then the meaning, that is, the narrative potential (which, as we have seen, in the positivist approach actually determines the causal power) of that occurrence arises from whether that is a big or small number for psychiatrists, given the past and given their other kinds of organizational life and activities. The meaning of this 40 percent *does not* arise from the fact that it is less than the 60 percent of lawyers in the ABA or the 75 percent of doctors in the AMA, etc. as in the population/analytic approach above, where attributes are independently defined.[25] The two approaches thus differ sharply in their reading of the ontological status of cases as social entities. The single-case narrative view is that cases may be deconstructed, they start off whole and get simplified. The population/analytic view is that they start out with mere existence, to which mutually independent properties are then added.

The two views also differ in that the case/narrative approach allows the "case" to be transformed in fundamental ways. Unlike Pavalko, a historian of welfare policy in Massachusetts might be quite interested in the implications of legislative turnover for workmen's compensation. Not only such

23. As David Weakliem has reminded me, this contrast is somewhat overdrawn. Even in the single-case narrative view, we must disregard many things about the case because so much is known. And historians themselves, again as Weakliem reminded me, often have recourse to the "what would a reasonable person have done in the circumstances" argument, which I shall consider below.

24. Hull 1975.

25. Abell 1987, chap. 2.

microtransformation is allowed, but also transformation in essence: from death to life or life to death, from one unit to two, from two cases to one to two split along some new line. That is, case narratives can mix demographic and (variable-type) analytic happenings in ways forbidden by the case concept implicit in the population/analytic studies discussed above. There, caseness has to do with endurance and thingness; appearance, disappearance, combination, and transformation are problematic and must be treated as censoring, group disappearance, or some other makeshift. (This reinforces the tendency in such methods to emphasize "irreducible" things like biological individuals as cases.) Thus in population/analytic approaches demographic and causal explanation can be and are explicitly separated and, with the hypertrophy of methods within each, there results a real problem when they must be combined.[26] Yet within the case/narrative approach transformation in attributes can be so extreme that a case which began as an instance of one category may complete a study as an instance of another; a state can become a nation, a craft can become a profession, and so on.

Thus the ontology of cases differs sharply in population/analytic and case/narrative approaches. The former requires rigidly delimitable cases, assigns them properties with trans-case meanings, builds cases on the foundation of simple existence, and refuses all fundamental transformations. The latter, by contrast, assumes cases will have fuzzy boundaries, takes all properties to have case-specific meanings, analyzes by simplifying presumably complex cases, and allows, even focuses on, case transformation. These differences in the ontology of cases are further magnified by the handling of narrative, by saying what it is that cases do. Describing what the case does or endures is what philosophers of history call the colligation problem. It has several subparts.[27]

The first is identifying the events involved. Events, like concepts in more familiar methods, are hypotheticals. Every historian considers dozens of indicating occurrences when deciding whether a given event has taken place. It is one thing to say that ten medical schools have been founded and another to say that the medical profession is deeply concerned about professional education. It is one thing to describe the course of ten battles, and quite another to identify the turning of the tide in a war. Moreover, these hypothetical events have varying duration and visibility. Interest in professional ethics codes, for example, spread much more rapidly than did interest

26. On separation of demographic and causal explanations, see Stinchcombe 1968.
27. See Abbott 1984 for an extended discussion and references.

in professional education, and thus "took less time" as an event. The drive for professional education was a long one and, moreover, was "happening" long before it managed to bear fruit in improved schools. Note the presumption, analogous to that about cases, that events are complex. Events are defined by a whole constellation of attributes and properties. The transformations discussed above are excellent examples of such complex events. Cases may thus do or endure a wide variety of things, each of which may be seen as an event arising either in agency (what they do) or in structure (what they endure).

These events must then be arranged in a plot that sets them in the loose causal order that we generally regard as explanatory. For Pavalko's workmen's compensation adoptions, this means finding out the crucial steps in the coming of the policy, finding out who had what kinds of agency with respect to each, what were the critical decisions and their consequences, and who made them, where, how, and with whose help. The coming of the policy is then seen as a sequence of major turning points (events or "kernels" in Barthes's terms) and sets of situational consequences flowing from those events.[28] An example closely comparable to Pavalko's paper comes from Sutherland's paper on the adoption of sexual psychopath laws by the various states.[29] There, the kernels are (1) a state of fear, partly national and partly induced by spectacular local events, (2) anxious agitated activity by diverse groups, (3) appointment of a committee, often dominated by psychiatrists, which usually produces a sexual psychopath law. What matters to Sutherland are the contingencies that push a state along this path or turn a state off it, not general variables that may or may not have importance depending on how far the process has gone.

By contrast, in the population/analytic approach, plot has a different definition and a different role. If we represent each case at each time by a point in a variable space, finding the plot is a matter of connecting the dots of time1, time2, etc. This plot is basically continuous. To be sure, population analytic methods must in practice treat the measures in each case's story—the measures of having control and being attached and seeking alternate employment for Halaby and Weakliem's workers—as discrete, because they are measured only occasionally. But they are in causal theory continuously measurable. (This contrasts directly with the case/narrative assumption of finite duration, which would treat these "measures" at time t

28. For a discussion of narrative theory, see Chatman 1978.
29. Sutherland 1950.

as "events." In such methods, no variable need be observed at all times; maybe the worker sometimes doesn't care about control or attachment!) There are many questions about similarities among these continuous tracks (narrative plots) that cannot be addressed by linear transformation models (with their continuity assumptions), because such similarities can be found only by looking "along the tracks" for similarities. It is striking that the population/analytic model does not perform this search for resemblance in "plot," in the case/narrative sense, but rather assumes (because it has to) an identical plot at an abstract level, that of the effect parameters. The parameters are implicitly justified by referring all the cases to a single isomorphic plot at the level of case narrative. The result is thus a peculiar bootstrapping, in which the theoretical dominance of the narrative plot is conceded, but its variety must be homogenized because the variables "plot" can only admit one narrative plot.[30]

The move from population/analytic to case/narrative approaches is thus a move first to a new way of regarding cases—as fuzzy realities with autonomously defined complex properties—and a move second to seeing cases as engaged in a perpetual dialogue with their environment, a dialogue of action and constraint that we call plot.

The idea that we ought to think about social processes in terms of complex cases going through plots has its own problems, however. There are three principal ones. The first is that plots intersect. A given event has many immediate antecedents, each of which has many immediate antecedents, and conversely a given event has many consequents, each of which has many consequents. One can write studies considering all the antecedents of a given event, a genre illustrated by Fay's celebrated analysis of the origins of World War I, and one can equally write studies considering the descendants of an event, as in Keynes's discussion of that war's economic consequences.[31] But of course these causes and consequences lie in the genealogies of other events as well—just as one's grandparents have other grandchildren and one's grandchildren other grandparents. The plots of the case/narrative approach must assume away this network character of historical causality.

Another problem with plot is its ontological status as a social reality.

30. Such methods do admit different narratives in a limited sense. In a system where two independent variables jointly determine a dependent variable, say with coefficients 0.2 and 1.0, a dependent value of 4.0 can arise from (20,0), (10,2), or (0,4); the transformation takes all the points on the line $x_1 = 5k - 5x_2$ into the point k. But the narratives all have the same "causal shape," that is, the same coefficients. I am grateful to Peter Abell for demanding this clarification.

31. Fay 1966; Keynes 1920.

Hayden White has argued that there are only four kinds of historical plots:[32]

1. Tragedy (everyone tries to be reasonable but gets in a muddle anyway), a genre illustrated by Tocqueville on the French Revolution.

2. Comedy (everyone is awful but things turn out all right in the end), a genre illustrated by von Ranke's historical writings.

3. Romance (light emerges from darkness), a genre illustrated by Michelet.

4. Irony (things always get worse, and the historian's writing about them won't help anyway), a genre illustrated by Burkhardt's writings.

White's paradigm is a little overdone, but still has important implications. Certainly sociologists are by now quite used to heavily emplotted (because heavily politicized) narrative theories; the labeling theory of deviance and the Marxist theory of class conflict are examples. We should thus be seriously worried about whether plot is ever anything other than an analyst's dream, ever really there in the social process.

A related problem is the implicit assumption that subsections of the social process have beginnings, middles, and ends, rather than simple endless middles. Why is Muncie in 1895 a beginning? What happens when *Middletown in Transition* is written, redefining *Middletown* (in the 1920s) as not a middle, but rather a beginning? Are there really ends? Of course, World War II comes to an end, but do its consequences? Now clearly, individuals can have finite life courses, as do some social entities. So, as in the population/analytic approach, there are some pressures here for studying biological individuals and other definite, finite social entities. But with other kinds of entities, like nations and commercial organizations, the issue of plot as having beginning, middle, and end—the issue usually called periodization—is a major problem.[33]

It is hardly fair to ask what cases do in population/analytic methods without asking the inverse question of what becomes of analytic concerns in case/narrative approaches: how in fact do narratives explain? In a curious way the answer to this question doesn't much matter. For narrative is where

32. H. White 1973.
33. The move to the single-case narrative is thus not a move without its own problems. As Harper (1992) argues, we gain a great deal in terms of fidelity to the material, in terms of allowing material to develop its own structuring, when we move to single-case narrative. Harper's conscious choice of narrative presentation, however, elides the problems I have raised here—whether the plot of his trip to the apple harvest is not actually the intersection of a number of offstage plots, whether that plot really is more than a literary convention (i.e., a real social process), whether it really has a beginning and an end.

positivists turn when reasoning in variables fails, and of course a particular narrative is what is rejected if an entailed set of variable relationships is implausible or incorrect. But still, in practice, variables are what matters in the positivist approach. The question remains of how explanation works in case/narratives, where we don't have the facile language of variables to help us ask questions about causality.

This problem has supported a celebrated literature in the philosophy of history. There are three basic models for "historical" explanation. The first is the covering law model of Carl Hempel. Historians, on this argument, use social science "laws" that cover a given case in order to further understand that particular case. Popper argued to the contrary that all social covering laws are trivial (the classic example being that people do what they are interested in doing), an argument he would undoubtedly apply to the interest-action law implicit in the first two studies discussed above. He ultimately came to believe that the covering law model was worthless because all the real explanatory action was in the side conditions specifying which covering laws hold, i.e., what the case is a case of.[34]

The covering law model has the further conspicuous disadvantage that historians themselves usually reject it. A more congenial model is the "understanding" model of Collingwood, Dray, and many others, which deals to some extent with Popper's issue of side conditions.[35] According to Collingwood, the historian aims to get inside a historical figure's own justification of action, to understand what was "reasonable" given that figure's tastes and conditions. (The reasonable is not necessarily the rational, although one might make rationality one version of reasonability, as Stinchcombe has recently argued).[36] The Collingwood position is thus a broadened version of current rational choice theory; the historian figures out "what it made sense for the actor to do," given the actor's beliefs, knowledge, and psychology. This view has been seen by recent philosophers of history as an extreme "idealist" one, given to dangerous subjectivism, and at present it is probably the most philosophically discredited view of historical explanation, precisely because of our difficulty in reconstructing past dispositions. It is thus quite paradoxical that this view is also at the heart of such narrative as we do see in analytic/positivist sociology. The two approaches differ only in how one finds the "context of decision": by intuition/reconstruction (in Collingwoodian history) or by positivist measure (in the articles analyzed here). It is

34. Hempel 1942; Popper 1962, chap. 25.
35. Collingwood 1946; Dray 1957.
36. Stinchcombe 1990.

also worth noting that while Collingwood's view is discredited among philosophers of history, the kinds of explanations it defends are used daily by historians.

The third principal view of narrative explanation is the "followability" view of W. B. Gallie.[37] Like Collingwood's constructionism, this view attempts to describe how narrative history actually works. On this argument narrative is itself explanatory by virtue of truth, consistent chronology, and a coherent central subject. Narrative is held to combine things that are determined by general laws with things that are contingent, producing a plausible, because followable, story. This notion of combination is much looser than the formalities of the covering law model, but still leaves a place for general determinism that is missing in the Collingwoodian position.

The case/narrative approach to explanation thus differs from the population/analytic one in important ways. It ignores "variables" (in its language, "types of events") when they aren't narratively important, whereas population/analytic approaches must always treat all included variables as equally salient (although perhaps differing in coefficient). This means that case/narrative explanation follows the causal action. Rather than assuming universal or constant relevance, it explains only "what needs to be explained" and lets the rest of things slide along in background. This selective attention goes along with an emphasis on contingency. Things happen because of constellations of factors, not because of a few fundamental effects acting independently.[38] And the roving focus of case/narrative has another distinct advantage over the population/analytic approach. It need make no assumption that all causes lie on the same analytical level (as in standard sociological models). Tiny events (assassinations) can have a big effect.

III Sociological Narratives

Not all narratives, however, concern only one case. Quite the contrary. Often we think that many cases follow similar narratives. A distinguished sociological tradition has considered this issue of universal narratives. Robert Park and a generation of his students developed a concept of "natural history" that generalized developmental narratives for gangs, marriages, revolutions, and occupational careers. Park's whole conception of social life was

37. Gallie 1968.

38. This does mean that case/narrative often unjustifiably takes as unproblematic the structures (like monarchy) that make contingency important. However, these are usually ignored altogether in covering law approaches, as in population/analytic ones. Thus neither side does well with structure and structural constraints or sources of those constraints. On the unreality of main effects, see the wonderful paper of Neyman (1935).

decidedly in terms of events. In his introduction to Lyford Edwards's *Natural History of Revolution*, Park wrote:

> [That there are tactics of revolutions] presupposes the existence of something typical and generic in these movements—something that can be described in general terms. It presupposes in short the existence of materials for a scientific account of revolution since science— natural science—in the long run is little more than a description in conceptual terms of the processes by which events take place, together with explanations which permit events to be predicted and controlled. . . . Like industrial crises, revolutions, when they do occur, tend to describe in their evolution a characteristic cycle of change. . . . What remains to be done is to reduce this revolutionary cycle not merely to a conceptual but to a temporal sequence, one in which the series of changes through which every revolutionary movement tends to pass are so determined and accurately described that they can be measured in temporal units.[39]

Thus, Park saw causal analysis as secondary to description, and saw description as narrative in its fundamental approach.

Among the strongest works of the natural history tradition were narrative studies of single cases, notably Clifford Shaw's celebrated studies of Stanley the jackroller and Sidney the delinquent.[40] Yet these great cases had less impact in upholding narrative analysis in sociology than one might have expected. In the first place, both Shaw and later commentators emphasized the rich detail of the data more than its narrative character per se. Second, although Shaw did argue that the meaning of current events tended to be dictated by past sequences of events, he in fact saw this process as less contingent than directed. In both his great cases, the fundamental image was one of convergence towards a personality type that sustained delinquent activities. He quoted W. I. Thomas on this subject:

> It appears that behavior traits and their totality as represented by the personality are the outcome of a series of definitions of situations with resulting reactions and their fixation in a body of attitudes or psychological sets.[41]

Shaw's purpose was

> to show that the habits, attitudes, and philosophy of life underlying these criminal acts were built up gradually through the successive

39. Edwards 1927: x, xiii.
40. Shaw 1930, 1931.
41. Shaw 1930:13, citing Thomas 1925.

social experiences of the offender over a period of years. . . . [One should see delinquency] not as an isolated act, but in its relation to the mental and physical condition of the offender, the whole sequence of events in his life and the social and cultural situations in which his delinquent behavior occurred.[42]

Delinquency studies took this "convergent" narrative form automatically, for they were concerned only with individuals who ended up at a particular point and with the paths that brought them to that point. The convergence narrative was one they shared with, for example, the great Freudian case narratives, by which they were indeed somewhat influenced. Only many years later did others become interested in what became of Stanley later on, that is, in the whole of the narrative of his life.[43]

Other writers in the Park tradition more explicitly emphasized the narrative approach. Park himself set forth the famous "race relations cycle" in a 1926 paper. Edwards's *Natural History of Revolution* appeared in 1927, as did Mowrer's *Family Disorganization* and Thrasher's *The Gang*. All three used "natural history" to refer explicitly to an expected order or pattern of events. For Park's colleague Ernest W. Burgess, however, "natural history" meant less a specific narrative or pattern of particular events than the general notion that biological and ecological metaphors effectively oriented the investigator. Hence in his work, as in much of the work derived from the Chicago Area Project, there was a sense of temporality, even of "succession," but a greater reluctance to identify a specific set of events in a specific pattern or patterns. Reckless's *Vice in Chicago* was a prototype of this looser view of natural history, which was also illustrated in the magisterial *Juvenile Delinquency and Urban Areas* of Shaw and McKay. A number of works, particularly Cressey's *Taxi-Dance Hall* but also Mowrer's and Thrasher's books, combined Park's detailed sequence model for one aspect of their topic with Burgess's looser "successional" approach for another.[44]

Even in Thrasher, Mowrer, Edwards, and Cressey the image of narrative was fairly loose. First, early stages were often defined in a deliberately vague way. For Edwards, for example, there were "preliminary" then "advanced" symptoms of unrest: mobility and rising expectations among the former, new intellectual allegiances and "oppression psychosis" among the latter. None of these was absolutely necessary, nor did they necessarily come in a particular order. Mowrer's early stages were "loss of respect" and

42. Shaw 1931:xiii.
43. Snodgrass 1982.
44. Edwards 1927; Mowrer 1927; Thrasher 1927; Burgess 1925; Reckless 1933; Shaw and McKay 1942; Cressey 1932.

"pattern of life tension" and he explicitly regarded each as a summary of subordinate sequences of events. Thrasher regarded a spontaneous play-group as becoming a gang when it began "to excite disapproval and opposition," but did not say whose the disapproval was or what its specific objects were. Park's own "assimilation" and "accommodation" were of course more abstract still.

Second, unlike Shaw with his convergence plots, the natural historians tended to see their "plots" as diverging. Thrasher ended up with five kinds of gangs arising in various ways, as well as numerous routes off the main track throughout the process (spontaneous disintegration, etc.). Many of Cressey's taxi-dancers dropped out without becoming recruited to the cyclical process of degradation he outlined. Mowrer argued that the same overall process of events obtained for marriages whether they culminated in organization or in disorganization.

This did not mean, of course, a surrender of the narrative approach, nor a denial of its utility. Rather, Park and his students recognized the complexities of social narratives and adjusted for them by avoiding a simple and rigid sequence theory. Subsequent writers in this line have followed the same approach. Probably the strongest single line of "natural historians" surviving after the Second World War were the students of occupations taught by Everett Hughes, himself a student of both Park and Burgess. Oswald Hall, Howard Becker, Rue Bucher, and others continued to apply natural history metaphors for decades. Usually, as in Bucher and Strauss's influential 1961 paper on professions, the image was Burgess's looser one of a competitive ecology. In Hall's equally influential paper on medicine, however, the image was again one of stages, loosely defined in the manner of Thrasher, Mowrer, and Edwards. Articles taking these natural history approaches to occupations have continued to the present and currently are central in the social problems literature.[45]

In a way it is clear why the narrative image survived best in the study of occupations. In the study of revolutions, its chief rival was the unique case history, which could retain immensely more detail. Indeed, when Skocpol wrote her comparative analysis of revolutions in 1979, Edwards was still a relevant reference, so little comparative work had been done since.[46] In the study of the family and of delinquency, by contrast, the immense number of cases meant that the chief competitor was aggregate, global analysis. Already in the 1920s, in studies of the family, for example, there were two

45. Bucher and Strauss 1961; Hall 1949; Bucher 1988; Spector and Kitsuse 1987.
46. Skocpol 1979:37.

schools. The "interactional" approach was founded on Meadean social psychology and rested on Burgess-type ecological analysis of differing rates. The "social change" approach looked at overall social developments and related these to society-wide variables.[47] The latter approach, under the leadership of William Ogburn and others, was to mature in the 1930s as the "social trends" approach and to dominate social research generally. In such an approach, there was only one narrative—that of the whole society—and so comparative narrative disappeared as a problem. That occupations survived as an island of natural history methods reflects the object of study itself. Too many for an exhaustive set of case studies, too few and too ill defined for aggregate or global analysis, occupations nonetheless showed fertile and complex historical developments that required some form of temporal theorizing.

The problem, in one sense, with the Chicago narrative approach at its best—exemplified by Cressey, Mowrer, or Thrasher—was that it retained so much information about individuals, about narratives, about groups. One way to reduce that complexity was to cut the narratives into pieces and investigate the "causal power" of each step. In studies of delinquency and race relations that is clearly what happened. The individual steps in the early Chicago narratives ultimately became the little plausibility stories justifying the analysis of this or that variable. These steps, that is, led to the rhetoric of analysis so clearly demonstrated in the opening section of this paper. Lyman's 1968 paper on the race relations cycle urged precisely this dissection of a "theory" into a set of "models" and Aldrich's later review of ecological succession recognized (there was no longer a real need to urge) the same thing.[48] This was not a rapid process, for clearly generations of writers survived to whom the variable-based analyses were supplements to the underlying narrative masterpieces. But it began in the Ogburn social trends era. Blumer wrote the first of several critiques of the concept of "a variable" in 1931, and clearly wrote it from a narrative standpoint.[49]

IV Multicase Narratives

This brief history of the fate of universal narrative models in sociology serves to introduce my closing discussion. We are often interested in universal narratives, that is in narratives we expect to observe, with minor vari-

---

47. Komarovsky and Waller 1945; Nimkoff 1948.
48. Lyman 1968; Aldrich 1975.
49. Blumer 1931.

ation, across a number of cases. As we have seen, the single-case approach permits narrative to function in a fluid and powerful way. By contrast, narrative functions virtually formalistically in most multicase positivist work, even though there, too, narrative is seen as the final, ultimate source of explanation. But I have implied throughout that we must disentangle these dichotomies. The difference between population and case approaches is not the same as the difference between analytic and narrative approaches. Hence we must consider the issue of multiple-case *narratives*, which can also be regarded as the issue of demonstrating common narratives across many cases or as the issue of what to do when one's "cases" are narratives. The Chicago writers dealt with all of these questions, but failed to articulate narrative study with the emerging forms of analysis one can loosely call "causal." It is that articulation—or in some cases the formal reasons for the lack of it—that I am seeking to outline in this paper.[50]

The Chicago work shows that there is no inherent reason why narratives can be given only for single cases, and indeed they are particularly important for analyzing small numbers of cases (Stinchcombe 1978). There is a simple reason for this. When a universe consists of thousands of cases, we are generally happy to separate the case study literature and the population/analytic literature—Halaby and Weakliem's workers versus, say, Michael Burawoy's.[51] But where the universe is smaller, as in Pavalko's forty-eight states, we are considerably less willing to make the sharp separation, in part because we are likely to have single-case studies of a substantial fraction of the universe. In such situations, population/analytic approaches seem to reject too much important information. Their discussions seem thin and insubstantial beside the vibrant richness of the narrative case studies. And since cases are fewer, it seems that population-level analysts ought to retain more of the relevant information. But strangely the constraints of methods (in particular of degrees of freedom) mean that the smaller the number of cases, the less the information quantitative methods can work with. The relation between the case study and population approaches thus becomes most difficult in this middle range.[52]

50. For a history of ideas of causality see Bernert 1983 and chapter 3 of this volume.

51. Burawoy 1979.

52. Stanley Lieberson (1992) has written about theoretical reasoning in precisely this middle range. We differ considerably, however, on what to do about it. Lieberson's examples—drunk driving, losing one's luggage—are in fact not small-N situations at all. More importantly, Lieberson's entire analysis comes at the problem of small-N situations within the context of causal theory and population/analytic methods, as, indeed, do the arguments of Skocpol that he is at such pains to refute. I argue, however, that comparative narrative analysis can get us out

Among the important information rejected by population/analytic approaches is the narrative sequence of events in the various cases. With appropriate methods, however, one can study this sequence and see whether universal narratives appear across cases. It is absolutely central to realize that we can become concerned about narrative without becoming concerned about all the other simplifying assumptions made in the population/ analytic approach. Thus we need not question the assumption that cases are not related to each other in some sort of structure (in which case diffusion, constraint, and dominance might determine things we otherwise attribute to the independent variables) or the assumption that case attributes have unique and distinguishable meanings (otherwise the complexity and ambiguity of each case and its properties requires hermeneutic methods). These, too, are fundamental simplifying assumptions in positivism, and, in what follows, I am going to continue making them. That is, I will deal with one problematic assumption of standard approaches but not the others. The networks literature—which deals with the structure assumption just given— does much the same thing for the structure assumption.[53]

There are different types of universal narratives, which can be ranked from strictly to loosely specified. At the highly specified end of the continuum are stage theories, where we believe in a common sequence of unique events. We may expect some deviations from it, but generally anticipate an autonomous, steady pattern. Familiar examples include developmental psychological theories (Piaget), developmental models of economies (Rostow), and, within sociology, theories of collective behavior (Smelser), family life cycle (Glick), professionalization (Wilensky), dialectical materialism (Marx), and comparative revolutions (Skocpol). Much of the literature on stage theories has focused on telling the stages apart—this was a major problem with Rostow—but the idea of stage theories is well established in social science.

A second, less specified form of universal narrative occurs in what I shall call career theories. Career theories emphasize the interaction of causes, the mixture of structure and determination, the dialectic of necessary and sufficient causality. Here there is less expectation of regular patterns, although such patterns are still to some extent evident. Events often repeat, durations

---

of the small-N dilemma. To me the entire vocabulary of "causes," "interactions," "multiple causes," and so on seems inappropriate.

53. I am here arguing (implicitly) for the possibility of a narrative positivism, an argument I have made quite explicitly in other chapters, notably chapters 1 and 6. A much more general analysis of the historical vagaries of these various assumptions is contained in Abbott 2001, chaps. 1 and 2.

are unpredictable, opportunity shapes history. Also, agency here plays a larger role. Examples are job histories (White, Spilerman) and processes of labeling for deviants (Scheff, Goffman). Perhaps because there are more cases available (the universes are larger), this area has seen extensive formal modeling, although most of it has disaggregated careers into individual transitions.[54]

The most indeterminate of narrative models are models I shall call interactionist. They are indeterminate partly because they emphasize structure; even more than in careers, patterned relations shape the developments of the future. Yet paradoxically they are also indeterminate because they emphasize interactants' agency, their ability to reshape, often through cultural redefinition, not only the future of a narrative, but its past as well. Some interactionist models emphasize the structure, the field of relations. Examples are the early interactionist analysis of cities (Park, Burgess), more general models of human ecology (Hawley), world systems theory (Wallerstein), and my own work on the professions. In these structural models, the actual telling of stories is avoided. Rather authors analyze the structure's ability to favor some kinds of stories and prevent others, the parameters that shape stories within it. Individual stories of cases are told, but largely to illustrate possible patterns. There is little expectation that such stories are characteristic except in illustrating possible patterns, since a fundamental premise of these models is that the various intrastructural narratives are not independent. These models provide not universal narratives themselves, but universal constraining frameworks for narratives.

There are also views of interaction that lack this emphasis on structural constraint. These emphasize the independent agency of interactants, their ability to twist and turn not only the interaction, but also the rules governing those moves and their pattern. This is the basic stuff of classic symbolic interactionism and of Goffmanian interaction, formalized in work on conversational analysis. The focus on rules (e.g., for turn taking) allows the analysts to escape the problem that possible narratives ramify endlessly through the free will of actors.

From a conceptual and methodological point of view, the stricter forms are the easiest types of universal narratives to analyze. Stage or developmental theories hold that a given set of events tends to happen in one of a number of common orders. As I have noted, this issue particularly arises in situations where there is much detailed knowledge of the individual cases as

54. For an elegant example combining several approaches see Faulkner 1983.

opposed to those in which cases number in the thousands and are not known in detail. Professions are a good example. If we are interested in characteristic orders of professionalization—from licensing to association to school to journal to ethics code—there are anywhere from twenty to one hundred cases, depending on our definitions. There are vast amounts of data on each case (since virtually all are objects of case studies), including exact dates of these and many other events occurring to all of them. Depending on one's assumptions about the relation between causality and the passage of time, there are a variety of directly applicable techniques. One can apply scaling methods to consider order of unique events, which I have done, for example, in studying the development of local American medical communities. The cases are cities and towns and the stories are the order in which various professionalizing events occur. And one can apply fancier techniques—the optimal matching/alignment methods of DNA research— to examine direct sequence resemblance in narratives where events repeat. I have done this with stories about the adoption of welfare programs in twenty developed welfare states (Pavalko's issue on a national scale). Here the cases are nations and the events are the coming of workmen's compensation, pensions, and other major welfare programs. I have also done it with job histories of eighteenth-century German musicians, where the events are holding one of thirty-five types of jobs in a given year. As these elliptical examples make clear, the move from single-case narrative to multicase narratives involves lots of assumptions about cases, plots, events, and their measurement. But it does retain the ability of cases to do something.[55]

In many ways the stage theory case is straightforward. It is much more challenging to develop narratives for the general "career" type of narrative. Here the assumption of a relatively plotlike development is unjustified because the narrative can take sudden, "interactive" turns under the impact of external constraints or indeed of other narratives. In methodology, this issue raises the difficulty of models for mutual constraint, models in which

55. On medical communities, see Abbott 1991b. On welfare programs, see Abbott and DeViney 1992. On German musicians, see Abbott and Hrycak 1990. Claude Fischer has rightly pointed out to me that stage theories often have a strong whiff of determinacy about them. There is a sense that it is only a matter of time till the next stage arrives, and so on. In practice, some of the processes I have investigated might be thought of as determinate, others not. Most national professions eventually acquire associations, licensing, and so on, but many local medical communities never acquire schools or journals. As for the German musicians' careers, these vary in terms of pattern and in terms of how far through the pattern they manage to get. Nonetheless, as the most regular of "narratively conceived" processes, stage processes do partake of some of the determinacy of analytically conceived social reality.

stories of the different cases aren't independent. There is a small literature on this problem (starting with Harrison White's *Chains of Opportunity*).[56]

But the more difficult problem is not methodological, but conceptual. The conflation of narrative with single-case analysis has hidden from us the importance of building conceptual models for narrative steps. In the single-case narrative, each step need only be told; it need not be conceived as a version of a more generic type of event. I have discussed elsewhere certain issues of conceptualization of events in multicase narrative research. These concern aggregating occurrences into conceptual events (as discussed above) and measuring the latter with the former. But those issues concern a very low level of generality. The more important problem in conceptualizing multicase narratives comes at the general level. We need generic models for types of causality and for "narrative steps." This issue is unfamiliar in population/analytic techniques, for there causal steps need little conceptualization. They are loosely attached to ideal-typical narratives, but themselves seen as unproblematic. "Worker control causes worker attachment" has its scientific ring precisely because the real problems of conceptualization are hidden in the implicit narrative. But with multicase narrative models these problems come out into the open.[57]

The issue of generic types of links in social causal chains was raised many years ago by Arthur Stinchcombe.[58] Stinchcombe laid out a series of causal processes that produce sequential patterns: functional, demographic, and historicist. These are one-step causal patterns that produce characteristic social sequences when iterated over the long term. The functional one, for example, produces sequences where fallings away from some equilibrium continually alternate with reestablishments of that equilibrium. Historicism produces sequences converging and stabilizing on a level. One notes other kinds of generic sequences—oscillating ones produced by "harmonic" causal links (Kroeber on fashion) and schmismogenetic ones produced by "conflict-exacerbating" links (Marx on class conflict).

At a somewhat less general level, any conceptual distinction produces a set of potential generic narrative links at a somewhat less general level. Thus, if we are interested in the relation between social structure and culture, Berger and Luckmann give useful names for narrative links in which the bonds of the two break down in certain ways.[59] The process by which

56. H. C. White 1970.

57. See Abbott 1984 for my discussion. For an interesting example of the multicase narrative problem, see McPhee 1963:184–234.

58. Stinchcombe 1968.

59. Berger and Luckmann 1967.

social structures lose their grounding in culture and develop an autonomous, continuing, often routine character, Berger and Luckmann call institutionalization. An "institutionalization link" in a narrative is thus one in which the chief event is a loosening of these bonds. Conversely, the process of reforging those bonds they (and many others) call legitimation, and such individual narrative steps might be considered legitimation links. The general hypothesis of authors like Weber and Troeltsch is that links of these two kinds tend to follow one another in long cycles rather than short ones, and that shorter cycles are often associated with ruptures in social structure. It may, of course, be that institutionalization is ultimately more certain if it alternates occasionally with (re)legitimation. But the central point is that consistent names might help formulate important hypotheses about patterned narrative changes in social and cultural structure. With terms like these, we can establish generic "plots" to investigate across many cases.

If one considers the micro/macro character of these social and cultural systems, one can create further terminology for generic types of narrative links. Links embodying macro shifts in cultural systems can be called paradigm or style shifts; links in which micro social structures align to produce macro shifts can be called collective action links; and so on. The point of developing these terms is that hypotheses like, for example, Diana Crane's about changes in science, could usefully be cast into the same terminology as, say, White and White's *Canvases and Careers*.[60] Rather than reducing these rich studies to justifications for a set of variables in the manner of population/analytic studies, we can encode their conclusions as predicting certain kinds of plots for stylistic or scientific changes across cases. Many hypotheses we have investigated with ill-fitting population/analytic methods could better be phrased as narrative models of this kind, allowing for agency and action among cases and for the unity of each case's history.

It follows from my earlier discussion of Pavalko's article that a very valuable set of concepts for generic links would deal with the issues of micro/macro relations tout court. I shall call these "entity process" links and close with a brief discussion of them.

The simplest entity processes are familiar from demography, the processes of birth and death. With "irreducible" actors like biological individuals, these tend to be nonproblematic; with emergents like occupations or pressure groups birth and death are difficult in both conceptualization and measurement. Among other important entity processes are merger and di-

60. Crane 1972; White and White 1965.

vision—again processes that are easily labeled, but not so easily modeled. All four of these processes are centrally important events in narratives of social processes, and, for emergents, at least, all four require far more careful conceptualization than is presently available.

Another fundamental entity process is microtransformation—transformation of the micro level of an emergent group with or without transformation of its macro identity or properties. A first type of microtransformation is turnover, which can happen through migration and replacement, through a restructuring of member life cycle in the group, or through new sources of recruitment, bringing new individuals with fundamentally different attributes into a group. All of this can occur with or without any formal change in macro properties like a group's self definition or ideologies.

A second version of microtransformation is internal metamorphosis, the change of member properties without turnover. This can happen through aging, collective action, or other processes in which the emergent properties of the group may (or sometimes may not) sharply change simply because of internal changes (often *common* changes) among members. Finally, microtransformation may occur through microstructural change. The internal arrangements of a group may change in ways that may affect its aggregate properties and its recruitment patterns. Internal hierarchies may lead to internal divisions. Or internal reorganization may fundamentally transform the acting character of a group.

Still another entity process is macrotransformation, fundamental change of the emergent entity without concurrent micro change. A first version of macrotransformation concerns change in basic properties of the emergent without constituent change. Occupational characteristics can change rapidly even though members don't change through turnover and other processes. In such cases macrotransformation may change the underlying meaning of the occupation for the individuals involved. A more subtle macrotransformation occurs when change in macro attributes occurs *without* affecting what we might call the "structural meaning" of the variables. The professions provide an excellent example. No nineteenth-century professional would regard any American professional of the late twentieth century as "a professional." The modern professional relies too much on others, works too often in congregate situations and too often for other people, advertises like a common tradesman, and so on. Yet the late twentieth-century professional occupies much the same *relative* place in today's labor force as did the nineteenth-century professional in yesterday's. Professionals still hold pride of place. The content of that pride is different, but its structural meaning remains the same. This kind of macrotransformation, which we might call structural isomorphism, is common in temporal studies.

This discussion brings me less to the end of this paper than to the beginning of another. To develop a serious catalogue of "narrative steps" that sociologists consider so often as to need standardized names for them is a substantial project. I have indicated some of the directions here, building on earlier work.[61] But the logical foundations of the effort lie in issues of case. It is because population/analytic approaches deal so poorly with the activity and ontology of cases that we tend to turn to single-case narratives. Only by analyzing single-case narrative in detail can we discover the aspects of narration and caseness that make it so attractive. But my contention here has been that we can and should disentangle the population/case distinction from the analytic/narrative one. By doing so, we may be able to construct new forms of population-level studies based on narrative, forms that retain some of the attention to case activity and case complexity that we find so enticing in the single-case narrative approach, but that at the same time allow us to create narrative generalizations across cases.

Some readers of this paper, Charles Ragin prominent among them, see this as a nearly impossible task. They question, too, who might be the audience for it. I think the "impossibility" stems from unfamiliarity. We have all grown accustomed to think in either the causality-variables-population-analytic way or the plot-events-case-narrative way. We have a hard time imagining what it means to generalize narrative, although, as I have said, our sociological ancestors were quite comfortable with it. So I think the impossibility will go away after we've tried narrative generalization a bit and found out what it can do.

This means being pretty simpleminded at first. We can't have complex and subtle analyses until we've had some stumbling and preliminary ones. But there are—and here is the answer to the audience question—many sociologists interested in typical narrative patterns. The life course theorists want to find out if there are life patterns. The stress analysts want to know if particular sequences lead to stress. The organization theorists want to know if particular patterns lead to successful innovations.[62]

61. Abbott 1983 contains another attempt to imagine a list of "unit processes" for social narratives.

62. A number of writers have been pursuing techniques of "narrative positivism." David Heise's work on events and responses to them attacks the problem from one angle. Peter Abell's homomorphic reduction techniques take another. My own use of optimal matching techniques is a third. (All three are discussed in chapter 6.) One could also view the growing use of simulation models, by Kathleen Carley and others, as part of this development.

Beyond these lies a broader, policy-minded audience that is presently under the complete sway of population/analytic methods. Regression coefficients now establish the parameters of public policy by providing both liberals and conservatives with "scientific" evidence of who is doing how well and how badly and what "causal forces" lie behind those outcomes. Political figures believe that if we change the parameters or increase people's levels of certain variables, then outcomes will change in some desirable way. If reality actually happens in stories, there is no reason why this should happen.

A social science expressed in terms of typical stories would provide far better access for policy intervention than the present social science of variables. Anybody who knew the typical stories of organizations under great external and internal stress would never have believed that breaking up AT&T would result in a highly profitable firm and a cheaper overall phone service. But policy makers saw economists' equations proving that profit equaled so many parts research plus so many parts resources plus so many parts market competition and so on. No one bothered to ask whether one could tell a real story that led from AT&T as of 1983 to the vision they had in mind. In fact there wasn't one. And so the phone bills that were to get cheaper got both more expensive and less comprehensible, the research laboratory that was to invent wonderful new devices was dismantled, and the firm achieves its current (short-run) profits by laying off the very scientists policy makers thought were the foundation of the future. AT&T's major new venture is in credit cards. The population/analytic approach is precisely the social science that said this would not happen. But it all makes great narrative sense.

Conceptions of Time and Events
in Social Science Methods

There are two sides to the question of why people have certain kinds of careers. We can focus on *why* people have certain kinds of careers or we can focus on why people have *certain kinds of careers*. That is, we can worry about causality on the one hand or narrative typicality on the other.

The difference is paradigmatic. Those worried about causality see no point in studies that don't discover causes. Those worried about typicality see causes as so much reification. The different views entail assumptions that make them mutually invisible. They are like two different paths through the same park; one sees the same things from each, but those things look very different.[1]

The contrast of causal and narrative analysis of course goes beyond the issue of careers. But careers provide an empirical referent for an otherwise abstract discussion. Careers are a particularly good example because they mix chance and determinism. Stage processes are widely theorized in social science but are usually conceived to be more regular than careers; the typical pattern is taken for granted and we seek the causes that propel it. By contrast, interactional processes, while equally well-known, are conceived to be looser than careers. There the focus is more on contingent developments, and typicality is presumed quite unlikely. In careers, we expect both a fair amount of pattern and a fair amount of fluctuation. They thus offer a particularly good example of the trade-offs between thinking about historical processes in terms of causality and thinking about historical processes in terms of narrative pattern.

This paper was originally presented at the Social Science History Association Annual Meeting in Washington, 17 November 1989. I would like to thank members of that audience for various useful comments. It was first published in *Historical Methods* 23 (1990): 140–50; reprinted with permission of *Historical Methods* and Heldref Publications.

1. I speak from personal experience, having submitted formalized narrative analyses to journals whose reviewers are trained to think causally. Nonetheless, the usual disclaimers apply to the following paper. I am overdrawing distinctions in order to underline important choices. Few analysts will take uniformly consistent positions on the assumptions I shall analyze. And good work can be done from either perspective.

This paper begins with a general portrait of the two different ways of imagining careers. It then considers the assumptions of the two views, focusing on major differences. These concern (1) the nature of the social process, (2) the working of causes, (3) the character and orderability of events, and (4) the nature of time. The paper closes with a short conclusion on what these differences mean for methodological development.

I Two Conceptions of Careers

There are two formal ways to conceptualize careers. On the one hand, one can treat them as realizations of stochastic processes.[2] On this argument, there is some sort of underlying process with certain kinds of parameters. These parameters may be determining causes like an individual's race or education, or they may be preferences that dictate an individual's choices.[3] This stochastic view sees the career as a realization; a career is simply the list of results that the underlying process throws up over succeeding time periods. It is, in that sense, an accident rather than a pattern, an appearance rather than a reality. Reality lies at the level of the underlying process of causes or choices.

As one might expect, career analysis methods that derive from this view focus on outcomes at particular points. For example, the Wisconsin status attainment model assumes that a set of variables predicts occupational outcome at a point, the time point of the dependent observation with which the path model ends. The much more sophisticated durational models based on event history data adopt the same idea, but predict outcome at a succession of points. Again there is no conception of the career as a whole. Some authors distinguish classes of cases that follow different sequences of outcomes,

2. I will use the phrase "stochastic view" hereafter as a shorthand for this view. I do not mean to imply thereby that the alternative "whole career" view is in some way a "deterministic view" as opposed to a "stochastic" one; "stochastic" here is short for "stochastic process."

3. It does not really matter whether we regard the underlying process as driven by "causes," as is customary in sociological modeling, or as driven by "choices," as is customary in economics. Logically, economists' preferences and opportunities function in a manner equivalent to "causes"; they are properties distributed among given actors that determine outcomes. The preference model simply adds the idea that actors choose what accords with their interest in a suitably sophisticated fashion. Both sociological and economic views of causality regard the fundamental determinants of behavior as external to the actor in some sense. In the sociological case, the determinants are reified "causes" like "race," "education," and "power." In the economic case, the determinants are the opportunities/constraints that set possible choices and the preferences that determine which of the choices is optimal. The individual per se simply acts as a locus where the intersection of these determinants takes place. For further discussion, see chapter 4.

then seek differences in causal parameters between those classes. Such models remain within the stochastic framework. Sequences of outcomes—for example, event "careers" of people entering the labor force—are used merely to separate subgroups; there is no idea that the causes themselves might be subject to differing orders in differing cases within the groups.[4]

One might alternatively conceptualize careers as wholes. That is, one could view a career as a single unit at its completion. The varying impacts of opportunities, constraints, causes, and choices are all then taken to merge their effects indistinguishably in a single thing, the career line. In this view, the career is a reality, a whole, not simply the list of successive realizations of an underlying stochastic process. It is important to recall that this is our commonsense construction of the history of persons and of many supraindividual actors. Thus, we consider academic careers to take this or that form. We make psychological predictions on the basis of particular life-event sequences. We talk about patterns in riots, revolutions, and other forms of collective behavior. Each of these discussions assumes that past careers—of individuals, social movements, organizations—can be treated as wholes, as units. Beginning, middle, and end are all of one piece, the one leading ineluctably to the next.[5]

Methods for analyzing careers as whole units are rare. Peter Abell has argued for a homomorphic analysis that reduces such narratives to a number of common shapes. It is not yet clear how Abell's methods would be applied empirically. Optimal matching techniques seem to be the only empirically practicable techniques available. They measure the resemblance of

4. But these writers at least regard different sequences of events as worthy of differentiated inquiry and hence show stronger sensitivity to the narrative character of social reality than do the more classical status attainment writers. For examples, see Hogan 1978; Marini 1987; Marini, Shin, and Raymond 1989. For a similar concern in the literature on stress, see Chalmers 1981.

5. I am uncomfortable with so strong a statement. Usually historical processes are regarded as open to chance, but somewhat constrained; then there will be typical patterns, yet no determination ab initio. We reserve the term "fate" for processes that unfold in real, contingent time but that have strong teleology and consider fate to be not a scientific, but a literary, concept. Thus, the inevitability of tragedy arises, for Aristotle, in the original hubris of the protagonist. The details of the plot are merely the working out—the career—of that hubris. In any case, the notion that careers and other historical processes can be treated as wholes goes back to the concept of "natural history" as set forth by Robert Park and others of the Chicago school of sociology. Park on race relations, Lyford Edwards on revolutions, Shaw on delinquent careers, Thrasher on gangs, Hughes on occupations, Burgess, Reckless, Cressey, and many others on neighborhoods: all these saw characteristic developmental patterns. In every case, "natural history" denoted development shaped by internal forces and environing constraints, but taking a characteristic pattern or form.

career sequences by counting the numbers of changes required to turn one sequence into another.[6]

There are thus two ways of seeing careers, indeed two ways of seeing historical processes more generally. One focuses on stochastic realizations and aims to find causes; the other focuses on narratives and aims to find typical patterns. This dichotomy holds as clearly in other fields of research as in the study of careers. Thus, one can imagine revolutions as the realizations of stochastic processes, in which case the history of a given revolution is actually just the listing of successive outcomes of some underlying causal processes. On the other hand, one can see revolutions as having a complete implicit logic running from start to finish, in which case the history of a given revolution is a logical narrative with an inherent telos. Similar arguments apply to life courses, organizational histories, occupational development, and so on.

II Major Differences in Assumptions about Time and Historical Processes

These two views of careers make a variety of assumptions about time and the embedding of social life in time. Of course any particular author makes a diverse choice of these assumptions. But reflecting about two polarized versions of the assumptions makes us more aware of the choices we do make. If the following argument seems overly schematic, then, one reason lies in its desire to excavate our views of the social process. To a certain extent, however, I have a polemical point as well. The stochastic view is overwhelmingly dominant in empirical social science. I wish to argue that, despite its real attractions, that view is not the only reasonable way to formalize social processes.[7]

6. Abell's principal work in this vein is Abell 1984, 1985, and 1987. The classic work on optimal matching techniques is Sankoff and Kruskal 1983. For the applications mentioned in text, see Abbott and Forrest 1986 and Abbott and Hrycak 1990. The stability of the methods under coding variation is shown in Forrest and Abbott 1990. For an overview of sequence methods, see chapter 6. See also Abbott and Tsay 2000.

7. I am not urging a turn away from positivist methods in the usual sense. Thinking about things narratively means thinking along cases rather than across them, as I have argued elsewhere (e.g., Abbott 1983). It does not necessarily involve a turn to interpretive methods, although the two have shown an elective affinity in the past. People who have argued for or assumed a necessary connection (e.g., Richardson [1990]) are conflating the problem of "multiple meanings" (that variables can have more than one meaning in a given model, in positivist terms) and the problem of temporality proper. I am avoiding that conflation. Therefore, in this paper narrative means narrative positivism. Even so, multiple meanings can in fact be formalized as well (as in Barthes 1974), so even there the assumption of "inherent unformalizability" is an error. If one does not recognize that the positivist/interpretivist dichotomy is a recursive

A. *Constitutive Assumptions*

Assumptions about the social process begin with constitutive assumptions about the nature of social actors and their world. That is, the first assumptions of the two views are less about time passing per se than they are about the social beings involved in that time.

In the stochastic or causal view of careers, as in the broader "general linear reality" that I have elsewhere analyzed, the social world is made up of fixed, given entities with variable properties. We usually call these entities "cases" and their properties "variables."[8] A career consists of the succession of the values of a dependent property or properties over time. The stochastic view aims to find the minimum number of properties necessary to generate these observed "careers," which are in fact most often considered one time point at a time, as in status attainment models.

Such a procedure builds up career from a minimum of mere existence. Its paradigms are the literatures of industrial reliability and epidemiology. In these fields existence itself is the dependent (and sometimes the only) property of interest; waiting time till death may, for example, be a function only of prior lifetime.[9] Of course the stochastic view of careers can envision considerably more complex matters. But it does so by adding more properties (more independent and dependent variables) to this foundation of mere being. It is striking that initiative and action in such "career" models belong to the variables, not to the cases. Variables do things, the cases themselves merely endure.[10]

By contrast, in the narrative or typical-pattern view of careers, the social world is made up of subjects who participate in events. The very language used to describe the position is radically different; "event" here means something quite different from "realization of a Bernoulli process." The subjects and events of the narrativist are inherently complex. Analysis occurs by directly simplifying them.

In order to make the two views commensurable, it helps to rephrase the

---

one, using it obscures rather than enlightens. See, generally, Abbott 2001, chaps. 1 and 2, on this issue.

8. See chapter 1, a general analysis of what may be called the philosophical assumptions implicit in standard linear models. The present paper elaborates the aspects of those assumptions that relate to the passage of time. For analyses of the idea of cases and variables, see also Abell 1987 and Ragin 1987.

9. Hence demography is the foundational science of the stochastic view. Note, however, that the tendency to sharply separate existence and other variable attributes implies a curious separation between demographic and causal models that in fact bedevils this kind of research.

10. See chapter 4.

narrative position in the terminology of the stochastic view. In that terminology, what the narrativists call "an event" may be defined as a combination of particular values of many variables. One moves from the stochastic state-space to the narrative list of "events" simply by creating a list of neighborhoods (for a continuous state-space) or combinations of properties (for a discrete one) that exhaustively cover (in the continuous case) or classify (in the discrete one) the state-space. This is the list of possible events.

To a narrativist, the justification for thinking directly in terms of these events (rather than in terms of the dimensions or the uncrossed categories themselves) is the surprising empirical fact that once we consider a state space of any real complexity, most events are null. That is, most combinations of particular values of discrete variables are never observed and most neighborhoods in a continuous variable space are empty. If it is the case that the state space is mostly empty—if most possible events don't happen— why should we design models covering all possible events? Such models (GLMs, for example) try to explain not only what did occur, but also lots of things that didn't or perhaps can't (because of constraints) occur. It is more parsimonious to define the actually observed locations as "events" and to investigate their narrative structure directly, without recourse to reified "causes." We usually justify the use of "variables" on the ground that reality is too complex to do otherwise. Maybe that isn't true.

An empirical example is useful to illustrate the assertion that most events don't occur. I have taken four variables on U.S. states at random from the *Statistical Abstract:* current expenditures per school pupil, crime rate per 100,000 population, percent of eligibles voting for U.S. representative in the last election, and energy consumption (BTUs) per capita. In order to provide a strong illustration of "emptiness," I have chosen these variables to be uncorrelated, for of course correlation would empty large areas of the space. (The highest correlation among these four variables, in absolute value, is an unimpressive 0.268.) To focus only on the relevant portion of the state space, I have located each state (fifty plus the District of Columbia) in a normalized four-dimensional rectangle by rescaling the variables; I have subtracted the respective minimum from each variable and divided the result by the variable's range. This gives us a cloud of fifty-one points in a four-cube with unit edges. We can divide each dimension of this cube into two or more parts and then consider how many of the resultant "grid cubes" have a case or cases in them.[11]

11. A two-dimensional analogy may help clarify the procedure. Considering a cloud of points in two-dimensional Cartesian coordinates, I am looking at the smallest rectangle that

Subdivide each Dimension by		2	3	4	5	6	7	8	9	10
	0	7	62	225	587	1253	2355	4047	6511	9949
Number of	1	4	10	22	30	36	42	47	49	51
	2	1	4	3	4	6	3	2	1	
cells with	3			3	3	1	1			
	4			1	1					
N	5		2	2						
	6		1							
Occupants	7	1	1							
	9	1								
	10		1							
	11	1								
	18	1								

Since there are four variables, there are sixteen grid cubes (or cells) if we divide each dimension in two and in general n^4 cubes for any "n-cut" of each dimension. Table 5.1 shows how many of the cells have specified numbers of occupants in this data. The number of empty cells is surprising. If we cut each dimension in two halves (a two-cut) 7 of 16 cells are unoccupied. Overall, of course, the number of empty cells reflects the disparity between the 51 cases and the hundreds or thousands of grid cells. But note the concentration in the cells that *are* occupied. In a two-cut, 45 of the 51 cases are in 4 (of 16) cells. In a three-cut, 33 of the cases are in 5 (of 81) cells. In a four-cut, 23 of the cases are in 6 (of 256) cells. Note, too, that one must divide this space into 10,000 cells to get each of the 51 cases in its own cell. Some of this clumping is, of course, random. But Poisson fits to this data show distinct evidence of further clumping, of real order. In a three-cut, for example, a Poisson model predicts that about half the cells should be empty; in fact, three-quarters are empty, distinct evidence of clumping in other cells.[12]

could contain all the points (there will be one or more points on each edge) and then squeezing that rectangle to make it a square that is one unit long on each side. I am then putting graph paper of various fineness over the square and seeing how many cases are in each cell of the graph paper.

12. Beyond the four-cut, the Poisson models virtually must fit because of the extremely small parameter. Some readers may suspect, as I did, that the emptiness of the state-space is caused largely by outliers, which stretch the boundaries and create empty internal space, as scatter plots often illustrate. However, "outlierness" does not appear to be at issue here. (Of course, there is a large literature on "regression diagnosis," which deals with issues of outliers.) In particular, I propose that outlierness is essentially a fractal property in many datasets; if the obvious outliers from a complex dataset are deleted, the result is a smaller dataset with equally obvious outliers. They could then be deleted, and so on.

I demonstrate this property on the present data, as follows. I calculated a centroid at the

The concentration shown in all these measures reflects local order un-measured by global measures like the correlation coefficient. Even when these global measures show minimal relations between "variables," most of the state-space is empty because there are in fact many local resemblances between cases. The three-cut—its 81 cells being of the same order of magnitude as the 51 cases—provides the fairest evidence. Only 19 of these cells are occupied, and over half the cases are in five cells. A purely typological approach to this data could cover much of the data with five simple descriptions.[13]

---

means of each of the four variables. I then calculated the Euclidean distances from each case to that point and selected the maximum distance as a standard radius. Next, I created ten concentric four-spheres: one with a radius at one-tenth the standard radius, one at two-tenths, one at three-tenths, and so on. (In two-dimensional terms this is like drawing bull's eyes around the center of the space.) I then asked what percentage of the cases lie in the outermost spheres, these presumably being the outliers. I deleted those in the outermost spheres, recalculated the centroid, the distances, and the decile spheres, and repeated the whole process. The table in this note shows the number of cases remaining, the number in the outermost sphere (to be dropped) and the percentages of cases in each of the three outermost spheres as I continued through this process of outlier deletion.

Remain	Drop	Sphere 8	Sphere 9	Sphere 10
51	3	.04	.02	.06
48	3	.06	.04	.06
45	4	.27	.04	.09
41	6	.27	.24	.14
35	9	.23	.23	.25
26	9	.12	.23	.35
17	4	.29	.24	.24

A sensible definition of outlierness, given an assumption of underlying multivariate normality, would be that the outermost cases are outliers (to be dropped) if there is empty space between them and the main body of the cases. Yet in the first three situations above, there are more cases in the tenth sphere than in the ninth. Deleting does not help. The data do not "properly tail off" until I have deleted 20 percent of the cases. The percentage of outliers does not significantly change until I have deleted a substantial portion of the data, because deleting some outliers just transforms other cases into outliers.

13. This is a cross-sectional example, as cross-sectional data were easiest at hand. The situation would be the same if I were to link up these measurements over several time periods; the state space would be a lot emptier than we might expect. In cross-sectional data, discovering the kind of local regularity here documented is the central task of descriptive methods like clustering and scaling, which create the typologies I have suggested here. I have clustered this data using a Euclidean metric in the four-space and find a number of clumps. Sometimes the members of a cluster are likely for obvious reasons (Louisiana and Texas), sometimes for less obvious reasons (Vermont, Wisconsin, and Pennsylvania), and sometimes quite unlikely (Illinois, Nevada, Michigan, New Mexico, Maryland, and Delaware, all closer to each other than are Louisiana and Texas). Note that narrative analysis as I am proposing it here is essentially an ex-

The narrative analyst therefore views events as the natural way to simplify the social process. Rather than disassembling complex particulars into combinations of (supposedly) independent variable properties (i.e., rather than locating the cases in a multidimensional or crossed-categorical state-space at all), such an analyst views direct conceptualizing of the observed events as the best way to simplify the complex flow of occurrences. Rather than building up its cases by assigning them minimal properties beyond a foundation of existence, the narrative view assumes a complexity from which it must "build down" or simplify. Existence of course still determines the ultimate beginnings and endings of careers, but it is inconceivable as a separate matter for inquiry.

A substantive example underlines the difference. Suppose we are considering the passage of workmen's compensation laws in American states.[14] To treat this problem from the stochastic view, one observes 48 states (the fixed entities) over some defined time period in which those laws are passed (say 1909–29) and notes when they don't and when they do have compensation laws. The goal (taking the event history approach) is to find the minimal set of state properties (types of economy, productivity of manufacturing, etc.) that will predict when the laws appear and when they don't. In the whole-career model, one establishes the basic events leading to workmen's compensation laws in the various states and tries to figure out the typical sequence of these events through which compensation laws come about. These events undoubtedly involve many of the "variables" used in the stochastic approach, but rather than treating them independently, the narrativist will view particular combinations of particular values of those variables as events in one or more patterns for the compensation story. The narrative process is justified because with, say, 14 variables, the vast majority of possible events must of necessity not be observed if we take the stochastic approach.

_____

tension of typological thinking to the temporal realm. One might further note that these results show how unrealistic are the scatter plots for "no correlation" typically shown in statistics texts. In such diagrams, the points are usually well scattered throughout the space. In fact, even on Poisson assumptions, there will be considerable clumping.

14. The example here is Pavalko 1989, already discussed in chapter 4. Pavalko analyzes 48 real cases (states), over up to 21 time periods (until adoption of a compensation act), which in the world of event history analysis serves as a dataset of 369 "state years," which are the analyzed "cases." There are 7 dichotomous variables, all of which have to take on both values at some point. There are 7 continuous variables; each of them is correlated with at least one other at an absolute value of .27 or more. Correlations as large as 0.40 and -0.67 are reported. Most of this continuous state space is undoubtedly empty.

B. *Assumptions about Causality*

These fundamental differences about how to simplify the complexities of social life are complemented by differences over how to understand causality. Ultimately, the two views accept the same ideas about explanation; both regard narration as the final form of social explanation. That the whole-career view does so is obvious. But stochastic writers usually appear to think that causality resides in variables. Yet careful reading shows that the language of "variables causing things" is merely a shorthand; stochastic writers fall back on stories ("plausible mechanisms") when they must defend or support particular assertions about the variables. Narrative is the fundamental recourse.[15]

This ultimate common reliance on narrative is entangled with other causality assumptions that are quite different. A first assumption concerns the pacing of causes. Although not required to, stochastic models generally assume that causes work "at equal speed" across all cases. Whole-career models, by contrast, imagine causal pacing as potentially varying. Consider two careers in which the same sequence of jobs is observed, but in one of which the duration of each job is exactly twice that in the other. Any model examining transitions or probabilities of motion will treat these durational differences as generating variance in estimates of the effect of the causal predictors on the careers. By contrast, if we consider the careers as a whole, we could propose that the causes are in each case the same, but that they are "working at different rates." Within the stochastic view, this is an assertion that some unmeasured variable(s) interacts with the observed variables, since time itself presumably causes nothing. A whole-career approach allows us to see that interaction effect (and hence raise the issue of unmeasured variables) relatively easily. Moreover, we might wish to consider the actual idea that causes can work at different rates. This is a standard assumption of working historians, and, as we shall see below, assuming uniformity of pacing involves problematic assumptions about the continuity of causal effects. It is for this reason that differences in assumptions about causal pacing matter.

A second difference about causality concerns relevance. As I have argued elsewhere, the stochastic view must make the assumption that causes are always relevant; once in the model they must remain. In formal terms, this means that any method employing linear transformations for modeling (whether directly or as an exponential term as in partial likelihood methods) has to assume that the dimensionality of the transform involved doesn't

15. See chapter 4.

change. Since the whole-career view looks at careers in terms of events, it can regard the causal factor of being black or female as affecting some of those career events but not others. There is no need to presume a perpetual importance. Of course in the stochastic view this problem could be formally handled by allowing the coefficients of the underlying transformation to vary continuously and by assuming that most of them are zero most of the time. But that procedure throws away the benefits of assuming the transformation model in the first place and precludes estimation in most situations. It would be a very cumbersome means of handling a problem confronted directly by the whole-career view.[16]

This difference is closely related to a more general difference between historiographical procedures and social science ones. Historians write their narratives to follow the causal action. If that action now seems to involve one or two principal causes and not other causes central just one or two events ago, then the historian simply ignores the present of those prior causes. They are assumed to be bubbling along in the background and not really affecting much. Such a view directly contravenes the views of most social scientists. The physical science model on which social scientists try to operate makes no allowances for causes that appear and disappear. One can hardly imagine a sociologist saying that "race simply didn't matter much except at a couple of crucial conjunctures." Yet this kind of argument is clearly implicit in standard narrative procedures in history.[17]

A third basic difference concerns the meaning of causes. The stochastic approach assumes, broadly speaking, that the meaning of a given variable doesn't vary with historical time and with the context of other variables. Interaction (the formal term for the latter context) is basically assumed to be secondary; main effects are primary. By contrast, the whole-career approach, with its focus on events, assumes that interaction comes first. For as I argued earlier, the whole-career approach sees as events what the stochastic view would call constellations of particular values of variables, particular values of interactions. Main effects are a fiction with which the narrativist dispenses, because social life doesn't actually occur in main effects, but rather in events/interactions. Gender, the disembodied characteristic, in fact causes nothing to happen. Men and women cause things to happen. And men and women never lack other characteristics than their gender. Life never occurs in main effects.

16. See chapter 1.

17. There is a large literature on how historical arguments actually work. See the sources cited in chapter 4, nn. 34–37.

This difference looks back to the constitutive assumptions earlier discussed. The stochastic approach starts with cases whose only property is existence and adds to existence as few other properties (mostly main effects, but sometimes interactions) as can explain the course of the careers. If main effects suffice, they suffice. By contrast, the whole-career view sees cases as inherently complex and uses typologies of events, cases, and narratives to simplify that complexity. Such typologies take complexity as primary, rather than deriving it as the product of crossed categorizations or dimensions, as would a "main effects" approach.

This focus on interaction means rethinking how we assign causal meaning to "variables." For in the narrative view, the meaning of a particular value of a "variable" is not fixed by its relation to other values of *this* variable among the other cases, but rather fluctuates with its status as one among the several values of different variables that make up various particular events. To take my earlier example of workmen's compensation laws, the impact of a given level of productivity in Massachusetts is not defined with relation to levels of productivity in other states, but with relation to the conjuncture of productivity, industrialization, and other variables in Massachusetts at a particular time. Main effects as such don't exist.[18]

The same argument applies to temporal context. A particular value of productivity may have no absolute meaning independent of time. Of course, the stochastic view can approach this problem via change scores. But the temporal contexts of variables may be more complex than change relations can capture. A given value may acquire significance because it is the first reversal of a long, steady fall or because it initiates a long steady state. In either case, it is the general temporal context, not the immediate change, that matters. Only when this preceding temporal context has a standard linear impact on the present can the stochastic view really handle temporal context, as in ARIMA methods, and even there the analysis of multiple variables is a central problem.

18. A serious controversy pitted Neyman against Yates on the latter's 1935 concept of "main effects" in factorial designs. For a discussion, see Traxler 1976. I am here following Neyman's argument that Yates's procedure made profound assumptions about the well-behaved character of reality. Yates's aim in adopting the concept of main effects was not, of course, to understand reality, but rather to decide whether to use a certain agricultural regimen. The main effects approach, that is, ultimately derives from the attitude of operationalism. The same of course applies to the modern social science usage of main effects, which is in many cases aimed at showing the positive or negative effects of various policies and personal characteristics rather than at understanding reality.

C. *Assumptions about Events and Their Orderability*

Although the stochastic approach to careers doesn't really think in terms of events, it does make distinct assumptions about the ordering of values of variables. To show how these assumptions work, I must introduce the concept of a variable's "time horizon," a time within which we can observe a meaningful fluctuation in that variable. The idea of "meaningful fluctuation" assumes that any variable is subject to measurement errors or "minor variation" (the two are probabilistically equivalent here) but that we know enough about those errors or variations to be certain, after some quantity of change in the variable, that an observed change is not error or random fluctuation, but substantive change. Time horizon is thus the period it takes to separate signal and noise or real and random change.

Time horizons fluctuate from variable to variable. They reflect in some cases the relation between the variance of the error process and the determinate coefficients of (say) autoregression. If a large error variance is superimposed on a slow determinate trend, it will take us longer to see the trend than if the superimposed error variance is small. This happens because of the practical strategy we use to identify changes in variables; because we wish to avoid mistaking random variation for true trend, we set our criterion for "real change" in terms of the error distribution.[19] To some extent, then, varying time horizons arise in measurement error and other forms of superimposed random variation. In this case they are a practical problem, but not a theoretical one.

But often, time horizons differ for substantive, theoretical reasons. For example, time horizon fluctuations can arise in relations of inclusion. The most obvious, but by no means the only, such example is the time horizon difference between a macro variable and its micro constituents. Intuitively, we think of aggregate measures as lacking ontological status in themselves; they are simply sums of individual level measures, in which case they would seem to have the same time horizon as the individual level measures. But in fact we are likely to notice a change in one individual's job satisfaction faster than we can observe a change the job satisfaction of a group of individuals. This is true for both conceptual and probabilistic reasons.

Theoretically, time horizons differ because emergents like group job

19. Filtering is a standard approach to this issue outside social science, but generally concerns cases where one can assume an underlying pure signal and hence can make some strong assumptions in order to clean it up. Nonetheless, filtering could well see wider use in social sciences (outside economics where it is already used widely).

satisfaction do have reality and can't be conceptually reduced to the sums of individual level measures that we use to indicate them. The job satisfaction of a group is a cultural construct with real consequences. Although we can measure it only by aggregating individual level measures, those are clearly but indicators of the fuzzy thing itself. The causal consequences flowing from recognition of a social fact like "workers are dissatisfied with their conditions of employment" are quite different from the causal consequences flowing from thousands of individual statements that "Jones hates her job." In the one case we may have revolution; in the other, burnout and neurosis, along with psychotherapy and other forms of individual response.

The mathematical argument that aggregate measures have longer time horizons requires no such emergentist assumptions and is therefore—to those who don't like such assumptions—all the more telling. In formal terms, time horizon is the waiting time until a result exceeding a certain limit is passed. Assume a standard normal distribution for an underlying individual variable to be aggregated and assume that we know the direction of change. In the usual way, we wish to avoid deciding change has occurred when it has not. So we set a criterion level, accepting such a false conclusion the usual 5 percent of the time. If the distribution has in fact moved m to the right, then the new mean is m, the variance remains 1, and the line drawn at the old 5 percent line (at $z = 1.65$) cuts the moved distribution at some point c. The portion of the moved distribution to the right of c gives the probability p of deciding that there has been a change, given that change has occurred. The expected waiting time for this decision, again given that change has occurred, is distributed geometrically, and hence its expectation is q/p.[20]

Now consider the addition of, say, ten such variables together to make an aggregate. Assume for simplicity that the variables are identically distributed. If they are independent, then the waiting time situation is exactly the same as before. The mean of the original sum is 0, and independence means that the variance of the sum is the sum of the variances (i.e., 10). The expectation of the moved distribution is $10m$. We can divide through by 10 and have the same z-criterion line, the same c, the same p, and the same expected waiting time q/p.[21] But if the variables in the sum are correlated, the

20. To this point the exposition follows that of the original article. However, the original article's argument about the time-horizon effects of aggregation was incorrect. The following two paragraphs replace it with a better argument.

21. The original paper used a convolution argument here. (See Feller 1968:266–69 for an application of convolutions to geometric distributions.) The argument assumed sequential trials of individual variables when by the conditions of the problem one trial of the aggregated variable entailed one trial of each individual variable.

variance of the sum will be greater than 10 and the summed distribution will be flatter. With a disproportionately larger denominator for z, we will be forced to go further out to the right to guarantee a 5 percent alpha error than in the uncorrelated case. When the summed distribution moves its $10m$ units to the right, we are "getting back" the next $10m$ units of the distribution to the left of our alpha level, but because the distribution is flatter, we get back less than in the uncorrelated case. As a result p will be smaller and the expected waiting time q/p will be longer.

There are many reasons to expect such correlations in aggregated variables. In situations of scale construction—multiple measures on a single individual—correlation is often deliberately sought. Even with summed measures on separate individuals correlation is common. In the just-mentioned case of job satisfaction, for example, contagion effects within workplaces can be almost guaranteed to generate such correlations. Period events reaching across whole populations will also produce serious cross-individual correlation. Local contagion and overarching events mean that in practice aggregated variables are very likely to have longer time horizons than individual ones.[22]

The concept of time horizons allows us to see important differences between the two approaches here considered. Stochastic methods must assume what is technically called partial ordering of the variables' time horizons. Causality can obtain between variables of equal time horizon or it may flow from variables of longer time horizon to those of shorter ones. But it cannot flow the other way. For one could then envision an observation interval such that the short-term variable would exhibit meaningful variation but not the long-term one. In such a case we could not believe that the short-term variable caused the long-term one, for we could measure only error in the latter.

Another assumption crucial to the stochastic approach is that, generally speaking, succeeding observations of all variables are what I shall call contingently independent. That is, we assume that if there is autoregression, it assumes a given pattern that does not vary through time periods. Values of a variable in succeeding time frames cannot be linked in arbitrary ways. Suppose we are estimating some dependent aspect of a job career with multiple independent variable regression done in time series format; successive years

22. My argument here is basically empirical. Note that survey analysis in general deliberately attempts to minimize correlation, although it is no doubt more successful with eliminating the effect of contagion than with eliminating that of broad period events. The sources of intercase correlation seem so strong, particularly in longitudinal analysis, that the lengthening of time horizons in aggregated variables seems very likely.

constitute the "cases" and some variable aspect of career (say income) is predicted from a vector of (potentially lagged) independent variables. If there are arbitrary patterns linking successive values of an independent variable (say temporary work assignments that last several observation periods and that reflect "events" in the economy lasting several observation periods), the varying autoregression in the independent variables does complicated and unspecifiable (because interactive) things to our parameter estimates. The problem is that certain succeeding values of various independent variables are linked in "events" that span several observation frames.[23]

The time horizon problem is handled differently in the whole-career view. Here all that matters is the list of events. They can be big or small in time horizon. In certain kinds of careers, for example, having a certain kind of patron at a particular stage determines the pattern of the entire rest of the career. This is an immediately determinable event, as opposed to other events of longer time horizon like "mastering fundamental professional techniques" or "holding various minor jobs." The only narrative assumption that need be made is that an event can affect only events beginning after it in the career.[24] Since the narrative moves from event to event, there is no necessity even to assume a regularly spaced observation framework such as observation every year. A small, highly specifiable event can be seen as affecting large, diffuse events. The only necessary assumptions involve event orderability.

The stochastic and whole-career views think about the sequence of events somewhat differently. In the stochastic approach, the standard assumption is that the fundamental order is an order of variables and that all cases obey this same order. In any multiple regression, for example, it is assumed that the pattern of causality is the same in every case. This is equivalent, given the relation of stories about "causal mechanisms" to path

23. This problem is not escaped by event history methods, which in their most common form (partial likelihood models) evade the normal problems of multicollinearity (which arise in the estimated parameter variances) by avoiding variance-based estimation. The writing of a likelihood equation, the fundamental step in maximum likelihood estimation, assumes the joint independence of the observations, something unfortunately impossible in an event history data array; what happens in Massachusetts in 1912 is obviously dependent on what happened there in 1911. Under certain conditions in the discrete-time estimation of event history models, the estimation equations do reduce to a situation of apparent independence. One condition is that the vector of explanatory variables explains all the variation in the hazard rate. The other condition is that of full rank for the matrix of explanatory variables. See chapter 4, n. 21. I have discussed the concept of time horizons in chapter 1 also.

24. One might imagine an event affecting an event already in process by making an analogy to catalysis. In that case an event would modify an already developing event of larger time horizon than itself. Certainly one can tell narratives this way. How to embody them in empirical practice is a different matter.

diagrams, to the assertion that every case follows the same narrative. One can, of course, use dummy variables (or simply split up one's cases) to avoid this assumption to some extent. But the characteristic aim is to find a pattern of causes that holds across all cases, rather than to find a variety of patterns. A related assumption holds that no particular sequence of particular values of variables has any particular causes or consequences. (Technically, this is part of the "main effects first" assumption.) That is, we can't say that whenever we see particular events a, b, c in that order we will always observe d. No statements are made about particular values a, b, c; statements are made only about variables A, B, C, and D.

By contrast, in the whole-career approach the order of particular events is the center of interest. Our first aim is to consider whether there is one or several characteristic sequences of events. Here the assumptions involve our ability to place a set of events in order. One version of the assumptions assumes strict order; there is no overlap between events. Another may permit some overlap, but places restrictions on its amount. Another strategy uses the basic observation framework of the stochastic method, but defines the observations in terms of events: the joint event of being of such and such an age and holding such and such a job, and so on.

Since order is central to the whole-career approach, we must be able to define order rigorously for that approach to work. There seem to be two basic strategies. One retains time horizon flexibility and defines events conceptually. It considers a reality of observable "occurrences" and imagines how these might be colligated into conceptual "events." Occurrences are things like taking courses or holding particular jobs; events are things like "getting an education" and "developing as a professional." Constraints on the orderability of the events can then be seen as issues of measurement given temporal patterns of occurrences within events. Alternatively, we may define events combinatorially within a standard measurement framework, as just suggested. This produces orderability automatically, but at the price of losing all information about the temporal "shape" of events—their duration, their intensity (in terms of producing occurrences), in short their time horizon. This last approach is thus a hybrid of a stochastic conceptualization and a whole-career one.[25]

25. For a formal analysis of these problems of colligation and measurement, see Abbott 1984. I have applied some of the techniques there described to sequences of welfare state development (Abbott and DeViney 1992) and of medical professionalization (Abbott 1991b). The literature on colligation is expanding. Scott Poole, in particular, has followed up the lead of Bales's Interaction Process Analysis approach. See Poole and Roth 1989a, 1989b.

D. *The Character of Time*

The stochastic and whole-career approaches differ, finally, with regard to the character and depth of causal time. The stochastic view implies a belief that the social process is continuous and causally shallow, while the whole-career approach sees it as discontinuous and causally deep. These are not, of course, conscious assumptions; rather they are implicit in the ways the two approach their problems.

The characteristic stochastic study of careers takes discrete repeated observations on its variables (i.e., panel data). If we are considering the effect of education at time 1 on income at time 2 (say five years later) our first idea would be to regard education as a step function, measured by degree (high school, BA, MS, Ph.D.), and to estimate its effect across cases in the normal way. But it would obviously be preferable to have annual measures of education, because education is not simply a matter of degrees but also of on-the-job training, and the latter might have its own distinct effect on income. If our measurement frame were annual, we could see the causal effect of degree in year 1 as falling on some intermediate variable—say, general occupation in year 2—and see that general occupation as providing access to other forms of education (on the job) which would then affect detailed occupational position in year 3 and so on. That is, the original education-income effect over five years would be regarded as interpolating a whole series of lesser processes. With those processes in the model, it seems unnecessary and perhaps even illegitimate to draw a causal arrow from education in year 1 directly to income in year 5.

It is this interpolation that makes us prefer more panels to less in longitudinal work and that makes the event history data framework, with its exact dates of events, so appealing. More data is better. Better dating is better.[26]

But in the limit, we have here the "continuity" of formal calculus. There is no time interval so small that independent variables are not affecting dependent ones within it. For if we continue unmasking the interpolative character of coefficients, we end up at daily or hourly measurement. But at this level we invariably think of reality in particular narratives. In those narratives, general variables like "my education" are simply resources in inter-

26. For a detailed discussion of this "more is better" issue see Tuma and Hannan 1984. They argue that the practically optimum spacing of waves is one that reduces the probability of two or more changes between waves to a negligible amount. Their argument rests on the conception that I have called "time horizon," the typical waiting time for a substantial change. They do not consider the issue of "disappearance of causes" at the micro level that is discussed below. That is, while they consider the time horizon of the dependent variable, they do not consider those of the independent ones.

actional facework; their consequences for one's income arise through privileging or disadvantaging one in interaction. And these daily narratives of real interaction generally don't involve most of the variables of "long-run" importance, or if they do, do so in infinitesimal ways indistinguishable, in any practical sense, from error. At such a fine temporal level, reality is quite discontinuous and choppy. Major changes (e.g., in job status) are likely to be quite abrupt; the record that justifies a major promotion may take years to build, but the promotion itself is instantaneous. That is, more panels are better, but only up to a point. If we look too closely, the effects of global variables like "my education" become very hard to specify meaningfully.[27]

This *reductio ad interactionem* presents the stochastic view of careers with a fundamental dilemma. The stochastic view's main assumption is that the career is simply a sequential list of the results of an underlying and real stochastic or choice process. A set of initial values face the model and produce new values that in turn face the model and so on; the immediate past is perpetually producing the future (much of it by reproducing constancy, of course). It is obviously better to have more iterations than less for such a model, and yet after a certain number of temporal subdivisions the assumption that every variable (or its constituents) is always in the model obviously breaks down. One requires a "micro temporal model" that addresses these local discontinuities, but that can somehow produce the appearance of a more continuous reality to be interpolated at the macro temporal level.[28]

27. The event history framework as usually used on historical data employs annual measurement because that is the typical framework of the records. Thus the micro reduction problem described in the text does not force itself on the event historians.

28. The relation of micro and macro structures is a widely discussed issue, in sociology at least. The best macro theories are relatively institutional and treat the micro level as relatively fixed. Marx, Weber, and Durkheim all tended to think this way, as have their current votaries. By contrast, by far the most exciting micro theories treat the micro level as extremely open and uncertain. The Chicago school and the ecologists and symbolic interactionists who descend from them all take this position. Despite some valiant efforts, no one has really managed to put Humpty Dumpty together again. Although there is a large literature on the issue in current sociological theory, most of it lacks data, applicability, indeed even comprehensibility. It consists of "theory fixes" that stick together a few general concepts and claim to have solved the problem. Some standard views of the micro/macro relation are (1) macro structures are simple aggregates of micro occasions, (2) micro occasions are mere instances of macro structures, (3) micro occasions are stochastic realizations of macro processes, (4) macro structures are constraints (alternatively, facilitators) for micro occasions, (5) micro is the level of freedom and macro that of constraint, (6) macro structures are simply stochastic limits of sequences of micro occasions, and (7) micro structures are psychological, macro ones social. None of this literature recognizes that the micro/macro problem is inherently temporal, that is, none of it recognizes the conceptual (as opposed to practical) problem of time horizons. The standard review of this literature is Alexander et al. 1987.

The whole-career view, like any narrative view, dispenses with this insistence on an absolutely continuous historical time altogether. Events have finite duration. They begin and end. There is less of a microtranslation problem because larger historical time has the same discontinuity as does micro time. Particular causes are not always present, but matter only when they are part of the complex particulars the narrativist calls events. It should be noted that while this view has all the weight of historiography behind it, it is quite shaky philosophically. Mead, Whitehead, and many others have argued that reality flows from deep past to immediate past to present and future, and that the deep past has causal effects only through having determined the immediate past. The stochastic view founds itself on this quite reasonable assumption. One's Ph.D. location, for example, may affect initial university placement, but its effects on later events should work through its effect on that initial placement.[29]

But there are a number of reasons for considering such historical "action at a distance." One of them is implicit in Mead's own theory of the past. The present is continuously reshaping the past in line with its concerns. In career terms, people constantly reinterpret their past job history in order to decide what to do now. Suppose a period of bad market conditions has sent people to jobs and organizations they would otherwise have ignored and then is followed by better market conditions. Some may then redefine their years on the periphery as useful preparation for current changes, while others view them as mere waiting time, and still others may have lost sight of their peripheral or undesired qualities altogether, perhaps seeing them as liberation from a career treadmill. These different analyses have varying implications for the individuals' future choices, even though all the people may have had what is "objectively" the experience of going to (what they at the time thought to be) the periphery. Because people are constantly assigning new historical efficacy to far past events (by reinterpreting their careers in light of them) we must consider the far past to have some sort of causal efficacy.[30]

29. Mead's general analysis of temporality is found in Mead 1932. Useful summaries are Tonnes 1932 and Eames 1973. See also chapter 7. Of course, state variables like Ph.D. location remain present, and so one may draw path arrows as if they had deferred effects. But the guts of the stochastic model of reality is that the entire situation at one instant produces the entire situation at the next. If part of that production is simple reproduction, then so be it. What matters is the continuity of career time and the reality of the underlying stochastic process.

30. Mead of course would argue that in fact all the causality is happening in the making of the immediate present. It is merely an analytical convenience or shorthand to regard the distant past as efficacious.

We must also assume that there is historical action at a distance because, as I have shown, it is difficult to do otherwise. Since insistence on the continuity of historical processes proves impractical, we must make do with the alternative view that events have finite and varying durations and that they may overlap. A career may be simultaneously shaped by ongoing events that began at very different times in the past: overall shifts in labor demand consequent on changes in the division of labor, recent vagaries of recruitment, changes of viability of individual hiring organizations, and so on. There is no need to reiterate these issues for those who have lived through the academic market since the 1960s. Note, however, that this position involves us in the assessment of multiple overlapping events.

III Conclusion

I have aimed in this paper to distinguish two fundamentally different views of historical processes. One views them as generated by stochastic processes. The social world consists of individuals with particular properties. Causes work at fixed rates in all cases, are generally rather than occasionally salient, and primarily work independently, although occasionally combining in interactive effects. Causality flows to some extent from context to detail but generally between variables of "equal" status. There are few or no patterns of causality reaching beyond a single iteration of the model and the patterns that are observed affect all individuals equally; everyone has the same causal history. Social time is essentially continuous.

The other view sees historical processes as whole stories. The social world consists of complex subjects to whom complex things—events—happen. Causality flows differently in different cases—perhaps at different rates, certainly in different patterns. Most causes work in complex bunches—the events—rather than alone. There is no necessity that these events be of a certain consistent temporal size or length and no restriction on relations between events of differing sizes. Events can come in a variety of temporal orderings—strict sequence, overlap, simultaneity. All of this means that historical processes are fundamentally discontinuous.

My first purpose in distinguishing these views has been to make them visible. The second is to establish the latter of them as a possible foundation for methods addressed to the question "what are the characteristic patterns in social narratives?" Our present approach to social processes following the first approach has been productive; I am certainly not denying that. But it makes many assumptions that restrict its vision.

The central restrictive assumption is that most events happen and hence that the variety of historical processes is overwhelmingly great. This assumption implies that the best models are global models aimed at global regularities, for it implies that they are the only feasible models. The idea that complexity requires global models in turn entails highly restrictive further assumptions: uniform causal pacing, relatively consistent causal effects, main effects dominating interaction, consistency of time horizons, single causal order across all cases. Thus, if we stop believing that most events happen, we can open new possibilities for formal analysis of historical processes.

These new analyses will not instantly produce results comparable to those we presently have. One can use optimal matching, for example, to examine the development of welfare states and develop measures of resemblance between those several histories. But causal interpretation of those resemblances presents problems. To find what overall causes determine the contrast between one group of welfare histories and another, one has to solve the problem of when to measure the causal variables: as of the beginning of the histories? as of a particular fixed date across all histories? as of the midpoints of the histories? The answers are not obvious. In the short run, a shift to narrative formalism means forgoing much of our customary interest in causes. Of course one can answer that most of our causal results, based as they are on the strict assumptions above, are little more than polite fictions. But still, narrative methods will provide no easy answers.

On the other hand, narrative positivism has some distinct and powerful advantages. It will facilitate direct communication between history and the social sciences, because it thinks about social reality the way historians have traditionally done. It will provide us with a method for directly addressing questions of typical sequence(s) that are central to a number of contemporary empirical literatures: life course, organizations, labor markets, revolutions. It will uncover regularities in social processes that can then be subjected to causal analysis of a more traditional sort. Eventually, it may more fully analyze the complex patterns of history than the causal methods can at their best. In the meantime, I think serious reflection about basic temporal assumptions can help us all improve our work.[31]

31. My current work attempts to use optimal matching to consider multiple case, multiple variable time series data. This is the problem of finding different "tracks" through the state space of variables. Citations to articles illustrating my other applications of narrative positivism may be found in earlier footnotes.

From Causes to Events

In the last decade a number of writers have proposed narrative as the foundation for sociological methodology. By this they do not mean narrative in its common senses of words as opposed to numbers and complexity as opposed to formalization. Rather, they mean narrative in the more generic sense of process or story. They want to make processes the fundamental building blocks of sociological analyses. For them social reality happens in sequences of actions located within constraining or enabling structures. It is a matter of particular social actors, in particular social places, at particular social times.

In the context of contemporary empirical practice, such a conception is revolutionary. Our normal methods parse social reality into fixed entities with variable qualities. They attribute causality to the variables—hypostatized social characteristics—rather than to agents; variables do things, not social actors. Stories disappear. The only narratives present in such methods are just-so stories justifying this or that relation between the variables. Contingent narrative is impossible.

There are of course empirical literatures within which process remains important. The various microsociologies—symbolic interactionism, inter-

This essay is dedicated to the memory of Bruce Mayhew, who wrote two interesting papers on sequences (1971, 1976) and who wrote me a wonderfully encouraging letter when I was trying to get some unorthodox work published early in my career. (As the reader can see, I am still trying.) I would like also to thank Harrison White for the original invitation to write this summary piece, for the "Interfaces Conference" at Enfield, New Hampshire, 16 August 1991, and I would like to thank the participants at that conference, whose hostile comments have forced important clarifications. I would like to thank Ron Thisted, John Padgett, Larry Griffin, and Larry Isaac for diverse comments and advice, and, finally, to thank Peter Abell for many forms of collegiality. This paper was first published in *Sociological Methods and Research* 20 (1992): 428–55; reprinted with permission of Sage Publications, Inc. I have left myself in the third person (which seems odd) as in the original, because that seems the only way to preserve the piece's unity of tone. Although I have removed the subtitles of these papers, this one in particular had a subtitle that got a lot of people's goats: "Notes on Narrative Positivism." The beginning of this paper covers ground analyzed in more detail in chapters 1, 3, 4, and 5. The latter part of the paper shows the connection between the theoretical argument and a particular body of methodological work and is my reason for including the paper here.

action process analysis, ethnomethodology, conversational analysis—all focus on social processes, and particularly on the branchings and turnings of interaction. Historical sociology, particularly in the study of collective behaviors like revolutions and strikes, likewise studies the unfolding of processes, although here the search is more for characteristic processes than for rules of interaction. (There are also literatures where process is of obvious conceptual importance, but where empirically no one has moved beyond the recipes of regression, the life course literature being the best example.)

But the main empirical traditions of sociology ignore process altogether, and this ignorance has gradually spread into much of our theory. Narrative methodology is a response to this twofold ignorance. In reviewing it here, therefore, I wish to propose an agenda of central questions in the conceptualization of process and to review the attempts, preliminary but exciting, to develop formal methodologies founded on such process conceptions. To that end, I shall first mention the status of process in classical sociological theories. I shall then discuss how process analysis gradually disappeared from empirical methods. This leads naturally into a discussion of the major theoretical questions raised when we reintegrate process into empirical practice. This discussion is followed by a review of the new methodological approaches proposed to accomplish this reintegration.

I Theory and Process

While action and process have largely disappeared from empirical sociology, they are by contrast central to much of sociological theory, both classic and recent. Weber made action central in his theoretical writings. He wrote numerous contingent narratives in the areas of comparative religion and economics and put the search for ideal-typical narratives at the heart of his methodological writings. Marx, too, conceived of the world processually, although his processes of interest were the grand tides of Hegelian history. But like Weber, Marx wrote explanatory narratives with both facility and felicity.[1]

In the American tradition it was above all the Chicago school that focused on process. Park and Burgess's textbook (1921) was organized around process headings. Their students gave "natural histories" of social processes, describing typical patterns observed in the development of gangs, occupational careers, even revolutions.[2] The central Chicago concept of

1. Weber 1947; Marx 1963.
2. Park and Burgess 1921. On gangs, see Thrasher 1927. On occupational careers, see Cressey 1932. On revolutions, see Edwards 1927.

"interaction" embodied an obsession with process, an obsession bequeathed to descendants like Erving Goffman and the labeling theorists. But Chicago was not the only theoretical tradition interested in process. Even Parsons, particularly in his early work, made action, if not process, central to sociology.[3] Today we see a recurrence of this longstanding sociological concern with action in yet another guise; rational choice theories focus directly on actors and decisions. Although many decry rational choice as "unsociological" in its resolute methodological individualism, the theory at least concentrates on agents and activity.

One might wish to summarize this common theoretical attention to process and action by saying that much of theory takes a "narrative approach" to social reality. But the word "narrative," unless it is seriously qualified, here obscures more than it reveals. We often assume that narrative necessarily involves complexity of meaning and that it is inherently unformalizable. Nonetheless, in approaching social reality through process one need not make either of these assumptions, however desirable they might be for other reasons. There is nothing about thinking processually that requires interpretive attention to complexity of meaning. And certainly there is nothing about thinking processually that forbids representing social reality in a formal manner. If we recall, then, that the word "narrative" is understood here in the broad sense of processual, action-based approaches to social reality, approaches that are based on stories, we can avoid these conflations and recognize that the great theoretical traditions of sociology have indeed taken a narrative approach to social reality.

II The Disappearance of Process in Empirical Sociology

But the dominant empirical traditions have not taken that narrative approach. The concept that has replaced process and narrative in empirical sociology is of course causality. Yet causality has a curious history in sociology. While it is now central to empirical sociology's self-image, it turns out that early sociological positivism avoided the concept.[4]

The contemporary concept of causality derives from logical positivism. Although Hume had held that causality was nothing more or less than correlation, early twentieth-century natural science nonetheless used the cause concept with distinctly pre-Humean overtones of determination and forcing. It was this concept that quantum mechanics challenged by asserting the essentially indeterminate nature of reality and by claiming "probable deter-

3. See, especially, Parsons 1937.
4. See Bernert 1983. This section covers material laid out in much more detail in chapter 3.

mination" (determination of probability distributions by probability distributions) as the best approximation to "real" causality. In response to this development, the logical positivists recast the causality concept as a predicate of statements rather than of reality.[5]

This recast concept of causality is the one taught in the best sociological methods courses today. To say "x causes y" is to say something about the equations relating x and y and about the implicit theoretical framework in which they are embedded (the temporal priority of x and so on). A good sociological methodologist will thus argue that "education causes occupational achievement" is essentially a shorthand for the union of three statements: (1) education generally precedes occupational achievement in the life course, (2) the two are highly correlated across individuals, and (3) it is plausible (because one can tell a "plausibility story" that "gives a potential mechanism") to see the latter as flowing from the former. In this idealized view, "education causes occupational achievement" is not a statement about some causal force—"education"—that determines in some transcendent fashion an equally abstract thing called "occupational achievement." Rather it is a quick way of summarizing many narratives in which education accounts for occupational achievement.

In practice, of course, such care is uncharacteristic. Many or most sociologists interpret statements like "education causes occupational achievement" in precisely the realist fashion, seeing in the social world causal forces that push on other forces in a terrain removed from human activity. One has only to read the journals to find such a rhetoric of determinate "causal forces," even though any serious methodologist falls back, upon challenge, to the idealized, "summary of narratives" view.[6]

The takeover of sociology by this reworked theory of causality began with the statistical revolution of Ogburn, Stouffer, Duncan, and Lazarsfeld. The first moves of this statistical revolution, in the 1920s, had been conducted in the name of association, rather than causation.[7] In true Humean fashion, this first version refused altogether to talk about "causes." But as sociology gradually adopted the new statistics during and after the war, the logical positivist notion of causality as merely a predicate of statements justified a renewed use of causal language. Since talking about causality was merely talking about equations, it was philosophically proper to do so, Hume notwithstanding. This interpretation gave rise to the "causal lan-

5. See, e.g., Reichenbach 1951, chap. 10.
6. See chapter 4 for a detailed exposition of this argument.
7. See Bernert 1983 and chapter 3.

guage as shorthand" view that I have just outlined as the widely taught philosophical foundation of standard methodology.

But in practice, sociologists never took the separation of statement and reality all that seriously. By the time of Blalock's *Causal Inference in Non-experimental Research* (1964), the language of determining causal forces acting in the real world yet without real reference to specific individual actions had become standard in the field. This metamorphosis was helped by the translation of Durkheim's *Suicide* (in 1951), with its seductive blend of resolute social emergentism and quantitative empiricism. Durkheim's almost medieval social realism seemed to justify ignoring agency and story altogether.

By this point the methods themselves had begun to constrain theoretical thinking with a set of implicit assumptions. The methods have gradually become such second nature to sociologists that these implicit assumptions have begun to dictate how sociologists imagine the social world to be constructed. It is useful to recall them here.[8]

1. The social world is made up of fixed entities with varying attributes (demographic assumption).

   1a. Some attributes determine (cause) others (attribute causality assumption).

2. What happens to one case doesn't constrain what happens to others, temporally or spatially (casewise independence assumption).

3. Attributes have one and only one causal meaning within a given study (univocal meaning assumption).

4. Attributes determine each other principally as independent scales rather than as constellations of attributes; main effects are more important than interactions (which are complex types) (main effects assumption).

Some of these assumptions have been attacked by various literatures. Thus, for example, the demographic assumption (assumption 1) has been attacked by some studies of merger and division. But the general drift in demography has been away from the study of flows of entities (formal demography) towards the fixed entities/varying attributes approach (social demography.) And while the organizational ecologists have addressed the question of merger and division, they treat these processes merely as the continuation of one group coupled with the death or birth of another, thus avoiding the central questions posed about the continuity between entity

8. See the extended analysis in chapter 1.

and attribute. Existence in such an argument becomes an attribute that it is somehow possible for an entity to lose, thus producing the philosophical monstrosity of an entity that can be defined as an entity but that doesn't exist.

The casewise independence assumption (assumption 2) has also been attacked, most forcefully by the network literature. This substantial literature focuses on types of interrelations and conceives of the social world in spatial terms. It leans towards scaling, clustering, and similarly descriptive approaches to social structure, but remains within formalistic approaches. By contrast, the univocal meaning assumption (assumption 3) has been attacked chiefly by the various interpretive literatures and thus has not been the focus of a formalizing or methodological literature, although one could imagine formal work on attributes with multiple causal relations to each other. In general, it is this third assumption that has provoked the major "soft" sociology critique of "hard" sociological empiricism.

The main effects assumption (assumption 4) has not been directly challenged by a major literature. To be sure, the network literature implicitly argues that social relations come in constellations rather than simple links. But it has been left to applied social scientists—predominantly market researchers—to argue that complexes matter more than do main effects and to follow the methodological implications of this argument to the point of making classification and description of reality more central than causal analysis of it.

More important for my argument than these four assumptions, however, are the assumptions implicit in standard methodology that involve time and temporality. For it is against these assumptions that the new "narrative positivism" has arisen.

5. Things happen in discrete bits of uniform length and are not aggregated into overlapping "events" of varying length (continuity or uniform time-horizon assumption).

5a. In cases where one must consider differential duration of attributes, determination flows from long-duration attributes to shorter-duration ones, from context to individual (monotonic causal flow assumption).

6. The order in which attributes change does not influence what changes occur (nonnarrative assumption).

6a. All cases follow the same "causal narrative" or model (homogeneous causality assumption).

Reflection will persuade the thoughtful reader that these are indeed the temporal assumptions basic to standard methods. A useful discussion of them, possibly the best in standard methodological sources, is found scattered through the pages of Blau and Duncan's *American Occupational Structure*. Applying regression methods for the first time to a massive social dataset, Blau and Duncan discussed these matters at length.[9]

In summary, the methods adopted by sociology since the Second World War not only embodied a concept of causality as forcing. They also brought a set of implicit assumptions that were gradually imposed on sociological theorizing. It is these hidden assumptions, and particularly those concerning time and temporality, that are the concern of the people I am here calling narrative positivists.

III Theoretical Questions about Narrative

The history of standard methods in sociology thus reminds us of a simple but important truth. Any methodological strategy (what we might call a Methodology with a capital "M") brings with it general constraints that are, properly speaking, theoretical. Since any social methodology must parse the social world in particular ways, it must contain elements of an implicit social theory. As one can see from the list of assumptions above, these elements comprise an ontology (assumption 1), theories of structure (assumption 2) and causality (assumptions 3, 4, and 5a), and a concept of time (assumptions 5 and 6).

Thus the first move in creating an alternative Methodology founded on narrative is to discover the theoretical strategy appropriate to such a methodology and to outline some central questions it poses for conceptual reflection. A narrative Methodology will of course itself make assumptions about social reality. The new narrativists claim no exemption from that necessity. Rather they wish to pose new questions based on new assumptions. That would give us two strings to our bow instead of only one, as we have at present.

At present the theoretical literature in this area is sparse. Although one can draw many theoretical insights from the scattered empirical literatures mentioned at the outset, none of these literatures is strongly interested in the creation of positive methods founded on narrative. The only self-conscious expositions are the various writings of Abbott and Abell. Both follow much the same logic in their attack on what Abell called "the variable-centered model," but from there they have gone different ways.[10]

9. Blau and Duncan 1967: 82–97, 121–28, 163–71, 177–88.
10. My own pieces are collected here (see also Abbott 1983 and 1984). Peter Abell's theoretical work includes Abell 1984, 1985, and, most important, 1987. Once the "narrative revo-

Abbott's original argument drew as much on literatures in structural literary theory and the philosophy of history as on sociology. He has focused on the issue of the coherence and followability of social stories, the issue of whether it really makes sense to think that "social reality happens in stories." Originally, Abbott proposed three major story properties.[11] The first was enchainment, defined as the nature of the narrative link from one step to the next; this was the narrative analogue of causality. The second was order, the degree to which a social story presupposed a particular, exact order of events. The third was convergence, the degree to which a social sequence approached a steady state, for which nonnarrative methods would then be appropriate. In later theoretical writing as in methodological work, Abbott has generally focused on the order property, and in particular on the typical sequence problem—finding a typical or characteristic order of events. By contrast with Abell's, Abbott's theoretical stance seems rather indeterminate; he leaves room for varieties of enchainment and has spent little time focusing that concept. This follows from Abbott's major empirical concerns as a historical sociologist of institutions. Enchainment is theorized in diverse ways in institutional analysis.[12]

Writing from a more formal background, Abell has grounded his approach to narrative much more explicitly on a theoretical model of action, a focused concept of enchainment. Like Abbott, Abell claimed a unity and coherence to stories. But he founded these chiefly on the philosophical literature concerning action. Abell defined enchainment explicitly in terms of individual action, which he categorized in terms of intention, positive activity, forebearance, and similar concepts. On this basis he has built a formidable algebraic approach to Abbott's typical sequence problem. For Abell, the central theoretical issues of narrative analysis lie in categorizing the types and modalities of action. Recently, he has become more explicitly wedded to the rational action paradigm, which he espouses as a "least worst alternative."[13] Although this commitment makes Abell's theoretical grasp more focused and thus perhaps less catholic than Abbott's, his exposition of the narrative problem in *The Syntax of Social Life* remains the best extended treatment of it in sociology.[14]

---

lution" got under way amid the general swing to the cultural in parts of the social sciences, we suddenly acquired a lot of company. See, for example, Griffin 1991; Aminzade 1992; Sewell 1996. Most of this work was not focused on the problem of generalization like Abell's and mine.

11. Abbott 1983.
12. I made many such arguments in Abbott 1988a.
13. Abell 1989, 1991.
14. Abell 1987.

Although Abbott and Abell have begun to develop an agenda of theoretical questions and issues for a methodology of narrativism, they have both turned to more explicitly methodological concerns in order to persuade empirical sociologists of their theoretical insights. (I review these methodologies below.) Thus, most of the theoretical agenda remains open for investigation. I shall here discuss some of the major problems. It is vitally important to note that these kinds of issues—issues of what we might call the "philosophy of method"—should not discourage us from seeing the social world in narrative terms. After all, the same kinds of issues exist for standard methods. They are simply ignored because of the paradigmatic quality of those methods. It is merely the novelty of the narrative approach that makes us conscious of these questions.

The first general category of theoretical problems concerns the handling of demographic questions within the narrative framework. Abbott calls this the issue of "entity processes."[15] These processes involve the transformation or fundamental change of the case itself. The most familiar (and best studied) are birth and death. But Abbott has also pointed to the importance of merger and division of cases, problems that disappear in Abell's rather strong methodological individualism, but that are conspicuously important at the institutional level that has been Abbott's chief concern. As I noted earlier, merger and division have been treated as death (of one case by merging out of existence) and birth (of one case by splitting off from another) in the event history literature, but this approach simply finesses an important theoretical problem.

Abbott has also argued that the micro/macro problem is inherently temporal and hence that there are a variety of entity processes relating change and nonchange at micro and emergent levels.[16] Again this problem arises out of the theoretical concerns of institutionalism. Professions, for example, can continue in a constant position in a division of labor while their personnel turns over totally, or, conversely, a constant personnel can experience, as a collectivity, a complete shift of collective identity or location through changes in the general professional division of labor. These kinds of problems raise issues of micro- and macrotransformation that are important subjects for theoretical analysis. We must discover reasonable rules governing the conception of cases and of their integration into macro entities. All these are problems of theorizing "entity processes."

After these demographic concerns, a second general class of theoretical

15. See the closing paragraphs of chapter 4.
16. Again, see the discussion in chapter 4 and also the consideration of this issue in the prologue. Micro and macro as purely temporal issues are discussed at length in chapter 7.

issues concern events. Because he draws on a relatively formalistic model of narrative and on rational choice with its methodological individualism, Abell tends to see events as simple, unproblematic exchanges and responses. Abbott, by contrast, regards conceptualizing events as a central theoretical problem.[17] For the literature in philosophy of history, events are particularly problematic because a given set of "happenings" (Abbott has usually called them "occurrences") can be emplotted in many different ways. (The analogous problem in standard methods is that a given empirical statistic can be used as an indicator of many different concepts.) Moreover, for the historian, events have duration and hence may overlap. This in turn raises havoc with the concept of order, which is central to that of narrative. Abbott's various writings have circled around these issues, but it remains a central question in applications.[18]

Moreover, once we take events as large, conceptual things indicated by "happenings" or "occurrences," there are then a whole variety of issues relating the two levels. To a large extent, these can be seen as measurement issues. Which are the crucial happenings that tell us that event x has taken place? Which new medical school, for example, finally persuades us that the medical profession is becoming committed to education? But they fold back into the problem of defining and theorizing events in the first place. Once we move beyond the simple world of action/response sequences to a world where events have duration and overlap and are known largely by the happenings that indicate them, we confront an enormously complex problem in deciding how the parts of stories go together. As Abbott has noted, there is a long and distinguished literature on this topic in the philosophy of history. It is nonetheless inconclusive for being long and distinguished.

A related set of theoretical issues concern the multiple plot structures of the social world. If we conceptualize the social world in terms of stories, we face immediately the problem that every event lies in many narratives at once. Every event has multiple narrative antecedents as well as multiple narrative consequences. (The same is of course true in standard methods with the word "causal" substituted for "narrative.")[19] That is, the full social process, when viewed in narrative terms, makes up a network of stories flowing into the present and future. Narratives vary in the tightness of this network. Certain narratives develop relatively independently of the others around them; these we call stage processes. Others are more contingent on

17. The conceptualization issue is discussed in Abbott 1984.
18. See Abbott 1991b. On multiple indication, see chapter 2.
19. Cf. Marini and Singer 1988.

those environing narratives—for example, organizational careers in the majority of cases. Finally, others take place in systematic structures that constrain their unfolding in radical ways. These last are "interaction systems" of mutually constraining narratives. Abbott's analysis of the evolution of professions takes this position as does Wallerstein's analysis of the world system.[20] This problem of the mutual contingency of narratives clearly requires extensive theoretical study before we can think about methodologies to address it.

We can generalize this issue by considering the theoretical problem of how the narrative (or causal) meaning of an event varies with the ensemble of environing contemporary events and with the past events leading to the present. A fundamental argument of narrative methodology is that narrative meaning (the "causal force" of enchainments) is a function of present and past context. Synchronically, this is the argument that "reality doesn't happen in main effects but in interactions." Temporally, it is the argument that narrative force is inevitably sequential, that order makes a difference. These problems, too, are topics for important theoretical reflection.

A final and particularly important theoretical problem is that of formally representing processes that involve multiple contingent sequences of events that are "moving at different speeds," what Abbott has elsewhere called the time-horizon problem.[21] This, too, is a theoretical problem raised chiefly by the literature in historical sociology. I once set out to explain why there are no psychiatrists in American mental hospitals. The exodus, which dates from 1900–1930, reflects not only rational individual mobility decisions that are specifiable annually, but also the attractions of outpatient communities that take decades to develop, and changes in knowledge and social control taking place over even longer periods. How are we to embrace all four processes at once?

There are a number of quick fixes to this problem; none is satisfactory. One is the traditional notion that historical study defines periods or intervals within which sociology studies causes in a basically synchronic manner. There is long-run change, within which we can specify short-run "causality." This argument (which dominates the historical sociology literature at present) unfortunately provides no way of accounting either for long-run (between period) changes or for the effects of long-run changes on short-run processes.[22] Another answer is the more subtle "Markovian" answer

20. Abbott 1988a; Wallerstein 1974.
21. See chapters 1 and 5.
22. See Abbott 1991a on the literature in historical sociology.

that there is in fact no depth to historical causality, that all the effects of the deep past are expressed through an immediate past that shapes the present. Characteristic of both many philosophies (e. g., Whitehead) and of certain methods (e.g., event history analysis), this view makes problematic continuity assumptions about history.[23] If events with duration really exist, which no sensible analyst would deny, the Markovian view has major problems. But beyond these two stopgaps, there is no easy answer to this issue of multiple sequences of differing speeds. Braudel's famous division of history into structure, conjuncture, and event is one way to start, but even there the narrative linkages between the three levels are not theorized. The multiple time-horizon problem remains the central theoretical barrier to moving formalized narrative beyond the simpleminded analysis of stage processes and rational action sequences. We cannot conduct serious institutional analysis without addressing it.

IV Methodological Approaches

Having sketched some basic conceptual issues involved in creating a narrative Methodology, I now turn to reviewing the methodological work in the area. There are three general approaches to narrative methodologies. The first involves some form of what we usually call *modeling*. In this view, although narratives and temporality are important, narratives themselves lack independent ontological status. Hence one aims to discover a stochastic process that has as its various realizations a set of observed narratives. The other two approaches take issue with this assumption. For them, the narratives are seen as viable realities in themselves, rather than simply as a means to uncover an underlying generating process. There are formal and informal approaches to studying these real narratives. *Formal description* seeks a detailed formalization of a relatively small number of stories. *Empirical description* or *empirical categorization* aims at finding classes among larger numbers of stories, which usually have a simpler structure than those of formal description.

A. *Modeling Strategies*

The modeling strategy is followed by a number of literatures. Some extend existing techniques "with a narrative accent." Others evolve new approaches. The three most important literatures involve time series methods, durational methods, and game-theoretic methods.

23. See chapter 5.

Time series methods remain within a fairly traditional variables-centered format. They take for granted the entities-with-attributes model discussed above. But their assumptions about causality embed causality directly in time by making the present of some variable depend on past values of that variable and/or on past values of an error term. They thus achieve a simple narrative character by revising assumption 6, on nonnarrativity.

A variety of writers have tried to make this simple narrative more complicated. A central paper in this line of work is Isaac and Griffin's argument that time series analysis as usually practiced ignores much historical information.[24] Conventional analysis makes profoundly erroneous assumptions about the historical constancy of causal models and thus about the kind of periodization that allows "sociology" within periods of constant cause and "history" across them. Isaac and Griffin argue that time series methods offer a natural format for empirical periodization. One applies the time series models to fractions of the data in a moving window and then analyzes the shifts in coefficients with time.[25]

Time series methods have a variety of strengths and weaknesses. Although models can be assembled across cases and with multiple variables (as in the combined "cross-sectional and pooled" time series models), the burden of statistical assumptions becomes great.[26] The methods are at their best with one case and one variable. Also, even under the Isaac-Griffin approach, they are seriously vulnerable when "events" reach across observation frames, violating assumption 5 above. But they have corresponding strengths. These lie not only in their simplicity and elegance, but also in their accessibility to the researcher used to standard, cross-sectional regression.[27]

The basic assumption of time series approaches, however, remains that there is an underlying process throwing up a realized surface of data. Reality, above all causal reality, lies at the level of the underlying model. Vari-

24. Isaac and Griffin 1989.
25. Isaac, Carlson, and Mathis 1991; Griffin and Isaac 1992.
26. Griffin et al. 1986.
27. In many ways, the new time series methods are part of a general development throughout statistics. Given the power of computers, statisticians increasingly urge recursive application of classical inferential procedures to subsamples of data. They recognize the frankly exploratory character of most applications of inferential statistics and treat the results as sophisticated description rather than as "causal analysis." This movement, associated with Tukey, Efron, and others, has produced important iterative procedures like the jackknife and the bootstrap. (For a discussion of this movement see Efron and Tibshirani 1991.) This impulse towards multiple, descriptive analysis finds its expression (in the general arena of time series analysis) in multiple analyses seeking the proper limits for time- and context-varying parameters. There is, in fact, a substantial statistical literature on finding these limits, which statisticians call the change-point problem.

ables retain their dominance over activity. While the new time series approaches are thus sympathetic to narrative positivism, they are only mildly so. But they do begin to take narrative contingency seriously.

A similar adaptation of existing techniques comes out of durational methods, or as they are usually called in sociology, event history methods. These waiting-time models were originally applied in sociology as part of a larger Markovian analysis of sequential data on marriage and divorce.[28] Later applications, however, have lost much of the implicitly sequential flavor of that application. They simply predict a single transition probability (within the full Markovian matrix) at a time. Narrative here is the waiting time until some event takes place, normally a drastic event like death, divorce, promotion, or organizational disappearance. There are thus two events in each narrative—start and finish—and one aims to predict how long it takes to finish, given various independent variables.

Event history methods have the advantage, for the traditionalist, of retaining the causalist framework "on one side." There are still independent variables. (These are occasionally time-varying independent variables, although the computational price is immense.) On the other side, however, we have events and times, the foundations of narrative. Philosophically, then, these are hybrid methods, with one foot in an event-based and one foot in a variable-based view of the world.

As a result, event history methods have some of the advantages and disadvantages of both sides of the methodological coin. The shifting of cases to a common abstract starting point obscures period effects, although these shifts may be entered as variables, up to a point. Past sequence effects, too, must be entered directly as parameters, rather than modeled directly. Event history models can be broadened to several events at once via the framework of competing risks.[29] However, they quickly become computationally brutal, a problem long noted with nth-order Markov models. The central problem here is one outlined at length by Abbott, but also considered by Ragin and others.[30] Once we start to multiply the variables of interest and to focus on effects of past sequences of events, we rapidly approach the point where most possible combinations of events and variables never occur. It becomes simpler to analyze the event/variable sequences individually as simple narratives; there are fewer of them.

28. General sources on event history are Tuma and Hannan 1984 and Yamaguchi 1991. The original empirical application was Tuma, Hannan, and Groenveld 1979.

29. See, e.g., Smith 1985.

30. See chapter 5 and Ragin 1987.

Nonetheless, event history methods offer another way to move towards narrative analysis within the traditional framework. They retain most of the causal assumptions of the traditional methods and certainly the ontological ones. But again they loosen up the temporal assumptions by embedding causality in the passage of time. Although they are hardly radical, they move towards the temporal pole.

The third strand of the modeling approach to narrative is that of sequential game theory. Game theory breaks with one of the central assumptions of the variable-centered world, assumption 1a on causality via attributes. Although game theory employs variables (in specifying preferences, for example), it articulates those variables through a stage of personal action (the game). Moreover, the whole idea of a game is to reject completely another of the variable-centered assumptions, assumption 2 about casewise independence. Thus game theory moves out of the variable-centered framework from the start, but in a different direction than does narrativism.

About temporality, game theory has a more divided attitude. Much of game theory concerns games "in strategic form." In this form, there is a presumption that all negotiations and exchanges occur before the actual play. The game proper begins with the specification of actors, preferences, rules, and payoffs. There is then one "play," whose optimal result is found (or sometimes shown to be unfindable) by a variety of solution systems. Game theorists have a variety of justifications for why the study of strategic games is in fact useful in temporal (extensive) contexts.[31] Indeed, one can argue that the major advances in game theory in the last decade arose precisely out of moving from temporal to strategic form.

However, a considerable area of game theory involves repeated or stochastic games, where there are repetition, negotiation between games, nested games, and, particularly, incomplete information, which usually prevents the reduction to strategic form. In this branch of game theory we move towards a more explicitly narrative conception of social life. Indeed one of the central figures of narrative positivism, Peter Abell, views his approach to formal description as reconcilable with sequential game theory. The most active exponents of rational choice and game-theoretic thinking in sociology are probably James Coleman and Michael Hechter.[32]

The strengths and weaknesses of game theory are well-known. Most criticism focuses on the unreal assumptions about rationality and preferences. But the central practical problems (of application) lie in two principal

31. See Shubik 1982:67–70.
32. Coleman 1990; Hechter 1987. A good review of sequential game theory is Kreps 1990.

areas. First, there are very many possible games (rules) applicable to a given social situation, with (sometimes) a corresponding variety of solutions. Put more broadly, most of the "explanation" in a rational choice explanation takes place not in the marvelously elegant syntax of strategies, but in the connection between what are usually called variables on the one hand and the actors' preferences and the game's rules on the other. It is all very well to know that some social choice situations are sensitive to small perturbations in parameters because of "tipping" in rational choices.[33] But what makes rational choice an "explanation" of a riot or set of riots is the demonstration that the parameters involved were in fact near those tipping points. This demonstration is a matter of measurement, not theory.

The second great problem for rational choice– and game-theoretic explanations lies in their normal failure to account for preferences in any serious way. There is of course research on this matter, but in practical applications, such explanations always make preference exogenous, thus again placing central aspects of explanation outside their reach. (It is also important to note that in most forms rational choice theory accepts the variable-centered assumptions about the strong definedness of actors and events.)

Rational choice and game-theoretic approaches thus form a useful bridge between extensions of traditional methods and direct narrative methods. They retain the belief in an underlying generating model, albeit a choice model. And they prefer strategic to extended forms. But sequential games with imperfect information are in fact important and well-studied narrative structures. They have the advantages of clarity and elegance and the disadvantages of indeterminacy and extensive assumptions about preferences. Their combination of substantive theory with clear applicability makes them perhaps the most interesting among the modeling techniques.[34]

Modeling strategies have a variety of strengths and weaknesses when applied to narratives; the analyst will wish to choose them, and choose among them, accordingly. They all take the common form of seeking a latent structure—a generating stochastic process, a set of game rules—that produces narrative patterns as something of a by-product. Within that framework they take a variety of different positions. Time series analysis tends to focus on small numbers of variables and on single cases because multivariable, multicase analyses with serious "contingencies" raise problems. Durational

33. On tipping models, see Rashevsky 1968 and Granovetter 1978.
34. For some illustrations of dynamic programming solutions to "dynamic choice theory," see the references in Abbott 1983: 144–45, n. 31.

methods look at lots of cases, and often lots of variables, but generally assume away period effects; they falter when asked to confront serious sequence effects, multiple events, and complex narratives. Game-theoretic methods can study sequences seriously, but only within a framework of fairly stringent assumptions and with surprising indeterminacy of application. It is not surprising, then, that these modeling approaches have been ignored by analysts deeply interested in narrative per se.

B. *Formal Description*

Both formal description and empirical categorization reject the "underlying generating process" approach. They treat narratives as generated by an inherent logic of events rather than by a transcendent logic of causal variables. Where they differ is in analysis of that logic. Those interested in formal description aim for a substantive, theoretical account of the event logic itself. In Abbott's term, they have a substantive theory of enchainment. Those interested in empirical categorization, chiefly Abbott himself, wish to leave the question of enchainment open. There are other differences, as we shall see. Formal description has tended to focus on a micro (in the general sense) level; narratives are for this approach exchanges between identifiable actors. Empirical categorization views narrative more as a set of events happening to a single and often amorphous actor. As a result, formal description tends to see more branching in sequences, while empirical categorization looks more at unilinear stages. As it happens, these are not likely to be permanent differences. Rather they arise out of the different empirical problems that served as stimuli for the various narrative positivists in developing methodological tools.

There are basically two practical versions of formal description. One is the "event structure analysis" developed by David Heise out of his interest in modeling small group interactions and formalizing ethnography. The other is Peter Abell's "comparative narrative analysis," arising out of Abell's attempt to model interactions within producer cooperatives in Africa.

Heise's "event structure analysis" has been under development for some time. His early work saw events as generated out of an attempt to restore harmony between desired and actual affect; it was not aimed at multistep narratives. Later, he moved towards a more general and multistep conception. An excellent recent application of the resulting event structure analysis to a classic "narrative" problem is Griffin's attempt to apply it to lynchings.[35]

35. Heise 1979, 1986, 1989, 1991; Corsaro and Heise 1990. For an application by someone else, see Griffin 1993.

Event structure analysis begins with definition of a lexicon of events. A formal description of some narrative of those events is then developed by an interactive computer algorithm that asks the respondent to tell the computer whether downstream event b required upstream event a, and so on across the time-ordered set of events. The computer uses this information on necessary causality to prepare a formal diagram of dependencies among the events, a diagram that captures the underlying narrative structure.

Heise's models have a theoretical foundation in the formal theories of Fararo, Skvoretz, and others.[36] These view social reality as generated by recipe systems that "produce" events and that are ordered in a set of priorities (that constitute institutions). The underlying model is in some ways close to that of rational choice—actors choose which recipe to invoke in accord with a set of priorities (preferences)—but differs in that action is not necessarily strategic. Rather events are triggered by their prior conditions' being met. The model is thus founded on a necessary cause conception of historical causation, which is both a strength (for its clarity and ease of analysis) and a weakness (since the most reasonable idea of historical causality probably involves some mixture of sufficient and necessary causality).

As developed by Heise, the system has a number of properties beyond this dependence on necessary causality. It assumes partial order of events; mixing events of varying durations is problematic. Events are thus bitlike and discrete (cf. assumption 5). Yet there is no rule against independent story lines; there can be multiple parallel narratives. However, nonrecursion (cycling) is not allowed. Simulations can be run—and the "generative grammar" of the narrative sequence revised—until there is a reasonable fit to observed sequences. Heise's system also provides for "generalizing" the narratives by making event descriptions more global ("colligating" more broadly) and repeating the event structure analysis.[37]

Abell's comparative narrative method is slightly different. Unlike Heise, Abell has focused on the development of pure formalism more than on that of computer programs. Also, his substantive theory is much closer to rational action theory. And Abell's fundamental goal is generalization; like Abbott, he is fascinated by the search for typical sequences of events.

Abell's methods proceed from a strong formal theory of action.[38] He starts with the "generalization of events" that with Heise comes at the end

36. Fararo and Skvoretz 1984; Heise 1989.

37. On colligation, see Abbott 1984 and Abell 1987. Griffin 1993 considers this problem also.

38. I summarize from Abell 1987, but see also Abell 1993.

of analysis. There are eight global types of activity, created by crossing three dichotomies: doing unintentionally versus doing intentionally, doing actively versus forbearing to do, and doing positively versus preventing. These eight activities are then allowed to various sets of actors in a narrative and placed in four separate contexts: intentional premises of action, cognitive premises of action, actual preconditions of action, and consequences of action. (This unpacks matters that Heise runs together.) Abell's theory thus leads to a highly formalized and abstracted representation of action.

To this Abell has latterly added substantive assumptions embodying his commitment to rational choice theory.[39] Thus for Abell, theory construction has three stages: (1) locate stable correlations, (2) provide narrative structures that show how those correlations arise, (3) derive these from the relevant games of actors. In practice, Abell has focused on steps 2 and 3. He begins with a "narrative table" locating actual and cognitive conditions of actions, actual actions, and narratively significant outcomes. He then produces a formal representation (in digraphs with suitable properties) of the narrative, which is then analyzed for abstraction (making the events more generic) and generalization (comparison with other narratives—note that Heise's "generalization" is Abell's "abstraction"). These analyses are stated in the formal language of set theory and hence lead to hierarchical classifications of resemblance rather than to the quantitative (metric) measures of Abbott's methods.[40]

Abell's analysis devotes less attention to actual elicitation of narrative connection than does Heise's. Rather than automated computer queries and an algorithm for generated narrative structure, Abell directly uses the sequential intuitions of himself and the group he studies to establish what "leads to" what. This conception of A leading to B in Abell is more a sufficient cause connection than the necessary connection of Heise. But perhaps by asking the question in such an open fashion, Abell leaves room for the INUS conditions (insufficient but nonredundant parts of unnecessary but sufficient conditions) of Mackie, which are probably the best approximation of our everyday beliefs about cause.[41]

Formal description is thus a well-served approach to narrative analysis. Heise and Abell give firmly grounded, analytically clear methods for examining social reality narratively. (I have not covered the extensive approaches

39. Abell 1991, 1993.
40. Some examples will be found in Abell 1987, although the explicit game theory connection is more recent (e.g., Abell 1993).
41. Mackie 1974.

to narrative analysis within the artificial intelligence community.)[42] At present, formal description does best when applied to small numbers of rich narratives. Its capacities for generalization and categorization are not yet strong. But the methods have a firm connection to substantive theory, thus beginning to cross the theory/methods chasm generated by our methodological devotion to causality. Above all such methods are explicit in their commitment to construing reality in stories.

C. *Empirical Categorization*

The chief proponent of empirical categorization is Abbott. Unlike Heise and Abell, Abbott has not based his methods on a particular substantive theory like production theory or rational choice. In part, this reflects a perspective on sequence and order originating in the historical sociology of institutions. As Abbott has argued from his earliest work, at the institutional level there are a variety of mechanisms propelling stories forward: choice, accident, functionality, institutionalization, historicism, force, and so on.[43] A flexible methodology must not commit to any particular enchainment. A second characteristic of Abbott's approach, its concentration on single-line sequences, also partly reflects origins, in this case Abbott's reliance on the philosophy of history literature and structural literary theory. Both are relatively focused on unilinear narratives. Although such narratives may have branching structures, at any given point only one branch is followed. Unilinearity also reflects a certain practical concern; many empirical literatures (e.g., life course, criminal and occupational careers) need unilinear methods.

Empirically, Abbott has divided sequences into two types.[44] The first are stage processes like professionalization where there is a temporal succession of unique events. The second are more complex "careers" in which events repeat. Abbott's methods themselves are borrowed from the interdisciplinary sequence comparison community. Following the lead of mathematical psychologists and archeologists, he has employed constrained unidimensional scaling for unique event sequences, as in his study of professionalization.[45] For repeated events, he has employed optimal matching techniques drawn from DNA analysis and related areas. These techniques begin by establishing a "distance" between sequences in terms of the num-

42. See, e.g., Schank and Abelson 1977; Dietterich and Michalski 1985.
43. See Abbott 1983.
44. The best review of my methods at the time this paper was originally published was Abbott 1990b. Since that time, there are Abbott 1991b, 1995b, and Abbott and Tsay 2000.
45. For the psychologists and archeologists, see Hodson, Kendall, and Tăutu 1971 and Hubert 1979. An example of the scaling approach is Abbott 1991b.

ber of insertions, deletions, and substitutions necessary to transform one sequence into another. By assigning varying costs to these insertions, deletions, and substitutions, the analyst can closely represent degrees of local resemblance. The algorithms then use dynamic programming to minimize the overall distance between two sequences. The matrix of these resemblances (across the dataset as a whole) is then used in various categorization procedures—scaling, clustering, and the like. Abbott has applied the technique to occupational careers, to histories of welfare states, to ritual dances, and to folktales. He has also begun to establish reliability information on the effects of coding perturbation on the method.[46]

In current work, Abbott is extending the techniques from the discrete events case to the continuous variables one, aiming to provide new weapons for the multicase, multivariable time series problem. This means reconceptualizing cases' behavior in the continuous variable space in terms of "trajectories" of "events." Events are here defined as neighborhoods in continuous space, and narrative methods are justified because the vast majority of these neighborhoods are empty.[47]

The various techniques of narrative positivism relate in a variety of ways. As I have argued, the most fundamental difference is between those techniques that are extensions or adaptations of variable-centered modeling techniques and those that are "direct narrative" techniques. In principle, the former treat narrative sequences as emanations from a model of causal variables while the latter treat them as possessing an inherent logic. Those inherent logics may themselves be "models" of action, however. In Heise's methods as in sequential game theory, there are underlying "models" of events that produce the surface sequences. These are, however, models of activity, not of reified variables. Thus the sharp distinction between modeling strategies and direct narrative ones is bridged to some extent by these techniques.

The decision between strictly narrative methods based on models of event logic (sequential game theory, Heise, and to some extent Abell) and those not (Abbott and to some extent Abell) involves a profound theoretical problem. The question is over the relation of generating mechanisms and types of sequences. If the categories of sequences related to a given generating logic are relatively separable from those related to another—if the gen-

46. These examples have been cited a number of times throughout: Abbott and Hrycak 1990, Abbott and DeViney 1992, Abbott and Forrest 1986, Forrest and Abbott 1990, respectively. On the perturbation issue, see the last of these.

47. See chapter 5.

erating mapping is "onto"—then attention focuses at once on generating mechanisms. If there prove to be many generating logics for any given sequence or sequence pattern, however—if the mapping is simply "into"—then attention shifts to patterns themselves and other things that might lead to their differentiation. At present this is an empirical question. Its answer may well vary from substantive area to substantive area.

There is also considerable variety among these methods in definitions of events. Under the event history approach, for example, there are two simple events: start and finish. Events have few characteristics. For Heise, events are a lexicon drawn from expert actors (who are taken as experts on events, but not on sequences of events). Abell, too, takes his events as simple interactive "doings" in stories (although he takes informants as experts on sequence as well). For Heise and Abell, events at this simple level may be represented at new levels of abstraction, gradually removing their content until they become, in Abell's system, absolute abstractions like forbearance. By contrast, Abbott's events have often been large historical happenings like "the rise of medical education" which he is concerned to indicate with "occurrences" like foundings of medical schools. Particularly as a theorist, Abbott has worried much more than others about the nature of events, a nature that has profound consequences for their measurement. Abbott's reconceptualization of complex combinations of variables as "events" has served as an explicit translation between variable-centered methodologies and narrative ones, an issue with which other authors have been less concerned.[48]

Yet the major techniques of formal description and empirical categorization are in many ways complementary. Heise's and Abell's techniques are basically addressed to actual interactions between identifiable actors. Abbott's are most effective with successions of things happening to a single actor. In both Heise and Abell, generalization takes place via simplification of the event representations to cover a broader variety of phenomena. Abell adds to this the use of homomorphism as a means of classification. Abbott generalizes directly by comparison of sequences, there being no analogue to simplification of events.

It is important to realize that none of these differences is absolute. Abbott *could* create models allowing for simplification of events, and there are in fact dynamic tree resemblance algorithms that could be used by Abell- and Heise-type methods to produce the direct resemblance measures that make Abbott's techniques more effective at empirical categorization. Put

48. See also Poole's work (Poole 1983; Poole and Roth 1989a,b) for this combinatoric conception of events.

more broadly, it is clear that "direct narrative" approaches will ultimately coalesce into a flexible package for direct analysis of narrative structures that allows for a variety of options and approaches within the general approach of narrative positivism. At present, Heise's approach is the best for uncovering narrative structure in particular events, Abell's seems to be the most effective for general comparison of complex interactions, and Abbott's is the best for analyzing unilinear careers like life courses and occupational histories.[49]

Five years ago there was no "movement" one could call narrative positivism. There were a few isolated workers addressing similar problems from different angles suggested by their own empirical interests. Today it has become clear that these efforts make up a fairly coherent assault on a central set of methodological issues, and, more broadly, an attempt to refound methodology on a clear articulation with sociological theories of action.

49. At this point in the original paper was a guide for where to find the methods. This guide is now completely outdated. For my own techniques, the current best guidance is in Abbott and Tsay 2000. CLUSTALG, a biological program for sequence analysis, has now been adapted for social science use, but Rohwer's TDA is probably the best generally available program.

PART THREE

Time and Social Structure

Temporality and Process
in Social Life

[S]o strange a dreaminess did there then reign all over the ship and all over the sea, only broken by the intermitting dull sound of the sword, that it seemed as if this were the Loom of Time, and I myself were a shuttle mechanically weaving away at the Fates. . . . this savage's sword, thought I, which thus finally shapes and fashions both warp and woof, this easy indifferent sword must be chance—aye, chance, free will, and necessity—no wise incompatible—all interweavingly working together. The straight warp of necessity, not to be swerved from its ultimate course—its every alternating vibration, indeed, only tending to that; free will still free to ply her shuttle between given threads, and chance, though restrained in its play within the right lines of necessity, and sideways in its motions directed by free will, though thus prescribed by both, chance by turns rules either, and has the last featuring blow at events.

Herman Melville, *Moby Dick*, "The Mat Maker" (chapter 47)

For years now, the renewed contact between history and the social sciences has promised revolutionary changes for both parties. Yet the changes have not come. This dawdling bewilders us. There is only one social process, and of that singular social process there should be a singular knowledge. Why have we not found it?

Of the many possible answers to this question, I would like to focus here on those that examine the relation of "past" and "present." One common way to distinguish between sociology and history is to say that the one studies the present and the other studies the past. I wish to investigate what is involved in speaking of present and past, in thinking about their connection to one another, in imagining a social process that connects the two to produce both change and stability.

I would like to thank Ragnvald Kalleberg and Fredrik Engelstad, organizers of the Fifth National Sociology Conference, at Tjøme, 6–9 September 1994, for both the invitation to speak and their hospitality whilst I was in Norway. As I noted in the prologue, the elaborate whaling example on which the paper is based derives from the conference site, near the great whaling center of Tønsberg. The paper was originally published in F. Engelstad and R. Kalleberg, eds., *Social Time and Social Change* (Oslo: Scandinavian University Press, 1999), 28–61; reprinted with permission of the Scandinavian University Press.

Rather than conduct this investigation through a purely formal analysis, however, I would like to use an ongoing empirical example, which I shall view through the three separate lenses provided by three important texts on the relation of past and present. The example is a local one: the invention by Svend Foyn of the grenade harpoon. The three texts are Bergson's *Time and Free Will*, Mead's *Philosophy of the Present*, and Whitehead's *Process and Reality*. I begin with a brief discussion of Foyn's invention. This leads into a discussion of "the present" as an epoch, in which I invoke the aid of Bergson. Bergson's work raises the issue of a purely mentalist account of the continuity of past and present, which in turns brings me to the work of Mead. In response to Mead, it becomes necessary to recast the issue of past and present entirely, a task for which I invoke the aid of Whitehead. The paper closes with a sketch of a concept of time reconciling history and sociology. In this complex itinerary, my aim is not to drown a defenseless example in the impracticalities of the philosophers, but rather to channel those impracticalities into a combined concept on which we could build a research practice presuming the identity of history and sociology.

I The Pasts and Presents of Svend Foyn

Let me begin with the example. Svend Foyn, so the tour guides tell us, invented the grenade harpoon. One immediately wonders when this invention took place. Yet the great historian of whaling in this period—A. O. Johnsen—does not make the date clear. From 1864 on, Foyn appears to have used grenade guns and harpoon guns, although usually as separate weapons. He had experimented with various combined versions from the early 1860s, when his highly successful sealing expeditions began to suffer under intense competition and he began to realize that, in gross profits, one blue whale was worth about four hundred seals. In 1870 he applied for and received a patent for the grenade harpoon. The episode of invention reached its practical culmination in 1873, when Foyn got a "ten-year patent on his catching system," guaranteeing him a monopoly on modern whaling in northern Norway through the 1882 season.[1]

1. Tønnessen and Johnsen 1982:32. This highly stylized example is of course chosen to honor the conference site of Tjøme, not because I have any knowledge of whaling, my entire contact with which consists of having eaten whale steak about thirty-five years ago at a Norwegian restaurant whose name I cannot recall but which was located in an alley between Boylston and Eliot Streets in Boston, right behind the old Trailways bus station. I wish I could claim connection with New Bedford, Nantucket, or some other New England whaling town, but although a New Englander, I grew up twenty miles inland. I must thank the conference organizers for an interesting tour of Tønsberg, where I first heard about Svend Foyn. Since my

If Foyn's "invention" could thus be said to have taken place over a six- or a ten-year period, depending on how we view it, its predecessors reached back many decades. William Congreve had apparently built, designed, and used shell harpoons fired from guns in the 1820s. In practice, however, Congreve's "rocket" proved an unaccountable failure. As Johnsen puts it, "a great many whales were killed, but they all sank, and further attempts were abandoned." Again, by 1860, there were in the U.S. 22 patents on versions of whale shells, including one with a shell-harpoon-line combination. The American Thomas Roys invented in the mid-1860s a rocket-powered shell harpoon that was launched from a dory, typically resulting in a Nantucket sleigh ride and, as likely as not, an irretrievably sunken whale. Roys had many imitators. In Denmark, Gaetano Amici patented a grenade harpoon fired from a cannon in 1867. In England, George Welch patented a grenade harpoon in 1867 that differed from Foyn's only in having a rigid rather than an articulated head.

Such a spate of predecessors may leave us wondering what exactly it was that Svend Foyn *did* do, besides acquire the ten-year monopoly of northern whaling that made him the richest man in Vestfold. But to truly understand the situation, we must resist our immediate urge to dig still further down into the details to find the "ultimate invention" that was "really" Svend Foyn's. Rather we must move in precisely the opposite direction, reflecting about Foyn's place in a larger change. As we read Johnsen, it becomes clear that there are two great epochs of whaling—premodern and modern. They differ in many ways: sailing vessels versus steam vessels, rowboats versus catching ships, right whales versus rorquals. What we *can* say with certainty is that the transition from the one to the other occurred in part through the person and the expeditions of Svend Foyn.

Each of these two periods of whaling was in some sense "a present." A historical epoch or present may be defined as a period within which something—in this case a set of social parameters prescribing the dimensions and character of whaling—does not change. Such an epoch might be as short as an afternoon for a group of children playing a specific game or as long as a century for Braudel contemplating the somewhat larger games of Phillip II.

interest in this example is purely theoretical, I have used only one source, the much shortened English version of *Den moderne hvalfangsts historie* of J. N. Tønnessen and A. O. Johnsen (Tønnessen and Johnsen 1982). All uncited facts about Norwegian whaling derive from its opening chapters. Since Johnsen actually wrote the portion of this history on which I rely (the first volume), I have referred to him as sole author in text.

Knowledge of the causal regularities of such a present is sociological knowledge. It is in this sense that sociologists often say that historians study particular events while sociologists study general laws governing events. The "general laws" are the causal regularities that govern such a present, that make it an epoch within which take place various "histories"—viewed by the sociologists as so many random chains determined by the sociological regularities. But the historians rightly argue that these general laws of the sociologists are themselves circumscribed by larger historical changes; they apply only within historically defined epochs or presents, and are thus, in their own way, particulars. Sociologists retort that there must be a general theory of how such epochs are produced, to which historians reply. . . . But you know the story. Every particular epoch is generated by larger universal laws, which hold true only with an even larger particular epoch, which was generated by still larger universal laws, which hold true only within . . . and so on and on.

Just such a set of Chinese boxes is involved in the story of Svend Foyn. At the first level, Foyn's sociological present is the world of marine mammal hunting in the early 1860s: the increasing competition for seals, the various failed expedients for catching rorquals, the strong markets for oil and guano. On the basis of these factors, one could envision, given sufficient information about weather and timing, a model predicting success or failure of whaling expeditions in the early 1860s. (As it happens, random variation was so great that such a model would be unlikely to explain much variance.) But the parameters of that model would soon be sharply changed by Foyn's inventions, by the falling price of oil after 1869, and by the arrival of new competitors within whaling itself. There would be, that is, a "new present" by the mid-1870s. (I shall later refer to these as Present 1 and Present 2, respectively.)

Only a historical argument—that is, a narrative—could move us from one of these presents to the next. In this "larger" narrative, moving along decade by decade, the sociological presents become particulars subject to the narrative of decadal social change. They are beads on a narrative string. But of course, sociologists could easily argue that such a narrative must itself obey a set of still larger, more general rules governing social processes in the whole of the nineteenth century. These rules might involve such things as levels of interdependence of markets, correlations of inventions in areas like shipbuilding and whale catching (through their common dependence on changes in steel or iron manufacture), and so on. But these larger sociologies would then be beads on an even larger narrative string; the one enigma repeats itself at each level. Historians would therefore speak of an epochal change of these larger rules that would itself require narrative explanation century by century.

Like many other temporal enigmas, this one is a version of paradoxes of the Eleatics. Consider the paradox of the arrow. While at any given instant the arrow is in one place, fully occupying that place and motionless, yet over time, the arrow moves from bow to target. Motion cannot lie in the motionless instants, and yet the arrow moves. For Zeno and Parmenides, such a paradox disproved the divisibility of time and space; it showed the universe to be a single continuum. But the application here is both more simple and more paradoxical. If sociologists can show a stable causal world in some present—an arrow complete and motionless in one place—how then can they explain the production of new causal coefficients in new presents? If historians by contrast can explain the changes, is the regularity of the sociological present simply a mirage, a focusing on the large digits on the odometer (which aren't moving) to the exclusion of the small digits (which are)? The "larger" versions of this problem—in which the whole nineteenth century becomes a causal "present"—are simply larger-scale versions of the same enigma.

Svend Foyn's invention thus raises the central issue relating history and sociology, the issue of the relation of past and present. Now a historical moment is not our most common idea of a present. We first think of a present as a moment in the conscious, personal experience of individuals. We denote by the word "present" that period of time to which we as individuals have immediate cognitive and conative access and we distinguish it in relation to a past and a future. The present is neither the past, cognitively accessible only in memory and conatively forbidden by its irrevocability, nor yet the future, cognitively available only to imagination and conatively dependent on chains of action yet undone. Like historical epochs, such present "moments" can be short or long; in speaking of a personal present, we can mean the duration of a lecture, or of a conference, or of a life stage. But the larger uses feel metaphorical. Our foundational concept of the present derives from the immediate personal experience of a certain kind of consciousness, the immediate sense of "here and now."

Rather than directly analyze the historical issue of past and present, then, we can perhaps borrow from writers who have addressed that question within the realm of personal consciousness. Our questions seem to be simple ones. How are the various presents are linked together? Is there, indeed, really such a thing as an extended "present," or should we rather imagine a sequence of disconnected instants? What are the relations of the various sizes of presents, the long and the short? Perhaps those who have studied the temporal flow of conscious experience can provide us with analogies applicable to the social process.

II Temporality in Bergson

One such author is Henri Bergson. The "Essai sur les données immédiates de la conscience," translated into English as *Time and Free Will*, was Bergson's first major work, written when he was in his twenties.[2] It comprises three long chapters: one on the problem of intensity and extensity, one on the sense of duration, and one on free will. The three chapters partly answer the questions just raised, but in the process, they raise new questions as disturbing as those they settle.

Descartes provides Bergson with his starting point, the relation between mind and body. Bergson asks whether the same concept of magnitude applies to mental states and physical things. (He will rest his entire analysis of time on the resounding no with which he answers this question.) Bergson from the start differentiates the measure of physical states, for which his model is the numerical contrast of greater or less, and the measure of mental states, which he defines as a "progressive stepping in of new elements, which can be detected in the fundamental emotion and which seem to increase its magnitude, although in reality they do nothing more than alter its nature" (11). Bergson follows this argument through a number of cases: the feeling of grace, responses to art, moral feelings like pity. All are changes that "correspond less to variations of degree than to differences of state or nature" (17). Even in more surface emotions like joy, the reality is of "a qualitative progress [of effort through more and more involved parts of the body] and an increasing complexity, indistinctly perceived" (26). In summary, "superficial or deep-seated, violent or reflective, the intensity of [these] feelings always consists in the multiplicity of simple states which consciousness dimly discerns in them" (31). This multiplicity, Bergson holds, is a matter of quality, not quantity.[3]

2. All parenthetical page references are to the Allen Unwin edition of Pogson's translation of Bergson (Bergson 1910).

3. Bergson even pursues this argument into the world of sensation, the classical site of the Lockean and Humean epistemology (36). In discussing heat, light, and sound, he is at pains to show that the only true magnitude involved is the muscular reaction we develop in response to stimuli; for example we measure the loudness of sound by a sense of the degree of effort required for us as individuals to produce such sounds (44 ff.). In a felicitous phrase, he contrasts the quantitative "increase of sensation" with the qualitative "sensation of increase" (48).

In its own time, Bergson's sharp differentiation of extensive magnitude from inner multiplicity (72) was sharply attacked. The set-theoretic theory of order and quantity then being created by Peano, Lebesgue, and others implied that there is no difference between counting inches of extension and counting the number of muscles involved in a sensation of effort.[4] But it is suggestive that important heterodox writers in diverse traditions have invoked precisely the same argument as did Bergson: that inclusion is a fundamentally different order relationship than ordinality. Whewell's concept of colligation is one of these heterodoxies. For Whewell, events were to be "colligated" into larger events as many battles make up a larger war, or many painters make up a larger style. Such colligation was quite different from classification with its ordered hierarchy of abstraction. Another example is Louis Dumont's analysis of hierarchy in classical India, which argues that the caste experience as lived by Indians did not correspond to the Western concept of an ordinal stratification, but rather to a notion of nested inclusions. We should also recall that there is some mathematical warrant for thinking inclusion to be different from ordinality; set inclusion is a much more general concept than is the arithmetic succession concept on which hang the Peano axioms and the resultant theory of ordinal ranking.[5]

Nothing is more crucial to Bergson's enterprise than this distinction of order into two types. For he feels that the association of "spatial," quantitative ideas of order with the inclusional "duration" of temporality profoundly warps our image of time. The different properties seen in the two different kinds of comparison—extension and intension, magnitude and multiplicity, quantity and quality—culminate in Bergson's second chapter in the two different dimensions of human experience, space and time.

First, Bergson argues that we are deceived when we fail "to distinguish between time as quality and time as quantity" (75). He recalls the argument of the preceding chapter that the multiplicity of psychic states is qualitative; we should therefore perceive them as whole units, much as we perceive a song by "gathering a qualitative impression of the whole series [of sounds]" (86). But all too often, when we measure time, we have recourse to arbitrary procedures that represent it in space. These arbitrary procedures violate the psychic states by reducing to nothing their interpenetration and permeation, thereby making them absolutely separable (89). Perhaps, Bergson argues, we can by reflection suspend all these remappings into the world of

4. See Dubbey 1970: 110, 118, on mathematical theories of order.
5. See Whewell 1968; Dumont 1980.

extension, and then begin to understand psychic states and indeed time itself—like the song—within the world of "pure duration."

On page 100, Bergson finally gives us his first definition of this "pure
duration":

> Pure duration is the form which the succession of our conscious
> states assumes when our ego lets itself live, when it refrains from sep-
> arating its present state from its former states. . . . Nor need it forget
> its former states: it is enough that, in recalling these states, it does
> not set them alongside its actual state as one point alongside another,
> but forms both the past and the present states into one organic
> whole, as happens when we recall the notes of a tune, melting, so to
> speak, into one another.

Duration is thus a world in which we smoothly move to experience whatever length of time is present for us at this particular moment. Again, Bergson has recourse to metaphor. If we hold a note of a tune too long, it seems
wrong not because of its own length, but rather because it redefines the
whole direction and shape of the phrase. Here, he says, we have "succession
without distinction" (105). This concept of duration, in which the immediate present's meaning is given by its place in a larger whole, is indeed very
closely akin to Whewell's idea of colligation.

No clock time seems possible within this "order" of duration. Bergson
specifically denies that succession, per se, is anything more than another
surreptitious mapping of temporal processes into space. "Before" and "after"—these reduce the integrated, permeated whole of duration to a succession of moments in a homogeneous medium, and hence to space. By
contrast, pure duration is the sense of succession a point would have when
passing along a line. That is, it is a zero-dimensional being's sense of one-
dimensional space. Any sense of that space that allows us to subdivide it,
that allows "separation" and "juxtaposition," presumes viewing the flow of
the line from outside it, from a point in two-dimensional space not on the
line. The zero-dimensional being's sense of the one-dimensional line can be
created only by imagining various line segments of various sizes, all of
which contain himself. These are multiple, overlapping "presents." Only
those *off* the line can see the line as made up of sequentially separable segments of equal lengths somehow pushed together to make a line.

Duration thus provides our first potential borrowing from the temporality theories based on consciousness. It has a number of properties. It is,
first, "centered" on a person or a moment, always located with respect to a
particular; in technical language, duration is "indexical." But while duration

is thus always located by reference to a particular point, it can denote periods of varying sizes. Durations can be multiple, overlapping; "now" can mean not one but many different periods. Third, duration is ordered. But this order is only in terms of inclusion; one duration includes another, but cannot precede or follow it. It is not clear how this inclusion works. If we follow Bergson's metaphor of the melody, we can think about motifs as "individual" durations within the longer duration of a melody. (Consider the three note descending and ascending figures at the opening of Grieg's first "Peer Gynt" suite, for example; move the motifs and the phrase is destroyed, move the notes within a motif and the motif is destroyed.) In summary, duration is indexical, multiple, and inclusive.[6]

Reconstructing our full experience of time, however, requires comparison of durations, and Bergson therefore next considers whether duration be measurable. This inevitably involves him in otherness. For the heart of duration as Bergson conceives it is the *inner* experience of psychic states "melting into one another" (like the overlapping presents). How then do we understand the duration of other objects, which have duration just as do we?

Even the simplest understanding of others' duration involves two movements, from other to self and self to other. But Bergson devotes his attention only to the first of these, which he regards as involving the fundamental error of taking external clock time as a measure of personal time. For Bergson, the imposition of clock time on inner experience is utterly arbitrary. The clock pendulum like Zeno's arrow has externality without succession; each position is radically distinct from the last, never coexisting with it. Our experience, on the other hand, has succession without externality; it never consists of radically distinct moments, but always of overlapping and inclusive presents. Temporal measurement as customarily understood, then, consists of an illegitimate correspondence of duration with space that is made possible by the connecting concept of simultaneity—the "intersection of time and space" (110).

Clock time thus cannot provide comparative measurement of durations. Yet Bergson offers no alternatives. His analysis of duration is completely depth psychological. It is the Freudian id that lives in the world of real duration, a world of interpenetration and melding. Duration seems confused,

6. This descent and ascent was a popular motif—used as a theme by Dvořák in the *Slavonic Dance*, op. 46, no. 8, by Mozart in the opening of the Clarinet Quintet, K. 581, and by Vaughan Williams as the first principal theme in "The Lark Ascending." In fact reversing its two parts doesn't make the whole meaningless. It produces the background vamp for the third movement of D'Indy's "Symphony on a French Mountain Air."

changing, and inexpressible by comparison with the clear and precise and impersonal world of the socialized ego. Even language, for Bergson, assists in the condensation process by which clock time regularizes the inner world of duration. Language, Bergson argues, teaches us to talk about mental states as if they did not interpenetrate and pervade one another.

Others' time is thus meaningless in Bergson's account. "Real" time is personal. Only the mechanical necessity of interaction requires the imagination of a homogeneous temporal medium—clock time—through which discussion becomes possible. Bergson writes bitterly of ideas that "float on the surface like dead leaves on the water of a pond. . . . Among these are the ideas which we receive ready made . . ." (135). It is because these social ideas are unimportant, unassimilated to the profound world of real duration, that they become capable of being categorized and logicized. In this Bergson writes small what is writ large in the creation of such things as time zones and official time. Social time is always enforced, always clock time. And Bergson felt that it ultimately created the personality it requires: "An inner life with well distinguished moments and with clearly characterized states will answer better the requirements of social life" (139). The sovereign self must surrender crucial temporal qualities to live in society.

Links between contemporaneous durations of different individuals are thus not provided in Bergson's account; we shall have to seek them elsewhere. But Bergson spends his third chapter addressing the connection of durations within the individual, the linking of past and present. This too is one of my central questions. And for Bergson as for so many others the central issue in links between personal past and present is that of freedom and determination.

Like most advocates of free will, Bergson admits to *some* immediate connection between successive states of mind, but will not admit to determination. Often, he says, what appears to be a sequence of determining mental states leading up to an action is simply something we discover in retrospect—a rationalization or justification. We deliberate when in fact our minds are already decided.

Even so, Bergson is not arguing for simple associationism, but for something quite the reverse, for the indivisibility of concrete particulars (cf. the Eleatics). He illustrates the dangers of particularist associationism with the example of a rose's smell bringing back memories of childhood. The smell is the same to all; but the result of the smell in his nose differs radically from the result in another's (161). A central postulate for Bergson is thus the transcendent unity of the self, the irreducibly connected nature of an individual's psychic states. Connectedness is, like containment, a recurrent Bergsonian notion. Indeed, the two imply one another. For Bergson immediately argues that the soul is not made up of generic, separable states like love and hate but that "each one of us has his own way of loving and hating and this love or hatred reflects his whole personality" (164). Thus the whole person appears in any part—again the Bergsonian idea of connectedness, containment, and inclusion.

Connectedness takes concrete form in free action. Freedom, Bergson argues, is merely the expression of the indivisible self; "the outward manifestation of this inner state" (165). Education, when it is not "properly assimilated," gives rise to a "parasitic self" within, which "continually encroaches on the other" (166). (Note the closeness of this doctrine, although with reverse valence, to Mead's concept of "the I and the me.") For Bergson, freedom is individual in its essence.

This radical individualism of freedom raises the issue of an individual's compromise of his own freedom, the idea that acts are not free but determined by prior acts. Libertarians rejected this position by identifying consciousness with the ability to conceive of doing other than what we actually do end up doing. (This is the game theory view of the world.) But Bergson notes that two alternatives facing us are not two absolute alternatives, but rather two directions. We turn first towards one possibility. But that very turning influences the way we think about the second possibility and so on. The choices never remain exactly the same.[7] Our process of decision thus involves "a self which lives and develops by means of its very hesitations until the free action drops from it like an over-ripe fruit" (176).

In a brilliant continuation of this analysis, Bergson demolishes the geometrical metaphors of paths and directions in decision making—the current foundation of game theory—on the ground that these "admit the possibility of representing time by space and a succession by a simultaneity" (180). Deliberation is not an "oscillation in space," in simultaneity, but a "dynamic progress in which the self and its motives like real living beings are in a constant state of becoming" (183).

On prediction, Bergson makes the same argument. To predict, the determinists say, is to know *all* the antecedents of an act. But if the order and succession and permeation of psychic states are integral to action, then it follows that to truly know *all* the antecedents of an act is to do it.

Now that it is completed by this analysis of freedom, one can see that the Bergsonian argument makes a coherent whole. For this analysis of determi-

7. Bergson is giving us a psychological version of the paradox of Achilles and the tortoise; one situation always changes while we act on the alternative.

nation and free will rests squarely on the concept of nested, inclusive durations. From the present action we look back over longer and longer durational units. Each unit contains the entire sequence leading from some past
point to the present, and each unit contains numerous shorter durations
within it. At various places, game theory would speak of a branch point; A
leads to B or C. But Bergson would say that even to lean towards one alternative is to change the way we view the other. Simultaneous alternatives are
a mirage. The route to the present is then a dynamic process by which a
coherent, indivisible self expresses and creates itself, a sequence of nested
durations. Bergson believed in constraint in various forms: not only immediate social or physical constraint, but the constraints of past durations. But
ultimately the individual is free to act, and the trajectory of his life is the trajectory of freedom within those constraints.

Once we place Bergson in the context of my example, the advantages
and disadvantages of his concepts of temporality become more clear. It is
evident, first of all, that the concept of duration as theorized by Bergson is
already at the practical heart of much historical writing. Most histories, like
Johnsen's history of Foyn, assume indexicality by organizing themselves
around crucial events that have explanatory chains of various lengths and
shapes leading up to them. These are Bergsonian "durations" and their con-
summate indexicality is shown in the fact that Johnsen, for example, does
not tell us what were the *other* consequences of high oil prices besides those
for the whaling industry. Johnsen has a particular "subject" of interest and
that subject, like any Bergsonian subject, lives in a set of nested durations.
Johnsen follows only these "durations," defined by his individual subject of
interest. Like Bergsonian durations, too, those durations are multiple and
overlapping. The history goes over the same "clock time" again and again,
at different paces, following the different chains of inventions, of prices, of
industrial structures, of labor markets. Finally, these durations are not "ordered" in some strict sense. Rather, they are more or less inclusive, involving greater or lesser periods. But between the different kinds of chains—
between writing about inventions and labor markets for example—they are
curiously disconnected. This disconnection echoes the resolute and problematic individualism of the Bergsonian account.

Freedom and determination in Bergson are again quite similar to freedom and determination in Johnsen's account of whaling. Foyn's durations
are shaped by forces around him, but he is always free to act. He vacillates
between alternatives, but does indeed continuously redefine those alternatives for himself, as when, his invention having led to the monopoly he so

much sought, he immediately began to license his inventions to others because it became clear that the monopoly from which so much was expected would prove less profitable, given the poaching and his own inability to process enough whales, than a franchising arrangement. It is, however, quite clear that he made more out of licensing once he had the monopoly than he would have made trying to license without having gotten the monopoly. The actual route to a present makes a difference when we get there; there were no simple alternatives.

One is heartened by these strong resonances between the Bergsonian account of temporality and that of a typical history. But there are two major problems left hanging by the Bergsonian account. The first is the role of determination. It is all well and good to think that actions drop from us like ripe fruits, but Bergson gives us little understanding of the farmer who mulches the trees, trims the branches, and perhaps picks fruit early to ripen on the way to market. That farmer is the force of determination, exercised across a whole orchard, and surely he has distinguishable, knowable effects.

Unlike this first problem of determination—which is deftly avoided by Bergson—the second great problem, that of solipsism, is built into the core of his thinking. Indeed, the central problem with Bergson's analysis of temporality is this firm solipsism. The concepts of duration and freedom are absolutely individual in nature. There is no social account of time other than as a dead mass of constructed clock time. True, at the deepest level people who construct a clock-time world are bound to live in it; situations that are real in their consequences are real in fact. But is this really a full account of the social nature of time and the present, on which we can found a general set of practices for studying the social process? I think not.

Recent attempts to theorize history have followed Bergson on this dangerous path of purely individualistic accounts of temporality. Indeed, most contemporary writers on that subject set out resolutely in the general direction of subjectivism and idealism. Ricoeur, for example, views time as incomprehensible without narrative. He therefore transforms the problem of the relation of past, present, and future into a problem of narrative understanding. By this he follows in the distinguished footsteps of Aristotle and Augustine. But this path leads away from a central goal in understanding the *social* process. For in the temporal riddles that Augustine contemplates in book eleven of the *Confessions*—riddles on which Ricoeur bases his analysis—society and interrelatedness play little role.[8]

8. Ricoeur 1984–88, in particular, vol. 1, pt. 1.

Even more extreme are those writers who forsake the rigors of Ricoeur for a more facile translation of historical contingency into a purely mentalist world ungoverned by the formalities of narrative. Aiming to overcome Cartesian dualism, they make of the social process a mere dance of cultural constructions in the perpetual present of consciousness. Since any arrangement of past, present, and future can exist in the mind, there is no need to worry about the actual temporality of the past. Indeed, there is in fact no such thing: the past has no temporality in and for itself.

Now this move into the mind does bind all time into the Parmenidean continuum; in Eliot's words:

> Time past and time future
> What might have been and what has been
> Point to one end, which is always present.
>
> Eliot, "Burnt Norton," lines 44–46

But while contemporary mentalism achieves that Eleatic continuity, it also reinvigorates the Cartesian duality it affects to despise by completely ignoring the contingent "stickiness" of past material reality. Retrospection can remake the past in many ways, but it is always constrained by a certain curious permanence of past things.

Consider the German attempt, in the 1930s, to identify Philipp Rechten of Bremen, along with his gunsmith-collaborator Cordes, as the inventors of the modern whaling. Rechten invented a double-barreled gun firing a harpoon out of one barrel and a bomb out of the other. This was patented in England in 1856, and on the strength of this, and of an apparently unpromising commercial experience with the device, Germans at one point claimed that they had created modern whaling. Dismissed as so much Nazi propaganda by Johnsen, this is a typical "constructing" of the past. In what ways is it "wrong"? True, the device failed commercially, but perhaps Foyn's commercial success simply reflected his better access to monopolized whaling grounds. Does that make him "more of an inventor"? Indeed, another of Foyn's predecessors—Roys—had considerable early commercial success with his hand-held grenade-harpoon gun, but then failed for reasons having mostly to do with the finances of his backers. Did this make him a bad inventor?

Out of this thicket of interpretations, however, certain sticky facts remain. There are the dates of the patents, the levels of commercial work, the diffusion of the innovations, the continued experimentation. All of these, too, are subject to "interpretation"; one inventor may have waited longer for a patent than another, and so on. But the stickinesses mean that while one can recast the story out of Johnsen's version so that Foyn is no longer the central focus, one cannot write him out of the story entirely. This is what I mean by the stickiness of empirical reality.

Unless we admit this stickiness and indeed its ability to intimately affect our mental constructions of the past, we take either a position of absolute idealism (in which the outside world is irrelevant to what we think about it) or we re-create a sharp, Cartesian dualism opposing the mind with its constructions to an inanimate world to be constructed. The first of these positions is untenable. The second is precisely what the constructionists had hoped to avoid. Their position is worsened by the fact that *past* action has a "doneness" that resists reinterpretation in a way that *present* action does not. That is, indeed, what makes it past.

Nor is the more sophisticated Augustinian temporality adopted by Ricoeur really a way out of this dilemma. While it is true that the irrevocable mass of the past and the unimaginable variety of the future are brought into the attentive present by memory and desire, this purely epistemological resolution of the conundrum of time leaves us without any ontological resolution at all. It gives us no account of the actual temporal relations of things unless we assume, with Whitehead and other strong organicists, that all things have consciousness after their own kind and that epistemology consequently *is* ontology.

Thus the subjectivists and mentalists fall into the same trap as did Bergson.[9] But we come away from Bergson with a strong concept of "duration," of indexical, multiple, and inclusive times. We also have from Bergson a loose, although ultimately unsatisfactory, sense of the dance of determination and freedom in those durations. Where Bergson really fails is in linking different people's durations together into a social whole, a failure ultimately traceable to the extreme mentalist position he takes on temporality. This problem involves Bergson in the general mentalist failure to construct a vi-

9. Note that the mentalist account also forgets that for all their differences, the constructions and imaginings of people do produce a common world of experience, as Eliot saw also, quoting Heraclitus in the epigraph to "Burnt Norton": "The Word yet being common to all, the many live as if each has a personal wisdom" (my translation). The problem of historical knowledge is thus not resolved but simply transformed by the move of mentalism. Rather than discussing the past for itself, we spend our time discussing the telescope through which we view it. The same relative distinctions between social and cultural reality are made, but now we speak of "routine, shared imaginings" versus "contested imaginings." The transfer of the problem to the realm of construction gains us nothing but an extra layer of distinctions to keep straight, the tax imposed by the new discipline of cultural studies as it attempts to control this particular route to knowledge.

able model of the past's nature for itself. I turn now to another author, and another philosophical tradition, in the hope of the answers Bergson has failed to give us.

III Temporality in Mead

Early twentieth-century American philosophy was dominated by pragmatism. The central pragmatic analysis of time is *The Philosophy of the Present* by George Herbert Mead. Auspiciously, Mead is perhaps best known for his elegant resolution of the problem of individual and society, in *Mind, Self, and Society;* we can therefore expect him to address head-on the Bergsonian problem of solipsism. Although unfinished, *The Philosophy of the Present* is Mead's only surviving personal work (unlike his other "books," which were reconstructed from lecture notes). It consists of four short chapters.[10]

Reality, Mead tells us, is always present; conversely, only the present exists. The essence of past and future is that they do not exist. The essence of the present is "its becoming and its disappearing" (1). "Existence involves non-existence. . . . The world is a world of events" (1). This seemingly innocuous opening argument seems to return us to the disconnected instants of the Eleatics. How can past influence present? Only through "becoming," Mead seems to say. But what of the distant past? How does it influence the present? Through memory alone?

Already, Mead seems to have disrupted the smoothly increasing inclusions of Bergsonian durations. Yet he then turns to the question of knowledge of the past, taking the mentalist turn so admired in Bergson by later subjectivists. But at the same time his cognitive account explicitly recognizes the stickiness of which I spoke earlier. On the one hand, every generation rewrites the past. Indeed, the future differs from the present in part because we constantly undertake this rewriting. Yet "the [past's] character of irrevocability is never lost" (3). Whatever way we rewrite the past, whatever account we give for it, to that account we always attach this "character of irrevocability," even though the importance of this irrevocability lies only in our present world, not in the world of the past we recount. Thus, Mead recognizes the dual nature of the past, on the one hand "open," free to choose for itself, on the other irrevocable.

This duality follows in part from his pragmatic account of cognition as

10. *The Philosophy of the Present* was published by the University of Chicago Press in 1932. Mead died before completing it, and A. E. Murphy produced the edition actually published. He appended several Mead essays to the original four-chapter text. All parenthetical page references are to this edition.

a mutual adjustment of mind and environment. For Mead, the presumption of a "world that is there . . . provides the basis for the inferential and ideational process of cognition" (5). "The very fact that . . . any accepted account of the past . . . may conceivably be thrown into doubt," he says, "seems to imply some unquestionable past" (6).[11] Now this might seem to imply that one could like Laplace imagine an infinite historian who knew all that had happened, "everything implied in our memories, our documents, and our monuments" (8), who would then possess asymptotically absolute knowledge of the past. But "from every new rise the landscape that stretches behind us becomes a new landscape" (9). From the perspective of the emergent present, that is, the past becomes a different thing. Mead's escape from "true history" comes via the pragmatist postulate that knowledge is always relational, that it varies with the knower as well as with the known.[12]

The Meadean analysis raises so many complexities that it is useful to recall our example. I argued for two "local presents"—marine mammal hunting in the early 1860s and in the mid- and late 1870s. Call these Present 1 and Present 2. Then there are the larger presents of premodern (pre-1870) and modern (post-1870) whaling. Call these Present A and Present B. What Mead is arguing is that an all-knowing historian writing in 1870 of the developments of Present A and Present 1 would write them differently than would an equally all-knowing historian writing in, say, 1900, or Johnsen writing in the 1950s. In this sense, what Svend Foyn "actually did" at the junction of Presents 1 and 2 or Presents A and B changes with time even though his "actual activities," for themselves, are irrevocably dead and gone. The same holds true for the relation of Present A and Present 1. Our understanding of how "the period of Foyn's immediate predecessors"

11. Mead's argument here is similar to that of Chuang Tzu on a similar point, our consciousness of the consciousness of others. Hui Tzu has just argued that Chuang Tzu's statement that the river fish are happy is baseless; Chuang Tzu is not a fish and thus cannot know what fish enjoy. Chuang Tzu replies: "You asked me *how* I knew what fish enjoy. The way you put the question shows that you already knew that I knew. I know it just as we stand here over the [River] Hao" (de Bary, Chan, and Watson 1964, 1:78, translating a passage from chap. 17 ["Autumn Floods"] of the Chuang Tzu).

12. Again and again, Mead answers the idea of a final, complete history, absolute in its plenitude, with the notion that a new knower will perforce know this history in a new way and thus as a new thing. For it has no meaning except meaning *for* someone, and its meaning for that knower must be different from its meaning for another. Put another way, it is in the process of rewriting the past from the perspective of the novel present (or "emergent" in Mead's term) that we make that novel present itself into a simple present that "follows from the past which has replaced the former past" (11). When we have understood the present, it has become the past.

emerged from the larger unit of "premodern whaling" changes as time passes, even though both presents are now irrevocably past.

How can these changes occur when the past is over—nonexistent, in Mead's words? There are two mechanisms. First, changes in our current interests can make past events more or less salient. This is the obvious force behind the Nazi reconstruction of Rechten as the inventor of the grenade harpoon. The political blatancy of that example should not blind us to the generality of this process in our understanding of the past; women's history and labor history provide the best examples of such rewriting of the past in recent decades. Second, the location of prior happenings within later "larger" events becomes clear only with time. Indeed, this is the foundation of Foyn's reputation. As of 1875, his invention was little more successful than that of Roys at an equivalent time after its discovery. It was the Foyn system's long-run success that defined it, retrospectively, as the successful invention. Whether this redefinition involves an internal but deterministic dynamic or mere chance depends upon our conception of events and determinism.

Events, in such an account, lack clear boundaries. Their definitions reach backward and forward. This leads Mead directly to the issue of connection and passage, and thence to the interweaving of time and free will that had fascinated Bergson. For Mead, determination of the future is accomplished by numerous factors, quantitative and qualitative, that relate things in their "passage" from past to future. Yet we do not directly experience this determination. (Mead like Bergson accepts Hume's and Kant's argument that causality is an attribute of knowing itself rather than a knowable phenomenon.) The problem is therefore to reconcile our experience of free will with our knowledge of determination, particularly given that, as Mead points out with devastating candor, "the emergent no sooner has appeared than we set about rationalizing it" (14).

Emergents are for Mead less important than emergence. He founds his analysis on "passage" itself, within which take place conditions that determine what emerges, although "not in its full reality." This conditioning occurs in the present, although we establish its roots in the past via memory and documentation. Most important, it is the conditioning, the *linkage* of past and present, that has ontological priority, not the past in itself, with what we sometimes call its "given causal implications."[13] Mead attempts to illustrate this concept of linkage with the example of the one suicide among

13. Mead draws here on chapter 3 of Dewey's *Experience and Nature*. Dewey 1958: 99 ff., 109 ff.

two thousand people exposed to exactly similar "disintegrating social conditions." It is, he says, "in the organization of tendencies embodied in one individual" that we find the emergent that leads to the suicide. This example is more or less equivalent to contrasting the many possible candidates for inventor of the grenade harpoon with the one Svend Foyn.

Now there are two ways of conceiving of the "organization of tendencies" in the suicide or the invention; it could be simply the complex conjuncture of forces or it could be some sort of special element beyond them. These reflect the two different ontologies within which we could take Mead's view. In the first, we take a Markovian view of time (precisely the reverse of the Bergsonian view), assuming that moments are infinitely divisible and that the past is determining the future in some sufficient way moment by moment. In this case, it is the mere conjunctural complexity of determining conditions that creates the suicide or the invention in the one case. This amounts to saying that Mead's posing of the problem is incorrect, that in fact conditions were not exactly the same for all two thousand cases.

Doubtless the other, Bergsonian view is what Mead intends, but within it his meaning is much less clear. With respect to historical *cognition*, to be sure, his argument is unexceptionable; in practice, we reason about causes by first comparing different outcomes of events. That is, the present of outcomes (the fact of one actual suicide) is the starting point for our analysis, and we proceed from it via a theory of its temporal (causal) connection with the past to establish an understanding of that past. But it still seems that Mead had wished here to make not a cognitive, but an ontological point, a point about "what was there" in the past. This point, however, is not yet clear.

Only when his analyses of cognition and determination are completed does Mead turn to define the present. For Mead it is by the happening of events that we know time, and our construction of a clock time of equal intervals is just that: a pragmatic construction designed to enable us to predict the future. Mead thus does not define clock time as inevitably social, like Bergson, but as inevitably operational. (And unlike Bergson, he clearly approves of it.) A present is, however, not an instant of clock time. It is rather that period which contains an emergent event, an "occurrence of something which is more than the processes that have led up to it" (23). That emergent event, through its conditioning relations to the past, marks certain antecedent processes as its causes; although later in time, the emergent event has logical priority.

For Mead, it is therefore events, patterns, and conditioning that have reality, not things at given points in time. His account is thoroughly relational. Because of this relational account, the size of a present varies; "its own temporal diameter varies with the extent of the event" (23). (In this he agrees with Bergson.) Past and future, Mead tells us, are fundamentally matters of ideation. They reach beyond the immediate conditions of the event, extended by memory and desire. The present, by contrast, is defined by activity, indeed the activity of the organism whose mind creates past and future (24–25).

The implication of this relational concept of time is that there is no "larger past" within which all these many pasts-defined-by-past-presents are reconciled. On the contrary, those pasts are reconciled only in relation to a particular event of a particular present (26). Moreover, not only is the past not a solid object against which we compare our hypothetical knowledge of it, the past is also *not* a series of unrolling presents. For to see it as such is to miss the conditions that link past to present, and therefore to make of time a list of unrelated moments. It is the conditioning, relational character of the past that makes it a past.

His first chapter thus shows Mead close to Bergson in some ways and far in others. They share a concept of time as multiple, inclusive, and, above all, indexical. Indeed, in Mead every new present rewrites all the past. But unlike Bergson Mead explicitly addresses the nature of the past and our knowledge of it. He notes the peculiar fact that while knowledge of the past is perpetually conditional on present interests, it perpetually invokes the character of irrevocability, of doneness. This fits well with the duality of freedom and determination in the past noted by Bergson, but from a presentist perspective.

Each writer, therefore, tells us little about the experience of the past for itself. Like Bergson's view, Mead's seems to be largely epistemological, not ontological. When he moves into ontology—in his characterization of passage and conditioning and in his example of the suicide—his argument becomes much less sure. Yet much historical knowledge takes the form of understanding the meaning of a prior past for some past present; this is the problem involved in explaining the impact of Present 1 (the early 1860s) on Foyn's invention, for example. Now Mead gives us no account of such activities. Yet when this task is considered generally, it becomes precisely the problem of understanding a set of continuous moments that Mead tells us is impossible. For example, surely we do not want to regard our analyses of the origins of Foyn's harpoon to be made "wrong" simply because we have later become interested in relation of Present 2 (the late 1870s) to Present B (the whole period of modern whaling), in which case Foyn's invention is no longer the past present to be explained, but a part of the conditioning past of the new explanandum. It is precisely this past of continuous moments that we must understand. A general view of the social process would be a view that treated a succession of moments as successive presents with all of their own relevant pasts understood.

With Mead's view, then, we come perilously close to the position that "the past is whatever we make it." In what lies the sticky character of the past, the irrevocability Mead himself notes, the importance of documents and testimonies, in such a case? Mead attributes it only to our cognitive acts. Moreover, the solipsistic jumble of presents in Bergson is now augmented by an equally solipsistic jumble of pasts. At every moment, every actor has a unique understanding of all parts of the past.

Only in the third chapter does Mead attempt to escape this solipsism, to find "the social nature of the present."[14] He begins with a definition of the social. Sociality occurs when a new actor enters a system and the system readjusts to it. The sociality lies not in the system-ness, the interaction per se, but rather in the moment of emergence, the moment *between* the old system and the new. But on the next page, Mead adds the qualification that sociality emerges when actors are conscious of mutual adjustment. This consciousness is, of course, central in Mead's *Mind, Self, and Society*. (Thus what is elsewhere central to the concept of social seems ancillary here.) Yet Mead soon defines sociality yet again, as "the capacity of being several things at once" (49). For example, the hunting animal is part of a worldwide distribution of energies, but also part of his pack, and of his couple. This is still another notion of sociality, founded on mutual inclusion as is Bergson's concept of duration. What all three definitions share—although Mead does not state this—is the idea of betweenness: between old and new, between actors, between roles, between systems.

Rather than reconcile these definitions, however, Mead goes on to give an account of emergence. He defines emergence through sociality as the co-presence of a single thing in several frames of reference, which produces "emergent" changes in that thing. He then transforms this argument, replacing "frames of reference" with "levels of analysis." Emergence is "the presence of things in two or more systems, in such a fashion that its presence

14. In the second chapter, Mead confronts the problem of reconciling relativistic time with his theories of emotion and passage. This investigation is of little interest to the sociologist or historian. When he does return to the issue of the social nature of the present, he does it quite seriously. This is not a facile argument that "time is a social construct," but is meant by Mead as a metaphysical argument.

in a later system changes its character in the earlier system or systems to which it belongs" (67). But with respect to the problem of relating emergence and sociality, these arguments are largely petitio principii. For they make emergence a concept definitionally indistinguishable from sociality, as Mead eventually admits.

Like Bergson, then, Mead has difficulty providing a substantial bridge between the presents of separate individuals. He can only define, not relate, them. But in his last chapter, Mead returns to his earlier work, his ontogenetic account of the self. Here we get the beginnings of a theory of this relation. Ideation, Mead says, begins with feeling, a naive response to the effects of one's actions on the environment. A primitive form of consciousness, feeling constitutes an "entering into the environment" (70). Here Mead begins to argue against Bergson, for the development of feeling into something higher is furthered by the "slower" responses of the organism to "distant" actions, which eventually give rise to "delayed and mutually conflicting responses," which are the "stuff of ideation" (71). That is, time is here spatialized, in a very physical sense. We are far from the interpenetrating durations of Bergson. For Mead, these "distant" experiences are the root of consciousness, for in responding to the choices presented by these conflicting responses the organism begins to create "purposive responses" that characterize a distant object in terms of "what we can do to it or with it or by way of it or what it can do to us." Such responses are "there" (in memory) and the organism responds as much to them as to actual sense perception. It is through organizing these responses—which Mead calls images—that we create our pasts, in order to create our futures.

"Distance" is thus the first hint, in Mead, of an effective approach to the social nature of temporality. A serious theory of how distance works would start us towards a real understanding of social time, one that would go beyond Bergson's mistaken identification of clock time as the only social time. It is of course true, even a truism, that "time is socially constructed." The problem is the exact topology of that construction, and, following Mead's earlier work, understanding how the constructing of social time is at the same time the constructing of the individual consciousness within which exist Bergson's durations.

IV Temporality in Whitehead

From our consideration of Bergson and Mead, then, we emerge with a clear list of the desiderata of a serious theory of temporality in society. From Mead, we can take the idea that temporality must—like mind, self, and society—emerge in interaction. Processes of interaction must produce a wide variety of temporalities, including among them the subjective pure duration of Bergson and the rigid clock time he so much despises. These temporalities must be indexical, multiple, and inclusive, as both authors argue. They must include both individual times and social times. They must arise in relations, in interaction, in moments. And the process that produces them must recognize both the workings of determinism and the moments of freedom and emergence.

Related to these requirements are requirements reflecting both authors' recognition of the granular, momentous quality of physical time. The past, Mead never tires of telling us, does not exist. Physical reality is Markovian, emerging from an immediate past instant to instant. No account of human temporality can afford to ignore this granular quality. Yet at the same time, the existence of inclusive durations clearly violates any simple notion of granular time. A theory of temporality must bridge this divide.

Our analysis of Mead and Bergson equally indicates pitfalls to be avoided. In both authors solipsism is a danger. So also is the tendency, in Mead especially, to regard the past as infinitely plastic, to give no account of the past's character for itself. Like the dilemma of freedom and determinism, to which indeed it is related, this problem of allowing the past to be irrevocable yet endlessly reinterpretable places central constraints on an account of temporality.

Mindful of these requirements, I turn now to the work of Alfred North Whitehead. A contemporary of Mead's, Whitehead developed over his life a "process philosophy" designed to overcome the problems of Cartesian dualism. It culminated in his labyrinthine *Process and Reality*, published in 1929. Although Whitehead does not specifically aim his book at the problem of temporality, he does aim it at a more general problem of which the temporality problem is a subset: the problem of finding an ontology viable in a postquantum world. Unlike Mead and Bergson, however, Whitehead does not lay this theory out in exposition, beginning to end; he starts in medias res and argues in a grand spiral. I therefore cannot undertake a front-to-back reading here. I rather begin with a simple account of the Whiteheadian ontology, and then use it to undergird the theory of temporality I have been developing from Bergson and Mead.[15]

15. I have used the 1969 Free Press edition of *Process and Reality*. It was only after undertaking a careful reading of that edition that I was made aware of the existence of the newer variorum edition edited by Donald Sherburne. The spiral argument structure makes *Process and Reality* extremely exasperating on first reading, although it forces a reader to a far more profound understanding of Whitehead than would be possible with a linear argument. For those who wish to start with a linear argument, Sherburne's *A Key to Whitehead's Process and Reality* abridges and rearranges the text into such a structure.

As this movement from ontology to temporality implies, one lesson I take from the texts so far is the notion that temporality does not exist ex ante. There is no theory of temporality without an ontology. Thus, in physical cosmology, there is no ultimate physical clock ticking off physical seconds in a uniform way across the universe; temporality appertains to matter and energy, not to emptiness. I approach human temporality with the same notion. Our only certainty is that something like local temporal order exists. That is, that within one interaction (within one locality) there are relations of relative time. Everything else is built up from this local temporality of interaction.

Neither temporality nor interaction, however, is Whitehead's principal subject. Rather, his aim is to replace Cartesian dualism and the ontology it presumes. He wants to replace a world of subjects that know objects by means of objects' enduring properties with a world of entities formed by their relations with other entities. For him, knowledge is merely one means of this formative relation. Indeed, relationism applies to formation in time as well; present entities come together out of convergences of relations to things past. As if to underline this perpetually renewed interrelation of everything with everything, Whitehead argues at two very different levels. The microcosmic world he calls the world of "actual entities." These "actual entities" are in fact events in the normal terminology. (One of Whitehead's refreshing qualities is a completely idiosyncratic and largely consistent terminology; most of his special terms are clearly defined and instantly recognizable as terms of art.)

Derived from this microcosmic level is the level of nexus or society (Whitehead uses the terms interchangeably). A nexus is a set of actual entities in some form of systematic relationship. In the standard terminology, a nexus is a set of events organized into some pattern. A nexus or society in time—what Whitehead calls a "personally ordered nexus" (40)—is what we would usually call an object or a thing. Thus, the Cartesian atomic basis of the world is in fact macrocosmic for Whitehead, because he, like Mead, takes the world to be "a world of events." Cartesian, enduring objects like stones and human individuals are simply events that keep happening the same way.

Yoking these two levels together are the relations of "order." However important their relations may seem to us, they are not well studied in *Process and Reality*. Neither are the relations of the macrocosmic "societies," under which we would place the relations of normal social interaction, but which Whitehead views as fully equivalent to the relations that create personal order. (Whitehead does not make a distinction in kind between my relation to, say, a randomly chosen Norwegian sociologist today and my relation to myself in 1967.) Rather, the process that yokes actual entities to one another at the microcosmic level—the relations of "prehension"—are Whitehead's central topic. ("Prehension" includes both those relations that standard Cartesianism would consider causal and those it would consider perceptual. Both are considered by Whitehead, but as parallel types of processes.) An actual entity (read event) occurs by a process of "concrescence." Concrescence begins with prehensions of other entities. These prehensions are then organized in various ways and culminate in the "satisfaction" of an entity, its finally "becoming what it is to become." As in Mead, at this point, when an entity loses what Mead calls "passage" or "becoming," it becomes in its turn an object, in Whitehead's terms the "datum" for a later "actual entity."

All this complexity—and it takes many obscure passages—creates a completely Markovian world at the microscopic level. The world is perpetually (re)creating itself. There are no fixed objects, only perpetual concrescence. The microcosmic world looks like chain mail, a network of prehensions in which actual entities are the intersects between links of prehension. In this network, the strong temporal lines are the "personal orders" by which enduring objects are created out of lineages of entities. But these lineages are no different in kind from other prehensive relations; indeed, in this identity lies Whitehead's rejection of Cartesian dualism.

Basing a view of social ontology on a Whiteheadian model seems quite attractive. The microcosmic/macrocosmic distinction allows us to have Mead's world of events at the microcosmic level, even as we have emergent structures, subject to perpetual definition and redefinition, at the macrocosmic level. At the microcosmic level, reality is granular. The world is perpetually creating itself. The emergent present is perpetually arising out of an immediate past. This side of Whitehead's ontology satisfies the probabilists and modelers for whom reality consists of a moment-by-moment chain of branching processes. Note, too, that we can allow irrevocability to inhere in such a microcosmic past. This deals with our difficulty, above, that we do not like to imagine that our rewritings of Foyn's discovery in 1880, 1900, and 1930 would change what Foyn actually did, for himself, at the time. The concept of the microscopic nature of action also captures Bergson's notion that alternative courses of action are not true alternatives, because inclining towards one of them redefines the other. If a person is not a thing that has experiences, but rather a historical trajectory of microscopic moments, then Bergson's idea becomes simple and comprehensible.

But there remain important problems that seem simply conjured away by the microscopic/macroscopic distinction. First, why is so much of the world personally ordered (that is, why does so much of it consist of things that stay the same)? This is less of a problem with the social than with the natural world, but remains a difficulty. Second, why do the parts of social reality that have personal order do so, and why do those personal orders sometimes collapse? In social terms, why are there enduring social structures and why do they sometimes fail unaccountably and sharply? More broadly, how does a Whiteheadian ontology confront the issue of the creation and dissolution of social entities and the complex relations of social entities of different sizes. How do small presents relate to large presents? Finally, what role is played by "constructionist" processes, by rewriting, by our own colligations of the past?

One premise holds the answer to many of these questions. That is Whitehead's implicit contention that the relation between small and large, between those occasions that acquire personal order and those that do not, is fundamentally an empirical relation. In Whitehead's view, it is not the case that enduring personal orders (acting social individuals) are somehow prior to more complex social beings. Rather, all relations of prehension take place within the same microcosmic universe, and acting social individuals possess coherent personal order (that is, they are sequences of events that become things) in precisely the same way that other kinds of social structures acquire order. At any given time, there is an immensely complex structure of prehensions linking up all the occasions of the social world. Some of that structure can be imagined as enduring "individual" trajectories. But other parts of it may be enduring networks of friends, bureaucratic relations that tie together "parts of people," even the complex links that Mark Granovetter has called "weak ties."

The future possibilities of this immense structure are purely empirical. In 1860, one large structure of links encoded the "premodern" form of whaling into the social structure of the whaling nations. By speaking of this form as "encoded," I mean that the overall pattern of links was such that innovation tended to be reflected back towards routine practice. An innovation might lack financial backing to succeed, or reputational factors might mean that the luck of weather and whale finding became central, or technical possibilities might not be available to those likely to see reason for using them. Or these things might not be available in an order that permitted change to unfold. The arrangement of events that allows an invention like Foyn's to have a decisive effect is a complex one. A "large" and long-enduring structure becomes vulnerable to change not because of some particular innovation, but because this structure itself becomes aligned in such a way that the usual reflection back towards traditional practices no longer occurs at its boundaries. Instead of constraining, the structure comes to facilitate change. Now although we speak of such an arrangement of links as a "large" structure, it is *central* to realize that its largeness lies only in its imperviousness to change, not necessarily in any widespreadness or uniformity. It is the empirical arrangement of links, the actual way in which local topologies of interaction hook themselves into something with this reflective impermeability to change that makes a structure large. There exists nothing but local interaction.

Thus it is that microscopic granularity is compatible with macroscopic regularity. The sheer empirical pattern of links creates some phenomena that look temporally large and others that look small. But since all are equally encoded in microscopic events, sudden change is just as possible in large structures as is gradual. Thus, when Foyn's invention, together with the conjuncture of other links around it, created certain new pathways and links in the structure of whaling, the past structures that had suppressed a dozen prior inventors no longer functioned. The system moved into flux for a while, then discovered what it was that the new arrangements permitted and forbade. That is what happened during Foyn's exercise of his monopoly, when he discovered franchising preferable to actual monopoly, and what happened in the decades afterward, as the possibilities of modern whaling were fleshed out.

In short, the "size" of the present is something encoded at any given time into the social structure. As such, a present is open to freedom and innovation, just as it exercises, in its own way, the forces of determinism, both immediate and "at a distance" through the larger networks of prehensions. Moreover, just as there are many social structures that overlap, drawing the same individuals into dozens of different intersecting structures, so too do the presents those structures imply overlap and intersect. Thus we have room for Bergson's multiple presents, but in this case not merely for one kind of "society" (individuals, or, in Whitehead's terms, "personal orders") but for any ordered system of links among prehensions. It is as possible, in such a model, to think about whaling in the 1860s as a subset of "premodern whaling" as it is to think about Foyn's personal experience as a matter of similarly overlapping durations. Evading Bergsonian solipsism is as simple (and as radical) as denying that "personal" prehensions are different from others.

Nothing in Whitehead's ontology, however, really addresses the question of how personal orders get started and why they have peculiar durability. Placing personal and nonpersonal orders on the same footing does well with the issues of small and large entities and with the general problem of relating social structure and temporality. But it does not address the question of personality per se. I might note that there are many possible theories for the generation of "persons," although they clearly go beyond the range of this paper. One might, for example, attribute personal order to some form of habituation. Or one might see its origins in larger phenomena; Whiteheadian "societies" acquire personal order because that order offers a partition of some larger structure that works more effectively than another partition. (This tends to be how we explain the division of labor, for example.) Or we might see the origins of personal order in names; personal orders arise when a set of occasions acquires a name as a thing. Calling a set of occasions an object makes it one. This "cultural" view of personal order moves us to the issue of construction.

Construction of the past seems another remaining problem in the social ontology I am taking from Whitehead. As I have so far presented him, Whitehead ignores the fact that our constructions of the past change constantly. He thinks only of the past more or less for itself. Does the foregoing analysis imply that we could in principle discover all relevant prehensions and hence actually understand the past for itself? Or is Mead right that we make the past what it is by defining its salience for us and that we are therefore constantly changing it?

Happily, Whitehead addresses these questions in a variety of ways. First, he recognizes the process of naming by which a set of occasions among which we see certain common abstract elements becomes a social thing. He calls this process "transmutation" and recognizes that it is done by particular entities, with their own particular interests, in their own particular ways. And transmutation can occur at a variety of time lags. The term would equally describe an individual prehending events in his immediate consciousness or a historian prehending past events through documents relating them. There is thus no absolute difference in kind between historical knowledge and immediate knowledge. However, there is a different mixture of types of prehensions involved, Whitehead having been careful to maintain a distinction between what he called "perception in the mode of causal efficacy," "perception in the mode of presentational immediacy," and "perception in the mode of symbolic reference." People at the time "felt" events causally and through immediate perception in ways that are extremely attenuated for the modern reader. Whitehead maintained on principle that every event in the world affected all later events—this paper is causally shaped by Foyn's discovery, for example—but he allowed for extreme attenuation in order to reconcile his pan-relationism with common sense.

In this distinction of types of prehension lie the seeds of an approach to the issue of construction. At the microcosmic level, prehensions of causal efficacy and presentational immediacy are continuously present. Once past, they are encoded in the satisfactions of entities, there to become data for new processes of concrescence. Once so encoded, these prehensions—the social facts and constructions of the time—are realities that can be known in two ways, either through some form of symbolic representation (recording) or through their own prehensive descendants. A much later writer may, as we have seen, see many actual structures of connections among microcosmic events that were obscure at the time. But he may also choose different structures of relevance (positive and negative prehensions) and so arrange the past quite differently than did those who experience it. Both in fact and in construction, therefore, the later writer is free, as Mead said, to rewrite the past in his own interests. At the same time, the causal connections of the past, and indeed its constructions of itself, are available as prehensible data, and about them one can be mistaken, or wrong, or misrepresentative. There is a sticky past, despite our ability to rewrite it.

Combining this analysis of construction with Whitehead's ontology and with insights taken from Bergson and Mead thus produces answers to most of the questions that have arisen in my analysis of Foyn's history, and, through it, of the larger relation of history and sociology. We have a local world built on a dialogue of freedom and determinism and a larger world that emerges from it by interrelations both cognitive and conative. We have granular time and larger time. We have constructions as realities and realities as constructions. We have a past that is sticky but interpretable, in which large can shape small and small restructure large. All this has come by moving to a fundamentally relational account of social objects and their meaning, and through recognition that the actual arrangements of social life encode histories and sociologies in an empirical relation (in any given case) that is ours to analyze.

At the last, however, there remains the central question of where temporality itself originates. Bergson and Mead's solipsistic temporality still seems a firm psychological category on which is imposed the dead social hand of the clock. But a model referring directly to Mead's other work escapes from this trap. In *Mind, Self, and Society*, Mead derives the personality from the experience of understanding how others react to one's own gestures, an experience that detaches the gesture from its actual performance and creates a significant symbol on which can be built a purely interior conversation with the self. A similar theory can account for temporality. The foundational experience in social life is of interaction, of turn taking. In the social process an individual could be defined as a site where various rhythms of turn taking—derived from various interactions in which an individual is involved—scrape against one another. This scraping is our primitive experience of temporality. It is purely relative between interactions. It matters not "how fast social change is occurring" but rather how fast it occurs *relative to* other things like the length of the life course. It matters not how fast computers enable people to play the stock market, but how fast computerized trading moves *relative to* changes in the underlying viability of firms and other economic indicators.

Generating stability within the welter of conflicting interactional rhythms is a crucial problem. Both solipsistic duration and clock time are in fact strategies for regularizing this rhythmic cacophony. On the one hand, solipsism simply prioritizes an arbitrary set of interactional presents around an individual. I may regard myself as still "present" with a friend when in fact that friend has redefined our relationship as past. My choice to define the duration as I see it is purely arbitrary, although a third party to whom I tell my version of things will not know that. Or, we are much more comfortable recognizing that arbitrary quality when the solipsistic individual involved is a social one: for example, an industrial corporation whose fixed hours and scheduled nonschedules dictate durational presents for many of its disparate employees. Note that there is nothing in a Whiteheadian view implying that the only individuals capable of pure "duration" are biological individuals. The literature on collective behavior has long focused on such behavior among groups.

On the other extreme, clock time is simply a minimalist approach to adjudication of rhythmic complexity across interactions. A choral singer follows the conductor's tactus only when the interplay of other voices momentarily offers no guidance for his own motion. Industrial firms treat lower-level employees with clock temporality but expect higher-level ones to accept their solipsistic definitions of "how long you ought to work today." Academics schedule appointments of fixed length when their interlocutors are less important to them but let the interaction find its own rhythm with those who are more. The imposition of clock time on duration that Bergson so much hated is merely a historical fact. The extreme separation of these strategies towards temporality—each of which in fact implies the other— arises out of the modern distinction of public and private. For Bergson's "pure duration" is not a primal experience, but a manufactured one, manufactured out of interaction by subtracting out all turns but our own.

With this brief analysis, I come less to the end of the present argument than the beginning of the next. The theory of temporality arising out of these three authors requires extensive development. Yet its outlines are clear. A world in process. A world of interaction. Temporality defined by relation. An entangling of micro process with macro order. A purely empirical relation between history and sociology, between narrative and cause, between small and large. Such a theory can interpret the transformation of Tønsberg in the 1860s. It gives us language to understand why Foyn, and not Amici or Roys or Welch, is regarded as the inventor of modern whaling, and how the varying overlaid presents of whaling make something that is not only a collection of separable epochs of apparent causal regularity, but also at the same time an ordered historical structure.

In the present, we live as if between endless past and future. Mead is right that we seem suspended in nothingness, the present an island of reality in a sea of ideation.

> Its steel arch floating
> above simplifying fog,
> does this bridge without
> supports link nothing to nothing
> or Nøtterøy to Tjøme?

But at the same time, the present stands as a connection between something we know, at least vaguely, and something we cannot yet descry. Even so, we cannot understand that present until it becomes past, and even then, will remake it as we see connections among its parts that were hitherto invisible.

> Hill to hill, gully
> to rocky field, the well-known
> landscape of the past
> splashes into the future's
> tides at the end of the world.

> Beyond spray-gilt rocks
> geography vanishes:
> field, hill, and gully
> all hid, like the rainy land,
> by water's calm ignorance.

On the Concept of Turning Point

In an important paper, John Goldthorpe has advanced three claims against what he calls the "case-oriented" approach in comparative macrosociology. First, he argues that problems created by small numbers of cases are just as important for case-oriented as for variable-oriented approaches. Second, he argues that Galton's problem (the impossibility of distinguishing heterogeneity and contagion in most data) arises equally in both approaches. Third, he argues that case-oriented approaches have no preferential access to the interior of the causal "black box"; where they do illuminate causal patterns they do not generalize; where they generalize, they have are no better than, and often worse than, variable-based approaches.[1]

Goldthorpe's points are well taken. And he argues them with magnanimity.[2] But he has chosen the easy target. The real critique of variable-based approaches comes not from case studies, but rather from approaches that characterize the social process through patterns of complex particulars. By avoiding this other critique, Goldthorpe is able to steer his discussion towards the old and familiar one of idiographic versus nomothetic, talk versus numbers.

But the variable-based approaches that Goldthorpe defends are not the only formal means of generalizing about the social process. They follow one among a number of possible generalizing strategies. They seek to understand the social process by developing linear transformations from a high-dimensional space (of "main effects" and occasionally of interactions between them) into a single dimension (the dependent variable). If this transforma-

This paper was prepared for a special symposium in *Comparative Social Research*, as a comment on a paper by John Goldthorpe. Since work of mine was one of Goldthorpe's targets, I have left in this version the prefatory section of my paper that responds to his criticisms; these are made clear in my response. I thank Frederik Engelstad for the invitation to write this paper, which originally appeared in *Comparative Social Research* 16 (1997): 85–105; reprinted with permission of Elsevier Science.

1. Goldthorpe 1997. On technical aspects of Galton's problem see Taibelson 1974 and Loftin and Ward 1981.

2. Cf. Lieberson 1992.

tion provides a sufficient approximation for the dependent dimension, the independent variables are said to "causally explain" the dependent one.

Now this strategy—which is effectively one of reducing by one the dimensionality of the data space—is useful only if the data space is more or less uniformly filled. It is then necessary to have a general model that applies everywhere in the data space and that is more or less the same everywhere in that space. But much or most of the time, the data space is not uniformly filled with data. On the contrary, most of the time most possible combinations of particular values of variables either don't occur or occur very rarely. Social reality usually has very strong local association of variables; data points are clumped within data space even in the presence of low values of global association measures like Pearson correlation coefficients.[3]

If most things that could happen don't happen, then we are far better off trying first to find local patterns in data and only then looking for regularities among those local patterns. Indeed, it is for this reason that cluster analysis and scaling, not regression, dominate big-money social science—market research—where the aim is to find, understand, and exploit strong local patterns. For these are methods that seek clumps and partitions of data and make no attempt to write general transformations. Put another way, clustering and scaling try to describe data by finding multivariable local regularities rather than by trying to select one data dimension for selective elimination.

Thus the real alternatives to Goldthorpe's variable-based approaches are not case-based approaches, but what I shall call, for want of a better term, "pattern-based approaches." Pattern-based approaches begin by establishing local patterns among the variables before setting out to generalize. These preliminary patterns are complex particulars: clusters of cases that have roughly the same values on many variables. In variable-based approaches, we don't seek such complex particulars, but rather generalize immediately on the basis of the given variables, which are treated as substantively independent of one another (i.e., as main effects). By contrast, pattern-based approaches use the variables to define types. They then seek more general patterns across types or relating types to one another. As I noted, this procedure will be most useful when much or most of the data clusters around a few types and a considerable portion of the data space is more or less empty. (This is an empirical issue, and one easily tested by straightforward methods.) In this case, we are best off establishing local associations first.

3. See chapter 5.

Note that these local associations need not be cross-sectional. That is, they need not be clusters in cross-sectional data space. They could equally be patterns of successions of values of one or more variables. In the simplest sense, an autoregressive scheme is such a pattern. In a more complex sense, any common succession of values of a variable (indeed any common succession of values of several different variables) would be such a pattern.

It is here that we arrive at "sociological narrativism," as Goldthorpe calls it. Late in his paper, Goldthorpe states that "for any kind of macrosociology, . . . 'history' will always remain as a necessary residual category." A footnote to this remark outlines Goldthorpe's worries:

> And I would take leave to doubt that the further attempt now apparently being made [to overcome the distinction between sociology and history] via 'sociological narrativism' . . . is any more likely to succeed. While one may sympathise with the efforts such as those of Abbott [1992a, 1992c] to establish analogues between narrative accounts and causal explanations, there are still basic differences to be recognized among the kinds of narrative that may be deployed. For example, one may understand rational choice theory in terms of narratives—but ones which, in contrast to historical narratives, are generalised rather than specific, set in analytic rather than real time, and implicative rather than conjunctive in their structure.[4]

I am less interested here in Goldthorpe's definitional relegation of history to the category of residuals than in his recognition that regular narrative patterns are in fact a reasonable way to generalize about the social process. That is, he concedes here the possibility of a pattern-based approach to social analysis based on temporal sequences, or, as I shall call them, "narrative patterns."[5] His last sentence calls useful attention to certain aspects of narrative patterns. We want them to be generalized (as indeed I argued in the papers to which Goldthorpe refers). We want them to take place in a temporality more flexible than clock time. (Goldthorpe's in-

---

4. Goldthorpe 1997: 22 n. 18. The papers he refers to are chapters 4 and 6 of the current volume.

5. When I first began to talk about analysis of sequential social patterns, in the early 1980s, "narrative" had not yet become the fashionable word that it later would. Hence I (somewhat lazily) used the word to refer to actual historical regularities as well as to narrated versions of them, specifying which meaning applied when necessary. Unfortunately, the word "narrative" has latterly become completely conflated with what the French call *discours*, the telling of a story. Throughout this paper, I use "narrative patterns" to refer to actual regularities in the social process itself and treat the entire issue of discourse and representation of such regularities as nonproblematic. This is of course a draconian assumption, but one necessary for my present purposes.

sistence on purely abstract time reduces pattern to mere succession, and we should retain the possibility of patterns involving duration.) And we want to have some sense that such narratives are "coercive" in the sense that after some point they imply a certain denouement, a certain result. (This last is my interpretation of what Goldthorpe means by "implicative rather than conjunctive in their structure.")

In this paper, I would like to take up this last issue of finality, of certainty, of implicative result. I view this finality within the broader issue of turning points in narrative patterns. Believing that after a certain point a narrative becomes coercive means believing that a turning point has been passed. We have moved out of a former pattern and onto a new trajectory. Turning points are commonly hypothesized in both quantitative and qualitative analysis in the social sciences. But we lack a sustained analysis of them. Indeed, the metaphors of "trajectory" and "turning" with which I have just conceptualized them may be completely misleading. I would like therefore to take up the logical and formal properties of the concept of turning point.

I begin with some illustrative references to literatures employing the concept of turning points. I then discuss some mathematical analogies for turning points and develop the idea of a narrative concept. This leads to a discussion relating turning points to trajectories and developing a social structural approach to turning points. The second section of the paper considers two particular problems in the theory of turning points: that of proliferating futures and that of instantaneous change. The substantive discussion of the paper closes with a multiple-contingency theory of unexpected social change.

I The Concept of Turning Point

In sociology, the concept of turning point is quite old.[6] It has had its main application in studies of the life course. Elder's widely cited review parses the life course into "trajectories and transitions."[7] Trajectories are interlocked and interdependent sequences of events in different areas of life. Transitions are on the one hand stages along such regular trajectories and on the other hand radical shifts. "Some events," Elder tells us, "are important turning points in life—they redirect paths." That turning points interrupted regular patterns was a major insight of the life course literature; earlier conceptions of the life course had spoken of a regular "life cycle," a

6. See Hughes 1971.
7. Elder 1985.

concept ultimately traceable to the Chicago school's concept of natural history.[8]

Although the life course literature will be my touchstone here, similar arguments are made elsewhere, for example in the criminological literature. Sampson and Laub argued that turning points played a central role in jolting delinquents into and out of trajectories that led to further criminality.[9] But the concept of turning point is not merely a life history or even a sociological concept. In political science, turning points have been sought in studies of political realignment and critical elections. In applied economics, studies of business cycles and other economic regularities have led to widespread analysis of turning points. In the history of science, revolution has been a central concept for decades or even centuries.[10]

In developing a concept of turning point that would support these various literatures, it is easiest to begin with concepts from mathematics. Imagine a continuous single-valued function of x. A turning point is a maximum or minimum point in this function, the point at which the slope of the function changes sign. (In practice, this is the operational definition of turning point in the applied economics literature.)[11]

However, we would not think of two such changes in quick succession as

8. Elder 1985:35. On natural history, see Park 1927. For a critical review of the life cycle concept, see O'Rand and Krecker 1990.

9. Sampson and Laub 1993.

10. On political realignment, see Lasser 1985. Critical elections consists of a large literature responding to V. O. Key (1955), e.g., Burnham 1970 and Clubb, Flanagan, and Zingale 1981. For examples from applied economics, see Chaffin and Talley 1989 and Zellner, Hong, and Min 1991. On scientific revolution, see Kuhn 1970 and Cohen 1985. The literature on political revolutions is so immense and familiar that I give no references. The historical antecedents of the concept of revolution are covered in Cohen's (1985, chap. 4) rather wooden history of the idea of revolutions. The idea of revolutionary turning points in historical processes is ultimately a Christian one (Collingwood 1946:49 ff.). Indeed the concept later developed for turning points in this paper—transition between relatively sharply differentiated regimes—is effectively captured by Paul's image of the turning point of incarnation separating the period of redemption from that of the law (AV Galatians 3:23–24):

> But before faith came we were kept under the law, shut up unto the faith which should afterward be revealed. Wherefore the law was our schoolmaster, to bring us unto Christ, that we might find faith. But after that faith is come, we are no longer under such a schoolmaster.

Paul's description of turning points in the life course is similar (AV 1 Corinthians 13:11–12):

> When I was a child, I spake as a child, I understood as a child, I thought as a child. But when I became a man, I put away childish things. For now we see through a glass darkly; but then, face to face.

11. See, e.g., Zellner, Hong, and Min 1991.

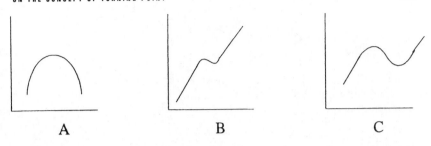

FIGURE 8.1

anything more than a minor ripple in a generally monotonic trend. But if the two changes were spread out from one another, we would think of the whole curve as divided into three segments, separated by the two turning points.

This homely example, illustrated in figure 8.1, captures a most important aspect of turning points. The concept of turning point is, in Arthur Danto's language, a "narrative concept."[12] That is, the concept has reference to two points in time, not one. What makes a turning point a turning point rather than a minor ripple is the passage of sufficient time "on the new course" such that it becomes clear that direction has indeed been changed.

Note that this "narrative" character of turning points emerges quite as strongly in quantitative and variable-based methods as in qualitative or case-based ones. If quantitative turning points could be identified merely with reference to the past and the immediate present, algorithms locating turning points could beat the stock market. It is precisely the "hindsight" character of turning points—their definition in terms of future as well as past and present—that forbids this.

Given this narrative quality, we can reformulate and generalize our concept of turning point to include simpler "bends" in a curve. What defines a turning point as such is the fact that the turn that takes place within it contrasts with a relative straightness outside (both before and after). Thus, as in figure 8.2A, there is no need for actual change of sign. What matters is the separation of relatively smooth patterns by a turn that is by comparison abrupt. Note that we wouldn't think of an undifferentiated smooth curve (figure 8.2B) as having a turning point, although it clearly involves long-term change.

12. Actually, Danto (1985, chap. 8) discusses "narrative sentences," which he defines as the class of sentences that have reference to two points in time rather than one. I am here extending his insight to cover concepts more generally and arguing that turning point, as a concept, inherently refers to two points in time.

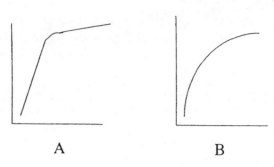

A   B

FIGURE 8.2

The same concept of turning point emerges if we think about reality as discrete and categorical rather than as continuous and numerical. In this view, we imagine social processes as Markov processes. Imagine a simple process that jumps around between various states, with each jump being probabilistically determined given the last location. For example, suppose a process takes on values 0 and 1, such that 95% of the time our next step is simply to repeat the last value. This is a Markov process with the transition matrix

		After	
		0	1
Before	0	.95	.05
	1	.05	.95

Such a process will produce long runs (median length about 15) of 0s and 1s. The turning points will be those relatively rare off-diagonal events that lead to changing the run element. Once in a while, we will get quickly repeated turning points. (In a sequence of six elements after a given start, at these probabilities, we will see two turning points only about 3 percent of the time.) But most of the time, turning points will be rare and clearly evident.

One can generalize this example by imagining a much larger state space with distinct clumps of states, the clumps being areas of that space within which the process wanders randomly while only occasionally jumping to another area. In this case, the Markovian transition matrix would be block-diagonal, with submatrices of substantial probabilities on the diagonal, and sparse submatrices off the diagonal.

This Markov formulation suggests that turning points are related to what Simon called "near-decomposability."[13] By a nearly decomposable system, he meant a system whose parts could be looked at more or less inde-

13. Simon 1969:99 ff.

pendently. Similarly, a process has turning points because it has regular subprocesses between which we switch only rarely. Those rare switches are what we call turning points. In this view, turning points are a second-level matter, governing changes between different first-level regimes, which can to a certain extent be understood on their own. A long-run career can be "nearly decomposed" into these constituent trajectories.

In the continuous formulation, then, turning points involve the separation of relatively smooth and directional tracks by relatively abrupt and diversionary moments. In the discrete formulation, turning points are those rare transitions that take us between different probability regimes. These two formulations both tie directly to traditional themes in the life course literature. The smooth befores and afters are trajectories, linked by a relatively abrupt "turning point." They are stable regimes separated by unusual transitions.[14]

Although the life course literature leads us to focus on the succession of trajectories within a single case, it is important to envision the social structure implied by (or entailed in) this view of turning points. The models given so far suggest a social structure in which there are numbers of trajectories of certain kinds and the life course consists of a person's attempt to hook those trajectories up into a reasonable sequence. People's lives are typically on a steady course, but at various times external and internal shocks mean that an individual must leap to a new steady trajectory.

This view applies well to elite career paths. Once one enters, say, an elite graduate school, one enters a stable trajectory from entry courses through exams and dissertation work. Graduate school is a strongly coercive trajectory: with minor internal variation, of course, but with an enormous amount of inertia. But it is followed by a quite chaotic turning point—entry into the job market—through which a graduate student leaps onto the next more or less stable trajectory: an assistant professorship, a research job, a postdoc, a job outside the specialty. The career constitutes a hooking up of a sequence of such inertial trajectory structures into a life course.[15]

14. The distinction of trajectories from turning points, in practice, will be less draconian. Every trajectory has little turnings within it, just as turning points—if extended—may have little trajectories in them. This fractal interpenetration will make identification difficult. The problems of hierarchically nested processes—which give rise to this interpenetration definitionally—are considered below.

15. It should not be assumed that the ultimate elite career is one that hooks together all the perfect elite trajectories. It may very well be that a Padgett-Leifer robust action argument applies here (Padgett and Ansell 1993; Leifer 1988). The most elite individual may be that person who maintains the largest number of possible future trajectories that s/he could jump onto, just as the most powerful actor is the one whose actions are the least predictable and least specifiable.

From a theoretical point of view, what is important here is the inertial, historicist character of the trajectories. These are life episodes with a capacity for self-regeneration and self-perpetuation. Such episodes are widely programmed into our social institutions: in graduate and professional schools, in internal labor markets, and still, to a surprising extent, in institutions like marriage. Thus, from this view of turning points emerges an implicit image of the social process as comprising a number of programmed inertial trajectories, with strong constraints on their number and desirability. Indeed, one might hypothesize that at extremes of the social spectrum these constraints are quite strong. There are only so many careers available for great opera singers, and these career trajectories exist quite independently of the voices generated and discovered in a given epoch. How the trajectories are actually filled is largely an arbitrary matter of what trajectories are open and who is ready to leap when. And at the other end of the social scale, Erikson's famous account of deviance suggests that there exist similarly inertial deviant trajectories, to which some persons' prior lives must end up being attached, even if that attachment is more or less random with respect to their own prior experience.[16]

In short, this conceptualization of turning points seems closely related to a structuralist view of social life. The focus is on constraints and vacancies, on availability and chance.

But this recognition of the social structural character of turning points should not blind us to the nature of the actors' individual experiences of them. There is for the individual actor a curious inversion of "causality" and "explanation" in the trajectory–turning point model of careers or life cycles. From the point of view of the actor moving from trajectory to trajectory, the "regular" periods of the trajectories are far less consequential and causally important than are the "random" periods of the turning points. The causally comprehensible phase seems unimportant, while the causally incomprehensible phase seems far more so. This paradox deserves elucidation.

What makes the trajectories trajectories is their inertial quality, their quality of enduring large amounts of minor variation without any appreciable change in overall direction or regime. Trajectories are trajectories precisely by virtue of what we might call their stable randomness, their causal character, in particular their comprehensibility under the image of cause implicit in regression thinking. Their inertia arises in stable, but localized, causal parameters.

16. Erikson 1966.

Thus, trajectories might be called "master narratives" in the sense Hughes speaks of "master statuses."[17] Just as a master status like race overrides subordinate statuses like occupation, eradicating them in a simple comparison, so a master narrative is an overarching social process that has the character of coercing processes within it, and indeed of preventing those processes from creating combinations that disrupt it. It is this coercive characteristic that makes trajectories master narratives.

By contrast, turning points are more consequential than trajectories precisely because they give rise to changes in overall direction or regime, and do so in a determining fashion. Thus, while we may want to think of them as "abrupt" and "chaotic," and indeed we may discover them because they appear as irregularities in what has hitherto been a stable trajectory or regime, in fact they are the crucial sites of determination in the overall structure of a life course or an organizational career because they change its parameters. Thus, ironically, trajectories are the periods within which standard statistical modeling might be expected to produce good predictions of outcome, because in a sense that is the definition of a trajectory. But the turning points, precisely because they are the more causally central shifts of regime, will not be discovered by methods aiming at uncovering regimes.

The concept of turning point as so far defined can be generalized in an important way. One can loosen the assumption about the nature of the trajectories on either side of the turning point by allowing one or the other of them to be a random process, rather than a fixed trajectory. (That is, in terms of the immediately preceding discussion, one or the other of them could be a period within which standard causal models did *not* help us predict future outcome.) In this situation, the turning point becomes either a "focal turning point," if the move is from a relatively random trajectory to a relatively fixed and directional one, or a "randomizing turning point," if the move is from a stable trajectory to a random one.

Focal and randomizing turning points are clearly important in life course studies. With Sampson and Laub's juvenile delinquents, for example, many crucial turning points towards "well-adjusted behavior" are focal turning points; they move individuals from random trajectories—involving occasional criminality, mixtures of employment experiences, and successions of social support and friendship networks—to stable trajectories organized around one job, one spouse, one way of life.

A number of writers have considered focal turning points whose out-

17. Hughes 1945.

comes are a function of the specific sequence or type of events within the turning point. Thus, in Thrasher's account of the natural history of gangs, a number of forces combine to coalesce a group into a gang, which then goes through a number of turning points that have varying outcomes depending on the nature of events within them.[18] It is thus important to add to the concepts of focal and randomizing turning points that of the contingent turning point, a turning point whose outcome is dependent on its internal event sequence.

Having characterized the standard, intertrajectory turning point as well as the focal, randomizing, and contingent turning points, we can reflect briefly on the empirical problem of discovering turning points in social processes. In the simplest sense—where we are not concerned about the problem of "quick shifts" (figure 8.1B)—an inspection of signs is sufficient. But within the broader conceptual framework sketched here, the problem is to establish some kind of moving window that can assess both the degree of "trajectoriness" in a currently ongoing trajectory and the "direction" of whatever trajectory does exist. In the broad sense discussed above, trajectoriness refers to some form of consistent causal regime: a constant slope, a constant set of transition probabilities, a constant set of regression coefficients. On the other hand, turning points are evidenced by chaotic internal regimes: varying internal slopes, irregular transitions, inconsistent regressions.[19] A true turning point, as distinguished from a mere random episode, has the further character that the trajectories it separates either differ in direction (slope, transition probabilities, regression character) or in nature (one is "trajectory-like," the other is random).

Recall that neither the beginning nor the end of a turning point can be defined until the whole turning point has passed, since it is the arrival and establishment of a new trajectory (or a determination that randomness will endure, in the case of randomizing turning points) that defines the turning point itself. This means that turning point analysis makes sense only after the fact, when a new trajectory or system state is clearly established. It is this quality that makes the moving window strategy for identifying turning points both practicable and necessary.

II Process, Instant, and Duration in Turning Points

The life course literature, however, has often taken a much broader and looser view of turning points. Writers in that literature have often defined turning points as "a process." Hareven and Masaoka write:

18. Thrasher 1927:56.
19. Griffin and Isaac 1992.

All transitions are potential turning points. Under certain conditions, transitions are perceived and experienced as turning points over the life course—as processes, which continue to influence subsequent events in various forms.

. . . .

A turning point is not an isolated event of short duration. Nor does it entail a sudden jump from one phase to another. A turning point is a process involving the alteration of life path, of [sic] a "course correction." A turning point requires, therefore, certain strategies and choices.[20]

There are several noteworthy aspects to this definition. First, it conforms to our idea that turning points are inherently narrative events, that they are defined as having happened only by observing things that occur after them in time. For example, transitions—which in the life course literature refer to normatively defined life changes like getting married or acquiring a first job—can sometimes be defined as turning points a posteriori by flows of events that proceed out of them.

Second, this definition regards turning points as to some extent subjective. Indeed, the rest of the Hareven and Masaoka article, along with much of the life course literature, regards as turning points those particular events that are defined as such by respondents themselves, however long the hindsight involved. However, while I would not deny that rewriting one's biography is an important aspect of turning points in empirical personal experience, such retrospective interpretive work is not necessary. The work of defining a prior moment as a turning point can as easily be accomplished by a social fact (as in the slope reversal concept of the economists) as by an interpreting human consciousness.

But most important, this definition asserts that turning points "are" processes and that as such they have duration in time. The statement that turning points are processes seems to me a muddled version of the fact that turning point is a narrative concept.[21] On the other hand, the idea that turning points have duration is quite important. The discussion above indi-

20. Hareven and Masaoka 1988:274.

21. In the passage quoted above, as in some other life course writing, the turning point becomes so extended that it no longer is a point in any sense, but rather simply a name for the fact that a change was made over some long period, thus including the situation shown in figure 8.2B as well as relatively sharp turns such as that in 8.2A. It seems best to distinguish these situations, indeed it seems that is the point of having a concept of turning point, as opposed to simply one of change or causality or succession, all of which would cover a turning point of this extremely gradual kind. For an empirical example using such a broad definition, see Pickles and Rutter 1991, e.g., p. 134.

cates that a turning point is always relatively small, compared to the longer (and usually more uniform) trajectories around it. At the same time, the notion of turning point developed here presupposes that turning points in fact have extension in time. Indeed, if we follow a causal theory of the social world, of whatever sort, it seems necessary to believe in this duration. Without it, we would have to assume that the social process sometimes took on new directions instantaneously. But then there would be no source, in some sense, for the change. It would simply arise de novo.

But this issue of instants actually arises even if we allow for turning points with finite duration. We still have to consider the delimitability of those turning points; they have to have a beginning. That beginning is either instantaneous or extended, and if extended, must have a beginning, etc. This Eleatic logic forces us to posit an instantaneous beginning to something (i.e., the beginning of the beginning of the beginning of a turning point) and thus leaves us unable to escape from the issue of how it is that change begins.

In empirical practice, of course, we expect the beginnings of turning points to be fuzzy. The turning point of figure 8.2A, for example, would be very hard to delimit if the entire curve were endowed (realistically) with some high-frequency variability. But the fuzzy character of the practical reality does not free us from requiring a philosophical account for an instantaneous change in an underlying regime. (Note that these considerations apply as much to the ends of turning points as to their beginnings.)

The life history literature's broader picture of turning point and duration thus raises the question of how turning points or beginnings of turning points may be instantaneous. A correlative problem arises when we try to think of turning points in the context of choice models of social life. In a choice model, we view the actor's experience as a perpetual branching process. The actor must first chose a or b, then, depending on that choice, a.1 versus a.2 or b.1 versus b.2. Now the choice-branching model seems to be an instant-by-instant model. But at the same time, the logical nature of the turning point concept—its narrative character—seems to forbid the one-step Markovian view implicit in branching models, since in the latter, choices are defined only with reference to the single moment of decision. A choice is made with respect to the expected future, but not in certain knowledge of whether or not the choice involved will prove to be a turning point.[22]

22. One aspect of turning points not considered at length here is the aspect of irrevocability. I have simply mentioned the concept of a "point of no return" in remarking on Goldthorpe's paper. But there are a number of kinds of threshold events that could produc-

ON THE CONCEPT OF TURNING POINT   253

But there is as well a second difficulty here. In a choice model, individuals are constantly facing decisions; some choose one way, some choose another. In this sense, individuals' experience seems to become ever more unique, ever more specific as time passes. Lives are like dendritic systems starting from simple roots and developing along tracks that always have more possibilities downstream than upstream; choice is always in the future and involves more different things than does the dead past.

The concept of trajectories urged here seems to deny this whole proliferating model. For in its strong form, it imagines a world of socially structured and generated trajectories linked by occasional turning points: a network in time. The social process is made up of overlapping generations of trajectories linked to past and future trajectories by turning points, resulting in sequences (e.g., careers) of "trajectory a, turning point 1, trajectory b, turning point 2, trajectory c," and so on. Such a process is no more complex or open downstream than up, because there are always about the same number of trajectories under way across the whole system, and each individual is either on a trajectory or in a turning point. The issue is merely who gets hooked up to what. That is, the trajectory–turning point model discussed here is a structural, social-level model, while the choice model assumes that there is a purely individual world, whose only "social" structure is something like a clearing market, not a constraining structure.

There are two responses to this question of branching and the proliferation of possible futures. One comes from the recollection that just as potential choices proliferate downstream, potential antecedents proliferate upstream. Individual choices may have more possible descendants with each passing generation. But any given trajectory could have been linked backward (by a turning point) to many different individual prior trajectories, and each of these, in turn, to many trajectories in the next preceding generation. There are dendritic systems going in both directions, and we care about the one or the other depending on whether we view the system from the viewpoint of an individual living into the future or the trajectory that comes to have a certain occupant.

But the second response is the more important. Choice is not an isolated act, but rather one made in a context of many others' choosings. To the extent that trajectories are constrained systemwide, everyone who enters a turning point at any given time is aiming for the same limited array of trajectories. Only a network, not a proliferating system, is possible.

---

tively be viewed within a branching framework. Making the choice to know the sex of one's unborn child is an example. Once known, the fact cannot be un-known.

But the apparent proliferation of futures is only the second problem raised by choice models. There remains the more important problem of instantaneousness, which is raised, as I noted, by turning point duration as well. The problem, again, is how it is that change begins. In particular, if turning points are the embodiment or extended process of change, how is it that *they* get started? This start must take place at a moment, and yet it would seem that given normal ideas about causality, an instant cannot see the production of enduring change. Similarly, since choice processes take place moment by moment, it is not clear how they can give rise to turning points, since we have defined those as necessitating reference to two points in time, not one.

A simple answer to this conundrum relegates turning points to the realm of the subjective, seeing them as post hoc interpretations of choices. This would be the view of most rational choice theorists, but it has the difficulty of failing to deal with turning points that don't arise in such immediate interpretation—turning points in stock prices and the like. Stock prices could of course be reduced to aggregates of individual choices, but changes in, say, an individual's ensemble of preferences could not. The relegation of turning points to the realm of the subjective doesn't work, even if it is clear, as I noted above, that turning points are central concepts in the subjective reinterpretation of the past.

A more effective answer addresses the problem the way Newtonian physics addresses Zeno's arrow paradox. We can't know from looking at an arrow for an instant whether it is in motion or not. But some arrows happen to be in motion while others don't; the passage of time tells us which. This answer worked well for Newton. He dealt with motion by deciding not to explain it, but rather to take it as a primal fact and find the fundamental regularities in which it is involved. ($F = ma$ says nothing whatever about causation; it is a purely descriptive statement.) But this strategy shies away from the fundamental issue of explanation; it suggests that we simply assume the existence of turning points as Newton assumed motion.

But Newton's answer to the Aristotelian question does suggest one way to approach explanation. We should assume that change is the normal state of affairs. The social world is constantly changing and reforming itself. To be sure, large parts of the social world reproduce themselves continually; much of it looks stable. But this is mere appearance. What transpires is reproduction, not endurance. The central reason for making this assumption is practical. It is possible to explain reproduction as a phenomenon sometimes produced by perpetual change; it is not possible to explain change as a phenomenon sometimes produced by perpetual stasis.

By making change our constant, we also exchange our explananda. It becomes necessary to explain reproduction, constancy, and entity-ness, rather than development and change. While I cannot give a full theory here, I shall sketch those aspects of it logically necessary to an account of turning points.[23]

The reproduced (or "constant") portions of the social structure are best imagined as made up of networks of relations between social actors. (They are made up of social relations between actors because, in the simplest sense, that is all there is in the social world. They are networks because the joint occurrence of such relations implies such networks.) Some of these networks of relations involve many actors, some few. Some are compact, some stringy. All are constituted by actors' actions in the present. For example, a university is produced by hundreds of people's coming daily to a set of buildings and talking and acting in certain ways. A great deal of individual variation within those activities is compatible with the endurance of the thing we call a university. That is the resilience of structure—to be impervious to large amounts of variation in teaching practices, ways of being a student, etc. (To discuss how this resilience is produced would take me beyond my subject here.)

That these networks of actions always take place in the present is crucial. The choice theorists and their ancestors the pragmatists are right that the past doesn't exist; it is dead and gone.[24] All its influence on the present comes through its structuring of the immediate past. Social structure is continuously enacted by actors doing things with others. They may do these things for any of a variety of reasons: habit, rational calculation, irrational commitment, etc. All that exists in the social process, however, is the momentary totality at any moment of these actions and the interlocked patterns that they create by connecting and disconnecting multitudes of actors in myriads of relations, of hundreds of types.

Note that any single action impacts many of these networked structures at once. No action accomplishes only one thing. (To believe that was the great error of role theory, as it is of the simpler versions of rational choice.) When I write this paper, I further my career (presumably), I connect my department to certain literatures, I identify my university with certain intellectual stances, I create rivalries with some of my colleagues, I provide employment for editors. The list is endless. These are not simply alternative emplotments. They are the real multiplicity of action. By doing many things, each action reconnects some existing structures, disconnects others,

23. See chapters 7 and 9.
24. Mead 1932. See also chapter 7.

and indeed creates some structures unseen before. These "structures" should not be reified as things; they are simply the patterns of relations (networks of connections) that are likely to reappear at the next iteration of the social process.

At any given time, structures have a particular arrangement—the total network made by them. Some parts of this network are "nearly decomposable," in Simon's term, and can be seen in isolation. Others are interwoven. Given the diverse arrangements of the various networks, there must inevitably exist some peculiarly essential junctures. By "peculiarly essential junctures," I mean junctures where action might make particularly consequential bridges by making or breaking links between many networks, with the consequence of at once rearranging the overall pattern of networked structures. Structure, that is, embodies arrangements that make certain actions or events particularly consequential. For example, it made no difference that some random eighteenth-century London pauper was insane. But encoded and created structures made it rather significant that George III was subject to fits of near insanity. We can think of peculiarly essential junctures as being like arrangements of tumblers in a lock; if an action sits just right under the tumblers, it becomes the key that opens, the agent of sudden advantage or disadvantage.

As I noted, not all parts of these structures are the same and, moreover, some parts will be more or less decomposable from others. In particular, some parts are arranged in such a fashion as to be very difficult to disconnect, to prevent from reproducing. They may acquire this quality because of their extent, their redundancy, their disconnection with other structures, or a number of other reasons. In Braudel's language, these difficult, resistant parts of the network of relations are *structure:* long-enduring patterns. (We often call them underlying, but that implies a hierarchy that is not necessary to enduring structures; they can as well be small as large.) In terms of macropolitics, examples of such enduring structures might be modes of production or regimes of nationhood. In life course studies, they might be "personal character." That these are long enduring means only that they are difficult to disconnect, difficult not to reproduce even if one consciously sets about stopping that reproduction. Often this will be because long-enduring structures are congeries of other shorter-enduring structures or local structures that provide reservoirs of redundancy that enable, indeed often enforce, reproduction even in the face of concerted effort. Hierarchy, that is, is often involved in reproduction. But, as I noted, it is not necessary.

However, hierarchy creates a particular version of the peculiarly essential juncture. Since all structures are continuously reenacted, it will happen from time to time that several local structures under a larger one might be simultaneously disconnected and their own reproduction prevented. This leaves an opening for action, a new juncture, that might assemble their constituent parts in a new way. If some actor takes that action, the result could be a minor turning point, the larger structure going on invulnerable. But once in a while, this minor turning point may line up with other minor turning points to create an opening in the overarching, master structure. Then we have a potential major turning point, in which a whole general regime can change if the proper action is taken. But just as all reproduction hinges on continuous action, so a potential turning point becomes actual only if the action is taken that makes it so. Many potential revolutions fail for want of attempt, just as many attempted revolutions fail for want of structural opportunity.

In summary, it is the nature of structures—partly interlocked with one another, partly hierarchical—that creates the possibility for sudden change in what seemed very stable. The heart of this suddenness is the merely apparent character of the stability in the first place. Change is the normal nature of things, but the effects of local habit and training, in the context of networked structures, mean that a substantial number of networks of social relations reproduce themselves, which makes us call them "large-scale structures." (My point is that such reproduction, and nothing else, is the defining characteristic of those structures.) But since structures always have a particular arrangement, and since that arrangement is always being reenacted in action, the possibility always exists for a pattern of actions to put the key in the lock and make a major turning point occur.

Thus the answer to the question of instantaneousness is that the social process is *always* instantaneous. Instants—the momentary steps of the dialogue of immediate past, present, and immediate future—these are all that exist. The world *is* Markovian. But the past is encoded into the present in patterns of connection that we call structure. The production of the next moment of social life happens from the basis provided by that structure. And the arrangements of structures always leave openings for actions, which if they fit the situation can change the longest-enduring structures quite quickly.

Only after the action has been taken that turns the key can we speak of the turning point as having occurred. It is in this dialogue of structural possibility and action that turning points are defined. Often, as in fall of the Soviet Union, it takes a long time for a system to settle back into structures once decisive action has been taken in a context of structural openness. At other times, the return to (possibly a new type of) stability is swift. But it is the necessity that potentiality be acted upon that makes turning points narrative concepts, in the sense earlier developed. Possibility must emerge before action. Possibility and action together provide the two moments necessary to the narrative structure of a turning point.

Finally, this argument implies that social structure is itself the memory of the social process. In the arrangements that we call social structure lie all the influences of the past. Of course interpretation adds a further dimension to this. Human memory contains much of the past and we act, always, on that basis of that memory. But even without it, the social process still has a memory. That memory is what we give the label of structure.[25]

III Conclusion

This paper has established a number of aspects of turning points. Turning points are best envisioned as short, consequential shifts that redirect a process. The concept is inevitably a narrative one, for a turning point cannot be conceived without a new reality or direction being established, a judgment that requires at least two temporally separate observations. Not all sudden changes are turning points, but only those which are succeeded by a period evincing a new regime.

There is a sense in which turning points are "second-level" moments that separate more uniform trajectories within which a "first-level" regime obtains. However, there is no necessary warrant for seeing turning points as organized or connected by an underlying or overarching (depending on your choice of metaphor) process. They could be simply random, but major, disturbances intervening in a life course. An individual actor (biological or social) experiences such a life course as a sequence of trajectories linked to one another via turning points: trajectory, turning point, trajectory, turning point, etc.

Linked to this view of turning points is a structuralist view of the social process. That process is organized into trajectories, many of which are programmed into institutions like schools, professions, marriage, and the like. These trajectories are often subject to various levels of constraint, ranging

25. In particular, not only is there the issue of actual human memory of the past. There is also the difficulty that the past can, literally, be rewritten. It can change after the fact because of new discoveries and new interpretations. Of course this is not a change in the past for itself, then, as it affected those actors. But it is a change in the interpreted, and hence presently consequential, past.

from pure vacancy constraint to looser class constraints.[26] Trajectories are strongly inertial, enduring substantial variation without change, because of consistent internal causal regimes.

Paradoxically, individual actors experience the causally comprehensible trajectories as less important and less consequential than the less comprehensible turning points. Indeed, there is no necessary reason for turning points to be systematic in their effects. In tightly constrained vacancy systems, for example, they will exercise a largely random effect.

Extended periods of nontrajectory experience are possible. In these, events are random or inexplicable. The turning points leading into and out of such periods are called randomizing and focal turning points respectively. We also recognize turning points whose results are determined by events within them, calling them contingent turning points.

While the concept of turning points is absolutely central to the normal process of autobiography, there is no *necessity* for interpretation in order for turning points to be recognized. Some turning points exist in se, without needing to be "discovered" or "invented."

Turning points have duration and extension. They take time. This follows in part from their inherently narrative character. Nonetheless, they are instantaneous in the sense that all social life is instantaneous. Allowing for the possibility of instantaneous change requires a social ontology founded on process and change, in which stability is a mere appearance. Turning points are thus best theorized as points at which the interlocked networks of relation that preserve stability come unglued and the (normal) perpetual change of social life takes over. This can happen in a variety of ways, particularly in hierarchically organized processes. A major turning point has potential to open a system the way a key has the potential to open a lock. In both cases, too, action is necessary to complete the turning.

My theory of turning points thus fits within a larger view of social structure as the encoded memory of past process. Since at any time the given structure of relations is all that exists (I ignore human memory for the moment), all influence of the past works through the shape given to those relations by the actions of the past. Memory of course provides a symbolic record of the past, which then reinterprets and reshapes it as a foundation for current action. But in the first instance, social structure is itself the memory of the social process.

Where does this leave us with respect to Goldthorpe's critique, with

26. Abbott 1990d.

which I began? This paper challenges Goldthorpe to say what a variable-based methodology would make of the social world if it were constructed in the way suggested here. (By methodology here, I mean not regression specifically, but rather the broader vision of the world implicit in it, what I have elsewhere called "general linear reality.")[27] Within trajectories, I have argued, variable-based methods might work. Identifying those trajectories, however, is a task for pattern-based methods, not variable-based ones. And once turning points are themselves introduced into the data to be analyzed, variable-based methods become even less useful. For through turning points constraint and contingency play roles that mock the presuppositions of variable-based analysis. If the world actually has turning points and trajectories, the only way to find them is to pursue the project of narrative positivism. Goldthorpe has little hope for this project. With due respect, I disagree.[28]

27. See chapter 1.
28. See chapter 6.

CHAPTER NINE

Things of Boundaries

In this paper, I shall argue that it is wrong to look for boundaries between preexisting social entities. Rather we should start with boundaries and investigate how people create entities by linking those boundaries into units. We should not look for boundaries of things, but for things of boundaries.

I begin with some problems that have driven me to think about boundaries. I then consider the logical and theoretical problems involved in my position that boundaries are prior to entities. I then turn to a particular example, the creation of social work in the late nineteenth century. Having discussed this example a bit, I then return to the main exposition, further specifying my argument. I close with a discussion relating this position to some other recent views of social structure.

I Interests in Boundaries

Problems of things and boundaries have arisen in both areas of my research: studies of professions and of temporality.

I theorized the professions as living in an ecology.[1] There were professions, and turfs, and a social and cultural mapping—the mapping of jurisdiction—between those professions and turfs. Change in this mapping was the proper focus of studies of professions and happened most often at the edges of professional jurisdictions. These edges could be studied in the three arenas of workplace, public, and state.

All of this presupposed much about boundaries of professions, of turfs, indeed of jurisdictions themselves. About boundaries, I presumed that they could be specified, that they did in fact separate professions, and that they were the zones of action because the zones of conflict. And indeed, I pre-

This paper was first given as a lecture at the Asilomar conference on organizations at the kind invitation of Richard Scott. I think him for the opportunity to develop these ideas. I thank Robert Gibbons for pointing me towards coalition theory and Michael Wade for discussions of runaway selection. The paper appeared in print in *Social Research* 62 (1995): 857–82; reprinted with permission of *Social Research*.

1. Abbott 1988a.

CHAPTER NINE

sumed a spatial structure to these boundaries, as did the many people who attacked my theory for covering mainly the exceptions in the lives of professions and not accounting for the stable life "at the core of a profession." Here was a notion of professions as convex bodies, with secure heartlands deep behind the boundary territories.

Beyond these implicit presuppositions about boundaries, I presumed something much more profound. In arguing mainly about interprofessional conflict I took for granted the existence of the professions doing the conflicting. This had been necessary, of course. One has to presuppose *something* and if I made interprofessional conflict the focus of attention, the bodies in conflict were the obvious thing to presuppose. But when I argued about the emergence of professions in border territories, or about the gradual dissolution of professions without jurisdictions, or about the transformation of professions via amalgamation and division, I was taking for granted the notion of acting bodies called professions, capable of being split or joined, capable of coming into or losing some kind of permanent existence.

A somewhat similarly linked set of issues about boundaries and entities arose in my work on temporality. One of my central concerns was how processes of different temporal sizes go together. The substantive issue again involved professions.[2] Why were there very few psychiatrists working in mental hospitals in the 1930s when psychiatry had begun as the profession of asylum doctors in the late nineteenth-century? I considered a number of responses to this question. One had to do with an annual mobility model of the behavior of doctors entering and moving within the nervous and mental disease area. Another had to do with the much slower growth of exciting local communities of neurologists and psychiatrists in major cities, communities that changed the very conditions of mobility. Yet another had to do with gradual changes in psychiatric knowledge, moving over a fifty-year period towards psychologism and Freudianism. And a final analysis invoked changes in social control that took more than a century to fall into place.

It was easy to set up these four explanations for the psychiatrists' move but hard to imagine how they went together. If one assumed that knowledge change was the central causal force, then it would determine the mobility choices of psychiatrists in, say the quinquennium 1880 to 1885, even though it itself would not be measurably complete until 1920 or 1930. Obviously that could not be. But it was equally ridiculous to think that such grand, contextual changes never mattered at all. Clearly, all these forces were

2. Abbott 1982.

working through the same present and yet contriving to somehow work independently.

All this drove me towards an intensely processual view of social structure. But if one took such a processual view—as did, for example, George Herbert Mead and Herbert Blumer—the problem of entities became acute. Was a social entity a merely accidental stability in a process, a kind of standing wave? Were boundaries in fact literally ever-changing, and hence not in any real sense boundaries at all?

Now it is easier to explain stasis as an emergent phenomenon in a fundamentally changing universe than vice versa. Social theories that presume given, fixed entities—rational choice being the obvious current example—always fall apart over the problem of explaining change in those entities, a problem rational choice handles by ultimately falling back on biological individuals, whom it presumes to have a static, given character. But it is very nearly as difficult to account, in a processual ontology, for the plain fact that much of the social world stays the same much of the time. Here, too, is the problem of entities and boundaries.

In both these research areas, then, arose questions of the relation between entities and boundaries and questions about the conditions under which social entities can be said to come into or leave existence. In this paper, I propose an answer to the latter question by proposing an answer to the former.

II Boundaries into Entities

I begin with a basic assertion about the relation of boundaries and entities: social entities come into existence when social actors tie social boundaries together in certain ways. Boundaries come first, then entities.

Let me restate this assertion in concrete examples. In the view proposed here, a geographical state is a set of frontiers which are later linked into what topologists call a closed Jordan curve (a continuous single boundary that defines an inside that is nowhere continuous with an outside). An organization is a set of transactions that are later linked into a functional unit that could be said to be the site of these transactions. A legal corporation is a set of market (and other) relations that are later linked in a certain, specified fashion. A profession is a set of turf battles that are later yoked into a single defensible position in the system of professions.

The major alternative to the position I am advocating takes the relation between boundaries and entities as a synchronic, even logical relationship. In this view boundaries are a logical correlate of thingness and vice versa. Therefore, indeed, saying that a set of closed boundaries exists is logically equivalent to saying that a social thing exists. This common view obviously cannot provide a temporal account of the origins of social entities.

It is not surprising that we never start with boundaries. The prototypical entity in modern social thought is the biological human being. We think about social entities as overgrown versions of such biological individuals, and thus have become accustomed to think that social entities have essences like biological individuals, that they have some internal plan or thingness or Aristotelian substance.[3] Moreover, we assign to human individuals a self-other boundary guaranteed by centuries of Cartesian philosophy and cannot imagine such boundaries without human entities, an inability all too easily generalized to the level of social entities.

I am here suggesting that we reverse the whole flow of metaphor. Rather than taking the individual human being as metaphor for the social actor, let us take the social actor as metaphor for the individual human being. Not only is there much biological evidence for this—the world is full of organisms like slime molds and jellyfish that appear to be individuals but are actually societies—but also, under such an assumption the fruitful belief that there might be social boundaries without social entities becomes possible.

Let me now turn to the logical issues of imagining boundaries without there being any entities for those boundaries to be the boundaries *of.* It will be helpful here to be formal. In algebraic topology, spaces are understood in terms of neighborhoods. The neighborhoods of a point x are arbitrarily defined "parts of the universe that are near x." In real (Cartesian) space, neighborhoods are typically circles or spheres or hyperspheres, loci such that all points in the locus are within a certain Euclidean radius of a point. But in general, given a set of neighborhoods and a set M, a boundary point of M is a point x such that every neighborhood of x contains at least one point in M and one point in the complement of M. (The complement of M [M′] is the rest of the universe once M is deleted.)

Note that this formal definition of boundaries requires the prior existence of entities—the set M and its complement—in terms of which the boundaries can be logically defined. Yet the direction of the definitions could be reversed. One could in principle define the neighborhood system and the potential boundary set and *then* construct the set of which the (po-

---

3. In the extreme version (e.g., in event history models), we are willing to think about existence as an attribute and to allow ourselves to imagine things that "are" but that lack the attribute of existence, as if the world were made up of myriads of potential entities, some of which have the predicate of actual existence.

tential) boundary set is the actual boundary. That is, given an assignment of points to neighborhoods and a complete list of potential boundary points, we would say that an entity M exists if we can find *some* assignment of all the points in all the neighborhoods to either M or the complement of M such that (1) each point has a unique location (in M or the complement of M) and (2) given these locations, the points in the potential boundary set all do in fact meet the definition of boundary points vis-á-vis M. This would define a set purely in terms of its property of being a thing that possesses a boundary and is a perfectly legitimate definition. But note that with the definition so constructed there is no guarantee of uniqueness. There might be several ways of assigning the points to a set (not M, but N, O, P, . . .) and its complement (N', O', P', . . .) that fulfilled the definitional conditions. Indeed, these different "assemblies of boundaries" would be many indeed if we allowed the definition of the neighborhood system to fluctuate.

Thus in formal topology, boundaries and entities are more or less logically equivalent. Either one could be primary. But in the logical sequence from neighborhood system to definition of boundary points to definition of set we see a logic of increasing specification that could easily be regarded as temporal, an account of the emergence of entities.

To postulate the temporal priority of boundaries, however, I must come up with a definition of boundary that makes sense even when there is nothing to bound. To do this, I shall replace the concept of set membership with the more general notion of "difference of character." Thus, I shall define a point x as a boundary point in space S if every neighborhood of x contains at least two points that differ in some respect: not one in M and one *not* in M, but simply two points that differ in some respect. (Note that the boundary point is defined "in a space S" rather than "of a set M.") In the simple case this difference will be a single known property—color, gender, creed, education. In the more complicated (and more likely) case, it will be a combination of properties or dimensions of difference.

I have not mentioned "boundary of" anything. These points are simply what we might call "sites of difference." Also note the assumptions, here, of "differences" and of some kind of atomic unit (the point) to which those differences can appertain.

These two assumptions are critical and problematic. The "differences" are things that emerge from local cultural negotiations. That is, local interaction gradually tosses up stable properties defining two "sides." These are not necessarily category labels, although the traditional argument (which starts with entities) would presuppose that. For me, the central requirement is rather that these differences be local and interactional.

But to whom or to what unit do these properties appertain? It would be easy to slide into the traditional argument; these units are preexisting entities—individual people, for example—who bring different, enduring qualities to interaction. In this case, my whole position turns into an elaborate micro-to-macro translation argument.

I wish to claim something more radical. I want to emphasize, with Blumer and other strong interactionists, that the units might be anything—people, roles, physical locations, shards of prior social entities, etc. Of course, any social interaction begins with what is in part a soup of preexisting actors and actions. But interaction is not merely actors' way of reproducing themselves. This is the seductive assumption that fools both functionalism and rational choice theory into accepting a social ontology that by making stasis primary loses its ability to explain change. If we would explain change at all, we must begin with it, and hope to explain stasis—even the stable entity that is the human personality—as a by-product. Previously constituted actors enter interaction, but have no ability to traverse it inviolable. They ford it with difficulty and in it many disappear. What comes out are new actors, new entities, new relations among old parts.

What are these parts? Is this a hidden assumption that there really are enduring, atomic units? It is not if we hold the world to be "a world of events." The parts are then events, instantaneous and unique. That some events have stable lineages, thereby becoming what we call "actors," is something to be explained, not something to be assumed.[4]

Having thus extended the logical foundations of my position, however, I readily admit that the example I shall use in this paper—the constitution of social work as a social entity—does happen to be an example that seems to fit into a micro-to-macro translation framework. But that accident should not mislead the reader. I could as easily have inverted the example, for the production of what are usually called micro entities (the personality, for example) takes place by precisely the same process, but with what we usually call *macro* entities playing the part of sites of difference. (I shall make discuss this example briefly later on. An analogous view of personality was held by Simmel.) Micro and macro are not equivalent to real and emergent. Interaction and events are real; both micro and macro entities are emergent. The world is a world of events.

4. The "world of events" quote is from Mead 1932:1. In this position, I am following Mead and Whitehead; see chapter 7.

III An Example

Let me move from algebraic topology and high theory to social reality in the late nineteenth century. In 1870, social work did not exist; the phrase didn't exist, the set of activities didn't exist, the "thing" didn't exist. There were some activities being done that would eventually be done by social workers but these were not being done by any group of people in particular nor were they aggregated even at the simplest level into the tasks they would be when social work later did them. For example, there were hospitals. Doctors, nurses, and others working in those hospitals sometimes contacted authorities at other institutions about patients they were discharging. But this work was not organized into a systematic set of tasks done by some one role in particular, much less was that role articulated with "similar roles" in other social institutions. Or again, "friendly visiting" by the wealthy to the homes of the poor existed as a behavior, but it was not articulated with anything like a systematic view of charity, but was rather seen as an outgrowth of earlier gentry-type obligations.[5]

Moreover, there were some tasks that would eventually be done by social workers that were not even imagined. Nobody was investigating family structures with an eye to their impact on health. Nobody was thinking about vocational education outside the trades themselves. Nobody was applying psychiatric concepts like stress to everyday life.

By 1920, all this had changed. The word "social work" was old and established. There were professional societies of social workers. There were schools for social work. There were journals for social work. There was an employment exchange and a clearly defined labor market. There were institutions hiring large numbers of such "social workers" and employing them in positions of that name. Most importantly, there was a fairly clear turf, a set of things to do.

If we then ask ourselves, "when did social work emerge?" we find that that question immediately disappears behind the more ominous question of "what does it mean to say that social work emerged?" Now we can address this latter question by turning it into the question of "what was the order in which certain institutions that we take as characteristic of social work emerged?" Then at least we know what came before what. This sequence-of-institutions view at least moves us from a static view of a profession's origins to a narrative one.[6] But the narrative is deceitful. For we build our

5. For specific references on social work, see the references in Abbott 1995a.
6. See Abbott 1991b.

narratives—at least our historical narratives—from back to front. We start with what we know emerged and then seek its origins. But history is lived front to back. Things emerge not from fixed plans, but from local accidents and structures.

In particular, the social work turf itself, the shape of the things to do and of things done, was by no means the relatively given factor that it appears in, say, the case of medicine. Nor should its origins be intuited by reasoning back from what appeared in the 1920s. Rather, we must ask ourselves why things like probation and kindergartens, which were originally part of this area of activity, disappeared from it in the final "thing" that emerged as social work.

Even worse, by the time we see major institutional events in social work, we are well past the real moment of structuration, the moment when the very shape of tasks began to become fixed. For example, the first local social work school arrived in New York, in 1898. The first professional associations arrived in the teens, typically specialty associations in areas like medical and psychiatric social work. The social work labor exchange also appeared in the teens, as one of the major activities of what would slowly become the national professional association in reality as well as name.

But the real action was long before. The area of charities and welfare began to take its first loose shape within the National Conference of Charities and Corrections, which began in 1874. At that original meeting were doctors, lawyers, clergymen, wealthy men and ladies, university faculty, and a whole variety of others. Under its consideration were things like vocational education and probation, as well as lunacy, tuberculosis, venereal disease, alcoholism, unemployment, child welfare, and who knows what else. The early institutions for social welfare—institutional churches, settlement houses, dozens of individual charities and charity societies—articulated between these and many other problems and services. Settlement houses provided kindergartens, cooking classes, adult education, and vocational guidance as well as several varieties of what we now think of as social services.

To the people of that time, all these different services, which seem to us like things that belong in schools and jails and hospitals and other such places, made sense together in one site. The emergence of social work as an entity was (i.e., can be defined as) the separation of those things into tasks that fell under social work and tasks that fell elsewhere. And it is my contention here that the separations themselves emerged as independent, unconnected boundaries long before it made any sense to speak of social work as a social entity.

Let me now return to the formal exposition. I had defined boundaries not as points all of whose neighborhoods contain both some inside and some outside, but rather simply as points all of whose neighborhoods contain sites of difference. I did not insist that all those differences be the same.

Such sites of difference are very common. Indeed, in many social states of affairs, they are quite random. Early social work is quite typical in this regard. If we look at John Mohr's data on New York charities organizations, we find that lots of adjacent charities differed in lots of different ways.[7] His main data happen mainly to involve client differences, but other data show many other kinds of differences.

These locally random sites of difference become proto-boundaries only when they line up into some kind of extended opposition along some single axis of difference. Thus we might have two kinds of people who do some task and find that difference lining up into a systematic difference across many work sites, or across several types of institutions. The kind of boundary that emerged between systems analysts and programmers in the 1970s and 1980s is an example of this. It appeared and reappeared independently in organization after organization. In this case, we have an extended set of boundary points that began to take a special reality by virtue of the precedence of one or a limited number of types of difference. The names were conveniences to describe the boundary, which emerged well before there was any really systematic social reality to the entity "systems analysis" or "programming." It was rather that a dimension of difference—in this case over how one approaches a computing problem—emerged across a number of local settings to produce a proto-boundary.

Note, however, that I have assumed, in the word "local," some kind of adjacency structure to the social space involved. That is, we imagine some kind of metric of propinquity that places institutions or areas. Examples of these metrics might be professional mobility between areas, or career structure linkages between areas, or relations of division of labor, or client exchange, or whatever. It seems to me that we should for the present leave the nature of propinquity open. I simply underline that I have assumed some kind of propinquity measure, which may or may not be independent of the dimensions of difference.

I am now poised to present a conception of the origin of entities. In my social work example, we have a zone of social space that we may loosely call welfare space or social order space in which various proto-boundaries are

7. Mohr 1992, 1995.

set up. These might involve gender, training, or prior profession. It is the yoking of these proto-boundaries that makes the entity "social work." Note that it didn't really matter what these boundaries were, at first. They began as simple, inchoate differences. They were not boundaries *of* anything, but rather simple locations of difference. They were not associated from one workplace to another; they were not consistent from one client type to another; they were not necessarily stable over time.

For example, kindergartens began in the 1880s to be conducted by people with a much wider variety of backgrounds than had appeared in the earlier Froebelian movement; some came from education, some from volunteering, some from churches. And these people also differed in some cases by gender, by class, by level of education. Rapid expansion from the earlier, smaller movement drove this differentiation. But the important distinction that emerged was in levels of special training; the older, specially trained Froebelians were overwhelmed by less trained workers coming into kindergartens via the settlement houses. But in the probation field the dimension of difference was different. In probation, the main difference was among clients, who were themselves differentiated by the state laws governing probation, and this difference of clients in turn drove a difference in the origin and orientation of people working with those clients; adult probation largely demanded legal professionals, while child probation was dominated by the newer aims of the child welfare movement.

Both kindergartens and probation thus became sites of difference, and hence boundaries in my sense, but the differences were not similar across the two areas, or even across given instantiations of a type of institution in a single area. In other parts of social welfare a gender proto-boundary emerged. The best example of such a boundary was in psychiatric social work, an area in which men (psychiatrists) and women (psychiatric social workers) did largely the same kinds of things under different professional banners. In other areas, what mattered was a similar opposition between people who had connections to churches and those who did not. Friendly visiting itself—the very root of social work—was such an area.

Social work as an entity came into existence when various social agents—the leaders of the settlement and charities organization movements, the heads of state boards, the superintendents of institutions—began to hook up these sites of difference into larger proto-boundaries, and then into larger units. (Other agents—particularly leaders of other environing professions and proto-professions—did so as well, the most important of these being the newly powerful occupation of school superintendents.)

[handwritten annotation:] Idea: the recognition of difference as significant to a context is what links it as a boundary. This is created, and mapped as part or not part for the actor. In aggregate, these differentiations negotiate to a new, socially stable, boundary

That is, social work emerged when actors began to hook up the women from psychiatric work with the scientifically trained workers from the kindergartens with the nonchurch group in friendly visiting and the child workers in probation. All those people were placed "within" social work, and the others ruled outside it. An image was then developed to rationalize this emerging reality as a single thing. Unfortunately, in the process of making such a hookup, certain areas (like probation) may have ultimately proved too distant, in some sense, to have one of their parties included in the emerging thing called social work.

This is not to argue that in some cases, along other dimensions, a single boundary may not have been crucial. One "edge" of social work illustrates this well. An important boundary in home economics, industrial education, and kindergartens was that between services that were school-based and those that were settlement house–based. All of these areas *could* have ended up "in" social work. But by linking the "school" sides of these boundaries together, school administrators achieved a much more secure location of certain welfare subjects into the school curriculum than did the emerging social work leaders into their own institutions.

Note that these various proto-boundaries may well reach clear out of what a functionalist might regard as social order space. Gender differences are an obvious example. A gender opposition in kindergartens, for example, was tied directly to similar oppositions in school systems via those particular sites where kindergartens had been started in schools. The social world is a crazy quilt in several dimensions, with many local regularities and edges, some of which peter out in quite small areas, and some of which run clear out of sight.

The making of an entity is simply the connecting up of these local oppositions and differences into a single whole that has a quality which I shall call "thingness" (which I will examine shortly). In a great many cases this connecting up is a matter of conscious agency. The process involved in creating the medical profession in mid-nineteenth-century England is a good example. There were four or five potential candidates for inclusion in the whole thing to be called medicine: the apothecaries, who had begun by selling medicine but were now organized into a tight, self-examining group; the chemists with their skill in drug manufacture; the surgeons with their physical expertise; the physicians with their university degrees. The preceding unities of these groups had broken up because a new dimension of difference—expertise certified by direct examination—was created by the apothecaries. On this new dimension, the kinds of things available to differentiate physicians from surgeons and apothecaries—things like university degrees and certain kinds of training periods—failed to provide continuing, effective differentiation. That is, the new dimension of difference collapsed preexisting differences. In this new way of looking at the medical world, the only effective, sharply differentiable entity one could create was one that would include physicians, surgeons, and apothecaries, which is precisely the group that became the modern British medical profession in 1858.

Note that what the apothecaries did was to change the way one looked at the space of differences. It was as if they forced a three-dimensional world into two dimensions, and in doing so moved themselves from the periphery into the center of the medical group. As a result of their act, other professions and actors beyond the professions moved to create a new unity. The emergence of social entities is often such an act, a drawing together of things. It could arise in any of the sources of action—charisma, tradition, optimization, accident, monomania, value rationality. We should remain explicitly agnostic about which is actually involved.

I need now to consider the term "linking up" or "yoking" that I have used throughout to refer to the connection of boundaries. What does it mean to say that an organization is a set of transactions which are later linked into a functional unit that could be said to be the site of these transactions? Or that a legal corporation is a set of market relations that are later linked in a certain, specified fashion? Or that a profession is a set of turf battles that are later yoked into a single defensible position in the system of professions?

Yoking means connection of two or more proto-boundaries such that one side of each becomes defined as "inside" the same entity. There seem to be two ways in which this can be done. In the example of British medicine just mentioned, the introduction of examinations had the effect of destroying a previous dimension of difference—broadly speaking, that of class, both of practitioner and client—thereby bringing things close together that had previously been far apart. In formal terms, such a yoking is a projection from a social space of higher dimensionality to one of lower dimensionality. (For example, Monterey, California, is right next to Monterey, Tennessee, if one ignores the difference in longitude, because the two are at the same latitude—$36°15'$ N.)

This kind of yoking is, I am persuaded, the central form used when a social space is already filled with entities, when a division of a social space into entities is already established and institutionalized in some way. Under such circumstances, the only ways to radically change arrangements in a social space are to delegitimize old differences or to emphasize new ones. The former strategy yokes entities together, the latter divides them.

But when a social space is empty or, rather, unstructured, as was the case with the area of social order and welfare in the late nineteenth century, yoking means literal connection of boundaries. That is, to create social work, a group of actors hooked up the female side of friendly visiting with the non-church-affiliated side of the provision of social services with the nonmedical side of patient work in hospitals and so on. The founding definitions of social work included one group from each of these disputes, placing that group "inside" the entity-to-be.

This second kind of entity emergence can be envisioned in two ways, one of which looks backward to the sources of my argument, the other of which depends on terms yet uninvestigated. In terms of my earlier definitions, the emergence of an entity is the assemblage of various sites of difference—boundaries in the loose sense defined earlier—into a set of boundaries in the topologically strict sense, boundaries that define an inside and an outside. But the work of creating an entity must also be seen as the work of rationalizing these various connections so that the resulting entity has ability to endure, as a persistent thing, in the various ecologies in which it is located.

IV Thingness

This brings us to the issue of thingness, entity-like quality, endurance, or whatever we wish to call it. In the processual ontology that I am here setting forth, the central quality of an entity is endurance. If "the world is a world of events," in Mead's ringing phrase, then what distinguishes entities is their property of repetition, of being events that keep happening in the same way. Repetition could arise either internally, through some structure of causes that internally regulates "enduring events," in which case I shall speak of internal reproduction. Or it could arise from an external structure, an ecology that leaves no real room for change in the individual, in which case I shall speak of ecological reproduction.

But entity-ness seems to me to go beyond mere recurrence. If one recalls my original question about the mutual effects of historical processes of different sizes, it is clear that what makes a historical event important is its independent standing as a site of causation, as a thing with consequences. It is this independent causal authority of large-scale and small-scale events that makes theorizing the social process so difficult. And what is true for large and small events is true also for large and small entities, which are, on my argument, a subclass of events. Thus, a second crucial property of entities is their ability to originate social causation, to do social action. But action here must be defined broadly, not merely as Weberian subjective action, but rather as any ability to create an effect on the rest of the social process that goes beyond effects that are merely transmitted through the causing entity from elsewhere.

An entity is therefore something more than a standing wave. It acquires, somehow, a coherence or internal autonomy. If that coherence is lacking, if we have pure ecological reproduction, to which is added no internal solidity, it may be less useful to think of a given recurrent event as an entity. At a minimum we must distinguish between such "internal" and "ecological" forces promoting entities.

For a set of examples, let me return for a moment to the theory of occupations. It is pretty clear that our ideal type of an occupation includes three things: a particular group of people, a particular type of work, and an organized body or structure, other than the workplace itself, capable of some kind of reproduction. The high professions and the guilds are of course the archetypical examples of such occupations. But we can easily imagine social entities that lack one of the three attributes, but that are, in fact, real social entities, in the sense that they can be continuously reproduced and can have independent causal consequences.

First, suppose that we have a particular group of people who are doing a particular kind of work, but who aren't organized. Such quasi occupations typically appear in the formative years of strong-form occupations. But they may also be permanently created, if there are organizational forces—laws against combinations of workers come to mind—that prevent worker organization.

But we can also imagine a particular group of people with an organized body and no work. Usually this situation arises from technological change or from displacement by other groups or from loss of demand. The railroad engineers illustrate the first of these, psychic mediums the second, and the clergy, at various times, the third. We can call such groups "workless occupations." And finally, we can imagine an organizational structure tied to a particular body of work, but no consistent group of people doing that work. These can be called "turnover occupations," for their chief characteristic is the intense turnover of workers within them. The nineteenth-century railroads offer examples of this, but more characteristic are modern life-cycle occupations, occupations served by individuals only at certain points of the life cycle—flight attendants in the early years of flying, for example.

I thus have four types of occupations, so far: strong-form occupations, quasi occupations, workless occupations, and turnover occupations. All of these are entities, in the sense that they can persist and that they can have causal consequences for adjacent social groups. It is clear that we are willing to think of them as social things.

But suppose I ask whether there are occupational entities with only one of the foundational properties of an occupation. What does it mean to think about a particular group of people in the work world, without either an organization or an area of work? How would such a group be identified? Such a situation could arise as an occupation was disappearing. An example might be canal boatmen, who up until a few years ago existed in dwindling numbers in rural New Jersey and Pennsylvania. There was an annual reunion, but no work and no organization. It was an occupation of memory, and in fact had no causal consequences for anybody. Similarly, it makes little sense to think of a mere organizational form surviving, without work to do or a consistent set of members. Surely this is not a social entity in any real sense.

But the third moment of occupation—an area of work to do—exists in some people's minds as a social thing. It is true that one might think of disaggregated tasks, at a very low level, as existing in discrete chunks, independent of particular people or organizations. (To imagine them aggregated is the enticing trap of simple functionalism.) Thus, in the social welfare area, things like teaching a mechanical arts class or contacting another welfare institution or directing a program for small children—these could all be seen as simple tasks. But how these tasks are connected up is precisely what constitutes the making of a social entity. It is all very well for the functionalists to say "doctors have control of everything that helps make the body well," thereby identifying the area of wellness. But this area did not exist ex ante; one has only to think of the exclusion from it, by the medical profession's definition of its turf, of the single greatest determinant of wellness—diet— which the profession has been quite content to leave to uninstructed family members for years. So this single dimension—of task—is also no warrant for defining an entity.

We can then draw an effective line between entities and nonentities in occupational life. I would like to raise two issues about this distinction, however.

First, the argument presented here is basically an argument about tiling, about dividing up a space in some way. Taking it as a general model for the creation of social entities seems to assume that the typical process of entity emergence in social life is division of labor or turf. To what extent do we in fact wish to assume this? Or are there rather several types of origins for social entities, one of which is division of labor? It is true that processes like amalgamation and division can be understood within a boundaries-into-entities format. Division, for example, is simply making an internal difference into part of an external boundary, putting that internal difference on the same footing as the inside/outside distinction.

But it would be harder to so construe cloning, the typical mechanism favored by the new institutionalists (like John Meyer) to account for the origin of entities. Suppose we create a new franchise or a new university. Aren't these simply clones of existing structures, and thus doesn't their origin lie rather in imitation than in association of differences? In a broader sense, cloning can be construed as a version of role theory, and thereby directly connected to the notion that social reality is produced by plans and scripts put into place by actors, á la Parsons. To me, however, it seems more useful to think about such scripting as a phase in the construction of entities. That is, in the view presented here scripting is one of several ways of conducting the action that pulls together a set of boundaries into a social entity.

Scripting cannot be seen as independent of boundaries because no social entity ever takes shape in a vacuum. Ecological constraints are always in position, and thus scripting alone can never produce an entity. Take the extreme case of the production of a human personality within a family. A first child enters a complex environment of two adults, with various boundaries placed between them in various dimensions and directions. And those of us who have children know well that the child's personality emerges as a pulling together of various of those existing oppositions. The Oedipus complex is precisely a contest over such a difference. There are many others, arising in different differences that divide the parents in different ways. From a hooking-up of these differences comes a new social entity—the child's personality—that in turn restructures the existing boundaries of the relationship between the adults, just as successive children will redraw the cozy threesome of parents and only child. A child's personality emerges as an assemblage of various sides of various sites of difference between parents and child, parent and parent, and child and other children.[8]

Thus, it seems best to retain the notion that the prestructure of an entity lies in the creation of zones of difference within the social process or social

8. This argument shows why replacing traditional role theory with a role theory based on structural equivalence is useful. Recipes and scripts can be proposed, but ecological constraints select among them. The result is a hybrid "role theory" that consists of a dialogue between scripts and surrounds.

space. These zones of difference gradually shape into proto-boundaries, which are then yoked by some kind of activity into an entity. If this proto-entity is to persist, it must have both internal reproduction and some kind of causal authority. We must, however, recall that this process is not in any way necessary. There are many ways a given set of boundaries could have been structured into an entity, and what matters is simply that the resultant entity have internal reproduction and causal authority, not that it be optimal in any way. Rather, it must satisfice. Boundaries are *always* being set up within groups, but only occasionally do these fall into defensible or coherent possible entities. Sometimes, action or accident takes advantage of that. But there is no guarantee of being "best."

I would like also to make another claim about the process of boundaries-into-entities. It seems to me quite significant that entity-status among occupations involves more than one dimension of difference or structure. It may well be that social entities cannot exist without the tension provided by the differing pulls of different structural dimensions. That is, what gives entities their structural resilience is their defensibility, their endurance in several different dimensions of difference. In a simple form, this might be seen as a sort of overlapping cleavages argument. Strength lies in overlapping cohesiveness of several kinds. Yet at the same time, an entity's causal influence or extent may reflect vast extensions along certain particular dimensions. That is, while it might seem that compactness (or heartlands or whatever metaphor we choose) would best allow an entity to reproduce and defend itself against redefinition out of existence by other entities, what produces causal authority may well be connection across long reaches of the social world.

The professions offer numerous instances of this phenomenon. A good example would be actuaries, who have a tightly organized, rigidly controlled, and quite small occupation. Entry is tightly structured, careers are tightly structured, task is tightly structured. In all three basic dimensions of people, work, and organization, actuaries are sharply bounded from the rest of the professional labor force. Yet it is in a sense because of this that their influence is so small. By contrast, consider the accountants whose "profession" is porous to the point of absurdity, whose careers lead in quite diverse directions, and whose task areas include heavily contested zones like tax law, unstructured areas like management consulting, and dying heartlands like public auditing. The accountants are in fact far more causally effective than the actuaries because they can bring their force to bear in so many different arenas, where they play so many different roles. It is precisely the structure of long tenuous boundaries anchored to a few more or less secure heartlands that enables accounting to be powerful. As in the Padgett-Leifer argument, openness provides strength.[9] Just as for Leifer skill means never having to make rational choices, for entities strong causal effect means never being pinned in any one heartland.

This strength refers to endurance, to the temporal dimension of entities, as well. Rigidity provides short-term safety, but long-term vulnerability, as is well shown by the rigid but self-defeating temporal structure of the English lawyers when compared with the open and tenuous layout of the Americans.[10]

V Conclusion

In closing I shall mention the relation between this view of social reality and certain others. I have already mentioned the new institutionalism, a view emphasizing isomorphism of entities and production of isomorphic entities both by ecological processes (so-called "coercive isomorphism") and by cloning (a version of "mimetic isomorphism").[11] I have elsewhere argued that much of the new institutionalism has failed to make the leap to a process theory of reality, a failure embodied in part in the emphasis on cloned institutions.[12] A simple reproduction model is far from the precarious, processual social world envisioned here.

Another theory of entities identifies them as congeries around an ideal type. Lakoff and others, for example, believe social entities are constructed by defining an ideal type and then identifying various entities that resemble it as members of its class.[13] "The professions" (as a class) is an excellent example of such a phenomenon, with medicine and law as the ideal types. But I believe this process of naming and metonymy comes much later, long after the structuration processes discussed here. Archetypal class images are central at that later moment, but do not play an important role in creating entities in the first place, except insofar as scripts play the role I earlier assigned to them. As in board games like go and chess, by the time the structures are clear enough to be labeled and discussed, they have long since been established.[14]

Another related theory is that branch of game theory dealing with coali-

9. Padgett and Ansell 1993; Leifer 1991.
10. Abbott 1988a, chap. 9.
11. Both terms are from DiMaggio and Powell 1983.
12. Abbott 1992b.
13. Lakoff 1987.
14. Leifer 1991.

tions.[15] To be sure, there are obvious ways in which game-theoretic concepts differ from the general view of social reality presented here. The world of game theory is not one of general flux and indeterminacy, of unbounded games in indefinite temporalities between players who themselves can be reconstructed and whose interests and resources differ in undefined and crosscutting ways. Nonetheless, coalition theory is among the most indeterminate in game theory: its foundations complex, its implications unclear, its solution concepts conflicting. There is some sense in which thinking of entities as "coalitions of units" accords well with the view presented here, particularly in a micro-to-macro context.

A final relevant theory is the theory of what we might call attractor structures. In social life, we often have situations in which runaway processes destroy the middle ground of indeterminacy around a group. A group's interest in compliance with extreme rules by its members reduces free riding and hence increases rewards for remaining members, who further strengthen the extreme rules, etc. Iannaccone notes such a mechanism among churches.[16] Similar runaway evolutionary processes leading to stable "entities" (in this case whole social structures) are discussed by Michael Wade and others.[17] These models are all organized by the same intuitive idea: that under certain conditions becoming a well-defined group strongly increases the rewards to constituents of that group. This intuition presumes a micro/macro character I have tried to avoid, but the overall structure of the theoretical argument is still closely related to the arguments made here.

In this paper I have set forth the view that social entities are often secondary to social boundaries. It is unclear whether this rule holds only in rare cases—unformed turfs like social welfare in the late nineteenth century—or is the general rule accounting for entities in social life. Addressing that question, however, means embedding this claim within a larger, general theory of social structure and temporality. Such a task takes me beyond the bounds of a short essay.

15. On coalitions, see Myerson 1991, chap. 9.
16. Iannaccone 1994.
17. Breden and Wade 1991; Wade 1995.

Time Matters

In this epilogue I shall try to bring together the themes of this book. As is necessary in such a summary, the discussion is often telegraphic. A full argument would be book length itself. Moreover, there are difficulties even in making a summary. The book's chapters were written over a twelve-year period in which I wrote about many other topics and over the course of which my ideas changed considerably. But nonetheless, there are underlying ideas and concerns that make something like a single whole.

I begin by setting these chapters in their larger context, discussing the audiences I had in mind and what I aimed to say to whom. I then summarize the critique of standard statistical sociology set forth in chapter 1 and elaborated in various ways by the chapters that follow it. I then turn towards the narrative alternative to standard sociology that I have urged throughout these papers, covering its assumptions and problems in turn. This discussion leads into a consideration of problems of explanation and causality. From this I emerge into a general theoretical discussion, first treating temporality per se, then turning to the question of time and social structure.

This design captures a logic that must be familiar to any reader who has come this far. In most of these papers, as in the course of my career, there is a progression from methodological critique to theory. In effect, the critical task of reflection about standard methods has stimulated my substantive work on the nature of the social process. There is thus a fractal character to the pattern, each article recapitulating in its own way the move that is also characteristic of the larger history of my thinking. I should note, finally, that I have throughout this chapter tried not only to summarize, but also to note in passing developments unmentioned earlier and to place the whole endeavor in a more general context.

I Audiences

In most of this work, I had two audiences in mind. The first of these comprised my colleagues in standard sociology. My conversation with them
very quickly settled into a fixed pattern:

ABBOTT: Social reality is more complicated than you think
and you might want to rethink your methodological
commitments.
COLLEAGUES: We already know everything you told us and
besides you offer no real alternative.

The various versions of this nonconversation over the years taught me a great deal and drove me towards a more profound understanding both of the methods I was trying to invent and of the paradigmatic nature of the assumptions involved in any attempt to formalize social reality.

But this audience's main contribution was to keep my critique honest. Unlike other sociologists engaged in similar projects, I did not label the mainstream as wrong or wrongheaded, dismissing their methods out of hand. Rather I attempted what is aptly called reverse engineering. I worked their methods through from back to front, sometimes down to the level of the programming, and asked again and again what became in those methods of the crucial elements of social theory. In the process I discovered a lot about social theory I would otherwise never have bothered to notice. All this because I did not lose sight of this audience and tried to make my critique stand on its own before them.

What I thought I was saying to them changed with time. My first papers aimed to sketch out a possible ground, to clear a space. By the time of the papers in part 2, however, I was busy protecting the little methodological plant in my greenhouse (optimal matching–based sequence analysis) from the chill winds of reviewers. I was making the same polemic, but using it to protect something. Also, I had begun to have philosophical misgivings about my own methods. By the later papers—chapters 2 and 3 and the papers of part 3—I was moving ahead to my own theoretical agenda; the critique of methods became less important than my new ideas about social structure.

My second principal audience comprised my qualitative colleagues. This was the harder group. Many qualitative colleagues—ethnographers, historical sociologists, theorists, and the like—simply wrote off quantitative work, usually on the basis of somewhat facile objections of principle. My conversation with this group, too, settled down to a fixed pattern:

ABBOTT: Social reality is more complicated than we think
and we might need to rethink our quantitative methodologies.
COLLEAGUES: We already know everything you told us and
then some. And why bother rethinking something that is
in principle useless?

My relation to this audience was odd. Although they often provided my sites of publication and certainly produced the majority of the citations to my work, that work became for them more a useful piece of propaganda than a matter of intellectual importance. I felt in the early papers that I was a leader of an offensive, parachuting behind enemy lines and ripping up the railroads. But as the 1990s wore on, qualitative sociology simply declared victory and moved on to other battlefields. I began to feel a little like those Japanese soldiers who occasionally used to turn up in the Philippines, still fighting a war everybody else thought was over. My exasperation showed in some of my later papers, in particular in chapter 2, which starts with the usual critique of positivism, but ends with an insistence that properly studied the vast output of positivism could support a profound quantitative inquiry into culture and multiplicity of meaning. Thunderous silence. Overall, my qualitative audience gave me little intellectual stimulation, since very few people in that audience had any belief they could learn something from the vicissitudes of quantitative social science, much less any interest in its reform.

One of the things I did learn from my audiences was that there were issues that neither side wanted carefully analyzed. In particular, neither side liked my position that we ought to disentangle a number of conflated dichotomies—narrative versus analysis, interpretation versus positivism, constructionism versus realism, situated knowledge versus transcendent knowledge. This particular gesture of analytical rigor makes a number of appearances in this book (in chapter 4 and particularly in chapter 6). But it greatly irritated both of my principal audiences. Each side wanted these dichotomies all run together like so much mush; mush apparently facilitated their reciprocal polemics, which were in general directed inward to rally the troops rather than outward as real acts of intellectual contest. Eventually my concern over this problem of conflation ran together with other ideas and produced the book *Chaos of Disciplines*.[1]

II Schemes of Social Science

A fundamental theme of these papers is that there are a number of ways to conduct quantitative or formal or generalizing or explanatory social sci-

1. One of the more amusing aspects of growing older has been to hear the younger generation in sociology declare victory by announcing that it sees no conflict between quantitative and qualitative, but can do them both. So can I, but not without a lot of internal gearshifting and double-clutching. Somehow, I don't think my younger colleagues have even begun to see the problem. Abbott 2001 contains extensive analyses of such declarations of victory.

ence. (The issue of which word is the right one will be dealt with below.) There is more than one way to skin this cat. The papers give a number of different versions of what the alternatives are to our standard procedure.

One clear alternative is a social science that mainly problematizes flows of units, of social entities, loosening up the standard assumption that the social world consists of fixed entities with variable properties. Our present example of such an alternative is formal demography, with its focus on birth, death, and migration of units. But I was not thinking merely about demography of people. Several of these papers insist that demography should generalize itself by studying birth, death, amalgamation, and division of organizations and other social-level entities. This generalization would give it more basic processes to think about, more complex objects of analysis, and a multilevel set of things to analyze. (Chapter 9 is a step in this direction.) I have by no means explored the possibilities of a serious demography of society, nor have the demographers, most of whom, under the banner of "social demography," have been seduced into abandoning their intellectual patrimony for the fleshpots of regression.

A second general alternative to standard methods is the structural one, which relaxes the fifth assumption of chapter 1 by emphasizing the mutual determination and interdependence of cases. This has been the program of network analysis and some related work. A number of my papers here mention it briefly, but it has developed considerably in the last two decades under the leadership of Harrison White and requires no further mention here.

The third general alternative relaxes the sequence and time-horizon assumptions of chapter 1: the assumptions that order makes little difference to social processes and that events are of uniform size and continuous. This is the narrative program that preoccupies me in this book, and to which I return below. Finally, implicit in chapter 2 is a multivocality program that would relax the univocality assumption of standard methods by letting variables have several meanings at once. Aside from a small amount of work applying multidimensional scaling to cultural systems, there has been little development here. (Little development in sociology: there is a quantitative study of culture—cultural evolution fits under this heading—but it is not really about formalizing conceptions of ambiguity, rather about treating cultural terms as objects in a univocal sense.)

While I have suggested that pursuing these various programs would be interesting simply in its own right, there are also some particular pragmatic reasons for doing so. These have to do with the nature of data. One of my ongoing critiques of the standard approach is that it tends to assume that most things that can happen do happen, that most of the potential data space has something in it. Moreover, the standard approach assumes that the patterns we expect in that data space are global, that they are the same at every point in the space. In this view, interaction effects at most slightly modify a basic underlying regularity. Often these assertions are true of our data, but probably more often they are not. When pattern is local, methods seeking global regularity don't find it. When the data space is mostly empty, one requires methods that ignore the empty space and focus on what is full. I have argued throughout that the structural and narrative programs—which aim at finding regularities and patterns directly rather than presuming a form for them ahead of time—probably work much better with datasets that have a lot of local order and empty data space. In this connection it is striking that standard methods tend to be applied to very noisy data spaces, a fact that Dan Smith pointed out many years ago.[2] We tell ourselves that we simply aren't interested in patterns that are "too easy." But in fact, as chapter 5 shows, much of our data is probably more locally ordered than we think.

Another important issue I have discussed is the question of why one should choose a particular variable (in a particular study) to be "dependent." If our aim is to understand the social process, there is no need to make one or another variable more important, and certainly, as chapter 2 shows, there is no particular reason to think that any particular indicator has a given status as dependent or independent. In fact, the impetus to call certain social variables more important than others in sociology comes overwhelmingly from meliorism; by far the most common dependent variables in sociology are those related to inequality. If we step aside from that project and simply ask "how should we understand the social system?" we have no real way to think about dependent and independent, and indeed, very little reason to, since our initial premise has to be that social life is an immense web in which everything is affecting everything else. From that point of view, our problem is one of data reduction. And from a data reduction point of view, the standard approach is worthless; as I have said many times, it boils down to reducing the dimensionality of the data space by something less than one. From a pattern search point of view, this is a waste of time. In summary, the nature of our data and the projects we pursue play an important role in guiding our choice of general methodological program.[3]

2. Smith 1984.
3. I have argued elsewhere (Abbott 2000) that we are about to be deluged by datasets of such size and detail that methods change will be forced on us willy-nilly. The commercial

Thus, I have argued throughout that there are several general programs for thinking about regularities in social life. They have different strengths and different weaknesses. They can all be imagined as relaxing certain of the basic philosophical assumptions of standard statistical sociology. We should see standard methods within this much broader context.

III The Standard Model and Its Assumptions

A basic concern throughout the book, appearing in nearly every chapter, has been the philosophical foundation of standard sociological methods. This foundation consists of beliefs about social ontology that are implicit, or sometimes explicit, in the methods as they are customarily used. These are not the more familiar statistical assumptions of standard modeling, although they are in several cases implied by those assumptions when applied to social data. They are rather philosophical assumptions, things that have to be true about the social process if we are to think that standard methods are giving us worthwhile information about that process. (I have given these assumptions in various orders throughout the book. Here, I give the basic entities assumption first, then the various temporal and causal assumptions, then the contextual and "meaning assumptions.")

The first of these is the assumption that the social world consists of fixed entities with varying properties. It is assumed that some subset of these varying properties determines another, single property, which is called the dependent variable. Rather than seeking to simplify entities that are at first apprehended in their full complexity, however, the standard system builds entities up from minimal properties by adding only those necessary to explain what it has set as the explanatory problem. In certain extreme forms, the variable property to be predicted is existence, and standard methods envision entities that have substantive properties but that lack the predicate of existence. In some forms, the methods assume that given cases at different times constitute independent entities.

The second broad set of assumptions involves causal flow. Between the variable properties of the fixed entities run some fixed "causal" relations. These are assumed uniform, in the sense that they must act the same way in

---

world already possesses, and we will soon be possessing, many datasets with population-level information in continuous time on whatever variables we like. Social science is no longer in the position of trying to make huge results out of little data—the purpose of hypothesis testing in the first place. Our present difficulty is quite the reverse. It is striking that in the commercial sector, where data overload hit some time ago, pattern search has long since dominated as the primary stance towards data analysis.

all cases. Moreover, the causes are constantly relevant; if the model exists over time, the underlying presumption is that their force does not vary with time. This can be changed by adding parameters to model it directly, but only at a large price in estimability and in the necessity of further assumptions about functional forms. In general, the causal relations hypothesized presume a partial ordering of variables in time, in that "small" temporal variables cannot cause "large" variables; short duration events cannot shape large ones. Moreover, variables must work at the same speed (over time) in all cases.

These causal assumptions are broadened in the third set of assumptions, which concern what I have called time horizon. The time horizon of a variable or phenomenon is that period which must elapse before we can measure a meaningful change in it (a change distinguishable from noise). Time horizons of variables have a number of important properties, not least of which is that the time horizons of aggregates are usually longer than those of their micro constituents. The problems caused by variation in time horizons across variables are exacerbated by the fact that standard methods must also assume that there are no "events" in the sense of dependencies between values of particular variables that extend across the temporal sampling frame, particularly when these vary from case to case, variable to variable, and time to time. In short, the standard method works most comfortably where all variables are conceived as instantaneous and temporally independent of the past.

A fourth assumption involves the absence of sequence effects. In general, standard methods assume that the order in which a set of events occurs doesn't shape the way it turns out. Put more generally, they assume that the data space lacks distinguishable temporal trajectories. They assume moreover that the causal trajectory (in the sense of the flow of determination among the variables) must be identical in all cases. This causal trajectory is generally justified by a set of pseudonarratives, usually about idealized actors of one sort or another.

The remaining assumptions concern context and meaning. A fifth assumption is that what happens to one case does not constrain or shape what happens to others. A variety of models—ranging from fairly simple class constraint models down to individualized vacancy models—have explored the possibilities of relaxing this assumption, but it remains overwhelmingly standard in quantitative work. Indeed, the very framework of survey analysis was in part designed to guarantee the validity of this assumption. But in small-N contexts—where regression has often been applied—this assumption creates major problems, and even in the survey context it has potential for disruption.

Sixth, standard methods assume that the (causal) meaning of one variable is in general not dependent upon that of another. The usual way of phrasing this is to say that standard methods put main effects first and add interaction as a necessary evil where required. This is the reverse of the pattern search strategy, which looks for constellations of particular values of variables as a way to simplify the data space.

Finally, the standard approach assumes that a given variable "means" only one thing, at least in a given study. This is of course a foundational assumption and gives rise to the phenomenon of "literatures," which are essentially trajectories of work within which there is a consensual understanding of the allowable meanings of certain variables. But of course, the causal meaning of variables changes wildly from one literature to the next, and even from one study to the next, a phenomenon investigated in detail in chapter 2. Indeed, even the locus of variables—the nature of the entity of which a given variable is a property—can change from study to study. It is by exploring the implications of this studied inattention to multiplicity of meaning that I develop in chapter 2 the concept of a serious quantitative attack on the problem of culture (construed as the problem of multiple meaning) via a meta-analysis of the multiple uses of variables across the entire body of social science. In this conception, the whole of social scientific literature constitutes a large web, within which particular literatures evolve as trajectories around particular focal variables of concern.

These assumptions—and their critique—form the armature of the book. The various chapters come at them in various ways and, no doubt, with varying degrees of success. Over the years that I have been setting forth my critique of the standard sociological empirical program, certain of these assumptions have been relaxed in minor ways. Statisticians, at least, have retreated from the causal interpretation of regression and its derivatives, which leaves them treating it either as purely descriptive (a task for which it is inefficient, even ineffectual) or, in the classical manner, as a pragmatic method for analyzing the impact of interventions in more or less experimental contexts, a task at which it is unsurpassed. Within sociology, the continued attempt to fix up and extend the standard family of models—to make them do things for which they are largely unsuited—has, in my view, had the effect of suppressing real methodological advance. High-quality

pattern search methods—of which there has been an enormous efflores-
cence in the last two decades—have been developed mainly in the private
sector and are virtually absent from sociology.

Overall, however, my basic critique of standard methods—that they are
applicable only under a fairly limited range of social ontologies—stands as
strong today as it did when I began setting it out. That these methods sur-
vive in such strength shows that Alvin Gouldner was right thirty years ago,
when he claimed that empirical sociology was becoming the technical eval-
uator of the welfare state.[4] As an evaluation program, a tester of the impact
of this or that intervention on a particular variable of immediate political interest, the standard format is quite good. But as a program for generally understanding how the social process works, it is quite weak.

IV The Theory of Narrative Analysis

Most of my own work on alternatives to the standard system has been de-
voted to a narrative-based program of explanation that would focus on regularities in trajectories over time. In the narrow sense of methodological
work, this led to a focus on the alignment methods discussed in the later
pages of chapter 6 and embodied in numerous papers elsewhere. But my
broader project was to think about a whole framework, an alternative ontology with which to envision the social world. It was the focused nature of this
project that my qualitatively inclined colleagues could not understand. They
wanted to reverse *all* the assumptions of the standard method and be done
with it. I wanted simply to recast the temporal assumptions (assumptions two
through four above) and leave the others more or less intact, even though
other parts of my own work (particularly my work on professions and the papers on ecologies that grew out of it) in fact did attack other assumptions.
And despite my supposed reluctance, the narrative explanatory program as I
imagined it conceptually did envision eventually relaxing nearly all of the
standard assumptions. It was when I came to the practical matter of trying to
develop actual narrative methodologies that a focused relaxation of the temporal assumptions proved to be the only practicable possibility. There is an
uneasy tension in the papers of this book, then, between the task of discovering all the crucial assumptions of standard methods on the one hand, and the
practical effort of trying to methodically relax one set of them on the other.

All that taken as given, a basic interest throughout the papers of this
book is what we might call a narrative program of research. In the most gen-

4. Gouldner 1970.

eral sense this grew out of my idea that the social process was itself narratively organized. I was insistent that this narrative organization be real; that is, that it be inherent in the social process itself and not merely in our talking about that process. So I focused from the start on patterns of successions of events (what I should have called trajectories from the start, but did not) that were actually evident in the social process itself. My first analyses tried to sketch out the ideas of enchainment (the processes moving the steps of the story along), order (the notion that the order of events varies across cases and makes a difference to outcome), and "convergence," by which I meant that some stories might "converge" on an outcome, while others might diverge into randomness.

It became evident that social processes varied quite widely in the degree to which they consisted of independent trajectories. A crucial issue throughout my papers on temporality became the degree of this interdependence, which we might imagine as the degree to which the fifth assumption of the standard system was violated across time. I have used varying terminologies for this, but eventually settled on the term "natural histories" for processes that had internal coherence as ordered sequences of events but were largely independent of other cases, "careers" for processes with some internal coherence and some contextual determination from other cases, and "interactions" (sometimes "interactional fields") for situations (like that in my analysis of professions) in which the cases were so interdependent that thinking of their histories as independent stories was nonsensical. In work not reprinted here I applied the equivalent distinction to *synchronic* intercase determination, envisioning three levels of spatial or structural determination to be the categories for the structuralist program analogous to these three for the narrative one.[5] Interactional fields were again the most complex structural system; I thought them to be governed by complex contextuality in both time and space.

Standard methods, as several of these papers imply, are the appropriate methods only when contextuality is low both over time and in (social) space. Survey analysis—where these methods were first developed—to some extent enforces that independence. Jim Coleman used to argue that this was appropriate because in more modern societies individuals were in fact more independent; we have the social science appropriate to our society. I used to argue back that the causality went the other way; social science had become part of the machinery enforcing that independence.

5. Abbott 1999a, chap. 7.

The particular utility of narrative methods in this array of varying contextualities is in the situation in which temporal contextuality (alone) is high: the situation where order and sequence—in short the past and its history—make a difference. Thus many of these papers circle around the concepts of stage theories, natural histories and the like, the various convergent narrative forms. I tried to set out the details of this conception in chapter 5, not with complete success. But this problem of finding natural histories became the place where I focused my own methodological work. A central issue was whether one conceived of a particular trajectory (confusingly, I called these "careers" in chapter 5, since I was not yet clear about the levels-of-contextuality problem) as a whole or as a stochastic process generated moment to moment. The only way the latter made real sense was if one privileged a particular outcome at a particular moment (by selecting a dependent variable at a time).

Thus, methodologically, I focused on a fairly narrow problem, as one must. But in setting forth the more general narrative point of view, I rejected, at least tacitly, most of the postulates of the standard model. I began by questioning the whole notion of entities. As several of these papers argue, the very issue of a "central subject" or entity of interest is problematized in most historical writing. Moreover, the central subject is generally a complex particular, which one sometimes simplifies in order to generalize. Historical writing often invokes demographic kinds of transformations, I recognized, although methodologically I have not yet produced any real marriage of demographic and narrative concerns. Theoretically, however, these essays move away from the standard view considerably with respect to the nature of entities, both in their views of contextuality and in the direct analysis of entities in chapter 9.

The narrative theory also had a different view of causality. Within the narrative conception studying the succession of steps was less a question of causality than a question of "followability." (This is a large topic, one to which I turn below at greater length.) The narrative view as I develop it here also reversed the other temporal assumption of the standard methods. Within a narrative program of explanation one would have to recognize variation in the time horizon and size of events. Defining and understanding events would in fact become the central task of conceptualization, cognate with theorizing variables in the standard program. I do develop (particularly in chapter 5) a translation of the concept of an event into the language of the standard program (a event being in that language simply a particular location in the variable state space). But in reality my notion of event on the narrative side was much more extensive. Events have duration; they can happen across observation frames. They have internal patterns of "occurrences" defining them. Although I elaborated this broad analysis of events more in papers not included here, this notion of a complex conception of events undergirds many of these pieces.[6]

So also does a sophisticated view of plots. At the simplest level, and certainly as a developer of methodologies, "one damn thing after another" was all I could afford; plot simply meant succession of events. But in a general narrative program of explanation plot must clearly play a central role. It is for that reason that various of these papers invoke the literature of literary structuralism, with its conceptions of limited numbers of plots. As part of the problem of plots, I also raise in some of these papers the problem of periodization. Plots have their arbitrary beginnings, middles, and ends cognate with the arbitrary dependent variables of the standard scheme. Clearly a serious narrative program must address the problem of periodization, the problem of deciding whether the beginnings of social sequences inhere in the social process itself or are simply an arbitrary aspect of the way we talk about that process. Related to this, in a number of these pieces, is the question of how we are to understand some of the other formalized historical discourses; the "ancestors plot" in which we consider all the antecedents of some one thing, the "descendants plot" in which we consider all its consequences, and so on. Yet all of these limit the networked character of the social process in itself.

I have explored these temporal questions in detail in the context of thinking about turning points in social processes. Here the notion of a narrative explanatory program is clearly expressed, because the idea of turning point is in logical and formal terms necessarily a narrative idea. Chapter 8 sets forth in detail the logical and explanatory implications of the idea of turning points, and I need not reiterate them here. The most general implication of the turning point conception was the notion that the social process could be parsed into trajectories and turning points. In this usage of the word "trajectory," I meant it specifically to refer not to a routine pattern (as above) but rather to a relatively stable set of rules governing outcomes; in short, a stable causal "model" for small variations. Such trajectories (periods in which there was such a stable model) were joined to one another by turning points, which were the points at which cases were delivered from one existing trajectory to another, that is, to a new regime of causality. The na-

6. See Abbott 1984 and 1991b.

ture of this transition was yet to be determined. Under this conception, standard and narrative methods could split the world, the one taking trajectories, the other turning points. Indeed, this argument led me to an analysis of the conditions under which such a parsable social system might emerge. One of the other utilities of this approach was that it offered a way of separating out the structural and nonstructural parts of social determination, the turning points offering a place for the intervention of the structural. In this sense, the turning point–trajectory model merged into my more general ideas, reviewed above, about formal ways to think about degrees of contextuality and interdetermination in social systems. This was another way of thinking of natural histories (trajectories, here), careers, and interactional fields.

There remain two important parts of the narrative program to mention. One of these was the idea that causal meaning was determined contextually. That is (putting it in standard terms), particular values of variables might or might not be narratively salient depending on the environment of particular values of other variables at the time. This was, in a sense, the natural consequence of thinking of plot as a sequence of events conceived as complex particulars, even within the standard program. Even if one defined events as successions of points in a state space, one had no need to assume that the succession was primarily determined by the values on this or that dimension conceived as main effects. It was the succession of fully dimensioned points that mattered, although one could, in principle, think about reducing the dimensionality until one had a coherent set of tracks through the (reduced-dimensional) space. Thus, while I have not directly developed the program emphasizing relaxation of the standard univocal meaning assumption, it was implicit in the way I theorized the narrative program generally.

Finally, a central issue—and difficulty—of the narrative program arose over the issue of the existence of the past. Particularly chapters 5 and 7 confront the problem of how we imagine causal or determinative influence from a past that has in fact disappeared. On the surface, this is an obvious assumption of any narrative program of explanation. Just as obviously, it presents central difficulties. I return to these below, in my discussion of encoding. At the same time these papers, particularly chapter 7, also consider the obverse of this problem—the curious stickiness of the past, its unwillingness to be reinterpreted arbitrarily.

There have been then a variety of themes in my exposition of a narrative program for understanding the social process. For the most part these involve reversals of postulates of the standard program, but there have been other concerns as well.

V Explanation and Causality

The topics of explanation and causality have made a number of appearances in the papers of this book. As several papers report, there is a longstanding debate over the nature of explanation and whether "causal" explanation is indeed the only form of explanation. Two alternatives have been raised throughout. The more extensively discussed is historical explanation. The less discussed, but nonetheless important, is description.

I comment on description first, since I have spent less time on it. The basic problem confronted by any empirical social scientist is the following. There is a data space of n dimensions, where n is the number of possible measured variables, and the cases move through it on trajectories that embody their course over time. (Alternatively, time is another dimension of the space.) A social scientist aims to say something comprehensible and parsimonious about the behavior of the cases in this data space. One way to do that is to vastly simplify the space, using any of the many forms of dimension reduction. In the standard terminology, this is a descriptive task. Here is not the place to debate whether that description constitutes a form of explanation, but it certainly does constitute a way of saying something comprehensible and parsimonious. The other way to say something about this space is to privilege one dimension of it (by calling it a dependent variable) and then to see if a (more or less) linear combination of information in the other dimensions can produce the information in this dependent dimension. In the standard terminology, this is called causal analysis.

The narrative program as I have carried it out methodologically has been explicitly descriptive. The idea is to find categories and patterns in social processes so that one knows, in the first instance, what regularities one is trying to explain. In this sense, it invokes the large body of pattern search methodologies that stand as alternatives to the standard approach to data.

But at the theoretical level, I have of course made throughout these papers a much stronger case for narrative: that it is a form of explanation. To this end I have set out the classical Hempelian account of explanation and have examined in detail the way in which our standard methods think they are following that account. Most of this is laid out in detail in chapter 3, and I do not repeat it here. I have in chapters 3 and 4 also laid out at some length the response of the philosophers of history to the Hempelian account, their notion of narrative as fully explanatory. When I have discussed these ideas directly with most of my standard method colleagues, I have found complete incomprehension. Apparently many of us are unwilling to think of explanation as having any possible meaning other than the narrow one assigned to it in our methods. But for philosophers narrative explanation is a serious possibility, and I have given several versions, taken from a very much richer literature. Also stemming from that literature, ultimately, are the discussions of colligation and central subjects—the historical equivalents of conceptualization (to include classification and measurement) and units of analysis—that are scattered throughout these papers.

There are two relatively undeveloped parts of this argument, however, which make only brief appearances. One of these is the problem—a central one for philosophers—of explaining things that didn't (or don't) happen. Peter Abell spent some time on this problem in *The Syntax of Social Life* and I have made methodological hay with it over the issue of empty data spaces.[7] But the broader issue of what it means to think about the social world by mainly attending to things that happen—or as Hart and Honoré put it, things that happen that are out of the ordinary—this I have not addressed at any length.[8] The other undeveloped issue is that of the possibility of "narrative links" in explanation. I mentioned in chapter 4 the importance of developing conceptual models for narrative steps, but this suggestion has not been seriously pursued elsewhere in these papers.

VI Time

I turn now to the more positive arguments that emerge from this body of work. Some of these involve the concept of time itself, which is discussed in detail in chapter 7, whose contents I can hardly summarize briefly. Chapter 5 makes an important pairing with chapter 7, for the former works at the methodological level on the same problems that the latter addresses theoretically. In particular, chapter 5 raises the problem that events seem to have structure over time, but that the social process seems in some absolute way to be instantaneous. It explores the problem that while on the one hand to have more data is clearly better, when we allow that "improvement" to proceed to the limit we are stuck with the problem of discontinuous change. Finer and finer focus simply impresses us with the discontinuity of things and the existence of events reaching across observation frames. Several papers raise the issue of temporal structures of varying sizes acting upon a

7. Abell 1987.
8. Hart and Honoré 1985.

single present, usually with the psychiatrists of my unpublished thesis as the example. This problem is an enduring one for me, one that I address in the theory of encoding.

Many of the early papers circle around the issue of differentiating causal time (the order of variables) from real time (the time of the life world). The later papers, particularly chapter 7, problematize even the latter. Newtonian time itself proves to have problems, and indeed the most practical concepts of time are probably relative rather than absolute.

I do not summarize here the details of chapter 7's analyses of time in Bergson and Mead. From them I take a notion of time as highly local, in the sense that it is proper to a particular place and moment, with larger inclusive presents reaching beyond it topologically and temporally. Time is indexical, because of this multiplicity of overlapping presents, yet inclusive, because their relations are of inclusion rather than quantity. From Mead comes the notion that time is relational, ultimately shaped by precisely this locality— one person's presents are not another's. Indeed temporality itself clearly arises from the scraping together of these different personal rhythms and the differing rates of interaction in social life. The impact of the new communications technologies is not that they make interaction faster, but they make certain kinds of interactions faster relative to others than they used to be.

In short, the notion of time as a series of overlapping presents of various sizes, each organized around a particular location and overlapping across the whole social process, provides a foundation for further argument. Clock time and solipsistic (Bergsonian) time are clearly two attempts to reduce this mass of overlap to single things, the first with an eye to specific kinds of social coordination, the second with an eye to a maximum of personal experience. The overlapping view gets us around the classic problem of how history relates to social science, which leads directly to the Chinese box view in which social science tells stories within fixed causal regimes and history explains how those regimes change. With luck, overlapping lets us evade the Eleatic difficulties that are the central problematic of chapter 7.

VII General Theoretical Matters

Out of all this reflection on methodology, as I have said earlier, has come slowly my sense of what a sensible social ontology really is. In this last section I set down the outlines of that scheme, which forms the basis of the book I am writing about time and social structure. The themes stated here come from various places in the foregoing papers.

I have already set out my concept of time. I imagine it as a set of many layers of fish scales, each scale a local present overlapping some others, every level consisting of larger scales overlapping a wider and wider space. We can think about the Newtonian present as a flat unknowable vertical plane cutting this huge phyllo dough of presents at an instant. Each actor is an implicit vertical pile of presents of varying sizes.

Within this complex world, change is the normal state of affairs. We do not see a largely stable world that changes occasionally, but a continuously changing world that has macroscopic stabilities emerging throughout it. This world is a world of events. When I say it is a world of events, I mean that quite literally. The micro level of this world is a completely eventful one. There are no preexisting actors. There is, of course, a biological substrate that means that there is a tremendous likelihood that more or less stable identities will emerge, out of this mass of events, within particular persons. But those selves arise in interaction; they are not in any sense given ex ante.

Stable entities emerge from this soup of events as lineages, as events that keep happening the same way. They pull together prior happenings in ways that become constant. Thus this micro world of events is completely Markovian, completely moment to moment. But there arise in it the more or less stable structures that we call social actors. The most obvious of these are the personalities of individual persons, but social groups are no less of the same kind. In this sense, the micro/macro problem is a delusion. In terms of the eventful world, everything is macro.

This does not mean that it is not worth thinking about the entity processes that I discuss in chapter 4. Many social entities are explicitly made up of individuals, and for these it makes sense to ask about the various processes I discussed under that heading: microturnover, internal transformation, paradigm shifts, collective action links, and so on. But as a philosophical issue the micro/macro problem is reduced, as we shall see, to a problem in theorizing social structure and its reproduction.

Lineages arise and acquire their stability through encoding. Encoding is essentially a name for the ways structures manage to embed themselves in the perpetual reproduction of social life so that they almost invariably are reproduced from moment to moment. These ways may include redundancy, distribution, interlocking patterns, and so on, but all have this characteristic of enabling reproduction in the routine passage from present to past. Turning points—in particular the destruction of structures—happen when these encoders get aligned in a manner that permits destruction. What we mean by an "enduring" or "large" structure is one whose encoding is particularly wide-ranging and effective. Social structure, as I said in chapter 8, is the memory of the social process. At any given time, the apparently synchronic social structure is in fact the embodied memory of the past, containing within it all the encoding that keeps the large structures (like capitalism, the United States, and gender roles) rolling along into the future. At the same time, the fact that everything—no matter how large—is perpetually being reproduced means that everything—no matter how large—is always on the line. So sudden large-scale change is not surprising. There were probably times before 1989 when the Eastern bloc was about to come apart (because the alignment of the encodings created the possibility), but no one had figured it out and turned the key in the lock. In 1989, someone finally did.

It is the differential distribution of encoding through the life cycle and the social structure that gives rise to the turning point–trajectory model of chapter 8. Indeed, much of our social structure is rather deliberately constructed in this manner; certainly much of education is, with its stable years and its sudden transitions between levels. Social entities all have their periods of vulnerability to change, and other periods when their encodings are more solid. It is also this flow of entities through time that allows the "things of boundaries" model of chapter 9. Differences between entities are continually appearing, and the continual pressure of eventful interaction creates the openings for actors who assemble boundaries into things. Indeed, the "things of boundaries" model is simply the most extreme form of the continuous way elements are woven into and out of the lineages that are social things.[9]

In chapter 9 I have also discussed somewhat the nature of these weavings. They are a form of action, which I thus take to be a more general phenomenon than simply things one given actor does to another. Actors are continually remaking themselves; the process of remaking the self is the same social process as interacting with others. This of course raises the question of what constitutes the "thingness," the solidity of social entities. This topic too is canvassed in some detail in chapter 9, which tries to distinguish between "ecological reproduction," where social structure continues solid because its environment holds it in place and the various forms of internal reproduction, which have their roots in encoding.

One of the implications of seeing the world as a world of events is that

9. I have attempted an attempt to chronicle a single lineage—complete with weavings-in and weavings-out—in Abbott 1999a, particularly in the discussion of the lineages we call "the AJS" and "the Chicago school."

each event is located in many lineages; my writing this chapter is an event for me, for Nuffield College (where I happen to be writing it), for men, for the University of Chicago Press, for my family (who are putting up with my absence), and so on. Events are always multiple—this is message of the "ambiguity of locus" discussion in chapter 2. And if by action we mean that collection of links tying one event to the next, then action too is inevitably multiple. Action has indeed been a topic of central importance in this book. For one of my longstanding objections to the standard approach is that human action basically disappears in it, to be replaced by the medieval shadowboxing of variables. Sociological theory, if it is nothing else, is generally about activity. Now action, as I have suggested in various of these papers, is a diverse business. Reasons for action include charisma, rationality, tradition, optimization, accident, monomania, value rationality, and many more. But the multiplicity of action, as I have said, is not merely of kind, but also of locus and lineage.

At this point, however, I find myself getting ahead of summarizing what was explicit and implicit in these papers and moving on to summarizing the draft chapters of the theoretical book that tries to assemble all this into a firm argument about the nature of the social process. Those chapters themselves are three years in the past, waiting while I have thought and written about other things.

Our intellectual life ends up like a shingle roof. Each article shelters much of itself under the findings of the last, but exposes its outer edge to the elements, keeping the rain off a few of the shingles below it. He would be a fool indeed who thought to keep the water out without such overlaps. I hope the present essay—a temporary ridge cap—will protect the apex of this particular outbuilding until I can get the main house up.

REFERENCES

Abbott, A. 1982. "The Emergence of American Psychiatry." Ph.D. diss., University of Chicago.
———. 1983. "Sequences of Social Events." *Historical Methods* 16:129–47.
———. 1984. "Event Sequence and Event Duration." *Historical Methods* 17:192–204.
———. 1985. "Professionalization Large and Small." Unpublished paper, Department of Sociology, Rutgers University.
———. 1988a. *The System of Professions.* Chicago: University of Chicago Press.
———. 1988b. "Transcending General Linear Reality." *Sociological Theory* 6:169–86.
———. 1990a. "Conceptions of Time and Events in Social Science Methods." *Historical Methods* 23:140–50.
———. 1990b. "Positivism and Interpretation in Sociology." *Sociological Forum* 5:435–58.
———. 1990c. "A Primer on Sequence Methods." *Organization Science* 1:373–92.
———. 1990d. "Vacancy Models for Historical Data." In *Social Mobility and Social Structure.* Ed. R. L. Breiger, 80–102. Cambridge: Cambridge University Press.
———. 1991a. "History and Sociology." *Social Science History* 15:201–38.
———. 1991b. "The Order of Professionalization." *Work and Occupations* 18:355–84.
———. 1992a. "From Causes to Events." *Sociological Methods and Research* 20:428–55.
———. 1992b. "An Old Institutionalist Reads the New Institutionalism." *Contemporary Sociology* 21:754–56.
———. 1992c. "What Do Cases Do?" In *What Is a Case?* Ed. C. Ragin and H. Becker, 53–82. Cambridge: Cambridge University Press.
———. 1993. "The Sociology of Work and Occupations." *Annual Review of Sociology.* 19:187–209.
———. 1995a. "Boundaries of Social Work or Social Work of Boundaries." *Social Service Review* 69:545–62.
———. 1995b. "Sequence Analysis." *Annual Review of Sociology* 21:93–113.
———. 1995c. "Things of Boundaries." *Social Research* 62:857–82.
———. 1997a. "Of Time and Space." *Social Forces* 75:1149–82.
———. 1997b. "On the Concept of Turning Point." *Comparative Social Research* 16:89–109.
———. 1997c. "Seven Types of Ambiguity." *Theory and Society* 26:357–91.
———. 1999a. *Department and Discipline.* Chicago: University of Chicago Press.

———. 1999b. "Temporality and Process in Social Life." In *Social Time and Social Change*. Ed. F. Engelstad and R. Kalleberg, 28–61. Oslo: Scandinavian University Press.

———. 2000. "Reflections on the Future of Sociology." *Contemporary Sociology* 29:296–300.

———. 2001. *Chaos of Disciplines*. Chicago: University of Chicago Press.

Abbott, A., and E. Barman. 1997. "Sequence Comparison via Alignment and Gibbs Sampling." *Sociological Methodology* 27:47–87.

Abbott, A., and S. DeViney. 1992. "The Welfare State as Transnational Event." *Social Science History* 16:245–74.

Abbott, A., and J. Forrest. 1986. "Optimal Matching Techniques for Historical Data." *Journal of Interdisciplinary History* 16:471–94.

Abbott, A., and E. Gaziano. 1995. "Transition and Tradition." In *A Second Chicago School*. Ed. G. A. Fine, 221–72. Chicago: University of Chicago Press.

Abbott, A., and A. Hrycak. 1990. "Measuring Resemblance in Sequence Data." *American Journal of Sociology* 96:144–85.

Abbott, A., and A. Tsay. 2000. "Sequence Analysis and Optimal Matching Methods in Sociology." *Sociological Methods and Research* 29:3–33.

Abell, P. 1971. *Model Building in Sociology*. New York: Schocken.

———. 1984. "Comparative Narratives." *Journal for the Theory of Social Behavior* 14:309–31.

———. 1985. "Analyzing Qualitative Sequences." In *Sequence Analysis*. Ed. P. Abell and M. Proctor, 99–115. Brookfield, Vt.: Gower.

———. 1987. *The Syntax of Social Life*. Oxford: Oxford University Press.

———. 1989. "Games in Networks." *Rationality and Society* 1:259–82.

———. 1991. "Narrative Analysis." Paper delivered at Interfaces Conference. Enfield, New Hampshire, 17 August.

———. 1993. "Some Aspects of Narrative Method." *Journal of Mathematical Sociology* 18:93–134.

Aldrich, H. 1975. "Ecological Succession in Racially Changing Neighborhoods." *Urban Affairs Quarterly* 10:327–48.

Alexander, J. C., B. Giesen, R. Munch, and N. J. Smelser, eds. 1987. *The Micro/Macro Link*. Berkeley and Los Angeles: University of California Press.

Alexander, K. L., and T. W. Reilly, 1981. "Estimating the Effects of Marriage Timing on Education Attainment." *American Journal of Sociology* 87:143–56.

Alker, H. R. 1982. "Logic, Dialectic, and Politics." In *Dialectical Logics for the Political Sciences. Poznan Studies*, vol. 7. Ed. H. R. Alker, 65–94. Amsterdam: Rodopi.

———. 1984. "Historical Argumentation and Statistical Inference." *Historical Methods* 17:164–73.

Alker, H. R., J. P. Bennett, and D. Mefford. 1980. "Generalized Precedent Logics for Resolving Insecurities." *International Interactions* 7:165–206.

Allison, P. D. 1977. "Testing for Interaction in Multiple Regression." *American Journal of Sociology* 83:144–53.

———. 1982. "Discrete-Time Methods for the Analysis of Event Histories." In *Sociological Methodology, 1982*. Ed. S. Leinhardt, 61–98. San Francisco: Jossey-Bass.

Althusser, L., and E. Balibar. 1970. *Reading Capital*. New York: Pantheon.

Aminzade, R. 1992. "Historical Sociology and Time." *Sociological Methods and Research* 20:456–80.

Ayer, A. J. 1946. *Language, Truth, and Logic*. New York: Dover.

Barthes, R. 1974. *S/Z*. Trans. R. Miller. New York: Hill and Wang.

Bates, R. 1981. *Markets and States in Tropical Africa*. Berkeley and Los Angeles: University of California Press.

Berger, P. L., and T. Luckmann. 1967. *The Social Construction of Reality*. New York: Doubleday.

Bergson, H. [1889] 1910. *Time and Free Will*. Tr. F. L. Pogson. London: Allen Unwin. Original title: *Essai sur les données immédiates de la conscience*.

Bernert, C. 1983. "The Career of Causal Analysis in American Sociology." *British Journal of Sociology* 34:230–54.

Bienenstock, E. J., P. Bonacich, and M. Oliver. 1990. "The Effects of Network Density on Attitude Polarization." *Social Networks* 12:153–72.

Bishop, Y. M. M., S. E. Feinberg, and P. W. Holland. 1975. *Discrete Multivariate Analysis*. Cambridge: MIT Press.

Blalock, H. M. 1960. *Social Statistics*. New York: McGraw-Hill.

———. 1964. *Causal Inference in Non-experimental Research*. New York: Harcourt, Brace.

———. 1984a. *Basic Dilemmas in the Social Sciences*. Beverly Hills: Sage.

———. 1984b. "Contextual-Effects Models." *Annual Review of Sociology* 10:353–72.

Blau, P. M., and O. D. Duncan. 1967. *The American Occupational Structure*. New York: Free Press.

Blumer, H. 1931. "Science without Concepts." *American Journal of Sociology* 36:515–33.

———. 1940. "The Problem of the Concept in Social Psychology." *American Journal of Sociology* 45:707–19.

———. 1956. "Sociological Analysis and the 'Variable.' " *American Sociological Review* 21:683–90.

Boorman, S. A., and H. C. White. 1976. "Social Structure from Multiple Networks II: Role Structures." *American Journal of Sociology* 81:1384–446.

Booth, A., D. R. Johnson, L. White, and J. N. Edward. 1984. "Women's Outside Employment and Marital Instability." *American Journal of Sociology* 90:567–83.

Boswell, J. 1981. *Christianity, Homosexuality, and Social Tolerance*. Chicago: University of Chicago Press.

Boudon, R. 1973. *Mathematical Models of Social Mobility*. San Francisco: Jossey-Bass.

Box, G. E. P., and G. M. Jenkins. 1976. *Time Series Analysis*. San Francisco: Jossey-Bass.

Bradshaw, Y. W. 1985. "Dependent Development in Black Africa." *American Sociological Review* 50:195–207.

Breden, F., and M. J. Wade. 1991. "Runaway Social Evolution." *Journal of Theoretical Biology* 153:323–37.

Brent, E. E., and R. E. Sykes. 1979. "A Mathematical Model of Symbolic Interaction between Police and Suspects." *Behavioral Science* 24:388–402.

Bridges, W. P., and R. L. Nelson. 1989. "Markets in Hierarchies." *American Journal of Sociology* 95:616–58.

Bucher, R. 1988. "On the Natural History of Health Care Occupations." *Work and Occupations* 15:131–47.

Bucher, R., and A. Strauss. 1961. "Professions in Process." *American Journal of Sociology* 66:325–34.

Bulmer, M. 1984. *The Chicago School of Sociology.* Chicago: University of Chicago Press.

Burawoy, M. 1979. *Manufacturing Consent.* Chicago: University of Chicago Press.

Burgess, E. W. 1925. "The Growth of the City." In *The City.* Ed. R. E. Park, E. W. Burgess, and R. D. McKenzie, 47–62. Chicago: University of Chicago Press.

Burnham, W. D. 1970. *Critical Elections and the Mainsprings of American Politics.* New York: Norton.

Burt, R. 1982. *Towards a Structural Theory of Action.* New York: Academic.

Cantor, D., and K. C. Land. 1985. "Unemployment and Crime Rates in the Post–World War II United States." *American Sociological Review* 50:317–32.

Carroll, G. 1984. "Organizational Ecology." *Annual Review of Sociology* 10:71–93.

Carroll, G., and J. Delacroix. 1982. "Organizational Mortality in the Newspaper Industries of Argentina and Ireland." *Administrative Science Quarterly* 27:169–98.

Cartwright, N. 1989. *Nature's Capacities and Their Measurement.* Oxford: Oxford University Press.

Chaffin, W. W., and W. K. Talley. 1989. "Diffusion Indexes and a Statistical Test for Predicting Turning Points in Business Cycles." *International Journal of Forecasting* 5:29–36.

Chalmers, B. F. 1981. "A Selective Review of Stress." *Current Psychological Reviews* 1:325–43.

Chatman, S. 1978. *Story and Discourse.* Ithaca: Cornell University Press.

Cicourel, A. V. 1981. "Notes on the Integration of Micro- and Macro-levels of Analysis." In *Advances in Social Theory and Methodology.* Ed. K. Knorr-Cetina and A. V. Cicourel, 51–80. Boston: Routledge.

Cliff, A. D., and J. K. Ord. 1981. *Spatial Processes.* London: Pion.

Clubb, J. M., W. H. Flanagan, and N. H. Zingale. 1981. *Party Realignment.* Beverly Hills: Sage.

Cohen, I. B. 1985. *Revolution in Science.* Cambridge: Harvard University Press.

Cohen, M. R., and E. Nagel. 1934. *An Introduction to Logic and the Scientific Method.* New York: Harcourt Brace.

Coleman, J. S. 1964. *Introduction to Mathematical Sociology.* New York: Free Press.

———. 1990. *Foundations of Social Theory.* Cambridge: Harvard University Press.

Coleman, J. S., E. Katz, and H. Menzel. 1966. *Medical Innovation.* Indianapolis: Bobbs Merrill.

Collingwood, R. G. 1946. *The Idea of History.* Oxford: Oxford University Press.

Collins, R. 1981. "The Microfoundations of Macrosociology." *American Journal of Sociology* 86:984–1014.

———. 1984. "Statistics versus Words." In *Sociological Theory 1984.* Ed. R. Collins, 329–62. San Francisco: Jossey-Bass.

———. 1987. "Interaction Ritual Chains, Power, and Property." In Alexander et al. 1987, 193–206.

Cornfield, D. B. 1985. "Economic Segmentation and Expression of Labor Unrest." *Social Science Quarterly* 66:247–65.

Corsaro, W. A., and D. R. Heise. 1990. "Event Structures from Ethnographic Data." In *Sociological Methodology, 1990*. Ed. C. Clogg, 1–57. Oxford: Basil Blackwell.

Coser, L. 1975. "Two Methods in Search of a Substance." *American Sociological Review* 40:691–700.

Crane, D. 1972. *Invisible Colleges*. Chicago: University of Chicago Press.

Cressey, P. G. 1932. *The Taxi-Dance Hall*. Chicago: University of Chicago Press.

Danto, A. C. 1985. *Narration and Knowledge*. New York: Columbia University Press.

Davis, J. A., and T. W. Smith. 1994. *General Social Surveys, 1972–1994: Cumulative Codebook*. Chicago: NORC.

de Bary. W. T., W.-t. Chan, and B. Watson. 1964. *Sources of Chinese Tradition*. 2 vols. New York: Columbia University Press.

Denzin, N. K. 1970. *Sociological Methods*. Chicago: Aldine.

Devine, J. A. 1983. "Fiscal Policy and Class Income Inequality." *American Sociological Review* 48:606–22.

Dewey, J. [1929] 1958. *Experience and Nature*. New York: Dover.

Dietterich, T. G., and R. S. Michalski. 1985. "Discovering Patterns in Sequences of Events." *Artificial Intelligence* 25:187–232.

DiMaggio, P. J., and W. W. Powell. 1983. "The Iron Cage Revisited." *American Sociological Review* 48:147–60.

Dray, W. 1957. *Laws and Explanation in History*. Oxford: Oxford University Press.

Dubbey, J. M. 1970. *Development of Modern Mathematics*. New York: American Elsevier.

Dumont, L. [1966] 1980. *Homo Hierarchicus*. Tr. M. Sainsbury, L. Dumont, and B. Gulati. Chicago: University of Chicago Press.

Duncan, O. D. 1951. "Proper Aphorisms for a Relativist Sociology." Typescript in the papers of E. W. Burgess (box 33, folder 4), Special Collections Division, University of Chicago Library.

———. 1966. "Path Analysis." *American Journal of Sociology* 72:1–16.

———. 1984. *Notes on Social Measurement*. New York: Russell Sage.

Durkheim, E. 1897. *Le suicide*. Paris: Alcan.

———. 1951. *Suicide*. Tr. J. A. Spaulding and G. Simpson. New York: Free Press.

———. [1895] 1964. *The Rules of the Sociological Method*. New York: Free Press.

Eames, E. R. 1973. "Mead's Concept of Time." In *The Philosophy of George Herbert Mead*. Ed. W. R. Corti, 59–81. Amriswil, Switzerland: Amriswiler Bücherei.

Edwards, L. P. 1927. *The Natural History of Revolution*. Chicago: University of Chicago Press.

Efron, B., and R. Tibshirani. 1991. "Statistical Data Analysis in the Computer Age." *Science* 253:390–95.

Elder, G. H. 1985. "Perspectives on the Life Course." In *Life Course Dynamics*. Ed. G. H. Elder, 23–49. Ithaca: Cornell University Press.

Empson, W. 1957. *Seven Types of Ambiguity*. New York: Meridian.

Erikson, K. 1966. *Wayward Puritans*. New York: Wiley.

Evans, M. D., and E. O. Laumann. 1983. "Professional Commitment." In *Research in Social Stratification and Mobility*. Ed. D. J. Treiman and R. V. Robinson, 3–40. Greenwich, Conn.: JAI Press.

Fararo, T. J., and J. Skvoretz. 1984. "Institutions as Production Systems." *Journal of Mathematical Sociology* 10:117–82.

Faulkner, R. R. 1983. *Music on Demand.* New Brunswick: Transaction.

Fay, S. B. 1966. *The Origins of the World War.* New York: Free Press.

Featherman, D. L., and R. M. Hauser. 1978. *Opportunity and Change.* New York: Academic.

Feller, W. 1968. *An Introduction to Probability Theory and Its Applications.* New York: Wiley.

Fligstein, N. 1985. "The Spread of Multidivisional Form Among Large Firms." *American Sociological Review* 50:377–91.

Forrest, J., and A. Abbott. 1990. "The Optimal Matching Method for Anthropological Data." *Journal of Quantitative Anthropology* 2:151–70.

Freedman, D. A. 1987. "As Others See Us." *Journal of Educational Statistics* 12:101–28.

———. 1997. "From Association to Causation via Regression." *Advances in Applied Mathematics* 18:59–110.

Freese, L. 1980. "Formal Theorizing." *Annual Review of Sociology* 6:187–212.

Freese, L., and J. Sell. 1980. "Constructing Axiomatic Theories in Sociology." In *Theoretical Methods in Sociology.* Ed. L. Freese, 263–368. Pittsburgh: University of Pittsburgh Press.

Freud, S. 1936. *The Problem of Anxiety.* New York: Norton.

———. [1915] 1963a. "Instincts and Their Vicissitudes." In *General Psychological Theory,* 88–103. New York: Collier.

———. [1915] 1963b. "Repression." In *General Psychological Theory,* 104–15. New York: Collier.

Galle, O. R., C. H. Wiswell, and J. A. Burr. 1985. "Racial Mix and Industrial Productivity." *American Sociological Review* 50:20–33.

Gallie, W. B. 1968. *Philosophy and the Historical Understanding.* New York: Schocken.

Giddens, A. 1979. *Central Problems in Social Theory.* Berkeley and Los Angeles: University of California Press.

———. 1984. *The Constitution of Society.* Berkeley and Los Angeles: University of California Press.

Goldberger, A. S. 1972. "Structural Equations Methods in the Social Sciences." *Econometrica* 40:979–1001.

Goldthorpe, J. 1997. "Current Issues in Comparative Macrosociology." *Comparative Social Research* 16:1–26.

Gouldner, A. 1970. *The Coming Crisis of Western Sociology.* New York: Avon.

Granovetter, M. 1978. "Threshold Models of Collective Behavior." *American Journal of Sociology* 83:1420–43.

Greeley, A. M. 1987. "Hallucinations of Widowhood." *Sociology and Social Research* 71:258–65.

Griffin, L. J. 1993. "Narrative, Event-Structure Analysis, and Causal Interpretation in Historical Sociology." *American Journal of Sociology* 98:1094–133.

Griffin, L. J., and L. W. Isaac. 1992. "Recursive Regression and the Historical Use of 'Time' in Time-Series Analysis of Historical Process." *Historical Methods* 25:166–79.

Griffin, L. J., P. B. Walters, P. O'Connell, and E. Moor. 1986. "Methodological Innovations in the Analysis of Welfare-State Development." In *The Future for the Welfare State*. Ed. N. Furniss, 101–38. Bloomington: Indiana University Press.

Haavelmo, T. 1944. "The Probability Approach in Econometrics." *Econometrica* 12: supplement.

Hage, J. 1972. *Techniques and Problems of Theory Construction in Sociology*. New York: Wiley.

Halaby, C. N., and D. L. Weakliem. 1989. "Worker Control and Attachment to the Firm." *American Journal of Sociology* 95:549–91.

Hall, O. 1949. "Types of Medical Careers." *American Journal of Sociology* 55:243–53.

Hareven, T. K., and K. Masaoka. 1988. "Turning Points and Transitions." *Journal of Family History* 13:271–89.

Harper, D. 1992. "Small N's and Community Case Studies." In *What Is a Case?* Ed. C. Ragin and H. Becker, 139–58. Cambridge: Cambridge University Press.

Hart, H. L. A., and T. Honoré. 1985. *Causation in the Law*. 2d ed. Oxford: Oxford University Press.

Hechter, M. 1987. *Principles of Group Solidarity*. Berkeley and Los Angeles: University of California Press.

Heise, D. R. 1979. *Understanding Events*. Cambridge: Cambridge University Press.

———. 1986. "Modeling Symbolic Interaction." In *Approaches to Social Theory*. Ed. S. Lindenberg, J. Coleman, and S. Nowak, 291–304. New York: Russell Sage.

———. 1989. "Modeling Event Structures." *Journal of Mathematical Sociology* 14:139–69.

———. 1991. "Event Structure Analysis." In *Using Computers in Qualitative Research*. Ed. N. Fielding and R. Lee, 136–63. Newbury Park, Calif.: Sage.

Hempel, C. G. 1942. "The Function of General Laws in History." *Journal of Philosophy* 39:35–48.

Hirschi, T. 1969. *Causes of Delinquency*. Berkeley and Los Angeles: University of California Press.

Hirschi, T., and H. T. Selvin. 1967. *Delinquency Research*. New York: Free Press.

Hodson, F. R., D. G. Kendall, and P. Tăutu. 1971. *Mathematics in the Historical and Archeological Sciences*. Edinburgh: University of Edinburgh Press.

Hogan, D. P. 1978. "The Variable Order of Events in the Life Course." *American Sociological Review* 43:573–86.

Howe, R. H. 1978. "Max Weber's Elective Affinities." *American Journal of Sociology* 84:366–85.

Hubert, L. J. 1979. "Comparison of Sequences." *Psychological Bulletin* 86:1098–1106.

Hubert, L., R. G. Golledge, and C. M. Costanzo. 1981. "Generalized Procedures for Evaluating Spatial Autocorrelation." *Geographical Analysis* 13:224–33.

Hughes, E. C. 1945. "Dilemmas and Contradictions of Status." *American Journal of Sociology* 50:353–59.

———. 1971(1950). "Cycles, Turning Points, and Careers." In *The Sociological Eye*. Ed. E. C. Hughes, 124–31. Chicago: Aldine.

Hull, D. L. 1975. "Central Subjects and Historical Narratives." *History and Theory* 14:253–74.

Iannaccone, L. R. 1994. "Why Strict Churches are Strong." *American Journal of Sociology* 99:1180–221.

Irzik, G., and E. Meyer. 1987. "Causal Modeling." *Philosophy of Science* 54:495–514.

Isaac, L. W., S. M. Carlson, and M. P. Mathis. 1991. "Quality of Quantity in Comparative-Historical Time Series Analysis." Paper presented at the Social Science History Association, New Orleans, 2 November.

Isaac, L. W., and L. J. Griffin. 1989. "Ahistoricism in Time-Series Analyses of Historical Processes." *American Sociological Review* 54:873–90.

Karesh, M. 1995. "The Interstitial Origins of Symbolic Consumer Research." Unpublished M.A. paper, University of Chicago, Department of Sociology.

Katzner, D. W. 1983. *Analysis without Measurement.* Cambridge: Cambridge University Press.

Kennedy, P. 1985. *A Guide to Econometrics.* Cambridge: MIT Press.

Key, V. O. 1955. "A Theory of Critical Elections." *Journal of Politics* 17:3–18.

Keynes, J. M. 1920. *The Economic Consequences of the Peace.* New York: Harcourt Brace.

Knoke, D., and J. H. Kuklinski. 1982. *Network Analysis.* Beverly Hills: Sage.

Kohn, M. L., and C. Schooler. 1982. "Job Conditions and Personality." *American Journal of Sociology* 87:1257–86.

Komarovsky, M., and W. Waller. 1945. "Studies of the Family." *American Journal of Sociology* 50:443–51.

Kreps, D. M. 1990. *Game Theory and Economic Modelling.* New York: Oxford University Press.

Kuhn, T. S. 1970. *The Structure of Scientific Revolutions.* Chicago: University of Chicago Press.

Lakoff, G. 1987. *Women, Fire, and Dangerous Things.* Chicago: University of Chicago Press.

Lasser, W. 1985. "The Supreme Court in Periods of Realignment." *Journal of Politics* 47:1174–87.

Laumann, E. O., and F. U. Pappi. 1976. *Networks of Collective Action.* New York: Academic.

Lazarsfeld, P. F., and M. Rosenberg. 1955. *The Language of Social Research.* Glencoe, Ill.: Free Press.

Leamer, E. E. 1983. "Let's Take the Con out of Econometrics." *American Economic Review* 73:31–43.

Leifer, E. 1988. "Interaction Preludes to Role-Setting." *American Sociological Review* 53:865–78.

———. 1991. *Actors as Observers.* New York: Garland.

Lieberson, S. 1985. *Making It Count.* Berkeley and Los Angeles: University of California Press.

———. 1992. "Small *N*'s and Big Conclusions." In *What Is a Case?* Ed. C. C. Ragin and H. S. Becker, 105–18. Cambridge: Cambridge University Press.

Loftin, C., and S. K. Ward. 1981. "Spatial Autocorrelation Models for Galton's Problem." *Behavioral Science Research* 16:105–28.

———. 1983. "A Spatial Autocorrelation Model of the Effects of Population Density on Fertility." *American Sociological Review* 48:121–28.

Lyman, S. M. 1968. "The Race Relations Cycle of Robert E. Park." *Pacific Sociological Review* 11:16–22.

MacIver, R. M. 1942. *Social Causation.* New York: Harper and Row.

Mackie, J. 1974. *The Cement of the Universe.* Oxford: Oxford University Press.

Marini, M. M. 1984. "Women's Educational Attainment and the Timing of Entry into Parenthood." *American Sociological Review* 49:491–511.

———. 1987. "Measuring the Process of Role Change during the Transition to Adulthood." *Social Science Research* 16:1–38.

Marini, M. M., H. C. Shin, and J. Raymond. 1989. "Socioeconomic Consequences of the Process of Transition to Adulthood." *Social Science Research* 18:89–135.

Marini, M. M., and B. Singer. 1988. "Causality in the Social Sciences." *Sociological Methodology* 18:347–409.

Marsden, P. V. 1983. "Restricted Access in Networks and Models of Power." *American Journal of Sociology* 88:686–717.

Marsden, P. V., and N. Lin. 1982. *Social Structure and Network Analysis.* Beverly Hills: Sage.

Marx, K. 1963. *The Eighteenth Brumaire of Louis Bonaparte.* New York: International Publishers.

Mayhew, B. H., L. N. Gray, and M. L. Mayhew. 1971. "Behavior of Interaction Systems." *General Systems* 16:13–29.

Mayhew, B. H., and R. L. Levinger. 1976. "On the Frequency of Oligarchy in Human Interaction." *American Journal of Sociology* 81:1017–49.

McCullagh, C. B. 1978. "Colligation and Classification in History." *History and Theory* 17:267–84.

McPhee, W. N. 1963. *Formal Theories of Mass Behavior.* New York: Free Press.

Mead, G. H. 1932. *The Philosophy of the Present.* Chicago: University of Chicago Press.

———. 1934. *Mind, Self, and Society.* Ed. C. Morris. Chicago: University of Chicago Press.

Mefford, D. 1982. "A Comparison of Dialectical and Boolean Algebraic Models of the Genesis of Interpersonal Relations." In *Dialectical Logics for the Political Sciences. Poznan Studies,* vol. 7. Ed. H. Alker, 31–47. Amsterdam: Rodopi.

Melville, H. [1851] 1957. *Moby Dick.* New York: Holt, Rinehart.

Miller, S. D., and D. O. Sears. 1986. "Stability and Change in Social Tolerance." *American Journal of Political Science* 30:214–36.

Mink, L. O. 1970. "History and Fiction as Modes of Comprehension." *New Literary History* 1:541–58.

Mohr, J. 1992. "Community, Bureaucracy, and Social Relief." Ph.D. diss., Yale University.

———. 1995. "Reinventing Asylums." Paper presented at the American Sociological Association, 21 August.

Morgan, M. S. 1990. *The History of Econometric Ideas.* Cambridge: Cambridge University Press.

Morgan, S. P., and R. R. Rindfuss. 1985. "Marital Disruption." *American Journal of Sociology* 90:1055–77.

Mortensen, D. T. 1988. "Wages, Separation, and Job Tenure." *Journal of Labor Economics* 6:445–71.

Mowrer, E. R. 1927. *Family Disorganization.* Chicago: University of Chicago Press.

Mullins, N. C. 1973. *Theories and Theory Groups in Contemporary American Sociology.* New York: Harper and Row.

Myerson, R. B. 1991. *Game Theory*. Cambridge: Harvard University Press.

Neyman, J. 1935. "Complex Experiments." *Journal of the Royal Statistical Association* supp. 2:235–42.

Nimkoff, M. F. 1948. "Trends of Family Research." *American Journal of Sociology* 53:477–82.

Offe, C. 1984. *Contradictions of the Welfare State*. Cambridge: MIT Press.

Olafson, F. A. 1979. *The Dialectic of Action*. Chicago: University of Chicago Press.

O'Rand, A. M., and M. L. Krecker. 1990. "Concepts of the Life Cycle." *Annual Review of Sociology* 16:241–62.

Padgett, J. F. 1985. "The Emergent Organization of Plea Bargaining." *American Journal of Sociology* 90:753–800.

Padgett, J. F., and C. K. Ansell. 1993. "Robust Action and the Rise of the Medici, 1400–1434." *American Journal of Sociology* 98:1259–319.

Park, R. E. 1927. Introduction to *The Natural History of Revolution*, by L. P. Edwards, xv–xix. Chicago: University of Chicago Press.

Park, R. E., and E. W. Burgess. 1921. *An Introduction to the Science of Sociology*. Chicago: University of Chicago Press.

Parsons, T. 1937. *The Structure of Social Action*. New York: McGraw-Hill.

Pavalko, E. K. 1989. "State Timing of Policy Adoption." *American Journal of Sociology* 95:592–615.

Pearson, K. [1892] 1937. *Grammar of Science*. London: Dent.

Peterson, R. D., and J. Hagan. 1984. "Changing Conceptions of Race." *American Sociological Review* 49:56–70.

Pfautz, H. W., and O. D. Duncan. 1950. "A Critical Evaluation of Warner's Work in Community Stratification." *American Sociological Review* 15:205–15.

Pickles, A., and M. Rutter. 1991. "Statistical and Conceptual Models of 'Turning Points' in Developmental Processes." In *Problems and Methods in Longitudinal Research*. Ed. D. Magnusson, L. R. Bergman, G. Rudinger, and B. Torestad, 133–65. Cambridge: Cambridge University Press.

Platt, J. 1996. *A History of Sociological Research Methods in America*. New York: Cambridge University Press.

Poole, M. S. 1983. "Decision Development in Small Groups II: A Study of Multiple Sequences in Decision-Making." *Communications Monographs* 50:206–32.

Poole, M. S., and J. Roth. 1989a. "Decision Development in Small Groups IV." *Human Communication Research* 15:323–56.

———. 1989b. "Decision Development in Small Groups V." *Human Communication Research* 15:549–89.

Popper, K. [1943] 1962. *The Open Society and Its Enemies*. 2 vols. Princeton: Princeton University Press.

Poulantzas, N. 1978. *Political Power and Social Classes*. New York: Verso.

Proctor, M., and P. Abell. 1985. *Sequence Analysis*. Aldershot, Hants: Gower.

Puterman, M. L., ed. 1978. *Dynamic Programming and Its Applications*. New York: Academic.

Rabinowitz, J., I. Kim, and B. Lazerwitz. 1992. "Metropolitan Size and Participation in Religio-Ethnic Communities." *Journal for the Scientific Study of Religion* 31:339–45.

Ragin, C. 1987. *The Comparative Method*. Berkeley and Los Angeles: University of California Press.

Rashevsky, N. 1968. *Looking at History through Mathematics.* Cambridge: MIT Press.

Reckless, W. C. 1933. *Vice in Chicago.* Chicago: University of Chicago Press.

Reichenbach, H. 1951. *The Rise of Scientific Philosophy.* Berkeley and Los Angeles: University of California Press.

Richardson, L. 1990. "Narrative and Sociology." *Journal of Contemporary Ethnography* 19:116–35.

Ricoeur, P. 1984–88. *Time and Narrative.* 3 vols. Chicago: University of Chicago Press.

Robinson, J. 1980. "Time in Economic Theory." In *What Are the Questions?* Ed. J. Robinson, 86–95. Armonk, N.Y.: M. E. Sharpe.

Rosenfeld, R. A. 1983. "Sex Segregation and Sectors." *American Sociological Review* 48:637–55.

Ruben, D.-H. 1990. "Singular Explanation and the Social Sciences." In *Explanation and Its Limits.* Ed. D. Knowles, 95–117. Cambridge: Cambridge University Press.

Sacks, H., E. A. Schegloff, and G. Jefferson. 1974. "A Simplest Systematics for Turntaking in Conversation." *Language* 50:696–735.

Salmon, W. C. 1971. *Statistical Explanation and Statistical Relevance.* Pittsburgh: University of Pittsburgh Press.

Sampson, R. J., and J. H. Laub. 1993. *Crime in the Making.* Cambridge: Harvard University Press.

Sankoff, D., and J. B. Kruskal. 1983. *Time Warps, String Edits, and Macromolecules.* Reading, Mass.: Addison Wesley.

Schank, R., and R. Abelson. 1977. *Scripts, Plans, Goals and Understanding.* Hillsdale, N.J.: Lawrence Erlbaum Associates.

Schelling, T. 1978. *Micromotives and Macrobehavior.* New York: Norton.

Schieve, W. C., and P. M. Allen. 1982. *Self-Organization and Dissipative Structures.* Austin: University of Texas.

Sewell, W. H., Jr. 1996. "Three Temporalities." In *The Historic Turn in the Human Sciences.* Ed. T. J. McDonald, 245–80. Ann Arbor: University of Michigan Press.

Shaw, C. R. 1930. *The Jackroller.* Chicago: University of Chicago Press.

———. 1931. *The Natural History of a Delinquent Career.* Chicago: University of Chicago Press.

Shaw, C. R., and H. D. McKay. 1942. *Juvenile Delinquency and Urban Areas.* Chicago: University of Chicago Press.

Sherburne, D. W. 1966. *A Key to Whitehead's Process and Reality.* Chicago: University of Chicago Press.

Shubik, M. 1982. *Game Theory in the Social Sciences.* Cambridge: MIT Press.

Simon, H. A. 1952. "On the Definition of the Causal Relation." *Journal of Philosophy* 49:517–28.

———. 1953. "Causal Ordering and Identifiability." In *Studies in Econometric Method.* Ed. W. C. Hood and T. C. Koopmans, 49–74. Chicago: University of Chicago Press.

———. 1954. "Spurious Correlation." *Journal of the American Statistical Association* 49:467–79.

———. 1969. *The Sciences of the Artificial.* Cambridge: MIT Press.

Simpson, I. H., R. L. Simpson, M. Evers, and S. S. Poss. 1982. "Occupational Recruitment, Retention, and Labor Force Cohort Representation." *American Journal of Sociology* 87:1287–313.

Smith, D. S. 1984. "A Mean and Random Past." *Historical Methods* 17:141–48.

Skocpol, T. 1979. *States and Social Revolutions.* Cambridge: Cambridge University Press.

Smith, K. R. 1985. "Work Life and Health as Competing Careers." In *Life Course Dynamics.* Ed. G. H. Elder, 156–87. Ithaca: Cornell University Press.

Snodgrass, J. 1982. *The Jackroller at Seventy.* Lexington, Mass.: D. C. Heath.

Sobel, M. E. 1983. "Structural Mobility, Circulation Mobility, and the Analysis of Occupational Mobility." *American Sociological Review* 48:721–27.

———. 1996. "An Introduction to Causal Inference." *Sociological Methods and Research* 24:353–79.

Sobel, M. E., M. Hout, and O. D. Duncan. 1985. "Exchange, Structure, and Symmetry in Occupational Mobility." *American Journal of Sociology* 91:359–72.

Southwood, K. E. 1978. "Substantive Theory and Statistical Interaction." *American Journal of Sociology* 83:1154–203.

Spector, M., and J. Kitsuse. 1987. *Constructing Social Problems.* New York: Aldine de Gruyter.

Stewman, S. 1976. "Markov Models of Occupational Mobility." *Journal of Mathematical Sociology* 4:201–45, 247–78.

Stigler, S. 1986. *The History of Statistics.* Cambridge: Harvard University Press.

Stinchcombe, A. L. 1968. *Constructing Social Theories.* New York: Harcourt Brace.

———. 1978. *Theoretical Methods in Social History.* New York: Academic.

———. 1990. "Reason and Rationality." In *The Limits of Rationality.* Ed. K. Cook and M. Levi, 285–371. Chicago: University of Chicago Press.

Stouffer, S. A. 1957. "Quantitative Methods." In *Review of Sociology.* Ed. J. B. Gittler, 25–55. New York: Wiley.

Stump, R. W. 1984. "Regional Migration and Religious Commitment in the United States." *Journal for the Scientific Study of Religion* 23:292–303.

Sudnow, D. 1971. *Studies in Social Interaction.* New York: Free Press.

Suppes, P. 1970. *A Probabilistic Theory of Causality.* Amsterdam: North Holland.

Sutherland, E. H. 1950. "The Diffusion of Sexual Psychopath Laws." *American Journal of Sociology* 56:142–48.

Taibelson, M. H. 1974. "Distinguishing between Heterogeneity and Randomness in Stochastic Models." *American Sociological Review* 39:877–880.

Thomas, W. I. 1925. "The Problem of Personality in the Urban Environment." In *Publications of the American Sociological Society: Papers and Proceedings of the Twentieth Annual Meeting,* 30–39. Chicago: University of Chicago Press.

Thornberry, T. P., and R. L. Christenson. 1984. "Unemployment and Criminal Involvement." *American Sociological Review* 49:398–411.

Thrasher, F. M. 1927. *The Gang.* Chicago: University of Chicago Press.

Tiao, G. C., and G. E. P. Box. 1981. "Modeling Multiple Time Series with Applications." *Journal of the American Statistical Association* 76:802–16.

Tonnes, A. 1932. "A Note on the Problem of the Past." *Journal of Philosophy* 29:599–606.

Tønnessen, J. W., and A. O. Johnsen. [1959] 1982. *The History of Modern Whaling.*

Tr. R. I. Christophersen. Berkeley and Los Angeles: University of California Press. Original title: *Den moderne hvalfangsts historie.*

Traxler, R. H. 1976. "A Snag in the History of Factorial Experiments." In *On the History of Statistics and Probability.* Ed. D. B. Owen, 283–95. New York: Marcel Dekker.

Tukey, J. W. 1954. "Causation, Regression, and Path Analysis." In *Statistics and Mathematics in Biology.* Ed. O. Kempthorne et al., 35–66. New York: Hafner.

Tuma, N. B., and M. T. Hannan. 1984. *Social Dynamics.* Orlando: Academic.

Tuma, N. B., M. Hannan, and L. P. Groenveld. 1979. "Dynamic Analysis of Event Histories." *American Journal of Sociology* 84:820–54.

Turner, R. H. 1953. "The Quest for Universals in Sociological Research." *American Sociological Review* 18:604–11.

Von Wright, G. 1971. *Explanation and Understanding.* Ithaca: Cornell University Press.

Wade, M. J. 1995. "The Ecology of Sexual Selection." *Evolutionary Ecology* 9:118–24.

Wallerstein, I. *The Modern World System.* New York: Academic.

Walsh, W. H. 1958. *An Introduction to the Philosophy of History.* London: Hutchinson University Library.

Weber, M. 1947. *The Theory of Social and Economic Organization.* Tr. A. M. Henderson and T. Parsons, ed. T. Parsons.

———. 1949. *The Methodology of the Social Sciences.* New York: Free Press.

Whewell, W. [1858] 1968. *Theory of Scientific Method.* Indianapolis: Hackett.

White, H. 1973. *Metahistory.* Baltimore: Johns Hopkins University Press.

White, H. C. 1970. *Chains of Opportunity.* Cambridge: Harvard University Press.

———. 1981. "Production Markets as Induced Role Structures." In *Sociological Methodology 1981.* Ed. S. Leinhardt, 1–57. San Francisco: Jossey-Bass.

White, H. C., S. A. Boorman, and R. L. Breiger. 1976. "Social Structure from Multiple Networks. I: Blockmodeling of Roles and Positions." *American Journal of Sociology* 81:730–80.

White, H. C., and C. White. 1965. *Canvases and Careers.* New York: Wiley.

Whitehead, A. N. [1929] 1969. *Process and Reality.* New York: Free Press.

Wilner, P. 1985. "The Main Drift of Sociology between 1936 and 1984." *History of Sociology* 5:1–20.

Wold, H. O. A. 1964. "On the Definition and Meaning of Causal Concepts." In *Model Building in the Human Sciences.* Ed. H. O. A. Wold, 265–95. Entretiens de Monaco en Sciences Humaines. Paris: Centre International d'Etude des Problèmes Humaines.

Wright, S. 1921. "Correlation and Causation." *Journal of Agricultural Research* 20:557–85.

———. 1934. "The Method of Path Coefficients." *Annals of Mathematical Statistics* 5:161–215.

———. 1960. "The Treatment of Reciprocal Interaction, with or without Lag, in Path Analysis." *Biometrics* 16:423–45.

Yamaguchi, K. 1983. "The Structure of Intergenerational Occupational Mobility." *American Journal of Sociology* 88:718–45.

———. 1991. *Event History Analysis.* Newbury Park, Calif.: Sage.

Yule, G. U. 1912. *An Introduction to the Theory of Statistics*. London: Griffin.
Zellner, A., C. Hong, and C.-k. Min. 1991. "Forecasting Turning Points in International Growth Rates Using Bayesian Exponentially Weighted Autoregression, Time-Varying Parameter, and Pooling Techniques." *Journal of Econometrics* 49:275–304.
Zetterberg, H. L. 1954. *On Theory and Verification in Sociology*. Stockholm: Almquist and Wiksell.
———. 1965. *On Theory and Verification in Sociology*. 3d ed. Totowa, N.J.: Bedminster Press.
Znaniecki, F. 1934. *The Method of Sociology*. New York: Farrar and Rinehart.

INDEX

This index does not cover the prologue. Nor does it include the names of individuals unless their work is discussed at length or they receive several mentions. Definitions and concepts are indexed under the heading "concept of."